CW01079794

Russian/Soviet Studies in the United States, Amerikanistika in Russia

Russian/Soviet Studies in the United States, Amerikanistika in Russia

Mutual Representations in Academic Projects

Edited by Ivan Kurilla and Victoria I. Zhuravleva

LEXINGTON BOOKS
Lanham • Boulder • New York • London

Published by Lexington Books
An imprint of The Rowman & Littlefield Publishing Group, Inc.
4501 Forbes Boulevard, Suite 200, Lanham, Maryland 20706
www.rowman.com

Unit A, Whitacre Mews, 26-34 Stannary Street, London SE11 4AB

British Library Cataloguing in Publication Information Available

Library of Congress Cataloging-in-Publication Data Available

ISBN 978-1-4985-1798-0 (cloth : alk. paper)
ISBN 978-1-4985-1799-7 (ebook)

∞™ The paper used in this publication meets the minimum requirements of American
National Standard for Information Sciences Permanence of Paper for Printed Library
Materials, ANSI/NISO Z39.48-1992.

Printed in the United States of America

Contents

Preface

Ivan Kurilla and Victoria I. Zhuravleva

Russian/Soviet Studies in the United States, Amerikanistika in Russia: Mutual Representations in Academic Projects is not a book about Russian-American relations as such; it is a book about their academic dimension that takes into account both their historical context and their prospects. This book is an interdisciplinary trans-Atlantic dialog concerning national and international agenda's influence on the process of understanding the *Other*, about the influence that the climate of bilateral relations, sociocultural traditions of the observer society, and the historical legacy of mutual representations have on this process. This book is also a reflection on the correlation of academic and expert knowledge within the context of foreign policy decision-making on both sides of the Atlantic.

The current crisis in Russian-American relations showed clearly that the loss of interest in the multilevel interdisciplinary study of another country is fraught with many mistakes in foreign policy expert knowledge and long-term negative consequences of strategic, economic, and sociocultural nature. The current confrontation between Russia and the United States is characterized by a critical misunderstanding of each other's motives and goals. This confrontation also shows the existence of a kind of a "civilizational rupture" at the state and public level, the kind of rupture that is deeper than it was even at the time of the Cold War. Given the circumstances, discussion regarding the shaping of academic knowledge about Russia in the United States and about the United States in the Russian Empire/the USSR/post-Soviet Russia is extremely relevant, as well as the exchange of ideas regarding the present-day state of academic studies of each other.

Both Russia and the United States have developed solid traditions of studying the opposing country and its people. Both Russia and the United States have established academic research schools and expert centers. This mixture of academic and expert knowledge should be shaping the foundations for decision-making at the government level. However, the history of Russian-American relations demonstrates that Russian studies in the United States and *Amerikanistika* in Russia have been, and still are, under the permanent influence of national agendas (both domestic and foreign) that dictate thematic priorities, hierarchy of approaches, and perception angles.

This is why our collection posits among its principal goals (1) to review the mechanisms shaping professional knowledge of Russia in the United States and of the United States in Russia on the basis of multicontextual approach; (2) to draw comparisons with other forms of perception of the *Other* that exist at the non-academic and non-expert level of public consciousness.

Knowledge of another country and another people exists in several forms. First, there is "common" knowledge maintained by the media; this knowledge rests on perception stereotypes developed by past generations, promulgated by mass culture, and used for propaganda purposes. It is this perception that forms the context which influences both academic and expert discourse. Politicians on both sides of the Atlantic largely embrace this first type of knowledge.

Second, it is academic knowledge which accrues within traditional academic disciplines such as history, political science, economics, sociology, and literary studies. Current concepts of the social sciences destroyed the image of the "ivory tower" or a metaphoric wall separating this knowledge from the problems that are of primary concern for society; however, even today, the tendencies and mechanisms of public interests that influence the workings of the academy have been barely contemplated by academics themselves.

Third, there is expert knowledge which emerges as a result of a direct demand the government and the public make on the academic community which, in response, strives to render its knowledge usable as "applied," or practical, recommendations. In the United States, academics often act as experts; they work for state agencies (the Department of State, or defense or intelligence agencies), and then they go on to work for think tanks or go back to university teaching (these career moves are called the "revolving doors" system). In Russia, the academic and expert communities are separated from each other to a much greater degree. A relatively narrow circle of academics acts as experts, and some of them cannot be termed academics as they do not publish academic articles or books and they do not teach in universities; yet, they are still considered experts in a particular sphere.

Professional study of Russia in the United States of America and of the United States in Russia is already more than one hundred and fifty years old. The first scholarly articles and books on the other country, about its history and politics, and about Russian-American relations appeared as early as the middle of the nineteenth century. At that time, prior to the abolition of serfdom in Russia and the Civil War in the United States, the two countries had many things in common, which inevitably led to mutual attention and first attempts to describe and analyze. However, academic Russian studies and *Amerikanistika* date back to the turn of the twentieth century and began to thrive during World War I. At that time, the first Russian departments emerged in the United States, American libraries started their "Russian collections," students began to study Russian and took courses on Russia, and the first Russian studies dissertation was defended. In their turn, eminent Russian sociologists, historians, and economists published books on the United States, including those books that could be classified as textbooks, and Moscow and St. Petersburg (later Petrograd) universities began to offer courses on the history and political institutions of the United States.

The next crucial stage in the history of mutual academic studies falls between the two world wars. In the United States, Russian studies were influenced by Russian historians and sociologists who had immigrated to the United States (Georgy Vladimirovich Vernadskii, Mikhail Mikhailovich Karpovich, Mikhail Timofeevich Florinskii, Pitirim Aleksandrovich Sorokin, and Nikolai Sergeevich Timasheff). They introduced into the American academe and into American university classrooms both knowledge of Russia and a certain vision of Russia. It was then as well that the USSR fell within the scope of interest of the first American expert center, the Council on Foreign Relations, and the "Russian theme" was given consideration by the *Foreign Affairs* journal that the center published.

In Soviet Russia, the development of historical *Amerikanistika* was connected with the names of Alexei Vladimirovich Efimov and Lev Izrailevich Zubok, the "founding fathers" of *Amerikanistika* in the Moscow State Institute for International Relations (MGIMO). As early as 1934, Efimov published a book *On the History of Capitalism in the United States*, inaugurating a series of publications which was completed in over thirty years with the publication of a fundamental work *The United States: The Development of Capitalism (Pre-Imperialistic Era)*. Zubok came to MGIMO as a full-fledged scholar with in-depth knowledge of American reality. (As a child, Zubok immigrated with his parents to the United States, joined the workers' movement. In the 1920s, he was forced to go back to Soviet Russia.) His academic interests were extremely broad and they included key issues of American history in the late nineteenth and twentieth centuries, from American expansion in foreign policy to the history of workers' movements. Both Efimov and Zubok were eminent scholars as well as brilliant teachers, and their lecture courses on American history were turned into educational books, and some of their students, upon graduating from MGIMO in the late 1940s through the early 1950s, formed the cream of the crop of the future Soviet *Amerikanistika*—for example, Georgii Arbatov, Yurii Zamoshkin, Vitalii Zhurkin, Robert Ivanov, Nikolai Bolkhovitinov, and Edward Ivanian. These and other *Amerikanistika* specialists (for instance, Raphail Ganelin, Alexander Fursenko, and Victor Furaev from the Leningrad school of *Amerikanistika*) succeeded in establishing in the 1960s through 1980s fruitful contacts with their colleagues from across the Atlantic due to the beginning of academic and cultural exchanges between countries. They also succeeded in significantly expanding the field of *Amerikanistika* in the USSR and in enriching its source base.

We can say that by the mid-1920s, American literary studies had emerged as a separate branch of foreign literature studies in the USSR. However, it was fully established only during the Cold War, when the first scholarly histories of American literature were published, and when Soviet literary scholars formed their own American literary canon, which became an important part of the ideological struggle between the USSR and the United States.

Both *Amerikanistika* in the USSR and Sovietology in the United States became full-fledged academic institutions during the Cold War. The Cold War pivoted on the ideological struggle for people's hearts and minds in various parts of the world, and Soviet *Amerikanistika* specialists, as well as American Sovietologists, played a very significant role in that struggle. Their ranks kept swelling, their multiple publications set the tone in area studies, humanities, and the social sciences. It was during that confrontation that use of *the Other* (American or Soviet *Other* respectively) became a fixture of public and political discourse in both countries, playing the role of a constitutive, that is, serving as a model for comparison within a dichotomic scheme thus highlighting one's own advantages compared to the opponent's drawbacks. The *Other* was located at the opposite extreme of the international order. Relations with the *Other* shaped the course of global development, and the need to address the experience of the *Other* during the Cold War demanded that expert knowledge be developed, and that it be useful in foreign policy decision-making. These needs led to the flourishing of area studies focused on studying the enemy.

When we look back at the Cold War, we can now see that during its first decade (the tensest moments of the late 1940s to early 1950s) the USSR mostly studied the United States through the intelligence community and not through academic institutions. Soviet *Amerikanistika* became an academic institution in the late 1960s (for instance, the Institute for United States and Canada Studies of the Academy of Sciences [ISKAN] was founded in 1967) largely due to Khrushchev's Thaw and the detente in Soviet-American relations, which demonstrates a clear connection between national agenda (both in domestic and foreign policy) and the dynamics of the academic studies of the *Other*. The 1970s saw the flourishing of university centers of *Amerikanistika*, first and foremost in Moscow State University (headed by Nikolai Vasilievich Sivachev and Evgenii Fedorovich Yaz'kov). The increased demand for expert knowledge about the United States was also linked to the expansion of rivalry dimensions: the USSR had to "catch up and overtake" America, and not only in military capacity. The same applied to the United States, as the country, due to the Vietnam War, civil rights movement, youth counter-cultures' challenge, and large-scale re-thinking of values, saw the emergence of a revisionist trend in American historiography, including American Sovietology as part of Russian/Slavic Studies. It destroyed the ideological consensus concerning the nature of the Soviet regime, which had been formed at the outset of the Cold War and had been influenced by McCarthyism. Both concepts, "totalitarian" and "revisionist," were harmful for Washington's foreign policy since the former exaggerated the USSR's expansionist ambitions, while the latter downplayed them in order to demonstrate the expansionist nature of the US foreign policy, which was, according to the revisionists, a greater threat for the world than the USSR.[1]

Academic history of Soviet-American relations during the Cold War demonstrates that both Soviet *Amerikanistika* and American Sovietology were closely linked with the interests of the respective states.[2] Looking back from the 1990s at the so-called totalitarian interpretation of Soviet history, Stephen Kotkin remarks that "the 'need' for totalitarianism as a devastating political weapon may well recede with those who engaged with serious battles of the Cold War."[3] The same applies to the Soviet *Amerikanistika* with its explanatory scheme based on the Marxist-Leninist paradigm.

Within the logic of academic disciplines, theory generally dominates country-related facts' analysis, notable exceptions being history which is traditionally subdivided in accordance with countries and areas studied, and literary studies linked to national literatures. It is not accidental that history and literary studies became the foundation of area studies programs in the mid-to-late twentieth century, despite governments being clearly interested in politics and societies (i.e., in the political science or sociology applied to the country being studied).

After the USSR collapsed in 1991 and the bipolar system of international relations disappeared, both academic and expert knowledge of the former enemies in the Cold War were pushed out by new countries and areas that took priority in accordance with the hierarchy of national foreign policy interests, global and regional challenges and threats, and the changing architecture of Euro-Atlantic security.

After Russia lost its "superpower" status and Russian-American relations took on an asymmetric character,[4] American Sovietology disappeared along with its study subject, and interest in Russian studies as part of area studies dropped significantly. The collapse of the USSR and the rejection of communism caught the majority of American area specialists unawares and undermined the general trust in the prognostic capabilities of area studies. The government's demand for expert knowledge about Russia dropped, and society no longer saw Russia as a potential enemy and was no longer afraid of it. As a result, the number of Russian studies departments in American universities decreased over the last twenty-five years, as did the number of professorships; there were fewer career possibilities for those who graduated in Russian studies, and a large number of talented and motivated students went on to study China or the Islamic world. Although the collapse of the "iron curtain" incredibly expanded the possibilities of doing "field research" in Russia, knowledge of Russia was no longer comprehensive and interdisciplinary. New university milieu challenges also played their part in the Russian studies crisis in the United States. As Kenneth Yalowitz and Matthew Rojansky stressed, "university curricula devoted to any cross-disciplinary regional expertise have suffered attacks from traditional social-science disciplines, such as economics and political science, which view language and regional knowledge as—at best—a secondary skill set." At the same time, the Russian studies expert base in the United States is quite good but good expert knowledge does not always translate into good policies.[5] There are still excellent Russian studies programs in the United States. However, as Angela Stent notes, "the problem of the relative depth of the Russian Studies bench lies not in the MA programs but much more in the PhD programs, and there is a real issue of whether there will be enough professors to teach the next generation."[6] This dangerous generation gap is a clear indication of the Russian studies crisis in the United States, since the field suffered greatly due to budget cuts. As Putin's Russia ascended, so grew American students' interest in studying it. However, the government, disregarding this academic trend, continued to cut financing for Russian studies programs. In 2013, the Department of State shut down the Title VIII Program, and later, the Department of Education shut down the Title VI Program; both programs offered grants to study Russia and attracted students to Russian studies programs. Private foundations also decreased funding. Only a full-scale crisis in Russian-American relations made the issue of the Russian studies programs relevant again. The crisis prompted some serious soul-searching on the part of the preeminent figures in the field and led to the re-instating of some federal financing for Russian studies in the United States. In particular, the Title VIII Program was reinstated.

After the collapse of the USSR, post-Soviet Russia was going through a major economic and political crisis and it simply didn't have the means to finance *Amerikanistika*. Russian *Amerikanistika* centers, both at universities and within the Russian Academy of Sciences, faced serious hardships. Academic financing was generally decreased; *Amerikanistika* was no longer viewed as a strategically important field, and academic institutes began to lose both resources and scholars. At the same time, this period (particularly, the 1990s to the early 2000s) witnessed a number of positive changes in *Amerikanistika* in Russia: disappearance of rigid ideological constraints that limited the expansion of its research and methodology scope; its geography changed significantly, too, thanks to the emergence of smaller American studies centers in regional universities; there appeared new possibilities for field research in the United States due to travel grants and university exchanges; universities introduced bachelor's and master's *Amerikanistika* programs, some of which were opened jointly with US universities; many translations of source materials were published (although not all of them were of sufficiently high quality) and classical works on American historiography were translated into Russian as well (mostly with the financial support of the US Information Agency); finally, access to original sources was expanded due to the appearance of digitized databases on the Internet.

However, this newly accumulated potential did not lead to a qualitative shift in the Russian *Amerikanistika* as a whole, although it did significantly expand its academic horizons, the more especially as in the late 2000s the intensity of the Russian-American academic dialog decreased, and funding from US sources dropped while Russian sources did not replace them. Besides, in the 1990s, the emphasis shifted toward idealizing America's history, toward moving away from old thematic priorities, and as a result, whole thematic fields were abandoned: first, those fields that had been linked to studying socioeconomic history. The professional level of published research decreased, too. On the whole, this thematic and professional balance still has not been fully regained, despite the publication of new comprehensive works by the older generation of Russian *Amerikanistika* specialists such as Vladimir V. Sogrin, Edward Y. Batalov, Vladimir O. Pechatnov, and Viktor L. Mal'kov, and despite the translation and publication of primary sources and the appearance of new textbooks, dictionaries and encyclopedias on US history and Russian-American relations.[7]

Government crises that afflicted Russia in the 1990s led, among other problems, to the loss of interest in *Amerikanistika* as part of the governmental demand. As in many other economic spheres, the government preferred to invest money into "ready-made knowledge" instead of developing independent research. The 1990s saw the publication of many translations of books by American historians of the "consensus" school of thought. Those works sought to shape a nonconflict version of American history, and in the 2000s, after the official attitude to the United States changed, the Russian book market was flooded with translations of radical American historians which shaped a critical attitude toward American history.[8] The same applies to translations of historical and political essays "exposing" American politics and policies.[9]

On the whole, it should be stated that in today's Russia, *Amerikanistika* specialists are much less in demand than they were in the USSR. In the USSR, ISKAN was one of the major think tanks, and journalists reporting about America had audiences in thrall.

Special attention should be paid to the fact that the new crisis in Russian-American relations and the new rise of anti-Americanism in Russia did not lead to additional financing for studying the United States (while in the United States, Russian studies did receive additional funding), which allows us to hypothesize that anti-Americanism in post-Soviet Russia is more closely connected with domestic policies issues, in particular, with the process of shaping national identity. This hypothesis is further buttressed by two developments. First, the low-quality journalism plays an increasing role in shaping the debates (to the detriment of academic *Amerikanistika*). Second, the Russian media actively discusses the crisis in American Russian studies as the reason for the US experts' "failures" in Russian and Ukrainian foreign policies (even those American specialists on Russia who are ready for serious self-reflection take part in these discussions). Both developments shift emphasis toward the United States in searching for the reasons for the current bilateral relations crisis and fuel anti-American sociopolitical discourse directly linked to the national I-concept of Putin's Russia.[10]

Our book is intended to draw particular attention to that aspect of the academic history of Russian-American relations which allows us to answer two interconnected questions: (1) how the agenda for academic Russian studies and *Amerikanistika* within area studies programs has been formed and is still being formed, and to what extent it depends on state policies and politics and on public debates; (2) how academic learning could contribute to this politics and to these debates. Turning to the academic history of Russian-American relations appears to be fruitful for discovering the interrelations between comprehensive area studies on the one hand and social and political "demand" on the other due to the long and intensive nature of mutual study of each other by Russians and Americans and at the same time due to their mutual "alienation," as well as to the permanent relevance of this comparison.

This is the reason why we chose as our methodology both traditional and sociocultural (imagological) approaches to studying Russian-American relations, which allows us to consider foreign policy discourse as identity one which allows us to consider foreign policy discourse as identity discourse. The *Other* (another country) is interesting first and foremost because it allows one to solve certain problems within one's own society. In regard to the imagology of Russian-American relations, the American or Russian *Self* is the point of departure for the perception of the *Other*, whether that *Other* is Russian or American. That is why, when we talk about studying the United States in Russia and studying Russia in the United States, we are interested not only in the research subjects and approaches used when studying another country, but in answering the question of motivations behind interpreting the development of the society that is being studied and stressing some of its aspects and marginalizing others. Studying the process of "using the *Other*," we shed more light both on waves of anti-Americanism and Russophobia giving ways to pro-American sentiments and Russophilia, and on the contents of foreign policy in regard to the *Other* as a derivative of these public debates.[11]

Sociocultural approach aimed at analyzing various contexts as a whole allows us to answer the question of the role of scholars as professionals in the shaping of the national identity, to understand to what extent people of learning are free when they study other countries and societies, to what extent academic research agenda follows public demand, and whether academic research can influence public demand itself.

Thus our book considers not only historiography, but the sociology of learning in its connection with the political and public agenda; it analyzes integration of studying Russian/Soviet studies in the United States and *Amerikanistika* in Russia as academic fields in studying the imagology of Russian-American relations as a whole.

Clearly, the contributors to the collection have different methodological approaches, and not all of them use the sociocultural approach. Still, the editors saw their task in bringing together texts which complement each other both thematically and methodologically. Traditional analysis of *Amerikanistika* in Russia and Russian studies in the United States as academic projects serves to solve the same scholarly problem.

The important feature of this collection is Russian authors analyzing both *Amerikanistika* in Russia and Russian studies in the United States, and American authors touching upon the role of Russian scholars in developing area studies in both countries. This situation of "double reflection" ("we study the *Other* studying us") helps the authors posit original research questions and see the area studies development in new contexts.

The collection is comprised of two parts; each is structured chronologically. The first part includes texts analyzing the interrelations between studying Russia in the United States, and the United States in Russia at different stages of the countries' historical development, starting with the first academic attempts at studying each other in the middle of the nineteenth century, until present day. Area studies is an interdisciplinary field, but that does not change the fact that each individual scholar belongs to a particular discipline. Our book analyzes the specifics of the work of historians and literary scholars, political scientists and sociologists, and thus it highlights the personal dimension of the knowledge of the *Other* becoming professional. This important aspect retains its significance for the authors who contributed to the second part of the volume. They, however, focus on the institutional nature of structuring the science of studying the *Other* in Russia (the USSR) and the United States. This work was carried out in universities and colleges, in research centers and think tanks in both countries. These bodies depended on state financing and the overall society climate in defining their research priorities. The contributors used the example of several large Russian studies (Sovietology) and *Amerikanistika* centers to investigate the tendencies and effectiveness of this influence.

While each of the academic disciplines that form the interdisciplinary research field of area studies has its own history, area studies as a whole essentially does not. The works focusing on Russian studies or *Amerikanistika* as a whole (as different, for instance, from the historiography of US or Russian history) are very small in number since studying the academic dimension of Russian-American relations using both traditional and sociocultural approaches is a fairly recent subject of academic investigation on both sides of the Atlantic. We hope that our volume will stimulate further consideration of both academics and non-academic experts and politicians who are engaged in searching for the ways for mutual understanding and rapprochement between Russia and the United States.

This volume is the second publication within the framework of the "Russian Studies in the United States, *Amerikanistika* in Russia: Mutual Representations" project that was initiated in 2008 by Victoria I. Zhuravleva and Ivan Kurilla. In 2009, they edited and published the first volume of the project, in which Russian and American authors analyzed various educational texts about each other published over a long period of time.[12] The first volume's intention was to discuss the ways that the nineteenth and twentieth centuries' scholars and textbook authors used in order to integrate educational book into the identity discourse on both sides of the Atlantic, to analyze the ways the I-narrative was constructed during various stages of bilateral relations with the help of the Russian ideas of the United States and the American ideas of the Russian Empire/the USSR/post-Soviet Russia as they are represented in school and university textbooks on history, literature, geography, international relations and political science on the one hand, and the domestic and foreign agenda on the other.

While working on the project, Victoria Zhuravleva also organized an international conference "Russian/Soviet Studies in the United States, *Amerikanistika* in Russia: Mutual Representations" held at the Russian State University for the Humanities,[13] and many of the conference participants contributed to the present volume. We also organized a series of round tables at the ASEEES conventions and other academic events in Russia and in the United States to exchange ideas with Russian and American colleagues.

The creation of the "Russian-American Studies" database in 2013 has become one of the main stages of this project. The Russian State University for the Humanities oversaw the development of this database in collaboration with the Institute of World History (the Russian Academy of Sciences) and the Kennan Institute (The Woodrow Wilson International Center for Scholars) and under the financial support of the Russian Ministry of Education and Sciences. This database includes information about scholars and experts on Russia in the United States and on the

United States in Russia, from the nineteenth century to the beginning of the twenty-first century, and contains an annotated list of academic centers, think tanks, and professional organizations (http://ra-studies.com). In the future, with the translation of the database into English, it will become a "two-way street," and will open up additional opportunities for the expansion of contacts between Russian and American studies specialists in both countries.

NOTES

1. Daniel Abele, *Looking Back at Sovietology: An Interview with William Odom and Alexander Dallin* (Washington D.C.: The Kennan Institute for Advanced Russian Studies, The Woodrow Wilson International Center for Scholars, 2009).

2. About American Sovietology, see David C. Engerman, *Know Your Enemy: Rise and Fall of America's Soviet Experts* (Oxford: Oxford University Press, 2009).

3. Stephen Kotkin, "1991 and the Russian Revolution: Sources, Conceptual Categories, Analytical Frameworks," *Journal of Modern History* 70 (June 1998): 424.

4. About the asymmetry in the bilateral relationship, see in details Angela E. Stent, *The Limits of Partnership: U.S.-Russian Relations in the Twenty-First Century* (Princeton, NJ; and Oxford: Princeton University Press, 2014).

5. Stephen E. Hanson and Blair A. Ruble, "Rebuilding Russian Studies," *Problems of Post-Communism*, 52:3 (May–June 2005), 49-57; Jason Horowitz, "Russia Experts See Thinning Ranks' Effect on U.S. Policy," *New York Times*, March 7, 2014; Kenneth Yalowitz and Matthew Rojansky, "The Slow Death for Russian and Eurasian Studies," *The National Interest*, May 23, 2014; Angela Stent, "Why America Doesn't Understand Putin," *Washington Post*, March 14, 2014; Dominic Basulto, "America's Russian Studies Programs: From Dostoevsky to Derivatives,," *Russia Direct* (January 30, 2015): http://www.russia-direct.org/opinion/americas-russian-studies-programs-dostoevsky-derivative. The most recent survey of the state of Russian Studies with accent on disparity between the rich intellectual capacity and shrinking funding for the research see in: Theodore P. Gerber. The State of Russian Studies in the United States: An Assessment by the Association for Slavic, East European, and Eurasian Studies (ASEEES), July 2015, available at https://pitt.app.box.com/FINAL-ASEEES-assessment.

6. Angela Stent, "How Deep is the Russian Studies Bench?" in *Best Russian Studies Programs 2015*. Russia Direct Report, Issue 8, April (2015): 25.

7. About post-Soviet *Amerikanistika*, see Victoria I. Zhuravleva and Ivan I. Kurilla, "Problemy razvitiya amerikanistiki v postsovetskoy Rossii,," in Nikolai N. Bolkhovitinov, ed., *Amerikanskii ezhegodnik, 2005* (Moscow: Nauka, 2007): 80–93; Ivan I. Kurilla, Victoria I. Zhuravleva, "Teaching U.S. History in Russia: Issues, Challenges, and Prospects," *The Journal of American History*, March (2010): 1138–44.

8. Max Lerner, *Razvitie tsivilizatsii v Amerike: Obraz zhizni i myslei v Soedinennykh Shtatah segodnya [America as civilization: Life and thought in the United States today]*, trans. V. Borisov et al. in 2 vols. (Moscow: Raduga, 1992); Arthur M. Schlesinger Jr., *Tsikly amerikanskoy istorii [Cycles of American history]*, trans. P. A. Razvin and E. I. Buharova (Moscow: Progress-Akademiia, 1992); Daniel J. Boorstin, *Amerikantsy: Kolonial'nyi opyt [The Americans: The colonial experience]*, trans. V. T. Oleinika (Moscow: Progress–Litera, 1993); Daniel J. Boorstin, *Amerikantsy: Natsional'nyi opyt [The Americans: The national experience]*, trans. Y. A. Zarahovich and V. S. Nesterov (Moscow: Progress–Litera, 1993); Daniel J. Boorstin, *Amerikantsy: Demokraticheskii opyt [The Americans: The democratic experience]*, trans. V. T. Oleinik (Moscow: Progress–Litera, 1993); Louis Hartz, *Liberal'naia traditsiia v Amerike [The liberal tradition in America]*, trans. G. P. Blyablin et al. (Moscow: Progress-Akademiia, 1993); Vernon L. Parrington, *Osnovnye techeniia*

amerikanskoi mysli [Main currents in American thought: An interpretation of American liter-
ature from the beginnings to 1920], trans. V. Voronin and V. Tarhov, in 3 vols. (Moscow: Izdatel'stvo inostrannoi literatury, 1962). Compare to: Howard Zinn, *Narodnaya isto-* *riya SShA: s 1492 goda do nashikh dnei [A people's history of the United States, 1492–present]*, trans. G. P. Blyablin et al. (Moscow: Ves' mir, 2006).

9. See, for example, Oliver Stone and Peter Kuznick, *Nerasskazannaya istoriya SShA [The Untold History of the United States]* (Moscow: Kolibri, 2014).

10. See, for example, Alexander Gabuev, "Iarye sovetchiki. Kto v Vashingtone raz-biraetsia v Rossii," *Kommersant.ru* (May 19, 2014), http://www.kommersant.ru/doc/2469723.

11. The genealogy of sociocultural approach differs from different viewpoints. From our perspective, the most important books include: Edward W. Said, *Orientalism* (New York: Knopf Doubleday Publishing Group, 1979); Tsvetan Todorov, *Conquest of America: The Question of the Other* / Trans. from the French by Richard Howard (New York: Harper & Row, 1984); Larry Wolff, *Inventing Eastern Europe: The Map of Civiliza-tion on the Mind of the Enlightenment* (Stanford, CA: Stanford University Press, 1994); David Campbell, *Writing Security: United States Foreign Policy and the Politics of Identity*, Revised Edition (Minneapolis: University of Minnesota Press, 1998); Walter L. Hixson, *The Myth of American Diplomacy: National Identity and U.S. Foreign Policy* (New Haven, CT: Yale University Press, 2008); Iver B. Neumann, *Uses of the Other: the "East" in European Identity Formation* (Minneapolis: University of Minnesota Press, 2008); Ted Hopf, *Social Construction of International Politics: Identities and Foreign Policies, Moscow, 1955 and 1999* (Ithaca, NY: Cornell University Press, 2002); Ted Hopf, *Reconstructing the Cold War: The Early Years, 1945–1958* (London: Oxford University Press, 2012). The examples of the U.S-Russian relations history based on this approach, see in David S. Foglesong, *The American Mission and the "Evil Empire": The Crusade for a "Free Rus-sia"since 1881* (Cambridge: Cambridge University Press, 2007); David C. Engerman, *Know Your Enemy: The Rise and Fall of America's Soviet Experts* (Oxford: Oxford Univer-sity Press, 2009); Ivan I. Kurilla, *Zaokeanskie partnery: Amerika i Rossiya v 1830–1950-e gody [Partners across ocean: America and Russia in 1830–1850]* (Volgograd: Izdatel'stvo VolGU, 2005); Victoria I. Zhuravleva, *Ponimanie Rossii v SShA: obrazy i myfy , 1881–1914 [Understanding Russia in the United States: Images and Myths, 1881–1914]* (Moscow: Izda-tel'stvo RGGU, 2012).

12. *Rossiia i SShA na stranitsakh uchebnikov: opyt vzaimnykh reprezentatsii*, pod red. V.I. Zhuravlevoi, I.I. Kurilly (Volgograd: Izd-voVolGU, 2009) [Victoria I. Zhuravleva and Ivan I. Kurilla, eds., *Russia and the United States: Mutual Representations in the Textbooks* (Volgograd: Kennan Institute, Volgograd University Press, 2009)]. Yurii Stu-lov's and Janet E. Dean's reviews on this book see in *Russian Journal of Communication*, 4, no. 1–2 (2011): 147–53.

13. For a conference report see, David Ayers, "Russian/Soviet Studies in the United States, American Studies in Russia: Mutual Representations," 16–17 February 2011, Russian State University for the Humanities (RSUH), Moscow," *Journal of American Studies* 45 (2011): 1–5.

Acknowledgments

The editors have worked on the project for several years, and during that time, they received support from various academic and educational institutions, and also from their colleagues and friends. We would like to express our gratitude to the Kennan Institute of the Woodrow Wilson International Center for Scholars, which supported the project at its inception, and we would like to thank personally Blair A. Ruble, the institute's director, and his successor Matthew Rojansky, and William E. Pomeranz, deputy director of the institute. We would also like to thank personally the staff of the now-defunct Moscow office of the Kennan Institute, including Galina Levina, Ekaterina Alexeeva, and Irina Petrova-Tsymbal. We also thank the organizations which supported the conferences we held while developing the project, in particular, the Russian Academic Foundation for the Humanities, the United States Embassy in Moscow, and the Fulbright Program in Russia. Special thanks for supporting our academic endeavors go to the administration of the universities where the editors worked during the project: the Russian State University for the Humanities and Volgograd State University. Due to considerations of space, we cannot list everyone, but we would like to give our thanks to our colleagues from the Russian Association of the United States Historians, and also to our American colleagues who study Russian-American relations and with whom we had many fruitful discussions in various venues, including the ASEEES conventions. We gladly share the project's achievements with all these people and institutions, while the project's drawbacks are entirely ours.

Part I

US Russian Studies and Russian *Amerikanistika* in Historical Retrospective

ONE

How Home Agenda Defines the Study of the Other

Russia and the United States in the 1850s

Ivan Kurilla

The period between the European revolutions of 1848–1849 and the emancipation of Russian serfs and the start of the American Civil War in 1861 was marked by intense political debates, both in Russia and in the United States, especially about the fate of the "special institutions" of serfdom and slavery, but also about the territorial expansion of the two countries and the future of the Vienna system of international relations. Increased contact and the similarity of the problems that the two countries faced lead to increased attention to the Other and the first appearance of special works published in each country about the other one. This chapter analyses the links between developments of political and social agendas and the ways each nation was represented in the home discourse that shaped biases as well as provided insights.

Mutual interest of Americans and Russians can be traced to the earliest periods of their interaction. By the mid-nineteenth century that interest started to take an academic shape. That was a result of several factors, including Emperor Nicholas's search for a source of industrial innovations independent from his rival England and the subsequent invitation of American engineers to assist Russian government in the technological modernization of the empire. The rapid territorial growth of both countries and the rise of the problems of serfdom and slavery also brought the two countries closer to each other through shared social problems.

Russian modernization and American participation in the technological rearmament of Russia were important driving forces behind the mutual interest and helped several important studies of the Other appear.

Thus, the first survey of America by Russians that went beyond
traveler's memoir was made in the late 1830s by the visiting engineers of
the Corps of Means of Communication (later Ministry of Transportation)
and Russian Navy officers who studied American technology in order to
apply it to Russian railroad and steamboat construction. Detailed reports
about railroads, steamboats, and other modern transportation technologies in the United States written by Pavel Melnikov in 1839 were published in the departmental *Journal of Ways of Communication* from 1841 to
1842.[1] Soon afterward American engineers were invited to Russia as con-
sultants and organizers of railroad and steam engines construction. The
United States became the most important source of the innovations introduced to the empire during Nicholas's modernization effort; by the end
of the period, a Russian journalist called the United States "a hotbed of
industry."[2]

At the time, Russian interest in the United States was driven by a need
for rapid industrial development. It is no wonder, then, that the first
Russian scholar sent to the United States, a member of Russian Imperial
Academy of Sciences, Joseph Hamel (Russian: Iosif Gamel'), was famous
most of all for his description of new inventions and organization of
industrial exhibitions. Hamel went to the United States on the eve of
Crimean War, and prolonged his stay there from 1853 to 1856. The Russian scholar was among the scientists invited to witness the first attempt
to set trans-Atlantic telegraph cable. Hamel visited, among other places,
Harvard University and the Smithsonian Institution. His goal was "to get
closer acquaintance of scientific institutions of America with the works of
our Academy, as people here possess very little knowledge about us."[3]
The Cincinnati *Daily Enquirer* wrote upon his departure:

> At all our fairs, cattle shows, school examinations, school openings,
> trial trips, ship launches, great castings, etc., as well as our anniversar-
> ies, and the lesser and greater celebrations of all our public institutions,
> the Doctor's face had become quite familiar, Our institutions were care-
> fully studied by him in order to give a thorough knowledge of
> American enterprise in science, art or public charity.[4]

The Russian government was especially interested in the applied side of
American science. It is telling that the Hamel's report to the academy
included technical rather than scientific achievements. That was probably
the reason for the negative review made by the new (since 1855) president of the Academy of Sciences Dmitrii Bludov: "it is questionable
whether further stay [of Hamel] abroad could bring any special benefit
for the technology or industry."[5] Engineers proved to be better equipped
to study technological advances than scholars.

Academician Hamel was not only interested in the modernization of the Russian state that was the target of enlightened bureaucrats of the Emperor Nicholas's administration. Upon return home he found a fresh atmosphere of expectations of liberal reforms from the new monarch (Alexander II inherited the throne from his father Nicholas I in 1855). Hamel published a series of articles in Russian magazines and newspapers about modern inventions of the Americans with special emphasis on the social impact of the novelties. Thus, while describing steam machines for newspaper production, Hamel pointed out the "extraordinary services that mechanics in America made to the rapid spread of knowledge, on the one hand, and facilitating that spread by applying it to locomotive and steamboat, on the other."[6] By including such an argument he managed to address Russian society's hopes for the reforms.

For the Americans, the technological advance of Russia was a less interesting theme, but American engineers' participation in the Russian efforts to build railroads, steamboats, and telegraph became the source of their compatriots' interest in the history of Russian modernization. Among the most famous works on Russia published by American travelers in the late 1840s were the historical survey of Peter the Great by young American diplomat John Lothrop Motley,[7] and a book written by another secretary of the US legation, John S. Maxwell, in which he compared two epochs of Russian modernization: "Nicholas sent to America for bridge builders and millwrights, as Peter sent to Holland for blacksmiths and carpenters."[8]

For the United States, the 1840s was a decade of rapid territorial growth that included the annexation of Texas, acquisitions of Mexican territory after the war of 1846–1848, the division of Oregon in 1846, and even dreams about acquiring Central America and Cuba. Such an agenda dictated an interest in the territorial expansion of other states, and Russia with its wars in the South gave Americans a good reference point.

Circassia; or a Tour to the Caucasus by George L. Ditson, published in 1850, was an account of Russia's war for territorial expansion.[9] Ditson compared Russian realities to those known to his US readers:

> The Americans require only to understand the condition of the people subdued and being subdued—the policy of the victors, and the result of their conquest, to recognize a picture of our wars with the Indians, the wresting from them their lands, driving them from the more sacred graves of their fathers—to assent to what all my observations bear me out in asserting, that Russia is doing much to civilize and christianize the eastern world.[10]

Ditson also quoted Russian prince Kotsohobey (probably Kotzebue?) as saying: "These Circassians are just like your American Indians—as untamable and uncivilized—and that, owing to their natural energy of character, extermination only would keep them quiet, or that if they came under Russian rule, the only safe policy would be to employ their wild and warlike tastes, against others."[11] Foreign reality could be best presented and explained by comparisons with home analogues.

European revolutions of 1848–1849 changed the political agenda in both countries for a while. Some Americans now believed that the "Spring of Nations" provided them with an opportunity to change the whole world order and to amend Americans' identity in order to align it with the new importance of their republican model for the Old World. Such an attempt was made by the "Young America" movement and some other politicians who aspired to elevate US international positions. Among other propositions, the leaders of the movement suggested a re-evaluatation of Russia's role in world affairs and called for American attitudes toward the Russian Empire to change. The northern empire was the main guarantor and defender of legitimist principles set by the Vienna system of international relations, but it was also a friendly power that provided assistance to American aspirations. That is why conservative American statesmen tried to improve US positions within the existing world order and considered Russia a diplomatic ally. "Young Americans," by contrast, wanted to overthrow the system that did not provide the United States with a high position in the world hierarchy; such an aim involved diminishing Russia—the guardian of the existing system. Their worldview was much more ideology-driven: the democratic and nationalist European revolutionaries looked at the United States as the model for their constitutional projects. The new generation of American politicians wanted to revolutionize the international order overnight and place their exemplary democratic republic at the top echelon of world power, instead of gradually climbing within the existing international system based on un-American principles of legitimization and monarchical rule.

The most comprehensive proposition to revolutionize the international system by antagonizing Russia was published by Congressman Henry Winter Davis in 1852. The book under the title *The War of Ormuzd and Ahriman in the Nineteenth Century* became, with historical irony, the first book devoted to US-Russian relations and one of the earliest American books on the international relations. The structure of the book explained the author's idea: starting with the history of the Holy Alliance created in Vienna, he proceeded to the sequence of "revolts against the Holy conspirators" in 1830 and 1848–1849, and continued by contrasting "American and English liberty" and "Russian Dictatorship." The last chapter was devoted to "The American Republic and the Last War of Freedom and Despotism."[12]

The author defined his task in a preface titled: "To the American People": "The American People have passed the season of youth when withdrawn from the eye of the world their pleasures might blamelessly be their pursuit. In the maturity . . . [t]hey cannot if they would be silent and neutral in that great controversy of the age which they opened on the field of battle."[13] Congressman Davis developed the idea of two central states of the world destined to set its fate. The idea was sharpened to its extreme: Russia in the book was a representation of evil, while America was a face of good.

"I insist," Davis wrote,

> that this power [Russia—I.K.] must from necessity, on principle, and by inclination, be devoted to the ruin of all free governments: that it is absolutely inconsistent with the existence of the English monarchy and the American Republic as free popular representative governments: and that they will be compelled sooner or later to defend by force of arms their freedom and independence against the intrigue, the diplomacy, the legislation, the hostilities of the despotic powers of Europe.[14]

The author saw the question of the day manifest:

> shall we wait till those powers, having utterly rooted out free governments from Europe, shall turn their might for our destruction, alone and without allies;—or shall we now size the first opportunity of a decisive outbreak in Europe to aid the cause of freedom with arms and money, fight our battle by the armies of European revolutionists on the field of Europe, and by the aid of our allies for ever settle the question between freedom and despotism.[15]

The author also reminded his readers that Russia possessed Alaska and was "therefore an *American power*—the jealous neighbor of this Republic—as insolent, aggressive, and tenacious as she has always proved herself on the opposite continent,"[16] but also pointed out that American "interests [we]re as directly opposed as our institutions, policy, and principles. Russia is a great wheat country of Europe. . . to cut off or to cripple the commerce of the United States, is to rid herself of her chief, and only dangerous competitor."[17] That is why, Davis insisted, Russia was a natural rival of the United States and that it needed to be contained.

Such a view suggested a radical change in Russia's image in American political debates; and many journalists, especially those agitated by exiled Hungarian leader Louis Kossuth's tour of the United States in 1851–1852,[18] readily joined the anti-Russian campaign.

Several magazines published negative reviews of George Ditson's book on his Caucasian travels. The reviewers blamed the author for his pro-Russian bias while, as *New Englander and Yale Review* put it, the Circassians were "fighting for their lives and their freedom." In a revealing manner the reviewer also relied on American analogues to explain Russian realities: "By the treaty of Adrianople in 1829 Turkey ceded to Russia all the littoral of the Black Sea; which is very much as if Mexico should cede to the United States Cuba or Porto Rico."[19] While Ditson in 1850 compared Circassians to American Indians, calling Russian advances in the Caucasus a "civilizing" move, an author of *US Democratic Review* doubted that Russia had a civilizing mission, and compared people of the Caucasus to "the followers of Leonidas at Thermopylae."[20]

Two years later, former editor of the *US Democratic Review* and one of the Young America leaders George N. Sanders, by 1854 US consul in London, invited exiled revolutionaries to dine at his house. Russia was represented by Alexander Herzen, who perspicaciously linked the "idea of giving a diplomatic dinner to the enemies of all existing governments" with the Americans' belief that they sent ambassadors "not to kings but to peoples."[21] That was a witty explanation of the "Young America" foreign policy worldview.

However, by that time the anti-Russian sentiments had proved to be short lived. "Revolutionaries" among American foreign policy ideologues were unable to challenge seriously the dominant conservative attitude that soon brought US diplomacy significant rewards. That was the time of Crimean War of 1853–1856, when American sympathies turned to the Russian side.

It was during that war when Russia and the United States signed a convention on Neutral Rights (1854).[22] The military defeat also made questions of international law very important for Russia. In 1855, one of the first Russian scholars of the field Kharkov professor Dmitrii Kachenovsky defended his doctoral dissertation about privateers and the rights of neutral commerce at Moscow University. He included in his thesis quotations from the opinions of US statesmen John Adams and Daniel Webster.[23] A year later Kachenovsky published his main work on American history, a biographical article about Daniel Webster.[24]

The content of the article exceeds the limits of a usual biography. Kachenovsky explained his choice of a topic: "Among the North American statesmen nobody had wider reputation than Webster." He continued,"He occupied an important place in the history of the United States for about thirty years."[25] That is why Kachenovsky's biography of Webster was in fact a detailed history of the United States in the first half of the nineteenth century. Two themes occupy the central part of the biography: the federative state and the diplomacy of a young republic. In the early days of a new emperor, Professor Kachenovsky defended the principles of the American Constitution: there is no "unbridled democracy" but a "complex system of checks and balances."[26] Kachenovsky acquainted his Russian readers with the essence of discussions about constitutional doctrine held in the United States in the 1830–1850s. He analyzed the Hayne-Webster debate and compared Webster's views with those of Southern ideologue John Calhoun.[27] The Russian professor was on Webster's side in those debates; he did not know yet that several years later Abraham Lincoln would use Webster's position as a legal basis for his fight against Southern rebels.

The second part of the biography was devoted to Daniel Webster's diplomacy. Kachenovsky's assessment of the Webster-Ashburton treaty

(1842) between the United States and England emphasized the peaceful solution of the international disputes. That was his principal position caused by the Crimean defeat. One of the Russian professor's colleagues quoted his credo: "Let the bloody specter of the countless people who died for Sebastopol urge us to pay attention to international affairs."[28] His conclusion was an example of wishful thinking caused by the comparison of Crimean War and Webster-Ashburton negotiations: "International problems must be solved by concessions and agreements; war should be the last resort and used only in the situations when independence and sacred rights are concerned, and not before diplomacy has exhausted its means."[29]

The end of the international crisis (with the signing of the Paris Treaty between the Russian Empire and its enemies in 1856) coincided with the aggravation of internal tensions in both countries. Russia and the United States turned to their home problems. "Russia was concentrating" as its Minister of Foreign Affairs Alexander Gorchakov stated, while the United States, since 1857 under the presidency of the former minister to Russia James Buchanan, was trying to check the coming Civil War.

These new agendas in the two countries also provided incentive for academics to use the other country in order to support their views regarding home developments.

Political agitation peaked in the second half of the 1850s, the "antebellum period" in the United States and the immediate aftermath of the Crimean War and eve of the Great reforms in the Russian Empire. During just a few years, Russian magazines published numerous articles about the United States. One of the reasons for such an interest was the softening of censorship at the beginning of Alexander II's reign. Finally, criticisms of slavery were permitted, but direct attacks on serfdom were still prohibited. It was then when Russian liberals published translations of *Uncle Tom's Cabin* by Harriett Beecher Stowe, analyzed problems of Negro slavery, and taught the history of slaveholding in the United States in Russian universities. The United States in Russian public opinion during that period was looked at as a friendly nation with a similar set of problems.

Notwithstanding the socioeconomic differences between serfdom and slavery, defenders and critics used examples of the other country's institution to support their positions regarding the institution in their own country. This interest brought the topic to university classrooms; probably for the first time in the countries' history, Russian professors lectured on America and US professors lectured on Russia.

Dmitrii Kachenovsky had by that time established close ties with a group of liberal intelligentsia—the famous circle of Professor Timofei Granovskii of Moscow University—and had become a popular professor at his own Kharkov University.

One of Kachenovsky's students, the famous sociologist Maxim Kova-levsky, recollected that in the late 1850s his mentor "for months in a row expounded on the history of abolition of negro trading, and hundreds of his students in his allusions fairly recognized an attack on serfdom."[30] Another student, future Odessa mayor Petr Zelenoi, remembered one of his lectures (that took place on November 10, 1857):

> The lecture of Prof. Kachenovsky that could not be mentioned in the press was delivered with the great ardor; it attracted so many listeners that they could not fit to one room and adjacent corridor; and it made tremendous impression. . . . There is no need to explain that every listener clearly understood and felt that telling about slaves' sufferings Kachenovsky meant whites as well as blacks.

The memoirist also quoted a verse that appeared the day after the lecture in manuscript copies: "I remember the moment: he narrated about negroes . . . and we felt shame and fear!"[31] During those years Kachenovsky included his criticism of slavery in all of his lectures and publications, even in his review of the works of the English sociological society.[32] When publishing the French translation of his biography on Webster in 1858, Kachenovsky added a preface, where he stressed the international importance of the US debates: "That struggle is especially important for humankind because it focuses on the problem of slavery; the solution of the problem will define the future of America."[33]

It is interesting that the story of professor Kachenovsky lecturing Russian students about the evils of American slavery in order to criticize serfdom had its direct parallel in the United States. Also in the fall of 1857, young Andrew Dickson White returned from his post as attaché to the US legation in St. Petersburg and lectured his compatriots on the evils of serfdom. White recollected in his *Autobiography* that he

> sketched, in broad strokes, the effects of the serf system, effects not merely upon the serfs, but upon the serf owners, and upon the whole condition of the empire. I made it black indeed, as it deserved, and though not a word was said regarding things in America, every thoughtful man present must have felt that it was the strongest indict-ment against our own system of slavery which my powers enabled me to make. . . . It would have been easy to attack slavery and thus at once shut the minds and hearts of a large majority of the audience. But I felt then, as I have generally felt since, that the first and best thing to do is to set people at thinking, and to let them discover, or think that they discover, the truth for themselves.[34]

Two educators used the same strategy to achieve similar aims in two different countries; the situation is even more revealing as there was no censorship in the United States; however, mainstream public opinion effectively played the same role as Russian state censors, thus providing incentives to bypass it with the other country's analogues. Still, the most interesting conclusion for our purposes is that the two educators' focus on the Other's institution was the direct result of their preoccupation with the social turmoil of their home countries.

During two antebellum decades, US and Russian views of each other were defined by the two nations' home agendas. The main themes of the epoch were modernization, expansion, and the fates of slavery and serfdom. Each of the themes discussed by the home society forced travelers and academics to focus their attention on the relevant experience of the other country. Sometimes those agendas coincided (like modernization, when Russians were interested in technological transfer and Americans were proud of the role their engineers played in Russian development). Sometimes agendas looked similar (like the fights to abolish slavery and serfdom), while other times the agendas were clearly different or even opposite (as they were during the European political crisis of 1848–1849), but always needed the Other as a reference point in home debates.

Academic interest was not excluded or isolated from the general agenda of society. Scholarly study of the Other was destined to play its own role in the processes of building national identities by describing and labeling the Other. After the end of serfdom in Russia (1861) and slavery in the United States (1863) the two countries stopped playing the role of mirrors for each other. They became closer to Europe and farther from each other. The institutions that brought them together disappeared, while principles that separated them became more prominent. This shift was a major factor in the process of alienation of the two nations in the last third of the nineteenth century. At the same time, the intensity of academic research on the other country also decreased during the subsequent era.

NOTES

1. See: Melnikov, Pavel P. "Nachertanie obshchei sistemy vodyanykh soobshchenii Soedinennykh Shtatov" (Review of the general system of water ways of the United States) (Extract from the report of travel of Colonel Melnikov), *Zhurnal putei soobshcheniya*, 3 (1841): Kn. 1: 1–119; Melnikov, Pavel P. "O parokhodakh na Mississippi i ee pritokakh" (On steamboats on Mississippi and its tributaries), *Zhurnal putei soobshcheniya*. 3 (1841): Kn. 2: 135–206; Kn. 3: 225–279; Melnikov, Pavel P. "Opisanie v tekhbicheskom otnoshenii zheleznykh dorog Severo-Amerikanskikh Shtatov" (Technical description of railroads in the North-American States), *Zhurnal putei soobshcheniya*, 2 (1842): Kn. 1: 15–85; Kn. 2: 95–197; Kn. 3: 209–265; Kn. 4: 285–374. 3 (1842), Kn. 1: 1–70; Kn. 2: 85–156; Melnikov, Pavel P. "Parokhody upotreblyaemye v chasti Mississippi nizhe N.Orleana" (Steamboats in use on Mississippi down from New Orleans), *Zhurnal putei soobshcheniya*, 3 (1841), Kn. 1: 285–362.
2. Rotchev A. G. "Vospominaniya russkogo turista. Iz puteshestvii A. G. Rotcheva" (Memoirs of a Russian Tourist. From the travels of A. G. Rotchev), *Panteon. Zhurnal literaturno-khudozhestvennyi*, 12 (December 1853): kn.12, smes', 65.
3. I. Hamel to P. Fuss, 28 March 1854; Hamel to Fuss, 18/30 April 1854, St. Petersburg branch of RAS Archives, Fond 2 Kantseliaria Konferentsii AS. Op. 1–1853. D. 5.

"O napravlenii akademika Gamelya s Angliyu i Severnuyu Ameriku" (On sending academician Gamel off to England and North America). L. 26–29 ob.

4. Cincinnati *Daily Enquirer,* 27 May 1856. Cit.: Saul N.E. *Distant Friends: the United States and Russia, 1763–1867.* Lawrence: University Press of Kansas, 1991, 232.

5. St.Petersburg branch of RAS Archives, Fond 2 Kantseliaria Konferentsii AS. Op. 1–1853. D. 5. "O napravlenii akademika Gamelya s Angliyu i Severnuyu Ameriku" (On sending academician Gamel off to England and North America. L. 47 ob.–48.

6. [Hamel I.] "Noveishie usovershenstvovania mashin, vvedennykh v Anglii i Amerike dlya pechatania gazet i drugikh periodicheskikh izdanii" (Recent improvements of the machines introduced in England and America for printing newspapers and other periodicals), *Syn otechestva,* 16 (1857): 366.

7. Motley, John Lothrop. "Peter the Great," *North American Review,* 61, no. 129 (October 1845): 269–319.

8. Maxwell J. S. *The Czar, His Court and People; including a Tour in Norway and Sweden.* 3rd. ed. New York, 1850 [1st ed. 1848], 128.

9. Ditson G. L. *Circassia; or, A Tour to the Caucasus.* New York: Stringer & Tounsend, London: T.C. Newby, 1850.

10. Ibid., x.

11. Ibid., 311.

12. Davis, Henry W. *The War of Ormuzd and Ahriman in the Nineteenth Century.* Baltimore: James S. Waters, 1852.

13. Ibid., iii.

14. Ibid., 275–76.

15. Ibid., 276–77.

16. Ibid., 361.

17. Ibid., 362.

18. It was during this intensive anti-Russian campaign that long-time Russian consul in New York Alexei Yevstafiev wrote a highly critical book about American democracy. The book, however, stayed unpublished and is kept in the Manuscript Division of New York Public Library. See: Eustaphieve A. The Great Republic Tested by the Touch of Truth (manuscript dated May 15, 1852), *Papers of Yevstafiev, Aleksyei Grigoryevich, 1783–1857.* New York Public Library.

19. "Caucasus," *New Englander and Yale Review,* 9, no. 33 (February 1851): 89, 107–8.

20. "Circassia and the Caucasus," *United States Magazine and Democratic Review,* 31, no. 172 (October 1852): 301–4.

21. Herzen A. *My Past and Thoughts* (Berkeley: University of California Press. 1982), 478.

22. Ponomarev V. N. *Krymskaya voina i russko-amerikanskie otnosheniya* (Crimean War and Russian-American Relations). Moscow: Institut Rossiyskoy istorii RAN, 1993.

23. Kachenovsky, Dmitry. *O kaperakh i prizovom sudoproizvodstve, v otnoshenii k neytral'noy torgovle* (On the Capers and Prize Proceedings as Related to the Neutral Commerce) (Moscow, 1855), 166.

24. Kachenovsky, Dmitry I. "Zhizn' i sochineniia Danielia Vebstera" (Life and works of Daniel Webster), *Russkii vestnik,* 3 (1856): 385–416; 4 (1856): 239–78; Katchenovsky D. *Daniel Webster. Etude Biographique.* Bruxelles & Ostende, 1858.

25. Kachenovsky, Dmitry I. "Zhizn' i sochineniia Danielia Vebstera," *Russkii vestnik,* 3, 385.

26. Ibid., 398–99.

27. Ibid., 411.

28. Yastrzhembsky V. Ya. "D. I. Kachenovsky kak uchenyi i prepodavatel" (D. I. Kachenovsky as a scholar and professor), in: *Pamyati Dmitriya Ivanovicha Kachenovskogo* (Kharkov, 1905), 13.

29. Kachenovsky, Dmitry I. "Zhizn' i sochineniia Danielia Vebstera," *Russikii vestnik, 4,* 275.

30. Kovalevsky M. M. "Moe nauchnoe i literaturnoe skitalchestvo" (My scholarly and literature roaming), *Russkaya mysl.* 1. (1895): 64.

31. Zelenoi P. A. "O poslednikh pyati godakh krepostnogo sostoyaniya." In: *Velikaya reforma*. Moscow, 4 (1911): 88.
32. Kachenovsky Dmitry I. "Trudy obshchestva, uchrezhdennogo v Anglii dlia razvitiia obshchestvennoi nauki," *Russkoe slovo*. 1860. Kn.12. (2nd pag.), 65.
33. Katchenovsky D. *Daniel Webster: Etude biographique*. Bruxelles, Ostende, 1858, iv.
34. White A. D. *Autobiography of Andrew Dickson White*. In 2 vols. Vol.1. (New York, 1905), 80–81.

BIBLIOGRAPHY

"Caucasus," *New Englander and Yale Review*, 9, no. 33 (1851, February): 88–109.
"Circassia and the Caucasus," *United States Magazine and Democratic Review*, 31, no. 172 (1852, October): 301–4.
Davis, Henry W. *The War of Ormuzd and Ahriman in the Nineteenth Century*. Baltimore: James S.Waters, 1852.
Ditson, George L. *Circassia; or, A Tour to the Caucasus*. New York: Stringer & Tounsend, London: T. C. Newby, 1850.
Eustaphieve, Alexyei. *The Great Republic Tested by the Touch of Truth* (manuscript dated May 15, 1852). In: Papers of Yevstafiev, Aleksyei Grigoryevich, 1783–1857. New York Public Library.
[Hamel, Iosif]. "Noveishie usovershenstvovania mashin, vvedennykh v Anglii I Amerike dlya pechatania gazet i drugikh periodicheskikh izdanii" (Recent improvements of the machines introduced in England and America for printing newspapers and other periodicals). *Syn otechestva*, 16 (1857): 365–67.
Herzen, Alexander. *My Past and Thoughts*. Berkeley: University of California Press, 1982.
Kachenovskii, Dmitry I. *O kaperakh i prizovom sudoproizvodstve, v otnoshenii k neytral'noy torgovle* (On the Capers and Prize Proceedings as Related to the Neutral Commerce). Moscow, 1855.
———. "Trudy obshchestva, uchrezhdennogo v Anglii dlia razvitiia obshchestvennoi nauki," *Russkoe slovo*, 12 (1860).
———. "Zhizn' i sochineniia Danielia Vebstera" (Life and works of Daniel Webster), *Russkii vestnik*, 3 (1856): 385–416; 4 (1856): 239–78.
Katchenovsky, Dmitrii. *Daniel Webster. Etude Biographique*. Bruxelles & Ostende: F.Claassen, 1858.
Kovalevsky, Maxim M. "Moe nauchnoe i literaturnoe skital'chestvo" (My scholarly and literature roaming), *Russkaia mysl'*, 1 (1895).
Maxwell, John S. *The Czar, His Court and People; including a Tour in Norway and Sweden*. 3rd.ed. New York: Baker and Scribner, 1850 [1st ed. 1848].
Melnikov, Pavel P. "Opisanie v tekhbicheskom otnoshenii zheleznykh dorog Severo-Amerikanskikh Shtatov" (Technical description of railroads in the North-American States). *Zhurnal putei soobshcheniya*, 2 (1842): Kn. 1: 15–85; Kn. 2: 95–197; Kn. 3: 209–65; Kn. 4: 285–374. 3 (1842), Kn. 1: 1–70; Kn. 2: 85–156.
———. "Nachertanie obshchei sistemy vodyanykh soobshchenii Soedinennykh Shtatov" (Review of the general system of water ways of the United States) (Extract from the report of travel of Colonel Melnikov). *Zhurnal putei soobshcheniya*, 3 (1841): Kn. 1: 1–119.
———. "O parokhodakh na Mississippi i ee pritokakh" (On steamboats on Mississippi and its tributaries). *Zhurnal putei soobshcheniya*, 3 (1841): Kn. 2: 135–206; Kn. 3: 225–79.
———. "Parokhody upotreblyaemye v chasti Mississippi nizhe N.Orleana" (Steamboats in use on Mississippi down from New Orleans). *Zhurnal putei soobshcheniya*, 3 (1841): Kn. 4: 285–362.
Motley, John Lothrop. "Peter the Great." *North American Review*, 61, no. 129 (October 1845): 269–319.

Ponomarev V. N. *Krymskaya voina i russko-amerikanskie otnosheniya* (Crimean War and Russian-American Relations). Moscow: Institut Rossiyskoy istorii RAN, 1993.

Rotchev A. G. "Vospominaniya russkogo turista. Iz puteshestvii A. G. Rotcheva" (Memoirs of a Russian Tourist. From the travels of A. G. Rotchev). *Panteon. Zhurnal literaturno-khudozhestvennyi*, 12, kn. 12 (December 1853): 65–76.

Saul, Norman E. *Distant Friends: The United States and Russia, 1763–1867*. Lawrence: University Press of Kansas, 1991.

White, Andrew Dickson. *Autobiography of Andrew Dickson White*. In 2 vols. New York: The Century Co., 1905.

Wikoff, Henry. *The Reminiscences of an Idler*. New York: Fords, Howard & Hulbert , 1880.

Yastrzhembsky V. Ya. "D. I. Kachenovsky kak uchenyi i prepodavatel" (D. I. Kachenovsky as a scholar and professor). In: *Pamyati Dmitriya Ivanovicha Kachenovskogo*. Kharkov, 1905.

Zelenoi, P. A. "O polednikh piati godakh krepostnogo sostoianiia." In: *Velikaia reforma*. Moscow: Izdatelstvo tov-va I.D.Sytina, 1911. 4, 86–94.

TWO

Russian Ideas of Cassius M. Clay

Vladimir V. Noskov

The period from the Crimean War to the Russo-Turkish War of 1877–1878 occupied a foremost place in the history of the development of Russian national self-consciousness and of Russian-American relations as well. The unprecedented rapprochement and obvious rise of mutual interest distinguished the period as a special one in the process of Russian and American perceiving each other. By the 1850s Russia was a practically unknown country to Americans and their ideas of the mysterious empire remained vague and uncertain. First of all, Americans understood Russia from international point of view and looked at her as a power holding an important place in the world balance of power. In the middle of the nineteenth century, interest in the internal life of Russia began to grow in America.[1] The most widespread ideas of Russia were borrowed by Americans largely from England, but they were inadequate and did not correspond to reality. Intensive development of interrelations generated in the American mind a need for acquiring more precise knowledge of Russia on its own.

The Crimean War was a turning point in the American attitude to Russia. New approaches were manifested by the Ohio Presbyterian minister Charles B. Boynton who later served as a professor of the US Naval Academy and chaplain of the House of Representatives. At the end of the war he published a book aiming to explain "a decided alteration" in American opinion "concerning the parties engaged in this bloody struggle." "A sympathy with Russia is fast springing up in the American heart," Boynton wrote, so it "will not harm us to look upon the great Northern Power from an American position; and this book has been undertaken in the hope that it may induce at least some of my countrymen, to examine, with fresh interest, the position and resources, the spirit and policy, of that European Power which, thus far, has been a constant friend of America."[2] The first chapter of the book was entitled "There should be an American Opinion of Russia founded, not upon European Prejudices, but on Facts."

"Until recently," Boynton stated, "the Empire of the Czars has awakened very little attention or sympathy in the American mind. Its remote position, and the channels through which we have obtained our scanty information, have prevented us from forming any correct and well-defined idea of its prospects, resources and policy." In his opinion, progress of Russia "follows the law of a life, and its development is after the model of a national idea." The United States had its own national idea and it was just the time when the thought should enter the American mind "that a mutual regard might spring up between the two Powers, and that they may yet become the friendly representatives of the two leading ideas of the world."[3] "The American mind expands with a vast idea—its 'manifest destiny,'" Boynton continued. This is universal idea of all great nations and "such an idea may possess the mind of a nation, and may become a reality in the course of its progress."[4]

Boynton wrote further concerning Russia: "Her territorial idea, which she is so rapidly working out, is the grandest conception of the kind, of modern times—perhaps of any age." He defined the Russian national idea as the "vast conception of an empire," so the Russian Empire was "the production of Russian thought."[5] Russia "has now so far emerged from her years of childhood as to have formed a distinct and individual national idea, upon which she has shaped a well-defined national policy," Boynton stated. The Russian "territorial idea" is "one whose grandeur stands unequaled by any idea of empire, whether of ancient or modern times, except by the American thought, which embraces the twin continents of the West." It was a "national idea of territorial greatness."[6] "Since Russia took her place among the nations as one of the great Powers of Europe, her policy has been shaped by one central idea—to recover the old Greek Empire from the grasp of the Turk, to possess herself of Constantinople, and thus extend the Greek Church again over its ancient territory," Boynton wrote ten years later. "She can not and will not abandon the national idea."[7]

The post-Crimean period was marked by growing aspiration of Americans with interests at stake for obtaining their own knowledge of Russia to counterbalance misrepresentations which prevailed in American public consciousness. As the US minister at St. Petersburg, Thomas H. Seymour, noted in December 1856, "Russia is not the barbarous nation which her late adversaries have represented her to be."[8] In the 1850s, ideas of a community of interests, of a common destiny, and a similarity of basic characteristics of the two powers began to enter the American mind. But it "should be noted, moreover, that the friendship, as it developed between the United States and Russia, during and after the Crimean War, was largely based on a belief of the South that Russia with her system of serfdom had interests in common with the South under its system of slavery."[9] In 1858, Minister Francis W. Pickens—the future secessionist governor of South Carolina—wrote in particular: "The highest classes of Russians are very hospitable and kind, and are as warm in their kindness as our Southern planters although so far North. The reason is that their domestic institutions are patriarchal like ours, as contradistinguished from the feudal system."[10]

In the early 1860s, ideas of a community of interests and a similarity of the two powers were developed on other foundations. The Civil War in the United States erupted just after news of the abolition of serfdom in Russia reached America. Both events were considered links in one chain and after the emancipation of American slaves both nations looked at each other as allies in a common struggle for freedom. The process of reconsidering started in the pre-war years. "After the grand and sudden emancipation of the serfs" in Russia, "at a time when the slave states of America were hoping to win in a great secession against the American Union, the admiration for Russia was assiduously cultivated in the North for intimate political reasons."[11] "The American crisis became Civil War just a few weeks after news had crossed the Atlantic of the Russian emancipation of the serfs," another historian wrote." "Now, the abolitionist element in the war aims of the North encouraged some of its journals to reverse completely their previous image of Russian despotism and of the absolute tsar."[12]

The evolution of the views of Andrew D. White, who was an attaché to the US diplomatic mission at St. Petersburg during the Crimean War, is significant in a sense. In the fall of 1855 he wrote privately about Russians: "Their whole ideas are the very reverse of ours."[13] The start of the Great Reforms made him modify his opinion of Russia. "In no other country on earth is there such unity in language, in degree of cultivation, and in basis of ideas," wrote White in 1862. "And, to an American thinker, more hopeful still for Russia is the patriarchal democratic system,— spreading a primary political education through the whole mass." Emperor Alexander II was depicted by him as "the Christian Patriot who made forty millions of serfs forty millions of men."[14] Many years later, after a two-year term as US minister at the court of Alexander III, White kept stating that the Russian reforms of the 1860s were "tending in the right direction."[15]

In the course of the 1860s, Russia and the United States were confronted with similar internal and foreign policy problems. It was a time when the two nations were drawing closer to each other much more than in any other time. For most of the 1860s, the post of US minister at the Russian capital was occupied by Cassius M. Clay, an extravagant Republican politician from Kentucky. Unlike most American diplomats, he deeply integrated into St. Petersburg society, had a lot of acquaintances in different social circles, and had access to various sources of information. That is why Clay was able to form a set of ideas of Russia of his own that he persistently tried to present to his countrymen. Clay made a noticeable contribution to American ideas of Russia. His contribution was of special importance because Clay was an immediate eyewitness of Russia's transformation as a result of the Great Reforms.

Clay became the first American author to use the set expression "Russian Ideas." It is worthwhile to note that, at the same time, the term "Russian Idea" appeared in the writings of Slavophils who were trying to elaborate a national ideology for Russia. For the first time the expression *Russische Ideen* (in German) was used as the title of the collection of Slavophil writings which the brothers Aksakov intended to publish in 1860 in Leipzig.[16] Certainly, Clay's "Russian Ideas" had quite another meaning in comparison with Slavophils' "Russische Ideen." The American politician used the expression to define his own statements about Russia as well as some characteristic ideas about educated Russian society as he understood them.

Clay found himself in Russia by chance and had a rather uncertain perception of the country. His mind was free from prejudices and preconceived opinions of Russia and was open to new knowledge. It was *tabula rasa* where any idea of the unknown country might be fixed. Clay's primary knowledge of Russia manifested itself in his words when he accepted the nomination to St. Petersburg: "Russia is a great and young nation, and must much influence this great crisis; I will go there."[17] According to another version of this story Clay declared to the president: "Well, Russia is a young and powerful nation, and must greatly figure in our affairs: I will accept."[18] The newly appointed minister was advised that he would represent the United States at "the most splendid court in Europe."[19] Comparing Russia with Great Britain and France, Clay wrote that "it is an equal power, becoming cosmopolitan, full of Americans and other travelers—and the most expensive Court in Europe."[20] He also knew that Russia was an expanding power and hailed "the Eastern march of her new-born civilization."[21]

The next stage in Clay's Russian education was the preparation of a speech to be addressed to Emperor Alexander II at an official presentation. The US minister went so far as to define the place of the czar-emancipator in all Russian history. Clay said in particular: "the great reforms which he was attempting in his empire, which . . . would add more to the physical power of his country than did Peter the Great by consolidation and extension; and that the success of his enterprise would, in the estimation of the western nation, place him even above that great ruler."[22] A bit later Clay wrote to the president: "In Russia also we have a friend. The time is coming when she will be a powerful one for us. The emancipation move is the beginning of a new era and new strength."[23]

"The Russians are advancing rapidly in the arts, and are very rapidly throwing off their dependence upon foreign talent," Clay reported to the secretary of state. "I find not only her leading men very shrewd, but her masses which have been denounced through all Europe as very stupid, not at all deficient in shrewdness and ingenuity." In March of 1862 Clay wrote to his wife: "Indeed, I have good reason to believe the more I see of Russia, that the people, great and low, are better and wiser and more civilized than we were led to believe by British columnists, who slander all whom they desire to crush!"[24]

It was evident from the first of Clay's impressions of Russia that he looked at her through the prism of American interests of the day. At the same time he reproduced in his reports many precepts of official Russian propaganda. From the very beginning, Clay adopted a rapturous view of everything in Russia and kept such an approach for the entirety of his diplomatic career. He especially praised the results of the liberal reforms in the most enthusiastic manner. Summing up the results of the first Clay mission to Russia, we may see that during a one year residence in St. Petersburg a specific matrix of his ideas about Russia was formed. These primary perceptions alongside the American agenda of the Civil War period greatly influenced further developments of Clay's views about Russia and everything Russian.

After returning home in August of 1862, the Kentuckian politician was causing the Lincoln administration considerable embarrassment by his intemperate speeches on behalf of emancipation. Striving for emancipation of American slaves, Clay, in his own words, represented "the Russian idea of home-policy."[25] "Russia had emancipated her serfs," he said, "Why does not democratic America liberate her slaves?"[26] His speech delivered at Odd Fellows' Hall in Washington, DC, excited the widest comments.[27] Arguing in favor of immediate emancipation Clay declared: "I think I can say, without implication of profanity or want of deference, that, since the days of Christ himself, such a happy and glorious privilege has not been reserved to any other man to do that amount of good; and no man has ever more gallantly or nobly done it than Alexander II, the Czar of Russia. I refer to the emancipation of the 23,000,000 of serfs." "Whilst I spent days and weeks in moving around, gazing at and admiring the people," he added, "I was surprised; for I had read in English journals of the Russian people being but little better than beasts of the field, but I have found that the Russians are a great race."[28] Throughout the rest of his life Clay was sure that Lincoln's decision to publish the Emancipation Proclamation in September of 1862 was much influenced by his efforts.

Awaiting his second nomination to St. Petersburg, Clay more than once made speeches in favor of the Russian-American alliance. In a speech made in February of 1863 in Albany, Clay declared: "Russia is with us upon the basis of common interests; and whilst the other monarchies may threaten us on one side, we are, on the other, safe in the defense of the greatest liberal of all Europe, Alexander II, who is more worthy of the name of «the Great," for the millions he has made free, than Alexander Macedon was for the millions he made slaves!."[29] Demonstrating the legality of the Emancipation Proclamation, Clay used such an argument among others: "The emperor of Russia, in the arbitration between England and the United States, decided that slaves were legal capture by the rights of war."[30] "My Albany speech of 1863 has been translated . . . into the Russian language, and widely distributed over the empire," Clay wrote in his memoirs.[31] It was translated "into their language, and distributed by thousands all over the Empire; for the Czar was engaged in the same cause at home, and the arguments were good in both nations."[32]

When Clay returned to St. Petersburg in the spring of 1863, he already had a set of clearly defined perceptions about Russia. In Russian society he was regarded as a true friend of the empire and a strong supporter of her policy.[33] The year 1863 was of special importance in Russian history. The Polish Insurrection and the threat of a revival of the Crimean coalition caused an eruption of national feelings throughout the country and led to an unprecedented national consolidation. The US federal government undoubtedly supported Russia in that moment. The Lincoln administration consciously went against the current because the image of "suffering Poland" was a standard American part of a set of perceptions about world and from generation to generation had been firmly established by school history textbooks.[34] But, during the Civil War, political considerations dictated support for the only US ally in Europe, so even the liberal American press justified Russian policy in relation to Poland. For example, "Harper's Weekly could go so far as to compare Alexander II's repression of the Polish Insurrection in 1863 with the attempt of Abraham Lincoln to prevent the South from seceding from the Union."[35] From its side, Russian patriotic propaganda readily supported such a comparison. In early 1864, Clay reported that he had received a note from the chief editor of the Russian Invalid "saying that by the order of the minister of war he sent me several numbers of that journal, comparing the Polish and confederate insurrections, and expressing the sympathy which Russia feels for America."[36]

The Polish Crisis of 1863–1864 was an important landmark in the history of Russia's foreign policy as well as in the development of her national self-consciousness. The Polish events greatly influenced the views of Ivan Aksakov, Nikolai Danilevskii, Fedor Dostoevsky, Konstantin Leont'ev, Mikhail Pogodin, and other creators of Russian national idea. The pro-Russian position of the US minister was manifested in that particular moment quite obviously. What is more, Clay's rhetoric, general orientation, and spirit of argumentation largely coincided with characteristics of Russian publicist writings. However, though he borrowed expressions from Russian thought, Clay was not acquainted with its basic foundations. Meanwhile the Russian attitude to Poland was much more sophisticated than what was available to a foreigner's understanding. The "rejection of the rebellion" did not "show sympathy with the Poles." The phrase illustrates complexity of the Russian mentality. There was one opinion in regard to the Polish Rebellion which was unanimously blamed in Russia as a crime against established order. At the same time the Russian thinkers recognized the Poles' right for any kind of national statehood but implemented by legal means. This idea was well manifested during the World War I. I think it would be better to substitute "was associated" for "get on." As in all other cases, Clay's ideas reflected not only the Russian agenda, but also the American agenda. In July of 1863 Clay wrote to his wife about Russia: "My sympathies are all on her side—for Poland is Catholic and of course antiliberal, and would be the tool of France in her European wars; and as Napoleon [III] has avowed himself our enemy—his enemies are our friends and the reverse." So, he stated in another letter, "I say once more what folly our press is guilty of in denouncing our liberal friend, the Emperor, for the sake of our *conservative enemy*, the New Poland."[37]

"In the mean time Russia does not relax her defences by land and sea, and the Emperor has made himself popular anew with the disaffected nobles, by the spirit with which he defends the integrity of the empire," reported Clay in September of 1863.[38] The next month, two Russian naval squadrons suddenly appeared in American ports. The US minister was sure of the anti-British character of this political demonstration because he knew quite well that the "rivalry of Russia and England may be said to be hereditary, if not natural."[39] "We get all our ideas of Russia and Russians through English sources, ever colored with implacable rivalry," Clay noted in that relation.[40] According to his memoirs, when the Russians "sent their navy into New York harbor, it was generally believed that there was an understanding of mutual aid. The ships could either there be safe, or assist the Americans; whilst Russia could advance toward India by land."[41] "March to India" was indeed one of the cherished Russian ideas that was being developed from the times of Paul I up to the conclusion of the Anglo-Russian *entante cordiale* at the beginning of the twentieth century.[42] In 1863, another plan of attacking the British in India was proposed by a Sevastopol hero, General Stepan Hrulev. Clay was well acquainted with him so his hint about India was of no surprise. A bit earlier he himself had projected a joint Russian-American expedition against British India and continued to be interested in the subject.

Russian expansion in central Asia, which was closely related to a Russian advance toward India, was another subject of Clay's immediate interest. Of course, the US minister did not know the details, but he felt rather well of leading motives of ideological justification for Russian expansion in the region. And once again his reflections were consonant with Russian official propaganda, though he failed to understand all nuances of its sophistication and interpreted the borrowed propagandistic precepts according to his own understanding. Russian expansion in central Asia began after the end of the Caucasian War in 1864 and Clay wrote:

> The world should not regard her progress into Asia with distrust, but with gratification. The new life must come from the west, and Russia is the only nation which can give it. No people are making more advances comparatively than the Russians in the fine and useful arts, in science and letters, and in general intelligence. A great destiny lies before her; let us be careful for our own sakes, and the cause of humanity, to reciprocate her friendly sentiments towards us. [43]

Summing up his reflections on the Cretean crisis of 1866–1867 Clay formulated his "ideas of Russian policy." "That there are some persons in Russia who would desire the possession of Constantinople and the straits, I doubt not," he wrote,

> But I think the ruling minds look upon that project not as a thing to be contended for, or bought at great price of money and blood, but acceptable, if good fortune should throw it into their power. Russia does not now desire war; neither her transition state of labor, nor her rail-ways, nor finances generally, make it now desirable. She does not desire, however, nor would she permit in my opinion, any great power to take Constantinople without a great war. She can carry on a great war even with all her backsets if the nation was much in earnest with it, and such a war would be that, ostensibly at least, for the protection of the Sclave and Greek Christian. [44]

In another report Clay stressed that "Russia does not desire war, but may be led into it at any moment. The Turkish civilization and religion are anachronisms in our days, and must perish sooner or later; the sooner the better." [45] One year later Clay repeated: "My opinion was that Russia neither desired nor anticipated war with Turkey; but was strengthening herself with the Christian populations of the south of Europe, as an offset to the discontented Poles of the Roman church." Returning to the central Asian problem he wrote that

> while Russia has been carrying on an aggressive or defensive war along the whole border of Asia at times, the commerce with that continent has steadily and is steadily increasing. Thus, while Russia is expanding her domain, she is at the same time enlarging her commerce. The result is civilization of Asia, by putting a part of it under a noble government, and consolidating the power and the peace of the Asiatic nations which remain independent, both of which processes inure to the common benefit of the Asiatic races. [46]

It's noteworthy that Clay's ideas about Russian policy in central Asia were in harmony with Ivan Aksakov's ideas, which he wrote of in May of

1868.[47] We may see the similarity of Clay's reflection relating to Constantinople with Nikolai Danilevskii's thought on the same subject expressed in 1869 in his book *Russia and Europe*.[48] The US minister also paid much attention to the pan-Slavistic movement as Danilevskii did in his path-breaking book. Such a consonance of Clay's political ideas and the reflections of the creators of Russian national idea are very significant for understanding the spiritual atmosphere of the time and is of importance for grasping the ideological legacy of the American politician.

Clay was a devoted protectionist and used every opportunity to propagate his views in society of Russian merchants and manufacturers. "I had all my life been a tariff man, under Henry Clay's lead; and during all my late Democratic schooling have not ventured into the deep waters of free trade," Clay wrote. Especially after his "tariff speech" in February of 1866 in Moscow "it began to be understood that I was the friend of home-industry—the 'Russian system.'"[49] Clay was also well acquainted with many Russian aristocrats including members of the imperial family. Some pages of his memoirs are read as a hymn in honor of Russian aristocracy. "The centralization of all the wealth, of all the learning, of all military achievements, of all the aristocracy of a great nation in one circle, under the most finished school of refinement, gives the Russian high-life the precedence over all others in the world," the ex-Minister wrote, "The aristocracy of Russia, men and women, are models of form and refinement; and, as an aggregate, excel all others."[50] Clay liked his Russian "surroundings immensely, for not only was he in an exotic land, but also he felt himself aristocrat among aristocrats at a time when they tried to be mankind's limited benefactors by giving their serfs and slaves freedom on their, the aristocrats', own terms."[51] Imaging himself an aristocrat Clay felt superior to his rival for a diplomatic post, Bayard Taylor, whose commoner's manners did not correspond with "the Russian ideas of sentiment and policy."[52]

Clay paid particular attention to the Russian revolutionary movement, which had its origin in the 1860s and was commonly referred to as nihilism. His first Russian mission was over at the very moment when the Russian capital was suffering from a lot of fires. It was "the immense fire in all the combustible part of St. Petersburg, the work of incendiaries," Clay remembered. There was "a reign of terror." In his opinion the discontented people

> were left without other resort than assassination and intimidation. This is the cause, I believe, of the origin of Nihilism. And its success would not save, but sink, the nation. For no progression can rest upon such basis of the sum of all crimes. The upshot of such a forcible overthrow of the central power would be universal anarchy, and the dissolution of the Empire back into petty governments, and old-time barbarism

Clay also wrote, "Were I a Russian, I should certainly be on the side of absolutism, and await such progress as came of general enlightenment and slow civilization."[53] Thus a striking representative of American democracy, republican and irreconcilable champion of emancipation, revealed himself as a strong opponent of revolutionary actions. Forcible overthrow of the Russian monarchy seemed inadmissible for him, for "a Republic, following in the wake of assassination, could produce no other result than the most disastrous anarchy, and a dissolution of the empire into petty tyrannies and ancient barbarism."[54] Small wonder that Clay supported ratification of the Russian-American Extradition Convention of 1887 and blamed George Kennan for his alleged intention to justify state criminals in Russia.[55]

Certainly, Cassius M. Clay was not a professional researcher on Russia; however, he contributed to educating the US political elite and the American public in general in all Russian matters. From 1861 until the early 1890s, Clay insistently propagated his "Russian Ideas" in official reports, private correspondence, public speeches, personal conversations, newspaper articles, and finally in his richly documented memoir, more than one third of which was devoted to his life and activities in St. Petersburg. This fact itself shows the great importance Clay attached to his sojourn at the Russian imperial court. His tenure as US minister in the Russian capital was the most significant event in Clay's biography and the crowning point of his political career. That is why everything connected with Russia was of special importance for Clay and was painted by him in the warmest colors.

In his later years the ex-minister was ready to refute the lies about Russia being spread by the American press. "I lived in St. Petersburg for nearly nine years, and made Russian life a study; mingling with all classes for that purpose," Clay wrote to the editor of the *Kentucky Herald* in December of 1883. "Perhaps there is no American living or dead who can speak with more authority than I can on the real character of Russia. I believe that there is no more charitable and humane nation on earth than Russia," he stated. Once again Clay reminded that "Russia liberated her slaves not by war, and gave them lands. America did neither." In his memoirs he mentioned several times "the humanity of the Russian nation" and declared: "I stand by my assertion, in the face of so much world-wide calumny, that the Russian is the most humane people in existence." "Hence Russian conquest is a civilizing assimilation, and unlike the British, where the conqueror virtually enslaves the conquered," Clay continued. "I did not hesitate to say that, of all the people I ever knew, the Russians are the most genial and hospitable," Clay wrote further and stressed "the humane spirit of Russia," which "fuses the whole into one national feeling, as in no other land."[56]

The "Russian Ideas" of Cassius M. Clay cannot be regarded as a system of objective knowledge. Trustworthy facts, expert estimates taken from reliable sources, dubious data, and his own subjective appraisals were combined in them in the most fanciful way. Clay made a significant contribution not to the scholarly investigation of Russia but to the shaping of certain stereotypes. His views became part of the more complicated image of Russia which was formed in America during the Civil War and Reconstruction period. Writing and speaking of Russia, Clay consistently developed two main sets of ideas. The first one concerned her image as a progressive state, where under the leadership of a liberal emperor beneficial reforms were conducted. The second set of Clay's ideas focused on Russian foreign policy which, in all its manifestations, was supported and justified by the U.S. minister whether it was the Polish Insurrection, the conquest of central Asia, or Russia's participation in the resolution of the Eastern Question. Every Russian step on the international arena was considered by Clay as beneficial for the whole of world civilization and for his own country. It's important to note that the same subjects—liberal vain attempts inside the country and territorial expansion—remained the most topical Russian problems for generations of Americans, although estimation of processes taking place in Russia as well as her foreign policy has radically changed in the course of time.

The "Russian Ideas" propagated by Clay helped to create the fundamental myth of "historical friendship" between Russia and the United States, which for many years exercised a marked influence on relations between the two powers. Clay's contribution to shaping such a myth may be considered his main service to keeping friendly relations with Russia. The analysis of Clay's "Russian Ideas" is of use because it reveals the information background and ideological context in which rudiments of the Russian studies in America were formed. The ideological legacy of Cassius M. Clay was the important contribution to a certain "proto-knowledge" of Russia which was the prerequisite and necessary precondition for origins of professional Russian studies in the United States. Their foundations were partly laid in the 1860s by aspirations of such scholars-diplomats as Bayard Taylor, Jeremiah Curtin, and Eugene Schuyler, who worked in Russia alongside Clay. Russian General Rostislav Fadeev, who was closely acquainted with Curtin, had all reason to state in 1870: "New concepts of Russia and the Slavonic question are now quickly spreading in America."[57] Cassius M. Clay certainly deserves recognition for his part in America's finding that new knowledge.

NOTES

1. See: Kurilla, I. I. *Zaokeanskie partnery: Amerika i Rossiâ v 1830–1850-e gody* (Volgograd, 2005), 374.
2. Boynton, Ch. B. *The Russian Empire, Its Resources, Government and Policy* (Cincinnati, 1856), iii–iv.
3. Ibid., 11–12.

4. Ibid., 126–30.

5. Ibid., 153–56.

6. Ibid., 185–90.

7. Boynton, Ch. B. *The Four Great Powers: England, France, Russia and America* (Cincinnati, 1866), 391.

8. Cit.: Saul, N. E. *Distant Friends: the United States and Russia, 1763–1867* (Lawrence, 1991), 294.

9. Robertson, J. R. *A Kentuckian at the Court of the Tsars* (Berea, 1935), 17.

10. Cit.: Saul, N. E. *Distant Friends*, 294–95.

11. Callahan, J. M. *Russo-American Relations During the American Civil War* (Morgantown, 1908), 1.

12. Dukes, P. "A Defence of Armageddon: Two Discourses Containing Some American Ideas of Absolutism in Mid-Nineteenth-Century Russia." In: *Russian Thought and Society. 1800–1917* (Keele, 1984), 34.

13. Cit.: Saul, N. E. *Distant Friends*. 230–31.

14. White, A. D. The Development and Overthrow of the Russian Serf-System, *Atlantic Monthly*. 10. no. 61 (November 1862): 551–52.

15. *Autobiography of Andrew Dickson White* (New York, 1905), I. 471.

16. Aksakov, Ivan S., to Koshelevu, Aleksandru I. 16 (28) yanvarya 1860 g. in: *Ivan Sergeevich Aksakov v ego pis'mah*. 3 (Moscow, 1892), 351.

17. *The Life of Cassius Marcellus Clay* (Cincinnati, 1886), 257.

18. "Cassius M. Clay." In: *Reminiscences of Abraham Lincoln* (New York, 1886), 627–28.

19. *The Life of Cassius Marcellus Clay*, 278.

20. Woldman A. A. *Lincoln and the Russians*.(New York, 1961), 103.

21. "Speech of the Hon. Cassius M. Clay." In: *Speeches delivered at the American Union Breakfast given in Paris* (Paris, 1861), 13.

22. C. M. Clay to W. H. Seward; June 21 [July 14], 1861, in: *Foreign Relations of the United States, 1861*, 305.

23. Woldman, A. A. *Lincoln and the Russians*, 109.

24. Cit.: Saul, N. E. *Distant Friends*, 317–19.

25. *The Life of Cassius Marcellus Clay*, 340.

26. Woldman, A. A. *Lincoln and the Russians*, 116–17.

27. Townsend, W. H. *Lincoln and the Bluegrass. Slavery and Civil War in Kentucky* (Lexington, 1955), 293.

28. *The Life of Cassius Marcellus Clay*, 308.

29. *Speech of Cassius M. Clay before the Law Department of the University of Albany* (New York, 1863), 20–21.

30. Ibid, 16.

31. *The Life of Cassius Marcellus Clay*, 414.

32. Ibid., 326; see: *Rech' Kassiya M. Kleya, chitannaya v Yuridicheskom fakultete Albaniyskogo universiteta, v shtate N'yu-York, 3-go fevralya 1863 g.* (St. Petersburg, 1864), 12, 16.

33. *Vospominaniya Dmitriya Alekseevicha Miliutina. 1863–1864.* (M., 2003), 126.

34. See: Zhuravleva, V. I., Kurilla, I. I. "Obrazy Rossii na stranicah amerikanskikh shkol'nykh uchebnikov istorii XIX–nachala XX veka," in *Rossiya i SShA na stranicah uchebnikov: opyt vzaimnykh reprezentaciy* (Volgograd, 2009), 24.

35. Dukes, P. "A Defence of Armageddon," 34–35.

36. C. M. Clay to W. H. Seward; January 25, 1864. In: *FRUS 1864*, 283.

37. Cit.: Saul, N. E. *Distant Friends*, 339.

38. C. M. Clay to W. H. Seward; September 2, 1863. In: *FRUS 1863*, 876.

39. *The Life of Cassius Marcellus Clay*, 294.

40. Ibid., 337.

41. Ibid., 334.

42. See: Noskov, V. V. "'Na sluchay voyny s Angliey': Indiya v voennykh planakh Rossii, in: *Sankt-Peterburg—Indiya* (St. Petersburg, 2009), 91–153.

43. C. M. Clay to W. H. Seward; June 27, 1864. In: *FRUS 1864*, 288.
44. C. M. Clay to W. H. Seward; March 20, 1867. In: *FRUS 1867*, Pt. I, 384.
45. C. M. Clay to W. H. Seward; May 24, 1867. In: *FRUS 1867*, 392.
46. C. M. Clay to W. H. Seward; April 17, 1868. In: *FRUS 1868*, 469–470.
47. *Sochineniya Ivana Sergeevicha Aksakova*. T. 1 (M., 1886), 206.
48. Danilevskii, N. Ya. *Rossiâ i Evropa* (St. Petersburg, 1995), 248.
49. *The Life of Cassius Marcellus Clay*, 415.
50. Ibid., 295.
51. Parry, A. "Cassius Clay's Glimpse into the Future," *Russian Review* 2. no. 2 (Spring 1943): 64.
52. *The Life of Cassius Marcellus Clay*, 328.
53. Ibid., 333–34.
54. Ibid., 441.
55. Zhuravleva, V. I. *Ponimanie Rossii v SShA: obrazy i mify. 1881–1914* (M., 2012), 186.
56. *The Life of Cassius Marcellus Clay*, 422–25.
57. Fadeev, R. A. "Prilozhenie k 'Mneniyu o Vostochnom voprose.'" In: Fadeev, R. A. *Sobranie sochineniy*. T. II, 2 (St. Petersburg, 1889), 316.

BIBLIOGRAPHY

Aksakov, Ivan S. *Ivan Sergeevich Aksakov v ego pis'makh*, tom 3 (Moscow: Tipografiâ M. G. Volčaninova, 1892).
———. *Sochineniya Ivana Sergeevicha Aksakova*, tom 1. Moscow: Tipografiâ M. G. Volčaninova, 1886.
Boynton, Charles B. *The Four Great Powers: England, France, Russia and America; Their Policy, Resources, and Probable Future*. Cincinnati, Chicago & St. Louis: C.F. Vent & Co., 1866.
———. *The Russian Empire, Its Resources, Government and Policy. By A "Looker-On" from America*. Cincinnati: Moore, Wilstach, Keys & Co., 1856.
Callahan, James M. *Russo-American Relations During the American Civil War*. Morgantown: West Virginia University, 1908.
Clay, Cassius M. "Cassius M. Clay." In: Allen T. Rice, ed., *Reminiscences of Abraham Lincoln by Distinguished Men of His Time*. New York: North American Publishing Co., 1886, 627–28.
———. *The Life of Cassius Marcellus Clay. Memoires, Writings, and Speeches*, vol. I. Cincinnati: J. Fletcher Brennan & Co., 1886.
———. *Rech' Kassiya M. Kleya, chitannaya v Yuridicheskom fakultete Albaniyskogo universiteta, v shtate N'yu-York, 3-go fevralya 1863 g*. St. Petersburg: Dom Dyusso, 1864.
———. *Speech of Cassius M. Clay before the Law Department of the University of Albany, N.Y., February 3, 1863*. New York: Press of Wenkoop, Hallenbeck & Thomas, 1863.
———. "Speech of the Hon. Cassius M. Clay." In: *Speeches delivered at the American Union Breakfast given in Paris, May 29, 1861, at the Grand Hotel du Louvre*. Paris: E. Briére, 1861, 11–15.
Danilevskii, Nikolay Ya., *Rossiya i Evropa*. St. Petersburg: Glagol, 1995.
Dukes, Paul. "A Defence of Armageddon: Two Discourses Containing Some American Ideas of Absolutism in Mid-Nineteenth-Century Russia." In: Roger Bartlett, ed. *Russian Thought and Society. 1800–1917. Essays in Honour of Eugene Lampert*. Keele, 1984, 23–29.
Fadeev, Rostislav A. "Prilozhenie k 'Mneniû o Vostochnom voprose.'" In: *Sobranie sočinenij Rostislava Andreeviča Fadeeva*, tom II, chast 2. St. Petersburg: V.V. Komarov, 1889, 304–27.
Kurilla, Ivan I. *Zaokeanskie partnery: Amerika i Rossiya v 1830–1850-e gody*. Volgograd: Izdatel'stvo VolGU, 2005.

28   *Vladimir V. Noskov*

Miliutin, Dmitrii A. *Vospominaniâ Dmitriya Alekseevicha Miliutina. 1863–1864*. M.: ROSSPEN, 2003.

Noskov, Vladimir V. "'Na sluchaj voyny s Angliey': Indiya v voennykh planakh Rossii." In: Evgenij N. Kal'ŝikov, ed., *Sankt-Peterburg—Indiya. Istoriya i sovremennost'*, 91–153. St. Petersburg: Evropeyskiy Dom, 2009.

Papers relating to the Foreign Relations of the United States (FRUS) 1861; 1863; 1864; 1867; 1868.

Parry, Albert. "Cassius Clay's Glimpse into the Future: Lincoln's Envoy to St. Petersburg Bade the Two Nations meet in East Asia." *Russian Review*. 2, no.2 (Spring 1943): 52–67.

Robertson, James R. *A Kentuckian at the Court of the Tsars: The Ministry of Cassius Marcellus Clay to Russia, 1861–1862 and 1863–1869*. Berea, KY: Berea College Press, 1935.

Saul, Norman E. *Distant Friends: the United States and Russia, 1763–1867*. Lawrence: University Press of Kansas, 1991.

Townsend, William H. *Lincoln and the Bluegrass. Slavery and Civil War in Kentucky*. Lexington: University of Kentucky Press, 1955.

White, Andrew D. *Autobiography of Andrew Dickson White*, vol. I. New York: The Century Co., 1905.

———. "The Development and Overthrow of the Russian Serf-System." *Atlantic Monthly*. 10, no. 61 (November 1862): 538–51.

Woldman, Albert A. *Lincoln and the Russians*. New York: Collier Books, 1961.

Zhuravleva, Victoria I. *Ponimanie Rossii v SShA: obrazy i mify. 1881–1914*. Moscow: RGGU, 2012.

Zhuravleva, Victoria I. and Kurilla, Ivan I. "Obrazy Rossii na stranitsakh amerikanskikh shkol'nykh uchebnikov istorii XIX–nachala XX veka." In: Viktoriya I. Zhuravleva, Ivan I. Kurilla, eds., *Rossiya i SShA na stranitsakh uchebnikov: opyt vzaimnykh reprezentaciy*, 16–67. Volgograd: Izdatel'stvo VolGU, 2009.

THREE

Zenaida Ragozin and Elizabeth Reynolds Hapgood

Two Remarkable Russian American Women

Norman E. Saul

My interest in Zenaida Ragozin and Elizabeth Hapgood derives from my research on Russian-American cultural relations in the nineteenth and twentieth centuries, and they featured in my published works on that subject.[1] They are also cited in my recent work on Charles R. Crane.[2] I became fascinated with Ragozin as a Russian woman in another world and thought she deserved further investigation and recognition for her contributions to the history and culture of Russia and America. Her god-daughter, Elizabeth Reynolds Hapgood, has also been virtually ignored in the literature on Russian-American cultural relations but made her own unique and quite valuable contributions. As will become clear, there are some mysteries associated with Ragozin as there are with Hapgood.

Most of the information in this chapter is derived from American sources, especially the papers of Norman and Elizabeth Hapgood in the Manuscript Division of the Library of Congress, and those of Charles R. Crane in the Bakhmeteff Archive at Columbia University. The former contains a number of letters from Ragozin in Russia to her American friend, Margaret Reynolds—Elizabeth's mother—written in immaculate and beautiful English, and usually addressed, "Dorogaya Mushka."[3] Ragozin and Reynolds appeared to have a sister-like or mother-daughter relationship.

Zenaida Alekseevna Verderevskaia was born on 16 June 1838 (though the Library of Congress lists 1835 as her year of birth) to a prominent intelligentsia noble family and was introduced as a young woman to the imperial court in St. Petersburg. She claimed to have danced with Tsar Nicholas I[4] and with Cassius Clay, the flamboyant American minister to Russia during the American Civil War. Her marital life remains unclear; she may have had as many as four husbands, the best known, Vasilyi Kel'siev (1835–1872), was a follower of Alexander Herzen. Kel'siev and his wife planned to seek refuge with other Russian radical populists in America shortly before his sudden death in 1872.[5] She did, however, come to the United States, with a new husband, a physician named Ragozin, in 1874.[6] Based on scanty information, he returned to Russia, where he also died suddenly. She remained in the United States, living mainly in New York City, and spending summers in Orange, New Jersey, or near Springfield, Massachusetts. According to a brief biographical note, published in 1895, she was descended from a Tatar prince on her father's side, had traveled in Italy and Greece, and had begun a literary career in Russia, writing for the newspaper *Golos*, under the name of her first husband, Agrenev, a noted singer and collector of folk songs.[7]

A talented linguist, artist, and musician, "Madam Ragozin" (she never used the feminine ending) supported herself in New York for a number of years by tutoring young women of New York society in foreign languages (French, German, and Italian), art, and music (piano and voice). She became a naturalized American citizen in 1883. At that time she was living at 356 West 42nd Street, a block from present-day Times Square. Introduced by her tutoring to the family of publisher George N. Putnam, she gained an opportunity to prove herself as a writer of English and as a professional historian by major contributions to Putnam's "story of nations" series. She soon gained an international reputation as an "orientalist" for the four books she wrote in the 1880s and 1890s on ancient Assyria, Babylon, Chaldea, and Vedic India, which were reprinted several times.[8] The last merited a review in the first issue of the *American Historical Review*.[9] For these Ragozin was elected to membership in the American Oriental Society, the Societe Ethnologique of Paris, and became the first woman member of the Royal Asiatic Society of Great Britain and Ireland.[10] She was the first important female Russian historian.

By the 1890s she attracted the attention of Russophile Chicago industrialist Charles R. Crane, who knew the Reynolds family from their mutual origins in Patterson, New Jersey. He was also interested in the history of the Middle East, as well as Russia, and urged Putnam to contract with Ragozin for the translation of a recent three volume work on Russia by French historian, Anatole Leroy-Beaulieu, and subsidized its publication by the purchase of twenty shares of Putnam's stock and two hundred sets of the printed books, while Putnam paid Ragozin a monthly honorarium.[11] Ragozin and Crane were thus partners in producing the first scholarly history of Russia in English, *The Empire of the Tsars and the*

Russians, with extensive annotations by Ragozin, amplifying and expanding on the original French edition.[12]

The publication had mixed results. Though favorably reviewed in newspapers and journals and by the recipients of gifts from Crane, sales were slow, owing at least in part to the steep price for the three large and thick volumes. A lengthy review of the second volume in the *New York Times* deemed it "the best presentation of the great problem [Russia] that has been printed in this country."[13] Mildred Page, a longtime friend of Charles Crane, after receiving the first volume commented, "Mdm. Ragozin is very interesting in her annotations. She rewards herself as well as the Russian people—when does the next volume come out?"[14]

As if these accomplishments did not task her linguistic and literary talents enough, she also wrote several volumes on early classical mythic heroes from their original sources.[15] With seemingly unlimited energy, she also wrote popular articles for journals, for example, one on Alexander Pushkin for *Cosmopolitan* in 1900, and a two-volume universal history of the world that same year.[16] Not surprisingly, having produced fifteen large volumes of history in fifteen years, she was known for "burning the midnight oil," her window lit into the early hours.[17] Though these publications, her tutorials, as well as some articles on America for the Russian press, provided substantial, if irregular, income, her life style and the acquisition of a considerable library often left her in financial difficulties. She even spent several weeks lecturing in Texas during the winter of 1886–1887 to make ends meet.[18]

Zenaida Ragozin was apparently a woman who could not be easily ignored in other respects. Six feet tall, she wore garish, bright colored outfits. For one description:

> Her appearance was made all the more striking by a slight peculiarity of dress. She wore gowns of the sheerest and best materials, but, doting on exceedingly bright and gay shades, managed to disturb many of her friends by adding a wrong touch. One dress, it was recalled, had as its foundation a material carrying the colors or purple, pink and red, and over it all was an over draping of exquisite handmade lace of black.[19]

She was also fond of wildlife and kept in her New York apartment a menagerie that included a number of birds and marmosets. She was also a chain smoker—cigarettes, cigars and pipes.[20] An observer described her:

> Personally Madame Ragozin is attractive both in appearance and manner. She is large in stature, her face is mobile and sympathetic, her fine dark eyes varying in expression with every change of thought. She is a delightful conversationalist, having a seemingly inexhaustible mine to draw from in her knowledge and reminiscence.[21]

Ragozin was also sought after for talks to women's clubs and afternoon teas on Russian culture, especially an illustrated one on "The Cottage

Industries of Russia."[22] As her small apartment at Second Avenue and 18th Street (207 East 18th Street) above a grocery store, was crowded with books and animals, noisy—and inconveniently located for New York society women—these engagements were usually held at more fashionable locations, such as one hosted by Mrs. Putnam in her large apartment on West 75th Street. Another venue was the presentation of a series of lectures on topics of her books in a public forum, quoting from the *New York Times*:

> The first of a course of six lectures on "The Old Religion of India" was delivered yesterday by Mme. Zenaida A. Ragozin at the Chapel of the Ascension, in West Eleventh Street. She was greeted by a large audience, which appreciated the spirited manner in which she delivered the discourse and her thorough knowledge of the subject.[23]

This self-made Russian scholar planned to return to Russia in 1895 to collect material for articles for the *New York Times* and another lecture series and sought Crane's financial support, but it fell through because of new publication contracts for Putnams.[24]

Around 1890 Ragozin met Margaret Reynolds, who was already a friend of Crane, and they bonded, especially since Margaret's husband, Edwin, was away on international trade ventures much of the time. After a daughter, Elizabeth, was born to the Reynolds in 1894, Ragozin became a frequent companion, babysitter, tutor, and godmother. The child was thus exposed to Russian language and culture at an early age and would became one of America's pioneering women teacher-scholars of Russian studies at Columbia University and Dartmouth, mainly due to Ragozin's influence.[25] In 1901 Ragozin returned to Russia primarily to reprint her several books in Russian,[26] but also to reconnect with family and friends. Another reason may have been that her relationship with Margaret Reynolds and daughter had become a cause of marital discord and separation.[27]

During her residence in America, Ragozin corresponded with friends in Russia, especially Sergei Syromiatnikov and Apollon Nikolaevich Maikov (1821–1897), a well-known poet, on her life in America.[28] More revealing are her letters to Andrei Kraevskii (1810–1889), a prominent editor, with whom she was associated before 1870 on the liberal newspaper *Golos*.[29] In one sixteen-page letter, she described meeting in 1876 a German ship officer, Emil Pohl, and marrying him.[30] This episode was apparently a brief affair in her active social life.

The story of Zenaida Ragozin sharpens in detail after she left the United States, owing to the frequent letters she wrote to Margaret and Elizabeth Reynolds and other American friends that were preserved by Elizabeth.[31] Though estranged from her only sister, Ragozin maintained close relations with nephews and nieces and especially with Syromiatnikov, a nationalistic philosopher who wrote a column for the St. Petersburg newspaper, *Rossiia*. With his encouragement she became a prolific translator and condenser of all kinds of American writings and reminiscences of her life in the United States. In almost weekly letters back to America she recounted her life in Russia and sought current materials from popular American journals such as *Cosmopolitan, Harper's Weekly, McClure's, Collier's, Munsey's,* and especially *Youth's Companion,* noting that less desirable were *Scribner's* and *Century,* the most widely circulated American journals, because all the Russian newspapers subscribe to them and rely heavily on them for American columns. She instructed that these should be sent through the American embassy in St. Petersburg to avoid government censorship.[32]

She wrote Margaret,

> Such odds and ends, and articles out of magazines are very precious material, and to have a person to watch the press for me — periodicals and books — is invaluable help; in fact such help, without which I could not do just what I want to in our press here; and you are literally the *only* person who can give me this help, because you alone are an *alter ego,* with all the word implies of sympathy, mutual identification, and absolute comprehension of me, my nature, my ends and my needs in spiritual and practical things.

Ragozin added that the quantity of material was important, because: "I shall be able to use very little, but to get that little, I must have the lot to fish in. . . . It is too fatiguing, because I do it too conscientiously, work too much for it, being absolutely incapable of giving less than my best in any line I undertake; and doing one's best *always, is* fatiguing."[33] She also hoped to do translation work but noted "that Russian standards are uncommonly high and sterling, a Russian taste for the fastidious to excess."[34]

Many of Ragozin's articles about the United States were published in the mass-circulation journal (350,000 issues printed) *Niva,* which paid well; the newspaper *Rossiia*; and a youth magazine, which she titled in English as "Young Crops." The topics ranged widely, including an account of her visit to Texas during the great Galveston hurricane, but tended to concentrate on contemporary themes and popular literature, especially on works by and about women and African Americans.[35] For example, she wrote a long review of Booker T. Washington's *Up from Slavery* and an abridged translation of Helen Keller's *Story of My Life* for *Niva,* as well as the New England short stories of Mary Wilkins.[36] This, she reported, "puts 'money in my pouch.'" She also translated into Russian the plantation stories of Paul Dunbar (1872–1906), a leading African American poet and short story writer, who, unfortunately, died of tuberculosis at the age of thirty-three. "They take much interest here in the 'coloured' question and problems," adding that Russians are very interested in reading about America in general.

Ragozin also noted that her articles on public "Carnegie" libraries that emphasized American promotion of children's literature created quite a stir. And her serialized world history for children even attracted the attention of the imperial family: "You have no idea what a sensation they made, and that too in very high spheres." In 1903, Nicholas II awarded her a thousand ruble grant to support her work on world history for children, somewhat to her embarrassment, not wanting this disclosed in America.[37] In her intimate letters to Margaret Reynolds, she pleaded for her to answer and reveal herself completely, adding that she destroyed all letters she received.[38] So apparently none of the return letters of Margaret and Elizabeth Reynolds to Ragozin survive.

Zenaida Alekseevna also wrote articles on Russia for the American press, though only a few have been identified, since they were usually published under the heading of "special correspondent." For example, in the *New York Commercial Advertiser* she compared the superior snow removal from streets in St. Petersburg with that of New York: "Of course, good care is taken [in Russia] to leave enough snow for good sleighing. Inside the yards the porters sweep the snow from the roofs and the ground into heaps, and it is carried away as well as that from the street somewhere out of town."[39]

During her years in Russia, Ragozin suffered from a number of ailments but especially arthritis that restricted her movements. She was able for several years, however, to spend summers on the huge (six square mile) Dubrovsky Ukrainian stud farm, the "home estate," Olissovo, of her sister, and at the dacha of Syromiatnikov at Orekhovo, near Novgorod. From Ukraine she described soaring behind a troika across the steppe, "like a sea, no landmarks, no roads."[40] But soon her health and writing demands confined her to the apartment in the capital. She planned to return to the United States in early 1904 for a lecture series but gave it up, even after passage had been booked, because of the Russo-Japanese War.[41]

Regarding that conflict, Ragozin expressed her dismay over pro-Japanese sentiments in the United States, noting "the incomprehensible attitude Americans generally have chosen to assume in their idolatrous worship of their yellow pets."[42] She also referred to Russia saving the Union in 1863 with the fleet visits but getting no thanks.[43] On the Revolution of 1905, she observed, "We are living a dreadful, an appalling page of history in my poor Russia; almost every day brings some fresh horror here in St. Petersburg, in Moscow, in the South."[44] But she continued to be a warm friend and advocate of a better understanding between America and Russia. Perhaps no Russian writer on America reached as many readers as she did over the period from 1902 to 1917. She used her American connections as conduits of information on current political affairs and advice on contemporary literary publications and wrote about them for *Golos* in Moscow as well as *Rossiia*. She was the first to translate the works of Jack London into Russian.

Ragozin repeatedly urged Margaret Reynolds and her daughter to spend a summer at Syromiatnikov's Orekhovo estate, where you can "see Russian life *from the inside* and have the kind of opportunity that foreigners never have . . . as I did in America,"[45] and they finally did so for two months during the summer of 1910, with the financial help of Crane, when the strikingly beautiful and talented sixteen-year-old Elizabeth, who already spoke good Russian, cut quite a swath through local Russian gentlemen, including Syromiatnikov himself, who later divorced his wife to become a suitor. Return visits by Elizabeth in 1913 and 1914 expanded her circle of Russian admirers. Ragozin's friends and associates by now included other Americans, such as the budding historians Frank Golder of Stanford and Samuel Harper of Chicago, who also had their eyes on the American beauty. Syromiatnikov, meanwhile, came to the United States in 1915 as a government agent to promote the Russian cause in World War I, as well as to fruitlessly pursue Elizabeth Reynold.[46]

After *Rossiia* closed in 1916, due to wartime inflation and the shortage of paper, she filled in with odd jobs, such as translating John Wesley's sermons into Russian for the American Methodist minister in Russia, George Simons.[47] She became more involved in the expanding American community in Petrograd that was centered around the Anglo-American Church on Vasilevsky Ostrov and its charity work, the Singer Building on Nevsky, which housed the American consulate, and the American embassy on Furstatskaia.

Elizabeth Reynolds graduated in 1914 from Bryn Mawr, enrolled at the School of Oriental Studies of the Sorbonne for post graduate work in Russian with Paul Boyer, and in 1915 was hired as the first lecturer in Russian language and literature at Columbia University.[48] There she met a considerably older leading American journalist and editor, Norman Hapgood; a mutual New York friend, Beatrice "Bice" Wood, conspired in their May–September "secret tryst,"[49] as did Charles Crane, who provided a retreat for them at his summer home at Woods Hole.

She cancelled a planned series of lectures on Russia at Columbia for the spring of 1917, and they were married in a civil ceremony in December 1916 (he recently divorced and forty-eight, she only twenty-two, and he having a daughter about the same age), much to the chagrin of many of her Russian and American admirers.[50] But Zenaida Alekseevna thoroughly approved of the progress of "my own baby girl" and her link with a prominent writer.[51] The Hapgoods were immediately off to Europe, where he was assigned to cover the war for the Hearst syndicate, and were mainly situated in London and Paris during 1917 through the Russian Revolutions and American entry into the war.[52]

Upon return to the United States in early 1918, Elizabeth Hapgood established the Russian Department at Dartmouth, where she became the first woman faculty member. She resigned after only a year, however, to care for their first child, Elizabeth ("Benny"), and to accompany her husband on a diplomatic mission to Europe.[53] As a loyal supporter of Woodrow Wilson, Norman Hapgood was rewarded with an appointment as minister to Denmark in the summer of 1919 with the mission of establishing communication with Soviet representatives in Scandinavia. This appointment, however, was not confirmed by the Senate owing to reports of his Bolshevik sympathies (Red Scare), so they returned to the United States after only six months in Copenhagen.

Norman Hapgood resumed his journalistic career, especially as a drama critic for the *New York Herald*, and authored several books.[54] His interest in theater before the war had already stimulated an admiration of Constantine Stanislavsky and the Moscow Art Theatre. His effort to secure their visit to America was cut short by World War I. His marriage to Elizabeth, fluent in Russian and well versed in Russian literature and culture, provided an additional incentive for advancing this overture, though the main catalysts were the success of the Russian vaudeville hit of "Chauve Souris" ("Fledermous" or "flying bat") and promoter Morris Gest. Stanislavsky and his theater, with the help of the Hapgoods and financing by Charles Crane, had a very successful American season opening in January 1923 at the large Jolson Theatre at 59th and Broadway, opening with Aleksei Tolstoy's "Tsar Fyodor," starring Chekhov's widow, Olga Knipper. Other performances including works of Gogol, Gorky, and, of course, Chekhov, all sold out. Will Rogers, starring in the Ziegfield Follies, the main competitor that season, quipped:

> These Russians are having a wonderful season in New York. . . . Nobody knows what they are talking about, so it has developed into a fad or game to make your neighbor, sitting around you, think that you know. Nothing outside of Grand Opera in a foreign tongue, has BORED the rich out of more money than these (so called) simple Russians. . . . The best acting I saw there was by the audience. When you take three thousand people that act like they like a thing when they don't know what it's all about, that's real acting.[55]

The Moscow Art Theatre tour of four months included Chicago, Philadelphia, and Boston. Stanislavsky enjoyed, as a respite, socializing with old friends Sergei Rachmaninoff, Feodor Chaliapin, and Leopold Stokowsky, and his own actors.

That summer, the Hapgoods journeyed to France to negotiate directly with Stanislavsky for a return visit the following year. They also paid a last and sad visit to Zenaida Ragozin, now an invalid in Petrograd after the hard times of the civil war and famine. The second Stanislavsky tour of America included a reception by President Calvin Coolidge at the White House on 20 March 1924 with Elizabeth acting as interpreter for the president. During the visit, the Hapgoods discussed with Stanislavsky the importance of putting his life and art in words, but the Russian remained committed to his current obligations until suffering a serious illness in 1930.[56] Elizabeth Hapgood reported, "His creative and artistic genius was never fully satisfied; it urged him on to the very day of his death to search for, to test, to choose new approaches to the art of acting, so that he hesitated to sum up any conclusions as final."[57] That summer the Hapgoods visited him while he was recuperating in the south of France to promote the importance of recording his legacy for prosperity.[58]

The result was a manuscript in two parts drafted by Stanislavsky in the 1930s that laid the foundation for method acting in America; as his writing proceeded, Stanislavsky agreed with the Hapgoods that it would be best to divide it into two parts. The first, *An Actor Prepares*, appeared in 1936, two years before the Russian original, edited by Norman Hapgood and translated by his wife.[59] Delayed by Stanislavsky's death in 1938 and the onset of war, the draft manuscripts finally reached Elizabeth from the family of the actor in 1946, resulting in *Building a Character*, published in 1948 to commemorate the fiftieth anniversary of the founding of the Moscow Art Theatre and the tenth anniversary of Stanislavsky's death.[60] *An Actor Prepares* was also published that year in a new edition with an introduction by British actor John Gielgud.

In the meantime, Zenaida Ragozin had become increasingly enmeshed in the troubles and worsening conditions of her native land, beset by civil war and revolution. Her old friend and publisher, George Putnam, came to the rescue with an offer for the translation of Russian short stories into English. She seized upon the opportunity to do as many as seven volumes for $250 each, in monthly advance remittances of $50, part of it shared with Syromiatnikov for writing brief biographical sketches of the authors. "This is not hack work you know," she wrote Putnam; though he wanted her to avoid political writers, she planned to include Gorky, who "could not be ignored, although he undoubtedly comes under the category which you very wisely deprecate; a very little of [this] will go a long way."[61] Despite difficulties of communication during the Russian civil war, four volumes finally appeared in 1920.[62]

World War I brought an increase in opportunities for contacts with Americans, due to a major influx of American personnel, such as those serving with the YMCA, the American Red Cross mission, and the Second Division of the Embassy that was involved with supervision of prisoner of war camps in Russia. Several other American students of Russia visited the country extensively on special missions, as journalists, or as scholars. One of the latter, Edward Ross of the University of Wisconsin, recorded notes of an animated dinner conversation in December 1917 that included Graham Taylor of Chicago, Dr. Simons, and Zenaida Ragozin on the comparison of Russian and American women. Ross and Ragozin praised the superiority of Russian women and emphasized the fault of the American males in keeping women secluded from the real world of business and politics, while Russian women were very much involved in both. Simons, however, was critical of the lack of morals, citing many young women students living with male counterparts.[63]

The conversation then turned to the arts:

> Mme Ragozin considers Russians superior in painting and music. But in regards [to] literature she is unable to say which is better. Both began in the early XIX century. She is certain that Am literature is more many sided and satisfying than Russ literature. The latter is too persistently earnest, often heavy and ponderous. A steady diet of it produces low spirits. She attributes Russian softness and want of energy to the influence of the Mongol domination. Slavs she says, have no bent for order, discipline, organization, lack of self restraint. [They] will not voluntarily conform to necessary rules. [They] resent all restraints on their freedom of will and therefore require a strong external authority if they are not to fall into anarchy and confusion. Hence she is a monarchist and considers autocracy necessary, pointing out the massive destruction going on, the plundering of churches.[64]

With reduced income and spiraling inflation, Ragozin's life style considerably diminished, even before October 1917. Now nearly eighty and increasingly afflicted with arthritis, she survived with the help of a faithful maid-companion (Natalie Stankeevskaia), Syromiatnikov, a nephew-engineer (who worked on the construction of the Murmansk railroad), and occasional charity from American friends, through the difficult years of the Russian civil war.[65] On the Bolshevik seizure of power, she commented succinctly that "anarchy has been established and taken to itself the name of 'government'" and then elaborated:

> This comes of blindly applying abstract theories and principles, which sound so fine and look so well on paper, without caring to know the nature of the material you have to work with and the practical facts you encounter, and, last but not least, ignoring totally the teachings of the history of their own country. Our people cannot exist and prosper and be great unless guided by a strong hand.[66]

More than anything she was tormented by lack of news from her American friends, though she continued to write letters of life in Petrograd during the civil war that provide more evidence of the virtually unbearable life of those times; they are not easy to read.

As an American citizen, she had an opportunity to leave Russia with the evacuation of diplomatic and other residents in 1918 but declined on account of health and a desire to stay in Russia through its troubles, one of the few Americans to live openly in Russia through the civil war and Allied intervention. By 1921 with communications restored she was able to receive aid through the American Relief Administration (ARA).[67] A poignant reflection of this period of shortages is a letter to Frank Golder, a historian with the ARA, providing a list of her doctor's and adding, "I am extremely desirous but very doubtful of obtaining in the first place any smallest quantity of alcohol, . . . if it is at all possible a few table-spoons of brandy (cognac)." The really important need: "Some real ink— perhaps from the office?—quite black, or, anyhow, dark. This [that I am writing with] is awful stuff, destructive to the eyes, for I hardly see what I write *while* I write." The other priority was candles, electricity being quite limited and kerosene non-existent. "Do try to get some more for me *soon!*" [68]

Essential assistance and moral support also came from Reverend George Simons, who had been forced to move his Methodist headquar-ters from Petrograd to Riga but was still allowed access to his former Russian congregation. In the summer of 1918 he arranged a special cele-bration of Madam Ragozin's eightieth birthday, which began with the singing of "America" and ended with "The Star Spangled Banner." This was certainly an unusual event in Bolshevik Russia. [69]

Though now confined to her small apartment with little or no heat, Ragozin continued to work, sending more Russian short stories to Put-nam and translating for the English edition of *Communist International*. "Beggars may not be choosers," she observed. [70] In May 1923 Margaret Reynolds and daughter Elizabeth Hapgood visited her in Petrograd for the last time, bringing food, seeds, and money. The seeds were primarily for Syromiatnikov to plant at Orekhova and consisted of particular American vegetables that he admired: turnips, parsnips, beans, and sweet potatoes—and he also welcomed the $125. [71] In her last letter to Margaret Reynolds, Zenaida Alekseevna complained of trouble she had in mid-winter writing in the dark, her lamp having given out, and that her eyesight had been dimmed by cataracts. [72] "Madam Ragozin" died a few months later at age eighty-six. An obituary, written by Elizabeth Hapgood, was delayed until the following year. Sergei Syromiatnikov memorialized his friend by depositing a special collection of her papers in Pushkinskii Dom in Leningrad in the 1930s. [73]

Elizabeth Hapgood, continued to lecture and write on Russian politics and culture and on Stanislavsky, well beyond her husband's death in 1937. [74] She also translated Russian children's books into English, until her own death in 1974, following Ragozin's example in Russia years earli-er. [75]

Zenaida Ragozin and Elizabeth Hapgood left a considerable legacy to the American knowledge and study of Russia and the Russian study of America for one hundred years, 1874–1974.

NOTES

1. Norman E. Saul, *Concord and Conflict: The United States and Russia, 1867–1914* (Lawrence: University Press of Kansas, 2001); Norman E. Saul, *War and Revolution: The United States and Russia, 1914–1921* (Lawrence: University Press of Kansas, 2006).
2. Norman E. Saul, *The Life and Times of Charles R. Crane, 1858–1939: American Businessman, Philanthropist, and a Founder of Russian Studies in America* (Lanham, MD: Lexington Books, 2013).
3. Ragozin's name for her American friend would remain with her for life, used regularly by children, as well as acquaintances who had no connection with Ragozin or Russia. In English it was usually spelled "Muszka."
4. Another reliable source cites her pleading with the tsar for the release of her father from Siberian exile. Frederick H. Martins to Margaret Reynolds, 25 September 1924, f. 3, box 9, Hapgood/Reynolds Papers, Manuscript Division, Library of Congress [hereafter, HRP, MD, LC].
5. V. V. Lobanov, "Predislovie," *Biblioteka Zenaidy Alekseevny Ragozinoi* (Novosibirsk: Siberian Section of Academy of Sciences, 1989), 5–7. It is not clear from this source how her American library ended up in Siberia. Going to America was popular among a number of Russian "narodniks." Some students of the University of Kiev, calling themselves "Amerikantsy" went there in 1872. For an account of one of them, see my "Through Curious and Foreign Eyes: Grigorii Machtet Chronicles the Kansas Frontier, 1872–73," *Kansas History* 17:2 (Summer 1994): 76–90.
6. Martins to Reynolds, HRP, MD, LC. Little is known about the background of Ragozin, though he is credited with drafting some reforms for Alexander II; Zenaida claimed to be descendant of the Riuriks and was often referred to as "princess." "Obituary of Zenaida Alexeevna Ragozin" [hereafter ZAR] by Elizabeth Reynolds Hapgood [hereafter ERH], 30 May 1925; ZAR to Margaret Reynolds [hereafter MR], 13 September 1923, box 9, HRP, MD, LC].
7. Carolyn Halstead, "Madame Ragozin," *Outlook* 51, 26 (29 June 1895): 1134. Dmitri Agrenev, adding the name Slavianskii, toured the United States with remarkable success in 1869–1870. For more on this, see Saul, *Concord and Conflict*, 51–53.
8. In chronological order: *The Story of Chaldea, from the Earliest Times to the Rise of Assyria* (1886), *Story of Assyria, from the Rise of the Empire to the Fall of Nineveh* (1887), *The Story of Media, Babylon, and Persia* (1889), and *The Story of Vedic India* (1895), all published by Putnam's Sons.
9. *American Historical Review* 1, 1 (October 1895): 103–5.
10. Halstead, "Madame Ragozin," 1134.
11. Anatole Leroy-Beaulieu, *Empire des tsars et les Russes*, 3 vols. (Paris: Hachette, 1891); George H. Putnam to Crane, 19 December 1894, reel 2, Crane Papers, Bakhmeteff Archive, Columbia University [hereafter CP, BAR, CU]. Copyright was retained by Crane in his own name.
12. Leroy Beaulieu, *The Empire of the Tsars and the Russians*, translated from the French by Zenaida A. Ragozin, 3 vols. (New York and London: G. P. Putnam's Sons, 1893–1896).
13. *New York Times*, 2 June 1894: 3.
14. Mildred Page to Charles Crane, 23 October 1893, f. 12, box 1, CP, BAR, CU.
15. *Odysseus, the Hero of Ithaca* (New York: C. Scribner's Sons, 1898); *Siegfried, the Hero of the North, and Beowulf, the Hero of the Anglo-Saxons* (1898); *Frithjof* (1899); *Herakles, the Hero of Thebes, and Other Heroes of the Myth* (1900); *Salammbo, the Maid of Carthage, Re-Told from the French of Gustave Flaubert* (New York: G. P. Putnam's Sons, 1900).
16. "Pushkin and His Work," *Cosmopolitan* 28 (January 1900): 307–14; Ragozin, *A History of the World*, 2 vols. (New York: W. B. Harison, 1899–1900).
17. Harriet Bliss Fuller, "Reminiscences of Mme Ragozin," *Springfield Weekly Republican*, 24 February 1921, clipping in box 9, HRP, MD, LC.
18. *San Antonio Daily Express*, 9 January 1887.

19. Fuller, "Reminiscences of Mme Ragozin," 24 February 1921.

20. Ibid.

21. Halstead, "Madame Ragozin," 1134.

22. "Cottage Industries of Russia," *New York Times*, 18 December 1894: 16.

23. "The Social World," Ibid., 8 March 1895: 2.

24. Ragozin to Crane, 23 March 1895, CP, reel 2, BAR, CU.

25. By all accounts, Elizabeth Reynolds was a precocious child, due in part to Ragozin's guidance. At age twelve she wrote the score to a song cycle by E. R. Kroeger: Elizabeth Reynolds, *Memory: A Song Cycle* (Newton Center, MA: Wa-Wan Press, 1906).

26. At least two were published in Russian: *Istoriia Assirii* (1902) and *Istoriia Midii* (1903) and soon went into second editions.

27. "It is a great misfortune for us both that Mr. E. L. R. [Edwin Reynolds] dislikes me so much!" ZAR to MR, 25 November/8 December 1903, box 9, HRP, MD, LC. It is not clear from the records whether Margaret and Edwin Reynolds were formally divorced.

28. Ragozin fond, Pushkinskii dom, St. Petersburg.

29. Kraevskii to Ragozin, 1886, Kraevskii fond, Manuscript Division, Russian National Library (Saltykov Shchedrin), St. Petersburg. For Kraevskii's important role in the establishment of a Russian liberal press, see Louise McReynolds, *The News under Russia's Old Regime: The Development of a Mass-Circulation Press* (Princeton: Princeton University Press, 1991), 30–51.

30. Ragozin to Kraevskii, 24 October 1885, Russian National Library. The marriage must have been a brief affair, since there is no mention of it in other records.

31. They are scattered, throughout the collection but especially found in box 9, HRP, MD, LC.

32. ZAR to MR, 25 November/8 December 1903, ibid.

33. ZAR to MR, 24 March/6 April 1903, ibid.

34. Ibid.

35. ZAR to MR3/16 February 1903, ibid.

36. "Shkola i zhizn'," *Niva* 1 (January 1903): 70–88; "Negry i belye v Soedinennykh Shtatakh," *Niva* 1 (January 1904): 75–106; "Istoriia odnoi dushi" (Helen Keller), *Niva* 5 (May 1904): 53–94 and 7 (July 1904): 343–70; ZAR to MR, 24 March/6 April 1903, box 9, HRP, MD, LC.

37. ZAR to MR, 24 March/6 April 1903, box 9, HRP, MD, LC. She asked that this not be revealed publicly, and also that she was suddenly flush with cash—2800 rubles.

38. Ibid.

39. "Snow-Clearing Methods in St. Petersburg," *New York Commercial Advertiser*, 8 March 1902, clipping in ibid. The article continued with a colorful description of the Russian celebrations of Christmas and New Years.

40. Undated fragment of letter to MR, ibid.

41. ZAR to MR, 16/29 February 1904, ibid.

42. 25 September/9 October 1904, ibid.

43. 19 September/2 October 1904, ibid.

44. 9/22 February 1905, ibid.

45. 20 May/2 June 1909, ibid.

46. For his sojourn in America, see Victoria I. Zhuravleva, "Rethinking Russia in the United States during the First World War: The American Voyage of Mr. Sigma," in Ben Whisenhunt and Norman Saul, eds., *New Perspectives on Russian-American Relations* (New York: Routledge, 2015).

47. ZAR to "Tina", 20 August/2 September 1916, ibid.

48. Elizabeth Reynolds performed with Beatrice Wood in pantomime and tableaux presentations for New York charities, and, besides being a precocious linguist, had published a volume of poetry: Elizabeth Reynolds, *On the Lake and Other Poems* (Boston: Gorham Press, 1915).

49. Series of letters, ER to MR, 1915, box 4, HRP, MD, LC. The daughter, Ruth, soon married Sewell Tyng, who served with the YMCA in Europe during the war.Beatrice

Wood would have her own adventurous life of romance; she married a Belgian count, divorced him, was an aspiring actress in Hollywood, then settled in California for a life of pottery, becoming well known nationally for her ceramics and eccentric social life, while maintaining regular contact with her New York friend; born in the same year as Elizabeth, she died in 1998 at the age of 105. Roberta Smith, "Mama of Dada Is Dead," *New York Times* 14 March 1998: A15. For colorful excepts of her long life, see *Playing Chess with the Heart: Beatrice Wood at 100* (San Francisco: Chronicle Books, 1994).

50. "Mrs. Norman Hapgood Divorced; Won French Decree Last Spring," *The New York Times*, 25 July 1915: 9; "Norman Hapgood Weds," ibid., 14 December 1916: 11.

51. ZAR to MR, undated fragment [1917], box 4, HRP, MD, LC.

52. Elizabeth gave several lectures on Russia to a group of British Members of Parliament and to the American Women's Society in London. She was especially impressed by getting to know her husband's friend, Herbert Hoover, writing her mother: "Mr. Hoover arrived Sunday night and is dining here tonight. He is full of much zeal and interesting things that we always have a fascinating time with him. He is shy, in a way and seems rather lonely now that Mrs. H. is in America, so we feel very much flattered that he should come to us and feel perfectly at home here so that he says on for hours and hours talking at a great rate." ERH (London) to MR, 3 April 1917, f. M and E, ibid.

53. According to younger son David Hapgood, his older sister "Benny" was still living a few years ago, in her nineties. Interview, New York, summer 2008.

54. Norman Hapgood had already written several popular biographies, including Daniel Webster (1899), Abraham Lincoln (1900), and George Washington (1901). After 1917, he wrote *The Advancing Hour* about the problem of facing a new Russia (1920), a biography of Alfred E. Smith (1927), and his own memoirs, *The Changing Years* (1930). He was better known for his outspoken and liberal views in many articles and editorials for a variety of journals and newspapers.The Hapgood family was well known at the time for their advanced "socialistic" views, especially Norman's brothers, Hutchins and William Powers Hapgood. Their father had founded a prosperous canning company, Columbia Conserve Company, in Indianapolis, that was a rival of Heinz and Campbell in food preservation and sales. The brothers, however, had passed majority ownership to the employees in the 1930s. It continued to exist into the 1950s, providing additional income for the family, until bought out by Sexton Company. The widow of Powers, Mary Hapgood, would be the first female candidate for governor of Indiana—for the Socialist Party. Hutchins Hapgood was as well-known as his older brother for his outspoken beliefs in anarchism, open marriage, and free love, along with his wife Neith Boyce. For more on the interesting Hapgood family, see Hutchins Hapgood, *A Victorian in the Modern World* (New York: Harcourt Brace, 1939), and Michael D. Marcaccio, *The Hapgoods: Three Earnest Brothers* (Charlottesville: University of Virginia Press, 1977).

55. Rogers, "Slipping the Lariat Over," *The New York Times*, 25 February 1923, XX2.

56. "Explanatory Note by the Translator," in Constantin Stanislavski, *Building a Character*, translated by Elizabeth Reynolds Hapgood, 21st printing, (New York: Theatre Arts, 1987), 1.

57. Ibid.

58. The result was the first book by Stanislavsky in English, translated by Elizabeth Hapgood under a pseudonym, J. J. Robbins. *My Life in Art* (Boston: Little Brown, 1924).

59. Constantin Stanislavski, *An Actor Prepares* (New York: Theatre Arts Books, 1936).

60. Stanislavski, *Building a Character*, translated by Elizabeth Reynolds Hapgood (New York: Theatre Arts, 1948).

61. ZAR to Putnam, 4/17 February 1917, Putnam Papers, Columbia University Manuscripts Collection.

62. *Little Russian Master Pieces*, 4 vols., chosen and translated from the original Russian by Zenaida A. Ragozin, with an introduction and biographical notes by S.N.

Syromiatnikov (New York and London: G. P. Putnam's Sons, the Knickerbocker Press, 1920). The contents by volume are: (1) Pushkin and Lermontov; (2) Saltykov-Shchedrein, Mamin-Sibiriak, Sluchevskii, Niedzwiecki, Uspenskii, Zeisiner; (3) Liskov, Dombrovskii, Dostoevsky, Tolstoy; (4) Staniukovich and Korolenko.

63. Edward Ross notes, 9 December 1917, vol. 4 (reel 29), Edward Ross Papers, Wisconsin Historical Society. The valuable Ross papers have been largely ignored by both Russian and American scholars.

64. Ibid.

65. ZAR to MR, 14/27 January 1918, and 3 March 1922, box 9, HRP, MD, LC.

66. ZAR to MR, 1/14 December 1917, ibid.

67. ZAR to MR, 4 May 1923, ibid.

68. Ragozin to Golder, 27 December 1921/9 January 1922, box 13, f. 59, Golder Papers, Hoover Institution Archives, Stanford. Hungry for news, Ragozin added to this letter: "And now, dear Friend, *don't* keep me long waiting for a real visit from you! We have *so* much to talk about, *so* many questions to ask and to answer." One gets the impression that perhaps the worst thing about this terrible period in Russian history was lack of communication, contact.

69. Printed program, 2/16 June 1918, box 9, HRP, MD, LC.

70. ZAR to MR, 22 February 1922, ibid.

71. ZAR to MR, 30 May 1923 and Syromiatnikov to ERH, 17 June 1923, ibid.

72. ZAR to MR, 19 January 1924, ibid.

73. Syromiatnikov to ERH, 30 March 1928, box 12, ibid.

74. Most notably, Elizabeth Reynolds Hapgood, editor and translator, *Stanislavski's Legacy, a Collection of Comments on a Variety of Aspects of an Actor's Art and Life* (New York: Theatre Arts, 1968). There is a small Elizabeth Hapgood collection regarding copyright issues in the Billy Rose Manuscript Collection of the New York Public Library for the Performing Arts at Lincoln Center.

75. For example, Eugene Schwarz, *Two Brothers,* translated by Elizabeth Reynolds Hapgood (New York: Harper Junior Books, 1973).

BIBLIOGRAPHY

Hapgood, Elizabeth, "Explanatory Notes by the Translator in Constantin Stanislavski," *Building a Character.* 21st printing. New York: Theatre Arts, 1987.

———, ed., *Stanislavsky's Legacy, a Collection of Comments on a Variety of Aspects of an Actor's Art and Life.* New York: Theatre Arts, 1968.

Leroy-Beaulieu, Anatole, *The Empire of the Tsars and the Russians,* translated from the French with explanatory annotations, 3 vols. New York and London: G. P. Putnam's Sons, 1893–1896.

Saul, Norman E. *The Life and Times of Charles R. Crane, 1858–1939: American businessman, Philanthropist, and a Founder of Russian Studies in America.* Lanham, MD: Lexington Books, 2013.

———. *Concord and Conflict: The United States and Russia, 1867–1914.* Lawrence, KS: University Press of Kansas, 2001.

Archival Collections Cited

Golder Papers, Hoover Institution Archives, Stanford, California.

Hapgood/Reynolds Papers, Manuscript Division, Library of Congress, Washington, DC.

Kraevskii fond, Manuscript Division, Russian National Library, St. Petersburg.

FOUR

Russian Studies in the United States and *Amerikanistika* in the Russian Empire

Imagination and Study of the Other in the context of Peace and World War

Victoria I. Zhuravleva

In 1916, Nikolai Andreevich Borodin, a statistician, economist, ichthyologist, and a co-founder of the Society for Promoting Mutual Friendly Relations between Russia and America wrote:

> Let us now remind the reader about the more or less well-known facts concerning our intensive trading with America, which led to intensified trans-Atlantic shipping, to the establishment of the Russian-American Chamber of Commerce and the American-Russian Chamber of Commerce, to the appearance of official commercial agents and attachés, to the founding of a Russian-American bank, to the opening of an American bank branch in Petrograd, to the publication of Russian-American periodicals, to lectures and courses being offered on America in Russia and on Russia in America, to English being studied in Russia, and Russian in America, to the publication of a large number of well-informed articles about America in Russia, and about Russia in America.[1]

He dwelled on the unprecedented mutual rapprochement of the two countries during World War I, which wasn't always entirely smooth (as happened with concluding a new treaty of navigation and commerce that was intended to replace the agreement denounced in 1911), but still took

place on a very impressive scale.[2] It was then, when cooperation in trading, economy, military, political, and humanitarian spheres was expanding, that the Russian-American relations agenda for the first time included the issue of destroying myths and stereotypes dominating the
countries' mutual perception, and also of developing academic study of
each other. Contemporaries admitted that for the most part, Russians
were more informed about the United States than Americans were about
Russia.

Richard Washburn Child, a military correspondent, lawyer, politician,
and later diplomat, gave a stark sketch of stereotypes about Russia promulgated in American society:

> We know so little about Russia and that little we know is so distorted!
> We know about spies, and secret police, ballets, massacres, exile to
> Siberia, the Jewish question, bureaucratic graft, and much of what we
> know is not so. We know a Yellow Russia. Most of our immigrants
> from Russia are not representative of Russia. They are not even Slavs,
> and three-fourths of Russia is Slav. They are not friendly to Russia, but
> nine-tenth of the real Russians, few of whom come here, are so friendly
> to Russia that they are willing to call it "Holy Russia" and believe it.
> More than that, most of the Americans who go to Russia and come
> back to report are not representative of the United States; they are
> adventurous journalists seeking to find the sensational mysterious Rus-
> sia of the moving picture scenario, and adventurous commercial agents
> who cannot speak the Russian language.[3]

Child told Americans that they "should be tolerant of Russians' intoler-
ance" in such issues as, for examples, "the Jewish question," if Americans
do want to develop cooperation, and he called upon Russians to expand
their knowledge of the United States with the aim of abandoning the
simplified ideas of "the land of smoke-spewing factories" and "the nation
of money-makers."

Many Russians, in turn, stressed the need for serious and multifaceted
study of the American historical experience, the need to shape a more
comprehensive image of America and Americans, which wouldn't just
reduce the country and its people to the stereotypes based on simplified
information promulgated by pulp fiction such as Nat Pinkerton novels.[4]
In August 1916, a reviewer of the Russian press in the *Literary Digest*
magazine paid particular attention to the many publications which posed
the question of the necessity to expand the knowledge of different aspects
of American life. *Novoe vremya*, a newspaper, called for closer mutual
business relations between the two countries and stated that such things
don't happen all by themselves and require serious preparations: "With
America, it is all the more difficult because we do not know her at all, and
America does not know us; even worse, she has a wrong and unfavorable
notion of us, owing to the circumstance that our enemies are conducting
there a wide propaganda against us, and we, as usual, pay no attention to

the falsehoods and calumnies which are spread about us there."[5] *Russkoe slovo*, the Moscow-based Russian newspaper with the lowest subscription price, emphasized that "those, however, to whom the interest of great Russia is dear and who wish to create conditions for the better development of the productive forces of the country so crippled by this burdensome war, cannot help greeting their efforts to bring about closer relations between us and the United States, based on mutual concessions" and mutual understanding.[6]

Another contribution to the process of mutual understanding was made by the Russian-American Chamber of Commerce, established in Moscow in 1913 under the chairmanship of Nikolai Ivanovich Guchkov, a businessman, politician, and former mayor. The chamber was under the supervision of the Russian Ministry for trade and industry.[7] Another prominent contribution was made by the American-Russian Chamber of Commerce established in New York in February 1916 under the chairmanship of Charles Boynton , who was married to a Russian and maintained close ties with Melville Stone, director of the Associated Press news agency, known for his Russophile stance.

In February 1915 in Petrograd, the Society for Promoting Mutual Friendly Relations between Russia and America started its activities aimed at developing "friendly public and business relations between Russian and the North American United States and Canada" by holding exhibitions and events, congresses and conferences, publishing periodicals and specialized literature, providing information and reference materials.[8] The society's director was Roman Romanovich Rosen, former Russian Ambassador to the United States; after he resigned in 1917, he was succeeded by Nikolai Andreevich Borodin. During its three-year existence, from December 1915 to February 1918, the Society published five issues of its *Izvestiya* dedicated to various aspects of Russian-American cooperation during World War I. Two questions should be asked while studying the development of *Amerikanistika* in the Russian Empire and Russian studies in the United States as academic disciplines based on the imagological (sociocultural) approach: (1) how much this process was influenced by both national and international agendas of the time; (2) has the process moved to that level of the perception of the *Other* which Tzvetan Todorov termed epistemological? While the praxeological level entails taming the *Other* by rejecting or appropriating "otherness," the epistemological level should entail studying it as a real, not imaginary, reality construed within the framework of discourses created by the texts about Russia and the United States.[9]

RUSSIANS STUDY THE UNITED STATES: THE AMERICAN *OTHER*

As an academic and educational field, *Amerikanistika* in Russia began to develop back in the late nineteenth century, when the United States became a staple of educational, scholarly, and social and political writings, and of university courses. In its early stages, *Amerikanistika* in Russia was moved forward by Russia's participation in the Columbia Exposition (Chicago World's Fair) in 1893. No other nation showed such an interest in the event as did Russians who were going through a sort of an "American craze." Never before had Russia seen such a number of publications about the United States. Newspapers, magazines, and journals gave the "American topic" pride of place; a series of books on American technological advances, production and capital management, education system and agricultural system was published; and not only that, Russia published reports on business trips of Russian professionals who represented various governmental departments at the exhibition; Russians published memoirs of the exhibition's participants full of observations about the US political system, interethnic and interracial relations, Americans' way of life and the traits of their national character which determined the economic flourishing and progress of the whole society.[10]

During World War I, at the time of the rapprochement between the two countries, *Amerikanistika* in the Russian Empire received a new development impetus. It occurred for several reasons. First, because of the intense teaching and writing of Pavel Grigorievich Mizhuev, a St. Petersburg sociologist, Stepan Fedorovich Fortunatov, a Moscow sociologist, and Maxim Maximovich Kovalevsky, a sociologist and historian who taught in Moscow and St. Petersburg universities.[11] Second, due to dissemination of knowledge about the United States by those who sought to further develop trading and economic cooperation between the two countries and organized special bodies which greatly contributed to the Russian-American rapprochement, mutual understanding, and study. Among those people we could name Nikolai Andreevich Borodin and Ivan Khristoforovich Ozerov. Third, it happened because the development agenda of the Russian Empire included the question of the prospects of liberalizing the political system and modernizing the economy and poised Russian liberal academics to study the American experience in their search for the ways to reform Russia. Pavel Grigorievich Mizhuev was active in the field of the popular education in Russia; after graduating from St. Petersburg university, he taught foreign languages and held the position of head librarian at St. Petersburg Technological Institute. He began to publish books, and social and political essays on America as early as 1891. He addressed various aspects of US development, such as the relationship between the British mother country and the American colonies, the issues of the political system, trade, education, charity, and the women question. All in all, Mizhuev wrote twenty-five books and essays on purely American subjects, and about fifteen works where the United States is characterized within greater comparative contexts.[12] Mizhuev's *The History of the Great American Democracy* was part of the university-published series called The History of Europe by Historical Periods and Countries in the Middle Ages and the Modernity edited by Nikolai Ivanovich Kareev and Ivan Vasilievich Luchitsky. Mizhuev's teaching allowed him to promote his views on US development in universities. It is hard to overestimate his role in disseminating knowledge about the United States in Russia, as well as his part in developing *Amerikanistika* as an academic discipline on the eve of, and during, World War I.

He was mainly interested in the subject of "the great experience of a democratic governmental reform" carried out in the United States.[13] Certainly, Mizhuev was inclined to idealize US reform, which was in general typical of the early Russian specialists in *Amerikanistika*, as they were focused on the issue of the influence political agencies had on a society's welfare. It is not accidental that both Mizhuev's book on American democracy and a whole series of his publications on the essence of parliamentary reforms, on the principle of the separation of powers, human rights and freedoms where the United States was given a special place, were published when Russia, during its first revolution, was puzzling over the question of modernizing its political system.[14]

Mizhuev turns to American democracy as an "unsurpassed experience of the power of the people," stressing the importance of the education system and of the free press in the United States both for the material welfare of American society, and for its intellectual progress the like of which humankind had never known before. And even such openly negative aspects of American life as the racial issue seemed to Mizhuev to be temporary, and a skillful selection of facts confirmed the growing education level among African Americans. As of 1900, the percentage of literate African Americans was higher than that of Russians in the European part of Russia (55 percent against 47 percent).[15]

The US experience in education was Mizhuev's second principal subject on the eve of, and during, World War I. This subject, just like the previous one, was supposed to evoke some kind of envy in the souls of Russian readers due to constant parallels drawn between the realities of the two countries. As one of the Russian reviewers wrote, "if we give money to fund education, the essential condition is that the education of the people shouldn't be too educating."[16] Besides many publications in magazines, Mizhuev summarized his observations in a book published in 1912. Its pages are full of references to the American *Other* in order to criticize the Russian *Self*. Mizhuev was a proponent of secular education since, as the American experience shows, all people agree on how to teach math, but they can have drastic differences about faith and teaching theology. Mizhuev called upon Russia to look up to America in education since "adolescents of fourteen or fifteen graduating from state schools in

America know more than some persons in Russia who are considered suitable to teach in state schools." [17]

During the war, Mizhuev was on the editing board of *Izvestiia*, the periodical of the Society for Promoting Mutual Friendly Relations between Russia and America, and its lecture committee. He disseminated his evaluation of the American development model through public lectures, magazine publications, and university teaching.

In Moscow, *Amerikanistika* developed due to the efforts of Stepan Fedorovich Fortunatov, a liberal Westernizer, professor of constitutional law and political history. In 1879, Fortunatov published his book *The History of Political Theories in the United States*. In the early twentieth century, he began giving courses on US history at Moscow University. Fortunatov admired American federalism, using the discussion of American political heritage to broach the issue of the need for reforms in Russia aimed at introducing self-government, the principle of the separation of powers, and giving Russians rights and freedoms. During the 1905–1907 revolution, he stepped up his social and political essay writing, trying to draw attention to the American experience of federalization and to the principles of structuring the legislative power in the United States when Russia debated the issue of introducing representational government.

During World War I, Fortunatov expanded his audience by lecturing to the students of the Moscow Higher Courses for Women. In the lectures addressed to them, Fortunatov stressed that only in the United States, democracy resulted in a harmonious union between the principles of freedom and equality, and drew a conclusion which is largely typical for the *Amerikanistika* specialists of the time:

> The United States is now facing two extremely difficult issues: one is the racial issue, and the other is the issue of harmonizing the economic system with the extremes of capitalist development, as well as harmonizing property inequality with political democracy. The future will tell how these issues will be resolved. Yet according to James Bryce, if we are talking the interests of masses and not individuals, the United States achieved the highest level of prosperity, intellectual development and happiness as no European nation has achieved. [18]

In his reading list for the course Fortunatov included the following books: Alexis de Tocqueville's classic *Democracy in America*; translation into Russian of *The American Commonwealth* (1889–1890), three-volume work by British politician, jurist, and historian James Bryce; Pavel Grigorievich Mizhuev's *History of the Great American Democracy*; 1897 translation of Harvard professor Edward Channing's *History of the United States of America*; the translation of the three-volume *History of the United States* (1870) by Édouard Laboulaye, French professor of comparative law; *The History of the North American United States* (1912), a two-volume work by Alexei Vasilievich Babine. [19]

Two authors are missing from this list, though both played a very significant part in the development of *Amerikanistika* in Russia: Moisei Yakovlevich Ostrogorsky and Maxim Maximovich Kovalevsky.

Ostrogorsky's fundamental two-volume book *Democracy and Political Parties* was undoubtedly the crowning glory of the pre-revolutionary *Amerikanistika*, and in the West, it was considered to be on par with the works of Alexis de Tocqueville and James Bryce. However, the book was published in French in Paris in 1898; German, Polish, and English translations followed, and in 1910 in New York, the revised version of the second volume was published in English under the title *Democracy and the Party System in the USA*. The Russian translation appeared only in 1927, in Soviet Russia. During his entire life, Ostrogorsky remained interested in American democracy whose drawbacks (linked with the parties' increasing bureaucratization, authorities' corruption, and people's alienation from political power) he criticized.

Ostrogorsky combined political theory with practical work aimed at transplanting the best features of Americans' democratic experience onto Russian soil. He applied his efforts, first and foremost, during his tenure in the First State Duma. He wasn't a member of any party, but he was engaged in deputy activities on behalf of the Constitutional democrats being in contact with its head and principal theorist Pavel Nikolaevich Miliukov, who visited the United States three times (the last visit was in 1908) and in 1905 published in the United States his book *Russia and Its Crisis*.[20] Constitutional democrats' publications focusing on progressive sociopolitical and economic developments in the United States were marked by profound analysis and strove to depict various aspects of American reality. Still, Ostrogorsky's criticism of the political party system was not welcomed by Russian liberals who were inclined to idealize the role of parties in a representative democracy.

While Ostrogorsky thought very highly of the US Constitution, he did not view it as a dogma. With great insight, he discerned the weak spots in the US sociopolitical system at a time when the United States was on the eve of progressive reforms. At the same time, he did not belittle the significance of the American model for humankind in general and for Russia in particular, and he pinned his greatest hopes on people's capability for critical thinking.[21]

Maxim Maximovich Kovalevsky, a sociologist, historian, jurist, professor of Moscow and St. Petersburg universities, leader of the liberal Democratic reform party, and co-founder of the Progressive party, was yet another scholar who combined both theory and practice in his work. He visited the United States twice,[22] published his course of lectures on the history of the US Constitution as a separate book in 1890–1891, and issued a series of articles in *Russkaya mysl* and *Vestnik Evropy* magazines.

In the memoirs he wrote in Karlsbad in 1914–1915, Kovalevsky stated that during both his trips to the United States he was primarily interested in the American education system and cultural and educational institutions from libraries and museums to literary clubs and art galleries.[23] Both his interest and his lectures and publications on agriculture and the national question in the North American republic and its local self-government bodies stemmed from the problems of the internal political development of the Russian Empire. In his commentaries on the Democratic Reform Party's agenda, Kovalevsky stressed that "our democracy will have to travel the same route as the United States, i.e., it will have to expand the functions of regional and municipal assemblies, to spread the system over the entire Empire, and to reduce the tasks of the central administration and of its bodies to carrying out monitoring functions in the provinces."[24]

His visits to the US, his reading the works of George Bancroft and Woodrow Wilson, a series of political publications edited by Herbert Adams, whom he met during his first trip, and by his acquaintance with the social critique offered by Henry George in his book Progress and Poverty were significant parts of the process. Observations and materials collected by Kovalevsky during his visits to the US, his reading the works of George Bancroft and Woodrow Wilson, a series of political publications edited by Herbert Adams, whom he met during his first trip, and his acquaintance with the social critique offered by Henry George in his book Progress and Poverty, formed the foundation for Kovalevsky's articles, presentations, and public lectures delivered in Moscow, St. Petersburg, and Paris. In 1883 in Moscow, he delivered a series of public talks on the specifics of the American national character which Russians should learn about if they wished to understand the inner resources which set the government machinery working.[25]

Although Kovalevsky admired Americans' achievements, he noted the negative aspects of America's development. Yet, since he was driven by his desire to use the United States to criticize Russia's political and socioeconomic system, more often than not he downplayed these negative aspects. He used coded (Aesopian) language in order to form in the minds of his students who worshipped him a permanently critical attitude toward the order of things in Russia, and he did so by drawing parallels with the Western way of things in general and the American way of things in particular, and for that, in 1887 he was denied the right to teach in the higher educational institutions of the Russian Empire.[26]

Kovalevsky would return to Russia cresting the wave of the first Russian revolution and would deliver a special lecture course for Moscow University students. The course was on the US local bodies with the emphasis on their truly democratic character.[27]

On the whole, his memoirs, written in the beginning of World War I, show us that despite his criticism of corruption in US political life, of the segregation of African Americans and Native Americans that struck him unfavorably, despite racial discrimination of Chinese immigrants, and despite his conclusion that "Americans entirely lack the ability to comprehend those public and political ideals that are different from their own," Kovalevsky believed in their competence to overcome all negative phenomena. He believed in their reformist spirit, which fully manifested itself in the Progressive era, in the constructive activities of the press and the public opinion, and on the whole, he believed in the rejuvenating power of that kind of sociopolitical system that was absent in Russia, which, in the United States, gave people a chance to hope that their pursuit of happiness would ultimately bring fruit.[28]

Kovalevsky's speeches in the Duma and then in the State Council both before and during the war (he died in 1916) abound with American contexts. The United States as the *Other* was a constant presence in Kovalevsky's thought, whether he was discussing the constitution, civil rights and freedoms, self-government principles, agrarian reforms, tariffs, railroad construction, academic and religious freedoms, the Finnish question, or Siberian development prospects.[29]

Kovalevsky was constantly inspired by American democracy, and in 1916, he planned to write a separate volume for a new edition of his *Origins of Modern Democracy*, but sadly, he died before he could do that. He believed that despite American society's difficult path from the colonial times to the twentieth century, it succeeded in making the right choice for the north-western/democratic and federalist development model (as opposed to the southern/aristocratic and separatist model), and thereby American society kept alive the best ideas of the English Levellers and federalists of the American Revolution.[30]

Before and especially during World War I, serious research into contemporary and historical US experience, as well as cooperation between the two countries, were promoted in the Russian Empire by two people who had contributed greatly to the development of the pre-war *Amerikanistika*: Nikolai Andreevich Borodin, who has already been mentioned, one of the founders of the Society for Promoting Mutual Friendly Relations between Russia and America, the First State Duma deputy from the Urals region and a member of the Constitutional democrats' faction; and Ivan Khristoforovich Ozerov, an economist, professor of financial law in Moscow University and in the Commercial University in Moscow, one of the founders of the Russian-American Chamber of Commerce.

For both Borodin and Ozerov, as well as for liberal Westernizers such as Mizhuev, Fortunatov, and Kovalevsky, the United States was not just a reality, but also a concept, and drawing parallels between the American and the Russian experiences (with the latter always coming off worse) allowed them to speak of those reforms which they believed the Russian Empire needed. All these scholars paid particular attention to the US education system, which laid down the necessary foundations for the civic consolidation of the society, for developing the country's productive forces, and for educating Americans. Multiple works on the subject appeared after the Chicago World Fair in 1893,[31] which Borodin had taken part in, and it was the exhibition that "blew his mind" about America. He visited America two more times in1913 and in 1917.[32]

Talking about the need to study the American experience at the time of a rapprochement between the two countries, Borodin stressed the significance of American achievements for developing Russia's productive forces and its renewal:

> It is obvious for everyone now that without an extensive development of our productive forces, Russia as a great power cannot exist, and in order to develop them we should work on the scale, and with the efforts broad and expansive, like America, and not small and meager like Europe. . . . We are profoundly convinced that there is no other path open to us than that of North America, and we must study it, moreover, we should use American experience and strive to attract its immense capitals and technical means for joint work on exploring Russia's untapped natural resources and for stimulating its poorly developed industry.[33]

During his second US trip in 1913 to attend an international congress on refrigeration engineering in Chicago, Borodin observed positive shifts that had taken place in the United States over the previous twenty years, and concluded that Russian readers had to be acquainted with various aspects of the American experience. As a result, in 1915 he published his book *North American United States and Russia* based on materials Borodin collected during his visit to America. In that book, Borodin shared with his readers his dreams of Russians learning from Americans, of effective US economic policy which was relevant for modernizing the economically and culturally backward Russian Empire, "whose present could be equated with the US past" of thirty to fifty years ago. Borodin traced similarities in the two countries' developments (this trend generally prevailed in mutual representations during World War I, especially in 1916 and in 1917 till the autumn) and thereby concluded that Russia could use the American model as its reference point, which poised Russians to study the American experience since it helped Russians understand the possible future development of their country and how to avoid possible mistakes. Borodin wrote not only about the socioeconomic development, but also about the lessons of American federalism. He believed that the American example clearly showed that the federative system allowed the United States to iron out contradictions of ethnic and religious conflicts, and that issue was particularly relevant for Russia.[34]

Depicting a collective portrait of an American as "a colonizer with all the attendant qualities"[35] and believing that a typical American was not a city dweller, but a resident of Illinois, Iowa, Wisconsin, and Minnesota, Borodin particularly stressed such positive features of the American national character as energy, individualism, respect for any kind of labor, managing talents, readiness to move around the country, the ability to assimilate people from different ethnic backgrounds, consciousness of their national unity and civic consensus, active patriotism which rested on their trust in their present and on their hope for the future (unlike the contemplative and mystical Russian patriotism which rested on the memories of the past). Borodin tried to destroy the stereotypes of Americans as a nation of money-makers and pragmatists, which emerged from insufficient knowledge of Americans' everyday life. Borodin stressed that an average American has a fairly high level of development, he perceives money as the symbol of success resulting from his work, and his pragmatism is combined with idealism. Schools were the principal mechanisms for shaping this national character; schools foster the public spirit and American patriotism, and the press spreads education. And that experience is also extremely useful for Russia.[36]

Borodin certainly idealizes Americans, and that is due to two reasons: (1) he attempts to create a generalized image; and (2) he constantly draws parallels between the two countries (even though sometimes these parallels remain in the subtext). However, that doesn't prevent him from discussing such "sores" of the current political life as political corruption and a venal press, the existence of negative phenomena in the economic and social life. Yet even these discussions bring the author to draw favorable conclusions about the American experience linked to the traditions of reformism aimed at returning American society to the state of balance it has temporarily lost.[37]

In April 1917, Borodin arrived in the United States as a member of Boris Alexandrovich Bakhmetev's Mission Extraordinary of the Provisional government to secure a loan and to guarantee sustainable fulfillment of orders for military and agricultural equipment. Upon his return in September, he gave a presentation at the Society for Promoting Mutual Friendly Relations between Russia and America, stressing that "now we have truly achieved rapprochement with Americans in the way that our society dreamed about: common interests and common global tasks will weld the two countries into a tight union which, we are certain, will continue for many years even after the war."[38] Alas, these hopes never came true, and neither did the dreams of Ivan Khristoforovich Ozerov, yet another active proponent of learning from the American experience and an ardent promoter of close cooperation between Russia and the United States.

Ozerov came from a poor peasant family, he achieved his professorship through his talent and hard work, but unlike Borodin, he never visited America. Yet the subject of America was important to him as he studied specific features of the development of consumer societies and cooperation in Europe and in the United States, and when he was preparing for his master's examination at Moscow University, he was supervised by Ivan Petrovich Ianzhul, a well-known economist who had visited the Chicago World Fair together with his wife. Ianzhul also wrote articles for *Russkie vedomosti* where he discussed American economy and the significance of education for successes in industry and trade.[39]

By discussing American progress and prosperity, Ozerov criticized the internal policies of the Russian Empire. Samuel Harper, a rising star of Russian studies in the United States, was a frequent guest in Ozerov's Moscow home on his visits to Russia. There, Harper listened to the Russian speak of and criticize the tsarist government.[40]

Ozerov started thinking about the secrets of capitalism's success in the United States as early as 1903 in his book *America Advances on Europe*. This book was reissued in 1908 with more emphasis on "American lessons for Russia" and was then titled *What does America Teach Us?* Ozerov stressed that America teaches us how not to starve, how to provide work for the population, how to follow the path of progress. It was possible to achieve these goals through intensive agricultural methods, through industrial innovations, as well as through disseminating new forms and principles of organizing manufacturing and sales of goods (trusts and syndicates for instance), as well as through stimulating the development of the transportation system, but first and foremost, through "cultivating people's minds." The ability to multiply human capital by developing education, the press, civil equality, and political activity—this is the American secret of success which "stems from the overall conditions of the American life." Such was Ozerov's conclusion.[41] "In America . . . people are taught to act, to shape new forms of life, to leave a bright, brave imprint of their own personality on life, everyone there is a creator, everyone there is an artist, in America they have space for the living creation of life and for the brave thinking," he mused and then continued, "In America, a businesslike atmosphere has been created, and everyone who is not working feels out of place, everyone feels responsible for what he is. This specific type of character is an achievement to go down the ages."[42] That was why Ozerov thought it necessary to learn from Americans. Thus far, he stated, Russia is awash in negligence, living in the old rut, practicing predatory business practices, thus far, there is no money "for people's education, for irrigating huge expanses of land, for small manufacturing," "apparently, there is no energy, no initiative, there is a shortage of . . . managing capabilities." Ozerov called for dispelling the darkness of ignorance and alcoholism, of the absence of civil and political rights that "shrouds Russia, and then the people's eyes will open, and wealth will literally spring from under the ground. We will drown in it."[43]

Certainly, Ozerov's discussion of the United States shows too many broad strokes; the American reality is idealized. Ozerov used the United States as a concept, and not as the entire agglomeration of all the positive and negative features of its development. But this concept was far too convenient for criticizing the way of things in Russia.

Ozerov promoted his views in his university teaching, and on the pages of the *Rech* newspaper published by Pavel Nikolaevich Miliukov, on the pages of *Russkoe ekonomicheskoe obozrenie,* and on the pages of American newspapers. In 1913, Yurii Petrovich Bakhmetev, Russian Ambassador to the United States, reported to the ministry for foreign affairs about one such publication in the *New York Sun*:

> He argues for the need for a closer rapprochement between Russia and the United States on the grounds of industry and trade, mostly, for tapping those of our natural resources that are yet untouched, using American money and American energy. He also hopes that Americans' influence on our people will serve as a foundation for a "just rule" which will see the establishment of the principles of "equality of all ethnicities and all confessions." The Jewish question which caused here a sad misunderstanding between Russia and America must be solved (but he does not say how exactly): "We must wake up from our centuries-long sleep and take a healthy dose of Americanism," and so on and so forth in the same vein.[44]

When World War I broke out, Ozerov channeled all his efforts into developing trade cooperation between the two countries. That cooperation was to be promoted by the Russian-American Chamber of Commerce, where Ozerov was vice chair, and also by the Society for Promoting Mutual Friendly Relations between Russia and America, whose publications gave voice to Ozerov's ideas.

Both Ozerov and Borodin certainly did criticize some drawbacks in the US development, but on the whole, the image of the American *Other* was romanticized and used to critically think about the Russian *Self.* However, both Ozerov and Borodin, as well as other representatives of the liberal Russian *Amerikanistika,* never doubted that once the conditions of life in Russia were changed, education, free press, transportation development, and new principles of industrial management would make it possible for Russia to be just as prosperous a country as the United States, and a Russian could be just as wealthy as an American.

Therefore, the Russian Empire's agenda dictated the priority subjects in studying the United States, and the favorable climate of Russian-American relations created the conditions for expanding and clarifying their knowledge of the American *Other* on the one hand, and, on the other hand, shifted the emphasis toward this *Other's* idealization.

Certainly, Russian society also had a radical discourse prompted by the US text.[45] Russian radicals grew progressively disappointed in the United States, especially in its social aspect, as early as the late nineteenth century, and this disappointment intensified during the First Russian Revolution. However, up until October 1917, it was the liberal Westernizers who made the largest contribution to the development of *Amerikanistika,* and their stance contributed to turning the space of the burgeoning

Amerikanistika into a realm dedicated to constructing a national concept of *Self* through the interpretation of another cultural experience.

Alexei Vasilievich Babine holds a special place among Russian *Amerikanistika* scholars. He was a conservative, and he was one of those who pioneered both *Amerikanistika* in Russia and Slavic studies in the United States. He received his MA from Cornell University, where he had worked as a librarian since 1891, and in 1896, he took a librarian's position at Indiana University.[46]

As a Russian studies specialist in the United States, Babine gave an introductory course on Russian language and bibliography at Stanford University beginning in 1898, and in 1902 he founded and headed the Slavic Section in the Library of Congress.[47] Babine spearheaded the acquisition, for one-third of its market price, of the famous collection of Gennady Vasilievich Yudin, a publisher and bibliophile from Krasnoyarsk. The collection numbered 80,000 printed books and 500,000 manuscripts. As a result, the Library of Congress became the holder of the largest "Russian collection" in the United States, although the collection remained unsystematized for a long time.

As a Russian specialist in *Amerikanistika*, Babine published a history of the United States in two volumes that traced back to Russia in 1910.[48] Scholars believe that of all the pre-revolutionary works on *Amerikanistika*, Babine's most conformed to academic research standards of the time.[49] Babine's book abounds with facts, and for that reason, it was recommended university reading.[50] Babine paid special attention to the political and economic history of the United States, and, as a conservative and an adherent of a strong central authority, he gave an overall negative evaluation of the American Revolution since he saw it as a disruption of the natural course of the common history of the Anglo-Saxon countries. He viewed the revolution as a period of desolation, anarchy, and the power of dishonest politicians seeking personal gain. Babine gave due credit to the "phenomenal economic progress" of the United States and to "the unprecedented growth of people's prosperity," yet he pointed out that Americans are consumed with a thirst for profit, that capitalism has a corrupting influence on government and the judicial system.[51]

Babine remained in Russia until 1922, working as a state school superintendent for the ministry for people's education, and after 1917, he lectured at Saratov University. Then he immigrated to the United States, and from 1927 to 1930 he headed the Slavic Section of the Library of Congress. He never accepted the October Revolution, and for that reason, his contribution to *Amerikanistika* in Russia was forgotten.

AMERICANS STUDY RUSSIA: THE RUSSIAN *OTHER*

Before World War I, Russian studies in the American academe was taking shape due to the work of Archibald Coolidge and Leo Wiener at Harvard University; George Noyes at the University of California; and also of Charles Crane, a well-known Russophile, businessman, and philanthropist, who stood at the origins of the Slavic program at the University of Chicago. Crane purchased books for libraries, supported various projects aimed at promoting Russian culture in the United States and financed Samuel Harper's personal "Russian program," helping him become a renowned specialist on the Russian question.[52]

On the whole, American Russophiles at the turn of the nineteenth to twentieth centuries made a large contribution to promoting interest in Russian literature and spirituality in American society. At the same time, they used American interest in "the Russia of Tolstoy and Tchaikovsky," which largely emerged due to the American agenda, to promote their own ideas of Russia. Russian literature, music, and art attracted Americans both as a way to understand the special features of a different national character and as a source of stunningly powerful realism in describing life and a special kind of spirituality which opposed the harsh reality. The study of Russian culture gave Americans a new religious and philosophical conceptualization of the humans' place in the world as well as the new vision of their own society and prospects of its reforming. At that time, the United States was going through socioeconomic, political, and moral renewals. Hence the fascination with Leo Tolstoy, a writer, a thinker, and a man with a peculiar social stance. The phenomenon of Tolstoy was the conduit for American knowledge of Russia and its history. Knowledge of Russian literature made clear the need to understand specific features of the development of Russian civilization.[53] It was not accidental that it was Isabel Hapgood and Nathan Haskell Dole, translators from Russia, who called for Russian studies in academe,[54] and Charles Crane and Archibald Coolidge, known for their Russophile leanings, who began to implement it. Crane and Coolidge explained the need for Russian studies through both the need to correct false ideas about the Russian Empire and through the emerging globalization process. A closer interaction between the United States and its eastern neighbor was to play a special role in global development. Archibald Coolidge could offer a realistic vision of Russia within the system of international relations based on his understanding of the history of diplomacy as the field of interaction of national interests, and also on the notion of the different nature of domestic and foreign policies, a view which was typical of the time. Coolidge initiated the Russian studies program in Harvard University. This program manifested the overall process of the professionalization of Americans' historical knowledge about the world.[55]

At the same time, Russian studies in the United States was influenced by the widespread myths and stereotypes in American society. Russian studies were closely connected with the domestic and foreign political situation (decreasing interest in the "Russian question" due to disappointment in the results of the First Russian Revolution, and the shift of American priorities after the Russo-Japanese War). Also, one should remember the influence of the explanatory schemes offered by European intellectuals (Alfred Rambaud, Anatole Leroy-Beaulieu, Wallace Donald MacKenzie), since American Slavists went to study first and foremost to Paris. For instance, a well-known French Slavist, Paul Boyer, was Samuel Harper's mentor in Russian language, history, and culture when the latter studied in Paris in the School of Oriental Languages.[56]

On the whole, despite the fact that there emerged a network of university centers and library collections, despite the fact that Frank Golder defended the first thesis in Russian studies the field only made moderate progress in the United States before World War I. Only Harvard and the University of California (Berkeley) systematically taught the Russian language; in the early twentieth century, occasional courses were also offered at the Universities of Chicago, Michigan, and Wisconsin, as well as Johns Hopkins University. Only Harvard and Berkeley had Russian history programs. In 1902, Harvard had only thirteen students enrolled in its Slavic department, and in 1912–1913, their number grew by two people.[57]

Before World War I, Russian studies in the United States was going through a preparatory stage. Americans were still looking for information in the verbal and graphic materials offered by the press, in travelogues, and in the writings of journalists and translators who, in turn, took part in shaping the discourses conditioned by the Russian text: the liberal universalist (optimistic) discourse, as offered, for instance, by George Kennan and Edmund Noble, progressive journalists crusading for the liberalization of Russia; the conservative pessimist (Russophobic) discourse, as offered, for instance, by Henry Cabot Lodge, a well-known politician, leader of the conservative "old guard" of the Republican party, and Frederic Palmer, American writer and military correspondent; the radical discourse, as offered, for instance, by gentlemen Socialists and journalists William English Walling, Arthur Bullard, Kellogg Durland, Ernest Poole; the Russophile discourse, as offered, for instance, by translator Isabel Hapgood and George Frederick Wright, geologist and professor at Oberlin College. Each of these discourses came with its own vision of the Russian national character, the modernization prospects of the Russian Empire, the construction of a "romantic" or a "demonic" image of the Russian *Other*, a set of mythologems and articulation practices.

The image of the romantic Russian *Other* was framed by the liberal universalist myths, which formed the repertoire of meanings for *the liberal universalist discourse*. Its components included the vision of the Russian Revolution that originated in the lowest classes of society, was directed by liberals, and followed the model of the great Western Revolutions. It included the beliefs that Russian society was capable of relatively rapid Westernization, that the Russian people were resisting its xenophobic authorities and waiting for help from overseas, and that Americans were responsible for the process of reforming Russia. It was argued that Russia had no other choice but to follow the path of democracy and capitalism already traced by the more developed Western countries, the United States first and foremost among them. The Russian liberals and radicals who visited the United States had made a special contribution in the maintenance of the American liberal-universalist myths about Russia, especially the "myth about the Russian Revolution." The image of the demonic Russian *Other* was framed by the conservative pessimist Russophobic myths, although the liberal universalists also contributed to its official component. These myths formed the repertoire of meanings of *the conservative pessimist discourse.* They emphasized the perpetual gap between "the Immutable Rus" and the West that was caused by insuperable cultural differences, the unalterable Russian national character that placed Russia in the Eastern/Asian camp, the aggressive and barbaric nature of Russian imperialism that threatened not only American interests, but also those of the entire civilized world. *The radical discourse* had acquired its final shape during the First Russian Revolution thanks to the efforts of the American gentlemen-socialists and other representatives of leftist ideologies, especially the Russian-Jewish emigrants of radical views. In this context, Russia was allowed to appear as America's mentor, but only in relation to its social message to humanity and the universal importance of its social revolution. *Conservative Russophiles* like Isabel Hapgood recognized that Russians had the right to be different, saw the ruler and the people as a unified whole, talked about the compassionate paternalism of the Russian autocratic state and the slow rates of modernization, and thus constructed its "Orientalist" image without becoming die-hard Orientalists themselves. *Liberal Russophiles* such as Charles Crane and Samuel Harper promoted studying Russia since they were enchanted by its unique culture, yet they banked on the liberalization of Russia's political system under the leadership of such figures as Pavel Nikolaevich Miliukov, the leader of Constitutional democrats.[58]

Russian-American rapprochement during World War I gave new impetus to the Russian Studies in the United States and to the process of demythologizing Russians' ideas of Americans and Americans' ideas of Russians.[59]

In 1915, Nikolai Andreevich Borodin stated:

> The events of the war powerfully influenced the new rapprochement between Russia and the United States on the basis of large consignments. . . . But besides this business-induced rapprochement, there is a cultural one, which is more important, and it begins, first and foremost,

with a more careful mutual study. Despite the dangerous and difficult journey, during this winter we welcomed not only businessmen, but also those American guests who are even dearer to our hearts, people of science, scholarship, thought, and press. We should mention S. N. Harper, Russian language and literature professor at the University of Chicago, Mr. Gr. Mason[60] from the *Outlook* magazine, Mr. Child,[61] and others. It was with great interest that they acquainted themselves with our domestic affairs, and we are certain that during their brief stay, they collected an abundance of materials which will form the ground-work for introducing to Americans both at universities and in press the true Russia and its mood during these difficult days. . . . This incredible influx into Russia of Americans from these fields indicates that the United States demonstrates a heightened interest in Russia and Russians.[62]

In September 1916, Borodin dwelled on "the new type of Americans learning about Russia not for financial gain, not for 'business,' but because they are interested in Russians and what they believe to be their undoubtedly great future."[63]

Russophiles were among the first who tried to correct the "distorted image of Russia" in American society, promoting the study of Russia and the economic interaction of the two countries.[64] On the whole, Russophile discourse was in demand in the United States given the Russian-American rapprochement, and it was particularly relevant to the need of an academic study of each other.

Charles Crane welcomed Russia's participation in World War I, he promoted the idea of the United States joining the anti-German coalition, and he wrote to Charles William Eliot, former Harvard University President: "Russia is fighting to become emancipated from Prussian domination and her whole heart is in this war. . . . I believe the next century is going to see the Slavs make great contributions to the culture of the world and that these contributions are not going to be wanting in a strong spiritual quality."[65]

Wharton Barker, a businessman from Philadelphia and an old friend of Russia, continued to publish articles in support of Russia in the local and central press, highlighting for Americans Russia's contribution to the fight against the German militarism. Barker suggested to Nicholas II and Sergei Dmitrievich Sazonov, minister for the foreign affairs, that they use Barker's connections and resources for the good of Russia, and from time to time, Barker acted as an intermediary between various American firms wishing to receive contracts to supply goods and weapons to Russia and the Russian Embassy in Washington, DC.[66]

In his turn, Samuel Harper wanted to use his knowledge of Russia to intensify the Russian-American rapprochement. He visited Russia in a private capacity in 1915, and in 1916, he traveled there on the same steamship as the new US ambassador David Rowland Francis (Harper had already declined an offer to take a post in the embassy). He also visited Russia as a member of Elihu Root's mission in 1917.[67] Antoni Moritsevich Volkov, Russian consul general in Chicago, highly praised Harper's work in a letter to Vladimir Antonovich Artsimovich, vice-minister for foreign affairs:

> In the United States, professor Harper has been very active and successive in acquainting Americans with the current events in Russia. Newspaper articles, public lectures in universities, and, finally, conversations about Russia with his many influential friends, all of these activities together should be credited to the young professor. I think I will not stray far from the truth if I say that professor Harper's pro-Russian activities made him very popular among Americans, and justly garnered him the reputation of an expert on Russia.[68]

In 1915, Leo Wiener, a trailblazer of Russian studies, the first American professor of Russian language and literature[69] who held that position at Harvard until retirement, published a book where he, as he put it himself, offered an objective evaluation of "the present and . . . the future of the great and gifted Russian people, the latest in Europe to carry high the banner of modern civilization." Wiener dwelled on the unity of opposites which was his explanation for perception stereotypes, and he deduced Russia's contradictory nature from "the unique jostling of mythical antiquity and stark reality." However, this negative factor no longer defined its history. Now Russia was defined by what Wiener called "the Russian soul," since he believed in its potential and special talents. Wiener called for unbiased study of Russia in order to discover those constants which had influenced the evolution of the nation and would allow the construction of reliable explanatory schemes.[70] Wiener offered Americans one such version of studying the history of the Russian people and their national character through art, music, religion, public and political thought, philosophy, and poetry and literature, through telling Americans about Russian peasants and the condition of women and non-Russian peoples. Wiener also traced the influence of American democratic impulses on the development of both social and political ideals, and of musical culture, stressing, however, their different manifestations and different results in the Russian cultural milieu.[71]

Nicholas II's government, in its turn, made consolidated efforts to destroy the stereotypical perception of Russia in the United States and to disseminate reliable knowledge about Russia among Americans. For that purpose, Sergey Nikolayevich Syromiatnikov, a Russian journalist and conservative public figure, Orientalist, and traveler, arrived in New York in February 1915 as an agent of the Ministry of Internal Affairs of the Russian Empire.

In the American press, Syromiatnikov called for establishing immediate trading and economic contacts between the two countries and for a serious study of Russia. He claimed that after the war, Russia would shift its trading priorities from Germany to Great Britain and the United States, and the development of Russian studies would enable the necessary foundations for this trade-based rapprochement. Syromiatnikov believed that Columbia University should become the principal seat of Russian studies.[72] In response to Syromiatnikov's article, the secretary of Columbia University, Frank D. Fackenthal published a letter to the editor of the *New York Times*, in which he informed the public about the creation of the Slavonic Department at Columbia University in 1913–1914 and about the growing number of students who took the courses taught by John Dyneley Prince, professor of Semitic and Slavic languages: from six students who took the "History of the Slavonic nations and races" course in 1913–1914 to thirty-nine students who took the Slavonic history course in 1915. These students were also attending a Russian language course that was first offered that same year. Fackenthal ended his letter saying that "of course, all this may seem a small beginning, but it at least indicates a healthy and growing interests along the lines so ably laid down by Mr. Syromiatnikoff."[73]

Yurii Petrovich Bakhmetev, Russia's ambassador to the United States, reported that two professors at Columbia University, John Prince and Michael Pupin[74] had supported Syromiatnikov's idea about creating Russian Studies courses. The ambassador emphasized that "Pupin who enjoys an outstanding position in the academic circles hopes to raise all the necessary funds for this undertaking among companies interested in the development of Russian trade."[75]

In 1915, Columbia University got its first Russian language professor—Elizabeth Reynolds. Since 1911, this talented American translator and promoter of Russian literature and culture had been in regular correspondence with Sergey Syromiatnikov. She was married to Norman Hapgood, a literary critic and editor of the *Collier's Weekly* and the *Harper's Weekly* magazines. The latter, owned by Charles Crane, became a forum for disseminating all kinds of information about Russia. Elizabeth Reynolds later founded the Russian Department at Dartmouth College (1918); in the meantime, she and Zenaida Ragozin, a Russian-born American and Syromiatnikov's old friend and colleague from the *Rossia* newspaper, had mobilized their contact networks to help him.[76] In New York, Syromiatnikov enjoyed the support and hospitality of Charles Crane. Syromiatnikov failed to establish good relations with Harper since the latter maintained ties with Russian radicals.[77]

What Syromiatnikov wanted to promote was not just the establishment of Russian Studies programs in the United States, but also the creation of student exchange networks for Russian studies majors from the United States and American studies majors from Russia. As he insisted in one of his publications, "our young men could learn much from you, and you Americans could gain a correct understanding of Russia through our universities."[78]

Initially inspired by Syromiatnikov's success, Bakhmetev petitioned for this trip to be extended. They fell out in November 1915, when Syromiatnikov published an article in the *New York Tribune* where he sharply criticized American Jews thereby breaking the rules of the diplomatic etiquette in the relations between two friendly countries.[79] In the end, the ambassador said that Syromiatnikov was too independent, unpredictable, and ambitious to carry out the mission of a public relations specialist and asked for his recall.[80]

Syromiatnikov's polemical ardor certainly hurt him, but one should keep in mind that his work fully fitted into the two countries' mutual movement toward shaping more multifaceted, more objective knowledge of each other, toward renouncing perception stereotypes, toward establishing academic study of each other and simultaneously intensified this movement.[81]

As far as the Russian studies in the United States were concerned, the war years were the time of their true take-off. At Harvard and Berkeley, more and more students took courses in Slavic studies. Meanwhile, Columbia University, where John Dyneley Prince championed the Russian studies program, opened the first Russian language program in the country. Like Syromiatnikov, Prince justified these innovations by pointing to the need for developing trade relations with the Russian Empire.[82]

The geographic reach of Russian studies in the United States also grew during World War I. In 1916, the University of Washington in Seattle inaugurated its Russian language program. The Russian consul in Nome and Seattle, Nikolai Viacheslavovich Bogoyavlensky reported to the embassy that the Russian language classes had "a demand that was surprisingly high," given the not-so-successful experience at the University of California. The program had twenty-three students in its midday classes and fifty-nine more in the evening slots, and the numbers just kept growing. "Under the current conditions," wrote Bogoyavlensky to the embassy in Washington, DC,

> it deserves to be mentioned as a peaceful Russian victory in America and furthermore as a means of fighting American prejudices against Russia. When I came to America three years ago, I was struck by the ignorance that even well-educated Americans with university degrees demonstrated with regard to Russia and everything Russian. . . . While our ideas of America were excessively rosy, Americans had gone too far in the opposite direction."[83]

The June 1916 issue of the *Russian-American Journal of Commerce*, which was published in New York in two languages and whose aim was to promote closer economic ties between the two countries, featured an editorial that said:

> Voices that call for a closer and more careful study of Russia sound
> ever more frequently and ever clearer in the American press and in
> private conversations. They call for a study that is neither mechanical
> nor limited to numbers, but that allows us to know Russia's aspirations
> and hopes, its potential forces and resources, its way of life—its very
> spirit. Hardly a month passes without several new works about Russia
> appearing in the American book market. Whatever the perspective of
> their authors, these books are all imbued with the same spirit—that of
> sympathy towards Russia.[84]

That was the time when Russia sided with progress, not regression, with light, not darkness, with freedom, not political slavery, because it sided with the fight against German militarism that threatened the world. In April 1917, already after the February Revolution in the Russian Empire, the United States itself was about to join this "democratic camp." It was against this background that "liberal crusaders" and Russophiles found themselves coming closer to each other in their heightened hopes connected with a new stage in Russia's renewal in the image and likeness of the West. Uncharacteristically, American Russophiles became engaged in "Westernizing" Russia by drawing parallels between the two countries' development.[85]

It was at that time that the Russian-American rapprochement peaked, and then it declined with the approaching October Revolution.

October 1917 marked the breaking point both in the history of *Amerikanistika* in Russia and Russian studies in the United States.

In *Amerikanistika* in Russia, its forward movement was interrupted, and ideological reasons led to many works by pre-revolutionary scholars being forgotten. The only exception was the work by Moisei Yakovlevich Ostrogorsky, which was translated and published in two volumes in 1927–1930 due to his criticism of the vices of American democracy. In the Soviet Union, *Amerikanistika* was inevitably influenced by the ideological *Other*, thus turning *Amerikanistika* into the field for constructing the Soviet identity. American studies in Soviet Russia was now dominated by the radical discourse conditioned by the Marxist paradigm, and not by the liberal universalist paradigm that dominated before the revolution.

In their turn, those members of the liberal Russian intelligentsia who immigrated into the United States after the October Revolution contributed to the flourishing of Russian studies in the United States. Russian studies was connected with the names of Georgy Vladimirovich Vernadskii (Yale University), Mikhail Mikhailovich Karpovich (Harvard University), Mikhail Timofeevich Florinsky (Columbia University) who brought to their classrooms not only knowledge but also a specific message which was both antimonarchic and anti-Bolshevik and tended toward the liberal-universalist sociopolitical discourse which now also became an academic discourse. American historians Donald Davis and Eugene Trani write that this fact resulted in American students studying "anti-Russian history of Russia," entering their academic, political and diplomatic life with notions that had been shaped by their professors from Russia and subsequently promoting anti-Russian sentiments in the United States. [86]

Social and political essay writings prompted by the "subject of Russia" back at the turn of the nineteenth to twentieth centuries are now integrated into the works of American specialists in Russian studies and Soviet studies, who continued the old argument about whether Russia is a "regular" country or an "exceptional" country, whether it is non-European or another Europe, whether the Russian way of development threatens the rest of the world.

Comparing the views of George Kennan and George Frost Kennan, Donald Davis and Eugene Trani conclude that "It is amazing how similar the overall perceptions of the two Kennans towards tsarist and Soviet Russia were: a despotic state that should be transformed into the image of American democracy. . . . The first Kennan's perception led to the Wilsonian policy of quarantine; the second Kennan's perception resulted in the Truman policy of containment." [87]

The liberal universalist (optimistic) discourse entirely accommodates the scheme suggested by American historian Martin Malia, who believed that Russia and Europe together made up "the West" conceived broadly. Consequently, Russia was destined to catch up with the countries that were ahead of it on the principal Westernization road. This movement was interrupted by the Bolsheviks and then it was restored after the collapse of the Soviet Union. Malia's vision of the Russian model contradicted that of his opponents, who promoted the idea of eternal "Russianness." [88] Richard Pipes was its most famous proponent among American Russian studies specialists. Pipes insisted on the fundamental tension between universal progress and national differences, which left Russia few opportunities to follow the West. In his works, Pipes followed conservative pessimistic discourse and insisted that Russia had an "Asian" nature and its political system would be inevitably authoritarian. [89] One could also remember a typical desire of Cold War American historiographers to speak of "the eternal Russia," to demonize the Russian national character, to link Soviet aggressiveness with a peculiar psychological reaction to the "close capitalist encirclement," with the historical tradition and the psychological traits of the Russian people. [90]

On the whole, one can state that during World War I, on both sides of the Atlantic, the perception of the *Other* shifted from that level which Tsvetan Todorov named epistemological; yet this shift did not diminish the significance of the praxeological perception vector in the shaping of the image of a different culture. In the academe, both the Russian *Other* and the American *Other* preserved their nature of an ideological and sociocultural construct and influenced thematic priorities, at the same time leaving enough space for constructing an imaginary reality which corresponded to the national development traditions and the agenda of the observer society and taking part in the interplay of meanings that shape the national I-concept. That trend emerged before 1917 and came to full fruition during the Cold War within the framework of that historiographical trend that was called "enemy studies."

Our research showed both the influence the particular climate of Russian-American relations had on the process of studying the other country and nation (at the time of a rapprochement, the academic space was inevitably pragmatized), and the direct correlation between the political and academic discourses. With the upswing of another cycle of hopes and disappointments that American society experienced in connection with a new stage of Russia's modernization (be it the Russian Empire, the USSR, or post-Soviet Russia), the liberal universalist discourse would become relevant, and then it would be supplanted by the conservative pessimistic discourse on the downswing of the cycle. In Russia, the preponderance of the liberal discourse in *Amerikanistika* inevitably coincided with the hopes for Russia's liberalization and modernization, and the upsurge of anti-Americanism used by authorities to construct the national idea, led, on the contrary, to the increase in the deeply critical approach to the historical past of the United States in the spirit of the radical discourse, and to the increase of the role of *Amerikanistika* as represented by social and political essays. As an example, we could quote the emergence of "transitology" in the United States, which is a separate trend in studying Russia after the collapse of the USSR, on the one hand, and the dominance in post-Soviet Russia of the 1990s of the "romantic version" of the US history Daniel Boorstin-style, and of the "demonic version" Howard Zinn, Oliver Stone, and Peter Kuznick-style during Vladimir Putin's presidencies. In both cases, the influence of the national domestic and foreign agenda turned into a crisis in the academic studies of another country and another nation.

NOTES

1. Nikolai A. Borodin, "Rossiia i Amerika do voini i vo vremia voiny," *Izvestia Obshchestva Sblizheniia mezhdu Rossiei i Amerikoi*, 3, September (1916): 2.

2. Reflections on the history of Russian-American relations during World War I can be found in the work of Rafail Sh. Ganelin, *Rossiia i SShA. 1914–1917: Ocherki istorii russko-amerikanskikh otnosheniy* (Leningrad: Nauka 1969) and Vyacheslav V. Lebedev, *Russko-amerikanskie ekonomicheskie otnosheniia, 1900–1917*. Moscow: Mezhdunarodnie Otnoshenia, 1964). American specialized research includes Benson L. Greyson, *Russian-American Relations in World War I* (New York: Ungar, 1979) and Norman E. Saul, *War and Revolution: The United States and Russia, 1914–1921* (Lawrence: Kansas University Press, 2001).

3. Richard W. Child, *Potential Russia* (New York: E. P. Dutton, 1916), 186–87, 200–1, 209.

4. In 1908, in St. Petersburg only, Russians bought 622,300 copies of the so-called "detective fiction": Kornei Chukovskii, "Nat Pinkerton," in *Sobranie sochinenii*, vol. 6.

(Moscow: Khudozhestvennaia Literatura, 1969), 139. It should also be noted that during World War I, Russia witnessed the beginning of the American cinema era, since Germany's movie industry was shut down, and Charles Pathé, France's cinematic trailblazer, whose movies were well-known and well-loved in Russia, moved his production to the United States. The Russian movie market was filled with crime movies, cowboy movies, adventures stories which played an important role in etching simplified ideas of America and Americans into the minds of the Russian movie-goers. For more on the subject see in: Robert V. Allen, *Russia Looks at America: The View to 1917* (Washington, DC: Library of Congress, 1988), 107–13.

5. "Russian Anxiety for America's Friendship," *Literary Digest*, August 5, 1916, 53 (1916): 295.

6. Ibid., 296.

7. Ustav Russko-amerikanskoi torgovoi palaty, 1913, in Grigorii N. Sevostianov, ed., *Rossiia i SShA: torgovo-ekonomicheskie otnosheniia, 1900–1930: Sbornik dokumentov* [hereafter *Rossiia i SShA: Sbornik dokumentov*] (Moscow: Nauka, 1996), 75–80; Nikolai A. Borodin, *Severo-Amerikanskie Soedinennye Shtaty i Rossiia* (Petrograd: Ogni, 1915), 312. The Russian-American Chamber of Commerce opened its Petrograd branch shortly thereafter.

8. Ustav Russko-amerikanskoi torgovoi palaty, 1913, in *Rossiia i SShA: Sbornik dokumentov*, 81–85.

9. Tzvetan Todorov, *The Conquest of America: The Question of the Other* (New York: Harper & Row, 1982), 185–86.

10. For more details about it see: Alexander S. Sokolov, "Rossiia na Vsemirnoi Vystavke v Chikago v 1893," in Nikolai N. Bolkhovitinov, ed., *Amerikanskii Ezhegodnik, 1984* (Moscow: Nauka, 1984), 152–64; Saul, *Concord and Conflict. The United States and Russia, 1867–1914* (Lawrence: Kansas University Press, 1996), 369–74; Allen, *Russia Looks at America*, 191–214; Victoria I. Zhuravleva, *Ponimanie Rossii v SShA: obrazy i mify. 1881–1914. [Understanding Russia in the United States: Images and Myths. 1881–1914]* (Moscow: Izdatel'stvo RGGU, 2012), 302–10.

11. Their works could be qualified as university textbooks on *Amerikanistika*: Stepan F. Fortunatov, *Istoriia politicheskikh uchenii v Soedinennykh Shtatakh* (Moscow: Tipo-litogr. N.V. Lubenkova, 1879); Stepan F. Fortunatov, *Istoriia Soedinennykh Shtatov Severnoi Ameriki* (Moscow: Litogr. Tityaeva, [1910]); Pavel G. Mizhuev, *Istoriia velikoi amerikanskoi demokratii* (Saint-Petersburg: Tipografia aktsionernogo obshchestva "Brokgauz i Efron,"," 1906); Maxim M. Kovalevsky, *Istoriia Amerikanskoi konstitutsii* (Moscow: Tip. t-va I.D. Sytina, 1890–1891).

12. About activity of Mizhuev as an *Amerikanist* see Irina R. Chikalova, "Russkii amerikanist Pavel Grigor'evich Mizhuev," in Tatiana V. Alent'eva, ed., *Amerikanistika: aktual'nye podhody i sovremennye issledovaniia*, 4 (Kursk: Izd-vo Kurskogo gosuniversiteta, 2012): 121–33; Vladimir V. Noskov, "Stanovlenie *Amerikanistiki* v Sankt-Peterburge ," in *Trudy ob'edinennogo nauchnogo soveta po gumanitarnym problemam i istoriko-kul'turnomu naslediiu.* (Saint-Petersburg: Nauka, 2007): 43–45.

13. Pavel G. Mizhuev, *Glavnye federatsii sovremennogo mira* (Saint-Petersburg: Izdatel'stvo G.F. L'vovicha, 1907), 248–49.

14. In 1906 alone, along with *The History of the Great American Democracy*, Mizhuev published the following books: *Popular Representation and the Legislative Assemblies in the Main Countries of Today's World* (*Narodnoe predstavitel'stvo i zakonodatel'nye sobraniia v glavnykh stranakh sovremennogo mira*); *Head of State. Structure of the Highest Executive Authority in the Main Countries of Today's World* (*Glava gosudarstva. Organizatsiia vysshei ispolnitel'noi vlasti v glavnykh stranakh sovremennogo mira*); *On the Forms and Essence of State Systems* (*O formakh i sushchnosti gosudarstvennogo stroia*); *The Rights of Man and Citizen* (*Prava cheloveka i grazhdanina*).

15. Pavel G. Mizhuev, *Istoriia velikoi amerikanskoi demokratii*, 1–3, 225–26, 275.

16. *Russkoe bogatstvo*, no. 5 (1912): 124.

17. Pavel G. Mizhuev, *Sovremennaia shkola v Evrope i Amerike* (Moscow: Pol'za,1912), 42, 44, 47, 144.

70 *Victoria I. Zhuravleva*

18. Stepan F. Fortunatov, *Istoriia Soedinennykh Shtatov*. Ch. 1–2. Kurs, chitannyi v 1915–1916 gg. po zapiskam slushatel'nits (Moscow: Ob-vo pri istoriko-filosofskom fakul'tete Moskovskikh vysshikh zhenskikh kursov, 1916), I, 44–45; II, 226.

19. Ibid., I, 43–47; II, 3.

20. Pavel Miliukov was among those Russian liberals and radicals who visited the United States have made a special contribution in the maintenance of the American liberal-universalist myths about Russia. See in details Zhuravleva, *Ponimanie Rossii v SShA*, 317, 456, 632–37, 664–65, 868–73, 920.

21. Max M. Laserson, *The American Impact on Russia — Diplomatic and Ideological — 1784–1917*, (New York: The Macmillan Co, 1950), 387–96; Noskov, "Stanovlenie amerikanistiki v Sankt-Peterburge," 46–49.

22. In 1881 he started his two-year long academic trip, and in 1901, he was invited to give a lecture course on Russia's political institutions in the Slavic lecture center of the University of Chicago. The center was inaugurated due to the efforts of Charles Crane, a well-known American businessman, philanthropist, and Russophile.

23. Maxim M. Kovalevsky, "American Impressions," *Russian Review*. vol. 10, January (1951), 38; vol. 10, N 3 July (1951), 178–79.

24. Cited after: Liudmila V. Selezneva, *Zapadnaia demokratiia glazami rossiiskikh liberalov nachala XX v.* (Rostov-na-Donu: B. i., 1995), 139–40.

25. The lectures were published in the March issues of *Russkie vedomosti*. See: Maxim M. Kovalevsky, "American Impressions," January, 181–82; July, 176–77; 181–82; Alexander S. Sokolov, "Amerikanskaia tema v nauchno-literaturnom nasledii M. M. Kovalevskogo," in Nikolai N. Bolkhovitinov, ed., *Amerikanskii Ezhegodnik, 1989* (Moscow: Nauka, 1990), 155–73.

26. *M. M. Kovalevsky—uchenyi, gosudarstvennyi i obshchestvennyi deiatel' i grazhdanin* (Petrograd: Artist. zavedenie t-va A. F. Marks, 1917), 27–28; Sokolov, "Amerikanskaia tema v nauchno-literaturnom nasledii M. M. Kovalevskogo," 172. Maxim Kovalevsky will permanently reside in France until 1905, although he will deliver lectures in both France and Great Britain.

27. Maxim M. Kovalevsky, *Istoriia amerikanskikh uchrezhdenii: Litograf. Lektsii* (Saint-Petersburg, [1908]).

28. Maxim M. Kovalevsky, "American Impressions,"January, 37–38, 41–42, 106; July, 112–13, 116–17, 183–84; Sokolov, "Amerikanskaia tema v nauchno-literaturnom nasledii M.M. Kovalevskogo," 162, 171, 173.

29. Laserson, *The American Impact on Russia* , 381–87.

30. Kovalevsky, "American Impressions," July, 182–83.

31. See, for instance: Petr E. Kovalevsky, *Narodnoe obrazovanie v Soedinennykh Shtatakh Severnoi Ameriki (vysshee, srednee, nizshee)* (Saint-Petersburg: tip. V. S. Balasheva i K°, 1895); *Ekonomicheskaia otsenka narodnogo obrazovaniia. Ocherki I. I. Ianzhula, A. I. Chuprova, E. N. Ianzhul, V. P. Vakhterova i dr* (Saint-Petersburg: tip. A. Benke, 1899).

32. Nikolai A. Borodin, *Idealy i deistvitel' nost'. Sorok let zhizni i raboty riadovogo russkogo intelligenta (1879–1919)* (Moscow, Gosudarstvennaia publichnaia biblioteka, 2009 (bazed on the edition of 1930), 92–108, 170–73, 189–206.

33. Nikolai A. Borodin, "Puti i sposoby sblizheniia mezhdu Rossiei i SShA," *Izvestia Obshchestva Sblizheniia mezhdu Rossiei i Amerikoi*, 1, December (1915): 2–3.

34. Nikolai A. Borodin, *Severo-Amerikanskie Soedinennye Shtaty i Rossiia*, 19, 21–22, 64.

35. Nikolai A. Borodin, *Amerikantsy i amerikanskaia kul'tura* (Petrograd: tip. t-va "Obshchestvo pol'za","," 1915), 3.

36. Ibid., 59–63, 71–72, 75–78, 80, 88.

37. Ibid., 99–101.

38. "Rech' tovarishcha predsedatelia N. A. Borodina o zadachakh Obshchestva sblizheniia mezhdu Rossiei i Amerikoi v sviazi s nastoiashchim momentom," *Izvestiia Obshchestva sblizheniia mezhdu Rossiei i Amerikoi*, 5, February (1918): 12.

39. V. L. Telitsyn, "Ivan Khristoforovich Ozerov. Zhiznennye ispytaniia russkogo uchenogo," *Voprosy istorii*, N 3 (1999): 135–36; Allen, *Russia Looks at America*, 204–10.

40. Samuel N. Harper, *The Russia I Believe In. The Memoirs of Samuel N. Harper. 1902 – 1941,* ed. by Paul V. Harper (Chicago: University of Chicago Press, 1945), 16.

41. Ivan Kh. Ozerov, *Amerika idet na Evropu* (Saint-Petersburg: tip. V. Kirshbauma, 1903), 1, 15, 40–47.

42. Ivan Kh. Ozerov, *Chemu nas uchit Amerika?* (Moscow: "Pol'za" V. Antik i K°, [1908]), 44–45, 128.

43. Ibid., 59, 127, 134–35, 151.

44. *Rossiia i SShA: diplomaticheskie otnosheniia 1900–1917. Dokumenty* (hereinafter: *Rossiia i SShA. Dokumenty*), Grigorii N. Sevostianov, ed., (Moscow: Nauka, 1999), 305. For a description of Ozerov's views, see also: Allen, *Russia Looks at America,* 214–23.

45. For example, we could turn to the sketches and travelogues of Vladimir Galaktionovich Korolenko, Vladimir Germanovich Bogoraz, Alexei Maximovich Gorky.

46. More about Babine see in: Evgenii G. Pivovarov, *A. V. Babine (1866–1930 gg.)* (Saint-Petersburg: "Petropolis,","" 2002); Donald Raleigh, *A Russian Civil War Diary: Alexis Babine in Saratov, 1917–1922* (Durham, NC; and London: Duke University Press, 1988).

47. Saul, *Concord and Conflict,* 391.

48. Aleksei V.Babine, *Istoriia Severo-Amerikanskikh Soedinennykh Shtatov. V 2-kh tt.* (Saint-Petersburg: tip. Trenke i Fiusno, 1912).

49. Noskov, "Stanovlenie amerikanistiki v Sankt-Peterburge," 45.

50. For instance, Fortunatov wrote that "the book is not without drawbacks; some issues are discussed at great lengths, and others, such as the slave issues, are all but skipped over, yet Mr. Babine's book is excellent for learning the history of the external events." Fortunatov, *Istoriia Soedinennykh Shtatov,* Ch. II, 3.

51. Babine, *Istoriia Severo-Amerikanskikh Soedinennykh Shtatov,* vol. 1, 489; vol. 2, 412, 426, 440–41.

52. Norman E. Saul, *The Life and Times of Charles R. Crane, 1858–1939* (Lanham, MD: Lexington Books, 2013), 39–77.

53. Zhuravleva, *Ponimanie Rossii v SShA,* 258–302, 311–19, 951–72.

54. Nathan H. Dole, "A Plea for the Study of Russian," *Harvard Graduate's Magazine,* vol. 3, no. 10 (1894): 180–85.

55. Archibald C. Coolidge, "The Expansion of Russia in the Nineteenth Century," in John B. Moore, Arthur G. Sedgwick, ed., *The 19th Century. A Review of Progress during the Past One Hundred Years in the Chief Departments of Human Activity* (New York, London: G.P. Putnam's Sons, 1901): 63, 64, 70, 74–75; Archibald C. Coolidge, "Across Siberia. III," *Nation,* 61, October (1895): 238; Robert F. Byrnes, *Awakening American Education to the World. The Role of Archibald Cary Coolidge, 1866 – 1928* (Notre Dame, IN: University of Notre Dame Press, 1982), 63–64.

56. Harper, *The Russia I Believe In,* 12–13; David C. Engerman, *Modernization from the Other Shore. American Intellectuals and the Romance of Russian Development* (Cambridge, MA: Harvard University Press, 2003), 25–27, 63.

57. For more details about Russian Studies in the United States at the turn of the twentieth century, see Albert Parry, *America Learns Russian. A History of the Teaching of the Russian Language in the United States* (Syracuse: Syracuse University Press, 1967), 45–64; Byrnes, *Awakening American Education to the World,* 5–19, 173–97; Saul, *Concord and Conflict,* 390–95, 461–64; Engerman, *Modernization from the Other Shore,* 54–66.

58. For a more detailed analyses of these discourses, see Zhuravleva, *Ponimanie Rossii v SShA,* 149–209, 337, 371–406, 535, 606, 738–61, 951–72, 1014–15.

59. Parry, *America Learns Russian,* 65–72.

60. Here Borodin speaks of Gregory Mason, a traveler and a military correspondent who worked for the *Outlook* magazine as an editorial writer. He visited the Russian Empire at the start of the war and was one of the first people to draw attention to the impending revolution.

61. Here Borodin speaks of Richard W. Child, an American military correspondent who has already been mentioned.

62. Nikolai A. Borodin, "Puti i sposoby sblizheniya mezhdu Rossiey i SShA," *Izvestia Obshchestva Sblizheniya mezhdu Rossiei i Amerikoi*, 1, December (1915): 1–2.

63. N. B. [Nikolai A. Borodin], "Nashi druz'ya amerikantsy," *Izvestiya Obshchestva Sblizheniya mezhdu Rossiei i Amerikoi*, 3, September (1916): 19. Borodin died in the United States in 1937. He became a professor at Harvard and a member of the Russian academic Union whose goal was to preserve the historical memory and culture of the Russian academe, to unite émigré scientists, scholars, and intellectuals in the United States for the future democratic Russia.

64. Saul, *War and Revolution*, 33–35, 53–58, 91–92, 94–96, 99–100.

65. Crane to Eliot, 15 December 1914 , The Bakhmeteff Archive (Columbia University), The Charles R. Crane Papers, Box 1, R. 1.

66. Letters of Wharton Barker to Nicolas II and Sergei Dmitrievich Sazonov see in Library of Congress, Manuscript Division, The Wharton Barker Papers, Box 12.

67. More details about Harper's activity during the World War I, see John Ch. Chalberg, "Samuel Harper and Russia under Tsar and Soviet, 1905–1943," PhD diss., University of Minnesota, 1974), Chapter 3, 4.

68. Volkov to Artsimovich, 1/14 April 1916, Archiv vneshnei politiki Rossiyskoi imperii [hereinafter AVPRI], f. Posol'stvo v Vashingtone, op. 170, d. 406, ll. 151, 153.

69. In 1902–1903, *Anthology of Russian Literature from the Earliest Period to the Present Time* in two volumes was published under editorship of Leo Wiener.

70. Leo Wiener, *An Interpretation of the Russian People* (New York: McBride, Nast, 1915), 10, 14–15, 17.

71. Ibid., 95, 99.

72. Sergey N. Syromiatnikoff, "America's Chance for Russian Trade," *New York Times*, March 15, 1915.

73. "A Slavonic Department," *New York Times*, March 25, 1915.

74. A physicist and a physical chemist by training, Michael Pupin is best known for his numerous patents, was a founding member of National Advisory Committee for Aeronautics (1915), and from 1911—the Consul General of the Serbian Kingdom in New York.

75. Bakhmetev's telegram, 13/26 March 1915, in *Rossiia i SShA: Dokumenty*, 607.

76. More details about the role of Zenaida Ragozin and Elizabeth Reynolds in US Russian studies see in Norman Saul's chapter, published in this volume.

77. Saul, *War and Revolution*, 32, 34; Saul, *The Life and Times of Charles R. Crane*, 131.

78. *New York Tribune*, April 10, 1915.

79. "Russian and American Public Opinion," *New York Tribune*, November 24, 1915.

80. Correspondence between Bakhmetev and Russian Ministry of Foreign Affairs concerning Syromiatnikov see in *Rossiia i SShA: Dokumenty*, 580–82, 608–9, 617–18; AVPRI, f.134 (Arhiv "Voina"), op. 473, d. 42, ll.195–96 ob, 234–36.

81. *Rossiia i SShA: Dokumenty*, 634–39, 706–7; Boris D. Syromiatnikov, *"Strannye " puteshestviia i komandirovki " SIGMY " (1897 . . . 1916): istoriko-dokumental'naia povest'-rassledovanie* (Saint-Petersburg: B.i., 2004), 89.

82. Parry, *America Learns Russian*, 65–71.

83. See reports dated 17/30 October and 25 November / 8 December, 1916, in AVPRI. f. Posol'stvo v Vashingtone, op. 170, d. 408, ll. 3-5ob; 7–7ob.

84. Quoted from: Nikolai A. Borodin, "Rossiya i Amerika do voini i vo vremya voini," *Izvestia Obshchestva Sblizheniya mezhdu Rossiei i Amerikoi*, 3, September (1916): 3.

85. David S. Foglesong, *The American Mission and the " Evil Empire ": The Crusade for a " Free Russia " since 1881* (Cambridge University Press, 2007), 47–50.

86. Donald E. Davis, Eugene P. Trani, *Krivye zerkala. SShA i ih otnosheniia s Rossiey i Kitaem v XX veke* (translation of *Distorted Mirrors: Americans and Their Relations with Russia and China in the Twentieth Century*) (Moscow: Vagrius, 2009), 25, 93–95; Nikolai N. Bolkhovitinov, *Russkie uchenye-emigranty (G. V. Vernadskii, M. M. Karpovich, M. T. Florinskii) i stanovlenie Rusistiki v SShA* (Moscow: Rossiiskaya politicheskaia entsiklopedia, 2005).

87. Donald E. Davis , Eugene P. Trani , "Povest' o dvukh Kennanakh: amerikanskie predstavleniia i politika v otnoshenii Rossii, 1881–1891," in Nikolai N. Bolkhovitinov, ed., *Amerikanskii Ezhegodnik, 2003* (Moscow: Nauka, 2005): 28.
88. Alen Bezanson, "Rossiia—evropeiskaia strana? Spor s Martinom Malia," *Otechestvennye zapiski*, 5 (2004): 246–65; Martin Malia, "Non Possumus. Otvet Alenu Bezansonu," *Otechestvennye zapiski*, 5 (2004): 266–71.
89. Richard Pipes, "Russia's Past, Russia's Future," *Commentary*, Vol. 101. N 6 (2006): 30–38. About Pipes's views also see his books *Russia Under the Old Regime* (New York: Charles. Scribner's Sons, 1974) and *Russian Conservatism and Its Critics: A Study in Political Culture* (New Haven, CT: Yale University Press, 2006).
90. Vladimir O. Rukavishnikov, *Kholodnaia voina, kholodnyi mir. Obshchestvennoe mnenie v SShA i Evrope ob SSSR/Rossii, vneshnei politike i bezopasnosti Zapada* (Moscow: Akademicheskii proekt, 2005), 164, 208–9.

BIBLIOGRAPHY

Allen, Robert V. *Russia Looks at America: The View to 1917*. Washington, DC: Library of Congress, 1988.
Babine, Aleksei V. *Istoriia Severo-Amerikanskikh Soedinennykh Shtatov. V 2-kh tt.* Saint-Petersburg: tip. Trenke i Fiusno, 1912.
Bezanson, Alen. "Rossiia—evropeiskaia strana? Spor s Martinom Malia," *Otechestvennye zapiski*, 5 (2004): 246–65.
Bolkhovitinov, Nikolai N. *Russkie uchenye-emigranty (G. V. Vernadskii, M. M. Karpovich, M. T. Florinskii) i stanovlenie Rusistiki v SShA.* Moscow: Rossiiskaia politicheskaia entsiklopedia, 2005.
Borodin, Nikolai A. *Idealy i deistvitel' nost'. Sorok let zhizni i raboty riadovogo russkogo intelligenta (1879–1919).* Moscow, Gosudarstvennaia publichnaia biblioteka, 2009 (based of the edition of 1930).
———. *Amerikantsy i amerikanskaia kul'tura.* Petrograd: tip. t-va "Obshchestv. pol'za," 1915.
———. *Severo-Amerikanskie Soedinennye Shtaty i Rossiia.* Petrograd: Ogni, 1915.
Byrnes, Robert F. *Awakening American Education to the World. The Role of Archibald Cary Coolidge, 1866–1928.* Notre Dame, IN: University of Notre Dame Press, 1982.
Chalberg, John C. "Samuel Harper and Russia under Tsar and Soviet, 1905–1943," PhD diss., University of Minnesota, 1974.
Chikalova, Irina R. "Russkii amerikanist Pavel Grigor'evich Mizhuev." In Tatiana V. Alent'eva, ed., *Amerikanistika: aktual'nye podhody i sovremennye issledovania*, 4, 121–33. Kursk: Izd-vo Kurskogo gosuniversiteta, 2012.
Child, Richard W. *Potential Russia.* New York: E. P. Dutton, 1916.
Chukovskii, Kornei "Nat Pinkerton." In *Sobranie sochinenii*, vol. 6, 117–47. Moscow: Khudozhestvennaia Literatura, 1969.
Coolidge, Archibald C. "The Expansion of Russia in the Nineteenth Century." In John B. Moore, Arthur G. Sedgwick, ed., *The 19th Century. A Review of Progress during the Past One Hundred Years in the Chief Departments of Human Activity*, 63–75. New York, London: G.P. Putnam's Sons, 1901.
———. "Across Siberia. III." *Nation*, 61, October (1895): 238.
Davis , Donald E., and Trani , Eugene P. *Krivye zerkala. SShA i ih otnosheniia s Rossiey i Kitaem v XX veke* (translation of *Distorted Mirrors: Americans and Their Relations with Russia and China in the Twentieth Century*). Moscow: Vagrius, 2009.
——— . "Povest' o dvukh Kennanakh: amerikanskie predstavleniia i politika v otnoshenii Rossii, 1881–1891." In Nikolai N. Bolkhovitinov, ed., *Amerikanskii Ezhegodnik, 2003*, 9–30. Moscow: Nauka, 2005.
Dole, Nathan H. "A Plea for the Study of Russian," *Harvard Graduate's Magazine*, 3, no. 10 (1894): 180–85.

Ekonomicheskaia otsenka narodnogo obrazovaniia. Ocherki I. I. Ianzhula, A. I. Chuprova, E. N. Ianzhul, V. P. Vakhterova i dr. Saint-Petersburg: tip. A. Benke, 1899.

Engerman, David C. *Modernization from the Other Shore. American Intellectuals and the Romance of Russian Development* . Cambridge, MA: Harvard University Press, 2003.

Foglesong, David S. *The American Mission and the " Evil Empire .": The Crusade for a " Free Russia " since 1881* . Cambridge: Cambridge University Press, 2007.

Fortunatov, Stepan F. *Istoriia Soedinennykh Shtatov.* Ch. 1–2. Kurs, chitannyi v 1915–1916 gg. po zapiskam slushatel'nits. Moscow: Ob-vo pri istoriko-filosofskom fakul'tete Moskovskikh vysshikh zhenskikh kursov, 1916.

———. *Istoria Soedinennykh Shtatov Severnoi Ameriki.* Moscow: Litogr. Tityaeva, [1910].

———. *Istoriia politicheskikh uchenii v Soedinennykh Shtatakh.* Moscow: Tipo-litogr. N. V. Lubenkova, 1879.

Ganelin, Rafail Sh. *Rossiia i SShA. 1914–1917: O c herki istorii russko-amerikanskikh otnosheniy.* Leningrad: Nauka, 1969.

Greyson, Benson L. *Russian-American Relations in World War I.* New York: Ungar, 1979.

Harper, Samuel N. *The Russia I Believe In: The Memoirs of Samuel N. Harper. 1902–1941,* ed. by Paul V. Harper. Chicago: University of Chicago Press, 1945.

Izvestia Obshchestva Sblizheniia mezhdu Rossiei i Amerikoi, 1–5 (1915–1918).

Kovalevsky, Maxim M. "American Impressions," *Russian Review.* 10, January (1951): 37–45; 10, N 3 July (1951): 176–84.

———. *Istoriia amerikanskikh uchrezhdenii: Litograf. Lektsii.* Saint-Petersburg, [1908].

———. *Istoria Amerikanskoi konstitutsii.* Moscow: Tip. t-va I.D. Sytina, 1890–1891.

Kovalevsky, Petr E. *Narodnoe obrazovanie v Soedinennykh Shtatakh Severnoi Ameriki (vysshee, srednee, nizshee).* Saint-Petersburg: tip. V. S. Balasheva i K°, 1895.

Laserson, Max M. *The American Impact on Russia—Diplomatic and Ideological— 1784–1917.* New York: The Macmillan Co., 1950.

Lebedev, Vyacheslav V. *Russko-amerikanskie ekonomicheskie otnosheniia, 1900–1917.* Moscow: Mezhdunarodnie Otnoshenia, 1964.

M. M. Kovalevsky—uchenyi, gosudarstvennyi i obshchestvennyi deiatel' i grazhdanin Petrograd : Artist. zavedenie t-va A.F. Marks, 1917.

Malia, Martin. "Non Possumus. Otvet Alenu Bezansonu," *Otechestvennye zapiski,* 5 (2004): 266–71.

Mizhuev, Pavel G. *Sovremennaia shkola v Evrope i Amerike.* Moscow: Pol'za, 1912.

———. *Glavnye federatsii sovremennogo mira.* Saint-Petersburg: Izdatel'stvo G. F. L'vovicha, 1907.

———. *Istoria velikoi amerikanskoi demokratii.* Saint-Petersburg: Tipografia aktsionernogo obshchestva "Brokgauz i Efron", 1906.

Noskov, Vladimir V. "Stanovlenie amerikanistiki v Sankt-Peterburge." In *Trudy ob'edinennogo nauchnogo soveta po gumanitarnym problemam i istoriko-kul'turnomu naslediiu,* 28–51. Saint-Petersburg: Nauka, 2007.

Ozerov, Ivan Kh. *Chemu nas uchit Amerika?* Moscow: "Pol'za" V. Antik i K°, [1908].

———. *Amerika idet na Evropu.* Saint-Petersburg: tip. V. Kirshbauma, 1903.

Parry, Albert. *America Learns Russian: A History of the Teaching of the Russian Language in the United States* (Syracuse, NY: Syracuse University Press, 1967.

Pipes, Richard. *Russian Conservatism and Its Critics A Study in Political Culture.* New Haven, CT: Yale University Press, 2006.

———. "Russia's Past, Russia's Future," *Commentary,* 101, no. 6 (2006): 30–38.

———. *Russia under the old regime.* New York: Charles. Scribner's Sons, 1974.

Pivovarov, Evgenii G. *A. V. Babine (1866–1930 gg.).* Saint-Petersburg: "Petropolis," 2002.

Raleigh, Donald. *A Russian Civil War Dairy: Alexis Babine in Saratov, 1917–1922.* Durham, NC; and London: Duke University Press, 1988.

Rossiia i SShA: diplomaticheskie otnosheniia 1900–1917. Dokumenty, ed. Grigorii N. Sevostianov. Moscow: Nauka, 1999.

Rossiia i SShA: torgovo-ekonomicheskie otnosheniia, 1900–1930: Sbornik dokumentov, ed. Grigorii N. Sevostianov. Moscow: Nauka, 1996.

Rukavishnikov, Vladimir O. *Kholodnaia voina, kholodnyi mir. Obshchestvennoe mnenie v SShA i Evrope ob SSSR/Rossii, vneshnei politike i bezopasnosti Zapada*. Moscow: Akademicheskii proekt, 2005.

"Russian and American Public Opinion," *New York Tribune*, November 24, 1915.

"Russian Anxiety for America's Friendship," *Literary Digest*, August 5, 1916, 53 (1916): 295–96.

Saul, Norman E. *Concord and Conflict. The United States and Russia, 1867–1914*. Lawrence: Kansas University Press, 1996.

———. *The Life and Times of Charles R. Crane, 1858–1939* . Lanham, MD: Lexington Books, 2013.

———. *War and Revolution: The United States and Russia, 1914 – 1921* . Lawrence: Kansas University Press, 2001.

Selezneva, Liudmila V. *Zapadnaia demokratiia glazami rossiiskikh liberalov nachala XX v.* Rostov-na-Donu: B. i., 1995.

"A Slavonic Department." *New York Times*, March 25, 1915.

Sokolov, Alexander S. "Amerikanskaia tema v nauchno-literaturnom nasledii M. M. Kovalevskogo." In Nikolai N. Bolkhovitinov, ed., *Amerikanskii Ezhegodnik, 1989*, 155–73. Moscow: Nauka, 1990.

———. "Rossiia na Vsemirnoi Vystavke v Chikago v 1893." In Nikolai N. Bolkhovitinov, ed., *Amerikanskii Ezhegodnik, 1984*, 152–64. Moscow: Nauka, 1984.

Syromiatnikoff, Sergey N. "America's Chance for Russian Trade." *New York Times*, March 15, 1915.

Syromiatnikov, Boris D. *"Strannye " puteshestviia i komandirovki " SIGMY " (1897 . . . . 1916): istoriko-dokumental'naia povest'-rassledovanie* . Saint-Petersburg: B.i., 2004.

Telitsyn, V. L. "Ivan Khristoforovich Ozerov. Zhiznennye ispytaniia russkogo uchenogo." *Voprosy istorii*, no. 3 (1999): 135–39.

Todorov, Tzvetan. *The Conquest of America: The Question of the Other* . New York: Harper & Row, 1982.

Wiener, Leo. *An Interpretation of the Russian People*. New York: McBride, Nast, 1915.

———. *Anthology of Russian Literature from the Earliest Period to the Present Time*. New York: G. P. Putnam's sons, 1902–1903.

Zhuravleva, Victoria I. *Ponimanie Rossii v SShA: obrazy i mify. 1881–1914 [Understanding Russia in the United States: Images and Myths. 1881–1914]*. Moscow: Izdatel'stvo RGGU, 2012.

Archival Collections Cited

Archiv vneshnei politiki Rossiyskoi imperii (AVPRI), f. Posol'stvo v Vashingtone.
The Bakhmeteff Archive (Columbia University), The Charles R. Crane Papers.
The Library of Congress, Manuscript Division, The Wharton Barker Papers.

FIVE

Russian Sociologists Abroad and Their Influence on Russian Studies in the United States in the First Half of the Twentieth Century

Marina B. Bulanova

This chapter is focused on the Russian émigré sociological community and its contribution into Russian studies in the United States. The "truth" about the native émigré country was "antidote," which stopped the mythogenesis and built an academic base for US Russian studies. From this point of view, it would be interesting to pay attention to three sociologist émigré who were contemporaries and whose academic authority was beyond all question.

Maxim Maximovich Kovalevsky (1851–1916)—the Russian historian, lawyer, ethnographer, sociologist, professor of the Moscow and St. Petersburg State Universities—made two study trips to the United States, in 1882 and in 1901, the last one thanks to the invitation of the Slavic Center at the University of Chicago.[1] During his first visit, the scholar and Western liberal, spent three months studying the civil, social, and political organization of the American community. As a result, Kovalevsky, in 1890, published his book *American Constitutional History* and prepared a special course of lectures about local American institutions' histories for the students of Moscow State University.[2] During his second visit, Kovalevsky gave a course of sixteen lectures under the title "Russian Political Institutions: past and present" at the University of Chicago, in which he associated the progress of Russian political institutions with the liberalization of political structures based on Western models and with the establishment of constitutional monarchy.[3] Kovalevsky provided compelling evidence, testifying that at the beginning of the twentieth century, Russia was precipitously moving toward liberalization, democracy, and constitution. These lectures were published as a book in 1902 and exposed the myth of historical backwardness of Russia.[4] In this way, American and English researchers of Russian political history obtained additional material for study. The Russian Revolution of 1905–1907 confirmed the tendencies identified by the sociologist. The scholar, inspired by the democratic perspective in Russia, published many articles on a variety of topics: freedom of expression, democracy, and policy. His optimism based on the belief into the future renovation of Russian social and political system according to the western principles of democracy. Kovalevsky was elected a deputy of the First State Duma, where, as an academic man, he hoped to help resolve issues of state and public concern.[5]

Kovalevsky introduced to American society an image of liberal Russia. He destroyed the historical myth of Russian backwardness, increased the assurance of Americans in the Russian people's ability to self-governing, and unwittingly contributed tor the formation of their "romantic" vision of the future Russian revolution.

Somewhat later, another Russian sociologist was able to "reap the fruits" of the "radical" image of the Russian revolution formed in Americans minds in 1905–1907 by the representatives of American radical discourse about Russia.[6]

Pitirim Alexandrovich Sorokin (1889–1968)—the lawyer, public figure, sociologist, and professor of the Petrograd Imperial University—arrived in the United States in 1924. He was exposed at once two "radical" myths—first one about "building of communist society" in Soviet Russia, second one about "Russian communist revolution.."

Sorokin was among that "bourgeois intelligentsia," "old-regime professors" that were expelled from Russia in 1922 on the so called "Philosophical ship." The reason for the expulsion was more than persuasive. The Soviet People's Commissar of Education Anatolii V. Lunacharsky, speaking to the students of the Moscow universities in autumn of 1922, explained the attitude to the pre-revolutionary professors: "They bring not just a science, but a science poisoned, falsified and unscientific."[7] Professors who did not share communist views were politically dangerous and ideologically harmful for the Soviet government.

Relative to the first myth about "building the communist society" in Soviet Russia, Sorokin in his memoirs *Dal'niaia doroga* describes the dialogue with the leader of the Bolsheviks—Georgii L. Piatakov just before his expulsion from Russia. This dialogue has academic and historical value, which is why it is important to discuss it:

> Pyatakov, may I ask you if you really believe that you are building a communist society?—Of course, no—he answered honestly.—Means,

you understand that experiment failed, and you build a common bourgeois society. Then why are we [intelligentsia — M.B.] being expelled? —
You do not accept the fact that in Russia are two parallel processes, — he
answered. One of them is in restoration of bourgeois society; the other — the adaptation of the Soviet government to this society. The first
one runs quicker than the other one. It poses a threat to our existence.
Our purpose is to slow down the development of the first process. That
is why you will be expelled from the country. Possibly, we will invite
you to come back in two or three years. — Thank you, I told, I hope to
return to my country without your invitation.[8]

Actually, the representatives of the first wave of emigration (including
Sorokin) believed that the Soviet government would not last for a long
time and soon the "brilliant minds of Russian intelligentsia" would be in
demand in their native country.

Because of the Soviet government's reluctance to accept the existence
of global tendencies in the development of Soviet Russia, Pitirim Sorokin's book, referred to the convergence of Russia and the United States in
the context of scientific and technical revolution, was banned from publication in the USSR in the middle of the twentieth century. This book
referred to the convergence of Russia and the United States in the context
of scientific and technical revolution, and was banned from publication
in the USSR.

Now we will refer to the second myth about "Russian communist
revolution." Having arrived in the United States, Sorokin, during his first
lectures at the Universities of Wisconsin and Illinois, faced a surprisingly
unfriendly reaction from the radical part of American intelligentsia,
which idealized the October Revolution. At the same time, the most part
of American people supported the "romantic" image of a liberal Russian
Revolution, created by Sorokin's predecessors such as Maxim Kovalevsky and Pavel Miliukov.[9] Sorokin described this unfriendly reaction:

> So long as I especially emphasized in my lectures the destructiveness,
> violence and brutality of the first five years of the communist revolu-
> tion, it caused a protest towards me and my lectures. This opposition
> lasted several years and manifested in various attempts to discredit not
> only my lectures and works on the Russian revolution, but also any
> academic activity and publications concerning other issues as well.[10]

Only mediation and support from such famous American sociologists as
Charles A. Ellwood, Charles H. Cooley, Edward A. Ross, and Franklin H.
Giddings saved Sorokin from accusations of scholarly incompetence and
political disloyalty.

Sorokin affirmed his scholarly name in the United States by the publication of his *Sociology of the Revolution*[11] in 1925. In that book, referring to
the facts, he clearly proved that any great revolution accompanies by the
riot of hatred and by the anarchical violence. Expanding the revolution

scenario the scholar noted that revolution's first phase is accompanied by aggression reflected which is reflected in revolutionary activity and society criminalization: "Revolution is not only the criminalizing factor, but also the essence and quintessence of the most bloody and violent criminality."[12] According to Sorokin, pre-revolutionary Russia acquired "legal forms" and most criminals became agents of special political service. The second phase of the revolution is followed by increasing anxiety and in this context the "vaccination of brakes" (conditioned reflexes that enable a person to control his behavior in accordance with social norms) is made by radical measures: "Whoever does not obey the government—will be executed. Who does not work—does not eat. Who steals—paying life or gravest punishment. Who performs his duties badly—will expelled. Who kills—will be killed without mercy."[13] A scared man does not belong to himself, and aspires to eliminate threats and avoid danger. Sorokin's conclusion is that a "Society that does not know how to live is unable to make timely reforms and is rushing towards embrace of the revolution, pays for those sins with lives of its members."[14] Thus Sorokin's sociology of revolution clearly demonstrates that any social revolution both, in its liberal and radical versions, is characterized by the destruction of social order, often with unexpected consequences.

Moreover, revealing the methods of work in Russia, Sorokin wrote that he never played politics in the lectures; he appealed to scientific facts no matter whether they maintained communist ideas or not. In theoretical research he followed the same principles—precise work with facts and abidance by the code of scientific ethics. He founded the best American school of sociology.

Sorokin introduced American society to a real image of revolutionary Russia in 1905–1907 and 1917.

Nikolai Sergeevich Timasheff (1886–1970)—the lawyer and sociologist—arrived in the United States in 1936 at the invitation of Sorokin. Timasheff worked with Sorokin at the University of Chicago, and taught a course in sociology of law. This researcher contributed to exposing the myth of "successful communist building" in Soviet Russia, actualized in American society during the Great Depression.

As an immigrant, Timasheff made all efforts to keep abreast of events taking place in Soviet Russia, whose fate worried him the rest of his life. As sociologist, he developed methodological approaches to analyze social processes, not only in Russia but also, in the whole world. These approaches included a multilateral approach to social reality, necessity in consideration of the entire complexity of social life, and analysis of both positive and negative aspects of any social process. For example, talking about the Soviet system and its great disadvantages, he also marked its achievements such as liquidation of illiteracy among the Russian adult population.[15]

The main principle for this sociologist was following the chronology of facts and events. The colleagues and disciples of Timasheff noted his amazing "veneration of facts," his submission to the logic of facts.[16] This enabled the scholar to observe the "great retreat" of communism in Russia, which according to him, began in 1934. Analyzing the facts, in particular, the recovery of free trade in bread, cancellation of the card system in 1935, return to national-historical traditions, Timasheff understood that, despite the persistence of communism, many things in Russia were not done according to the communist doctrines, but based on the requirements of common sense and national security.

In his book *Velikoe otstuplenie* he wrote that the move away from communism caused great progress in Russia. Timasheff claimed that Russia had found itself again under the concessions to historical tradition. The Russian people finally had something to fight for: national pride, and, even very limited, but nevertheless, real economic well-being, and, more important, hope for a better future. Soviet Russia had provided its own dynamics due to the "great retreat" toward the "natural" order of things in economy, politics, and culture. Timasheff concluded that the great retreat saved Russian independence and its government at once. This was the expected reward for the ability to see real process in the society.[17]

One should note, again, that Timasheff chronicled the events and persons related to Russia from 1917 to the last days of his life. He was assured in the democratic future of Russia. According to the sociologist, people in Russia were not waiting for the "strong government" regime, but the regime without "intolerable guardianship of public structures, which would give everyone full confidence in the impossibility of arbitrary interference in the personal life." He imagined a democracy as closely related to the idea of the inherent value of the individual, "the person, whose constant interaction with the others results in a democratic system born, rises and falls down by democratic government."[18] Timasheff claimed that everyone was responsible for the election of the most worthy persons in a democracy. It was not by chance that the US State Department considered him one of the leading authorities on issues related to the USSR.

Timasheff introduced American society to a real image of the Soviet Russia, which was far from the propagandized image projected by the Soviet government.

In accordance with the projections of Maxim Kovalevsky, Pitirim Sorokin, and Nikolai Timasheff, Russia (the pre-revolutionary one, revolutionary one, and Soviet one) has developed according to the evolution of an industrial society. This idea was the real contribution of the sociologists from Russian émigré community in the United States. Russian studies in the United States in the first half of the twentieth century were inside the so-called American liberal-universalist discourse about Russia. This discourse became the academic one in the period under review thanks to the writings of Georgii Vernadsky, Mikhail Karpovich, and Mikhail Florinsky as well as to the works of mentioned Russian sociologists.

NOTES

1. Victoria I. Zhuravleva, *Ponimanie Rossii v SShA: obrazy i mify: 1881–1914 [Understanding Russia in the United States: Images and Myths. 1881–1914]* (Moscow: Izdatel'stvo RGGU, 2012), 451–53.
2. Alexander S. Sokolov, "Amerikanskaia tema v nauchno-literaturnom nasledii M. M. Kovalevskogo," in Nikolai N. Bolkhovitinov, ed., *Amerikanskii ezhegodnik*, 1989 (Moscow: Nauka, 1990): 155–73.
3. Maxim M. Kovalevsky, "Poezdka v Ameriku," *Russkie vedomosti*, no. 171–80 (1901).
4. Maxim M. Kovalevsky, *Russian Political Institutions: The Growth and Development of These Institutions from the Beginnings of Russian History to the Present Time* (Chicago: The University of Chicago Press, 1902).
5. Maxim M. Kovalevsky, *Moia zhyzn'. Vospominanniia* (Moscow: ROSSPEN, 2005).
6. About this discourse, see Zhuravleva, *Ponimanie Rossii v SShA*, 728–32, 749–61.
7. Natalia L. Safrazyan, *Stanovlenie marksistsko-leninskogo gumanitarnogo obrazovaniia v Moskovskom universitete (Oktyabr' 1917–1925)* (Moscow: Politizdat, 1987), 78.
8. Pitirim Sorokin, *Dal'niaia doroga* (Moscow: TERRA, 1992), 144.
9. About American trips of Pavel Miliukov and his contribution into the American liberal-universalist discourse, see in details: Zhuravleva, *Ponimanie Rossii v SShA*, 317, 456, 632–37, 868–73.
10. Ibid., 154.
11. Pitirim Sorokin, *Sotsiologiia revolutsii* (Moscow: ROSSPEN, 2008).
12. Ibid., 142.
13. Ibid., 137.
14. Ibid., 412.
15. Marina B. Bulanova,*"Metodologicheskie podkhody k izucheniiu sotsialnoi realnosti N. S. Timasheffa,"* in Vladimir Kozlovskii, Ruslan Braslavskii, eds., *Rossiiskoe obshchestvo v sovremennykh tsivilizatsionnykh protsessakh* (St. Petersburg: SPbGU, 2010), 22–25.
16. Shoyer John, "Sotsiologiya N.S. Timasheffa," *Na temy russkie i obshchie* (New York: Izd-vo obshchestva druzei russkoi kultury, 1965), 44–54.
17. Nikolai S. Timasheff, *The Great Retreat* (New York: Dalton Press, 1946).
18. Nikolai P. Poltoratsky, *"Professor N. S. Timashev o putyakh Rossii"* in Nikolai Timasheff, ed., *The New Review* (New York: New Review Inc., 1966), 84.

BIBLIOGRAPHY

Allen, Philip J., ed., *Pitirim A. Sorokin in Review*. Durham, NC: Duke University Press, 1963.
Bulanova, Marina. "Metodologicheskie podkhody k izucheniiu sotsial'noi realnosti N. S. Timasheffa." In Vladimira Kozlovskogo, Ruslana Braslavskogo, eds., *Rossiiskoe obshchestvo v sovremennykh tsivilizatsionnykh protsessakh*, 22–25. St. Petersburg: SPbGU, 2010.
Cowell, Frank R. History, Civilization, and Culture: An Introduction to the Historical and Social Philosophy of Pitirim A. Sorokin. Boston: Beacon, 1952.
Gnatyuk, Olga. *Nikolai Sergeevich Timasheff*. St. Petersburg: "SPbGPU," 2003.
Kovalevsky, Maxim. *Moia zhyzn'. Vospominanniia*. Moscow: ROSSPEN, 2005.
———. *Sochineniia v dvukh tomkhj*. St. Petersburg: ALETEIA, 2003.

————. *Russian Political Institutions: The Growth and Development of These Institutions from the Beginnings of Russian History to the Present Time*. Chicago: The University of Chicago Press, 1902.

————. "Poezdka v Ameriku," *Russkie vedomosti*, vol. 171–180, 1901.

Kozlovskii, Vladimir, and Braslavskii Ruslan, eds., *Rossiyskoe obshchestvo v sovremennykh tsivilizatsionnykh protsesakh*. St. Petersburg: SPbGU, 2010.

Nichols, Lawrence T. "International Solidarity in the Creation of Science: The Ross-Sorokin Correspondence, 1921–1931," *Journal of the History of Behavioral Science*, 32 (1996): 135–250.

Poltoratsky, Nikolai P. "Professor N. S. Timashev o putiakh Rossii." In Nikolai Timasheff, ed., *The New Review*, 84. New York: New Review Inc., 1966.

Safrazyan, Natalia. *Stanovlenie marksistsko-leninskogo gumanitarnogo obrazovaniia v Moskovskom universitete (Oktyabr' 1917– 1925)*. Moscow: Politizdat, 1987.

Shoyer, John. "Sotsiologiia N.S. Timasheffa." In Pitirim Sorokin, Nikolai Poltoratskii, eds., *Na temy russkie i obshchie*, 44–54. New York: Izd-vo obshchestva druzey russkoi kultury, 1965.

Sokolov, Alexander S. Amerikanskaia tema v nauchno-literaturnom nasledii M. M. Kovalevskogo in Nikolai N. Bolkhovitinov, ed., *Amerikanskii ezhegodnik, 1989*, 155–73. Moscow: Nauka, 1990.

Sorokin, Pitirim A. *Sotsiologiia revolutsii*. Moscow: ROSSPEN, 2008.

————. *Glavnye tendentsii nashego vremeni*. Moscow: Nauka, 1997.

————. *Chelovek. Tsivilizatsiia. Obshchestvo*. Moscow: Politizdat, 1992.

————. *Dal'niaia doroga*. Moscow: TERRA, 1992.

Sorokin, Pitirim, and Poltoratskii Nikolai, eds., *Na temy Russkie i obshchie. Sbornik statey i materialov v chest' prof. N.S. Timasheffa*. New York: Izd-vo obshchestva druzei russkoi kultury, 1965.

Timasheff, Nikolai S. *War and Revolution: A Sociological Analysis*. New York: Sheed and Ward, 1965.

————. *The Great Retreat*. New York: Dalton Press, 1946.

Tiryakian, Edward A., ed., Sociological Theory, Values, and Sociocultural Change: Essays in Honor of Pitirim A. Sorokin. New York: Free Press, 1963.

Zhuravleva, Victoria I. *Ponimanie Rossii v SShA: obrazy i mify. 1881–1914. [Understanding Russia in the United States: Images and Myths. 1881–1914]*. Moscow: Izdatel'stvo RGGU, 2012.

SIX

Between Moscow and the West

Constructing the Soviet Self in the American Studies in Soviet Russia and Ukraine during Late Socialism (1956–1991)

Sergei Zhuk

A founder of the first Soviet Ukrainian center for American studies in Kyiv, Arnold Shlepakov noted in April 1990,

> In doing their research of the United States, using various discursive strategies in their research presentations and publications, Soviet Americanists not only discovered and constructed their own understanding of American modernity. They also discovered and constructed their own intellectual Soviet self. Therefore, a community of Soviet Americanists could be used as a special micro prism for a scholarly analysis of the history of Soviet intellectuals.[1]

Ten years after the dissolution of the Soviet Union, in a conversation with me in May 2001, Nikolai N. Bolkhovitinov, a founder of another Soviet school of American studies in Moscow, noted,

> According to Stalin, Moscow became a show case of mature socialism, demonstrating to the entire world the achievements and advantages of the Soviet socialist system. All the best of socialism, including its culture, scholarship and science, was concentrated in Moscow. This affected the development of American studies as well. The first centers of American studies with all their resources and academic privileges were concentrated in Moscow rather than provinces.

And he continued,

Sometimes we, here in Moscow, misunderstand the attitudes of the intellectuals from provinces. Take for example, our Soviet American-ists. Many of our Moscow Americanists came from the Soviet prov-inces. The best students of US history that I used to work with came from provinces. At the same time I noticed certain tensions between provincials and Muscovites. To some extent the relations of provincial scholars with Moscow as an academic center for the entire Soviet schol-arship became an indicative of the new developments in the authority of knowledge in the Soviet Union. To understand what happened with the provincial intellectual Soviet elites during late socialism and how these elites contributed to the collapse of the Soviet Union, we need to study the relations between Muscovites and provincials. These rela-tions, including academic ones, could be used as a model for a serious research of the transformations of our Soviet intellectuals into the new post-Soviet intellectual elites.[2]

So following suggestions of Shlepakov and Bolkhovitinov, and using various Soviet—Russian and Ukrainian—studies of the US history, cul-ture and politics, personal correspondence, and more than one hundred interviews as its historical sources, this chapter will concentrate on how Russian and Ukrainian scholars, who studied the US history, politics, and culture, employed different ideas of the North American civilization as the elements for a construction of Soviet and post-Soviet modernity in both Russia and Ukraine during the period of late socialism after Stalin. Combining the methods of oral history, symbolic anthropology, and his-torical sociology, this chapter will explore how the Soviet practices of history writing interacted with the ideological orthodoxy and centralist infrastructure of American studies in the USSR and contributed to the intellectual opposition of the Soviet peripheries (Ukraine) to the Soviet center (Moscow) during the perestroika.

Both contemporaries and scholars noted that the Cold War confronta-tion between the United States and the Soviet Union led to the intense "ideological offensive" when thousands of historians and social scientists in both countries became involved in the special fields of the area studies such as Soviet studies in the United States and American studies in the USSR. The common feature of all these efforts was an attempt to combine the techniques and insights of new historical research and "social sci-ences (intelligence on demographic and cultural trends, public opinion data, media manipulation, and so on) with advanced engineering (in command and control, weapons, transport, and so on) to manage, defuse or in some cases obliterate local challenges to superpower influence."[3] But in contrast to the American side of the Cold War story, where the US government and various corporations had funded the college-based cen-ters for Soviet studies as early as the 1940s, the Soviet centers of American studies were organized much later and only in the Moscow-based and Kyiv-based institutions of the USSR Academy of Sciences. From the early beginning, in the United States various Russian and Soviet research centers were spread all over the country in a decentralized fashion and were affiliated with different colleges and universities. All these American centers were professionally organized, well-funded, and they immediately became integrated in so called academic-national security complex in United States, especially during the late 1940s and the 1950s.[4] Paradoxically, the first professional Soviet centers of American studies appeared much later, only after Stalin's death, during the relaxation of international tensions and the improvement of US-Soviet relations. The beginning of institutionalization of the Soviet centers of American studies according to the directives of the Soviet state and the KGB took place in the special research institutes of the USSR Academy of Sciences only in the 1960s and the 1970s.[5] But the real peak of popularity and wide spread of American studies in the USSR during the late 1970s and the 1980s was a result of individual efforts by local college professor-enthusiasts who created their own schools for studies of US history, politics, literature and films at the major universities in big industrial cities of the Soviet Union.

At the end of the 1980s, almost 70 percent of all one thousand prominent Soviet Americanists (including economists, sociologists, and literary and film critics) were college professors who taught American studies in major universities of Soviet Russia and Ukraine, in big industrial cities such as Moscow, Leningrad, Kyiv, Odesa, and Dnipropetrovsk. By 1991 it was the largest community of the professional Americanists in the world outside the United States. The Chinese Americanists (so-called America Watchers) created the second largest community of American studies experts with almost seven hundred specialists concentrating in fifteen college centers. More than 60 percent of the Soviet college Americanists represented Russia and almost 40 percent represented Ukraine.[6]

From 1966 to 1970, among 150 Soviet books about US history published by the central Moscow publishing houses only two were written by the Ukrainian historians.[7] By 1991, more than 30 percent of all Soviet publications in American studies were written by Ukrainian authors. By the end of perestroika the Ukrainian experts in US history and politics became the leading Soviet researchers in such areas as the colonial period of US history, American Indian history, and the history of immigration in United States and Canada.[8]

SOCIALIST MODERNITY AND IDENTITY OF A SOVIET AMERICANIST

From the beginning, the creation and institutionalization of American studies in the Soviet Union was directly connected to a self-perception of socialist modernity and limits of its "openness" among Soviet intellectuals. As Volodymyr Yevtukh, a Ukrainian Americanist and politician, noted in December 1995, "to be a Soviet Americanist, a Soviet expert in US and Canadian history, meant to be a very special, real modern scholar, who was different from a boring and traditionalist scholar, an official Communist expert of the Soviet past and Soviet realities." And he continued,

> Everybody understood that despite all our official anti-Americanism in the Soviet Union, for us, Soviet intellectuals, American civilization symbolized a modernity of the entire humankind. According to Communist ideology, the Soviet Union also was a modern, progressive civilization. That is why, we, Soviet scholars, studied the United States not only to criticize Americans, but also to learn from American experience how to be a part of modernity. At the same time to study America for us was an attempt to avoid our Soviet "closeness" and associate with "open" western civilization.[9]

More than 90 percent of former Soviet Americanists, whom I had interviewed since the 1990s in both Russia and Ukraine, acknowledged how attractive for them were the images of modernity (*sovremennosti*), ideas of cultural and technological progress, they always associated with the United States and the English language as a signifier of the connections to American modernity, to the "opened" Western world. Even the first post-war generation of Soviet intellectuals, whose representatives became the founders of the first Soviet schools of *Amerikanistika* in Moscow and Kyiv, grew up under the influence of the controversial images of the United States as the Soviet allies in World War II, as a progressive modern country that developed forbidden but very popular trends and fashions, especially in music and films.[10] All subsequent generations of the Soviet Americanists from the 1960s, the 1970s, and the 1980s were influenced by the similar images, sounds and ideas of the western modernity they associated mainly with the United States.[11]

To some extent, the entire Soviet Americanist's identity was built around this notion of Western (American) modernity and its English linguistic expressions. To be *sovremennyi* (modern), "cool" was a major point of an academic career for many Soviet Americanists, especially after Stalin. The different representatives of Soviet Americanists, such as N. Bolkhovitinov, M. Vlasova, A. Yarygin, A. Sergounin, V. Zubok in Russia, and A. Shlepakov, V. Kalashnikov, V. Yevtukh, A. Belonozhko in Ukraine, emphasized their desire to be modern, to be progressive, when they selected a field of American studies for their academic career. For many of them, this notion was also connected to certain material privileges—travels abroad, access to Western (especially American) cultural products. To be an Americanist for them was to be "a very special (*osobennyi*) scholar, to be ahead of times, to be an agent of intellectual progress, part of the open world (*chastitsei otkrytogo mira*)."[12]

In building their identity, Soviet Americanists distanced themselves not from American scholars, but from their Soviet colleagues, who represented the more conservative, traditionalist and orthodox fields of scholarship, especially a Communist party (CPSU) history and a recent history of the Soviet Union. They constructed their scholar ideal as the opposite to an image of "*k-p-esesnik*" (a historian of the Communist party, *KPSS* in Russian abbreviation). A representative of the most numerous group of college history professors in the Soviet Union, a Soviet expert in communist party history was an object of ridicule by the representatives of more progressive (and more modern) Soviet field for historical research, which was known as "*vseobshchaia* universal (world) history." Soviet historians who studied US history were part of this westernized modern school of Soviet scholarship. Soviet Americanists always criticized "*k-p-esesniks*" and specialists in contemporary Soviet history as the "Marxist-Stalinist crammers," the conservative memorizers of "Marxist classics," "retrograde defenders of Soviet closeness," and ridiculed them for a lack of cultural (including historical) erudition and for their bad linguistic skills. Paradoxically, a traditional Soviet dichotomy *kul'turnost'* vs. *beskul'turie* from the Stalin era became a major building block for an identity of Soviet Americanists. To be cultured was associated with open-mindedness.[13] The very act of pursuing American studies in the Soviet Union signified a modern, cultured Soviet intellectual vis-à-vis a boorish and ignorant pedant from the field of CPSU history or the recent history of the Soviet Union. A notion of the special role of the Soviet Americanists as agents of modernity affected their attitudes not only toward their colleagues, CPSU historians, but also to other Soviet scholars who were engaged in official propagandist fields of political science and social studies known as *nauchnyi kommunizm*. They sometimes even criticized their colleagues from ISKAN because they did their research on the request of the communist ideologists and the KGB, therefore losing their status as agents of modernity and defending "Soviet closeness." Historians from a Bolkhovitinov center (formerly the Sevostianov center) sometimes distanced themselves as "serious academic researchers" from the experts from the Institute of the USA and Canada, calling them "*koniukturshchiks*," who worked for so-called "*directivnyi* organs."[14]

PERESTROIKA AND DISCURSIVE LEGACIES OF THE BREZHNEV ERA

Overall, Americanists affiliated with research institutions, tried to concentrate on mere facts and avoid ritualistic references. Even during the 1970s, *SShA: ekonomica, politika, ideologiia* (hereafter—*SEPI*) demonstrated more liberal discursive strategies than other Soviet periodicals, covering American studies. Only from 20 to 30 percent of this journal's publications appealed at least once to the authority of the "classics of Marxism-Leninism." (Compare with *Voprosy istorii* and *Novaia i noveishaia istoria*, where from 80 to 90 percent of all articles ritualistically cited Brezhnev, Lenin, and Marx.) At the outset of perestroika in 1987, less than 10 percent of all *SEPI* publications contained any direct reference to Marxism, in mostly editorial articles written by senior scholars (*doctor nauk*) and by historians, who demonstrated a more conservative approach than political scientists, economists or literary and film critics. None of junior scholars (*kandidat nauk*) quoted the "classics." The same trend was obvious among Soviet historians who published their essays on US history in this journal. In his article about class struggle in revolutionary America (Shays' Rebellion), a young (then) historian B. M. Shpotov did not cite any reference to Marx or Lenin, while an established senior colleague of his, A. A. Fursenko, referred to Marxist classics in his essay about political history of the American Constitution of 1787.[15] In 1987, a year of the fiftieth anniversary of the Great October Socialist Revolution, 30 percent of all *SEPI* publications were devoted to problems of class struggle and revolutionary (working class and communist) movements in the United States and solidarity of the American workers with Russian workers.[16] The next year, these topics completely disappeared from the pages of this periodical. In 1988, only four in fifty-four *SEPI* articles contained any direct reference to Marxism, meaning that less than one percent (0.8 percent) referred ritualistically to the "classics." It is noteworthy that only senior scholars from ISKAN followed this ritual. All representatives of the young generation of scholars, including Andranik Migranian and Vladislav Zubok, who later became famous figures in the post-Soviet era, the first as an advisor of Yeltsin, and the second, after his immigration to United States, as an American expert in Soviet history, ignored the ritualistic games of quoting Marxist works. Even such a prominent senior scholar like Yurii Zamoshkin avoided Marxist citation in his essay about "a usage of class antagonism category in the analysis of Soviet-American relations."[17]

The historians who dominated in *Amerikanskii ezhegodnik* (hereafter— *AE*) publications were more conservative and traditionalist. In 1986 seven *AE* articles from fourteen (50 percent) contained the direct references to Marxism. Two articles had indirect reference to Marxist literature by citing books written by American communists. If young Muscovites like Sergei Stankevich ignored ritualistic citations from Marx, all historians from provincial schools, including young scholars like myself, demonstrated their ideological skills and loyalty with numerous quotations from the classics of Marxism-Leninism.[18] During the peak of perestroika, in 1990, five from twelve *AE* articles (almost 41 percent) appealed at least once to the authority of the "classics."[19] Compared to a discursive inertia of the central historical journals, in which almost 50 percent of the material contained ritualistic referral to either Marx or Gorbachev, Americanists' periodicals, especially *SEPI*, still looked more modern and progressive. In contrast to this "discursive modernization" in Moscow, a discourse of major Ukrainian Americanists in Kyiv was still based on Marxist phraseology even in 1991.[20]

The most important legacy of discursive strategies from the Brezhnev era was a particular Soviet style of historical narrative—internalist, factological, and discussion-avoiding. As perestroika opened formerly forbidden areas for exploration and discussion, a remarkable thematic shift followed that now stressed creating a social and, especially, cultural, history of the United States.[21] If in 1986 *AE* had more than 80 percent of all articles covering traditional "factological" political and economic history of the United States, in 1989 it had almost 60 percent of such material. Only in issues prepared in 1991 this domination of Soviet discursive tradition was challenged by emergence of a new social and cultural history on the pages of AE. According to my calculations, 90 percent of all publications in Amerikanskii ezhegodnilk for this year covered themes of cultural, religious, and social history, and 10 percent—traditional political history. To some extent it was a result of publication of foreign authors in a former Soviet periodical for US history. In the last Soviet issue of *AE* (it was prepared during the spring of 1991, before the collapse of the Soviet Union), titled *New Views on American History*, six articles from eleven were written by American and German historians such as Horst Dippel, Bradford Perkins, Durret Rutmen, and Walter LaFeber.[22]

Unfortunately, the major trend in American studies, especially US history, during perestroika was "merely adding new facts." This ("factological") approach presumed a model of history in which the general picture had already been drawn, only some "dark spots" were left. As historians discovered forgotten facts, the dark spots would disappear, and the picture would finally become clear and complete. This view of history required recollection not reinterpretation. In the intense process of restructuring the field of power/knowledge relationships, any new interpretation of the role of historians in shaping discourse about the United States was "a statement laden with political values." To some extent as some contemporary observers noted, Soviet readers had "been given an updated textbook of political history in which the previous black-and white history" of the United States "often becomes white-and-black."[23] Perestroika reduced ideological barriers and opened new theoretical horizons that certainly implied changes in the thematic discourse of Soviet experts in US history. It was time "for historians to realize that not only themes, but also research methodologies, ought to change." The factological tradition was now being challenged by those historians who began to put more emphasis on the cultural and social context of US history. In 1993–1995 a few former Soviet Americanists published more theoretical and innovative articles, a majority of which were written during the last years of perestroika, especially in 1990 and 1991. So technically speaking this material also reflected the situation of late Soviet scholar-ship.[24] But overall, in post-Soviet time the Soviet legacy of factological approach still dominated the field of American studies.

Another Soviet legacy was the influential role of research institutions in shaping research agendas for American studies in colleges and univer-sities. Some scholars argued that communist ideology "has played a less significant role than we have tended to assume, and structure played a more significant role." To some extent, ideological shifts without structu-ral alterations (research institutions' influences) produced very little ef-fect on research work done in Soviet American studies; "structural changes without ideological concomitants have played a much greater role."[25] Bolkhovitinov's sector of North American studies in Moscow at the Russian Institute of World History influenced many young Americanists from provinces (in both Russia and Ukraine), and after 1988 this organizational structure of Soviet American studies contributed to radicalization and revisions in post-Soviet historiography of US history.[26]

SOVIET AMERICANISTS AS MODERNITY AGENTS AND THE "ENVY OF MOSCOW"

Soviet Americanists employed flexible discursive strategies to convey de-sired meaning without violating the constraints of the then politically acceptable language. According to some scholars, Soviet academic dis-course was "not as a container of a particular ideology or theory, but rather as a mechanism for advancing a certain agenda via disciplinary knowledge." As Slava Gerovitch noted, "Instead of depicting the Cold War solely as a clash of ideologies, it may be more productive to examine the discursive strategies that were employed to shape the image of the opponent and to build up 'our' ideology against 'theirs.'"[27] In this con-text, Soviet Americanists actively developed various discursive strategies to appropriate the image of the opponent to the needs of the current situation. At the same time they connected the opponent's image to their mental construction of progressive modernity and to their assumed role of the agents of this modernity in both Russia and Ukraine.

Both these mental constructions and assumed roles were affected by the psychological complex of tensions, which had existed between Soviet provincial populations and Muscovites since the Stalin era. Historically, the tensions between provincials and Muscovites created a unique and mass psychological phenomenon of mature socialism in the USSR known as the "envy of Moscow." This phenomenon was Stalin's legacy, a result of the creation of Moscow as a show case of the socialist achievements for the entire Soviet Union. With all limitations in socialist production, distri-bution and consumption of manufactured goods and cultural products in Soviet provinces, from a provincial point of view, Moscow looked like a "socialist paradise" with the best food stores, best schools, theaters, libraries, and museums. Moscow was a symbol of the entire Soviet civilization, a trendsetter for all provinces, but at the same time an object of intense envy for the millions Soviet provincials.[28]

In September of 1999, Sergei N. Burin, a younger colleague of Bolkhovitinov, noted an important development that affected the intellectual history of American studies in Russia and Ukraine:

> Envy has always been a fundamental element in constructing the Soviet personality since Stalin's times. Beginning with Yurii Olesha, all Soviet writers noted this. Provincials envied Muscovites because Moscow had the better living conditions. Muscovites envied provincials, if they made successful careers and traveled abroad. In my opinion, envy killed the Soviet Union, when the local intellectual elites from national republics transformed their envy of Moscow into their new national politics. Envy became the most important factor in shaping the entire intellectual history of the Soviet Union, including its academic life and, to some extent, effecting the development of American studies as well.[29]

In the USSR provincial intellectual elites tried to join the Muscovite elite. If they failed to do so, they eventually began developing certain anti-Moscow feelings. This phenomenon influenced the attitudes of various provincial Americanists toward their colleagues from Moscow. The major perception of the provincial intellectuals was that ISKAN (since 1967) and other Soviet centers for American studies offered jobs only to the representatives of the Moscow elite, to the young members of the ruling families in Moscow. For people from the provinces, all young (and sometimes not very young) Americanists from Moscow were "the golden youth," *mal'chiki mazhory*.[30] This "envy of Moscow" became a significant element in formation of the regional version of Soviet intellectual self among the Ukrainian Americanists.

A UKRAINIAN AMERICANIST AS A REGIONAL VERSION OF SOVIET INTELLECTUAL SELF

In 1986, Viktor M. Kalashnikov, a Ukrainian scholar who studied the social history of the American Indians during the European colonization of North America in the seventeenth and eighteenth centuries, complained about a centralization of American studies in the Soviet Union, about a concentration of all American literature only in Moscow libraries, and particularly, about high academic standards for research established by the Moscow Americanists:

> I am tired of this Muscovites' condescending attitude toward historians from the Soviet provinces. It is very easy for them to criticize the provincials, sitting among American books and historical sources at the

Moscow central libraries and using American literature for their own research. We, provincial scholars, can visit Moscow libraries only occasionally, because it is very expensive to travel to Moscow, to find accommodations in Moscow and do serious research in Moscow libraries, when you have very limited time and budget.[31]

In 1990, another prominent Ukrainian historian, an expert in the history of migration and working class movement in the United States and Canada, Arnold Shlepakov, noted a different source of conflict between Ukrainian and Moscow Americanists:

Muscovites are cynical hypocrites. In public, they tried to demonstrate their loyalty to the Soviet politics of international peace, they always required from us, provincial scholars, to follow the official Marxist interpretations of US history, which they had developed. But in real life, they laugh at our blind following Marxist-Leninism, they do no not believe any more in Marxist ideology they had imposed on us here in Ukraine. Criticizing privately our loyalty to Marx's teachings, Muscovites ignore our research of US history as too "ideologized," provincial, and the second rate comparing to their own confusing and changing revisions of the American historical developments.[32]

Many Ukrainian Americanists expressed their misunderstanding of Moscow politics in the field of American studies, especially during the 1980s. In 1990, Aleksei B., a graduate student of Semyon Appatov, a scholar of the US international politics from Odesa State University in Ukraine, complained about the privileged position of Muscovites in the area of American studies,

Historians from Moscow have the direct access to all recent literature in US history and politics. Therefore they can criticize us, historians from the provinces, as ignorant scholars. But look at who is travelling to America, who is taking part in scholarly exchange with the United States. They are predominantly Muscovites. They have the best schools of English language, a direct exposure to American influences, almost unlimited access to American literature and historical sources. Therefore they monopolize American studies in the Soviet Union and control us, the scholars from the Soviet provinces, through various central administrative structures.[33]

As a result, this element of envy of Muscovites co-existed with more conservative and cautious professional discourse (including ritualistic references to the "classics") of Ukrainian Americanists, which was still dependent on Moscow authoritative discourse even during the perestroika.

During the 1970s and 1980s many of these Ukrainian scholars gradually developed their own critical attitudes toward the Soviet center of academic power in Moscow. These attitudes took a wide variety of forms— from an obvious misunderstanding of changes in ideological practices of their supervisors from Moscow to an attempt to carve their own cultural and research niches in Soviet studies of North American civilizations. Eventually the history and culture of Ukrainian migration to Canada (with traditional emphasis on class struggle) became a research niche for many Ukrainian Americanists. This emphasis on the Ukrainian ethnic and cultural elements in Canadian history was enforced by strengthening the connections between the Soviet Ukrainian intellectual elite, whose regular visits to Canadian soil were sponsored by the Soviet government, and the Ukrainian Diaspora (mostly with the representatives of the Canadian Left, like Petro Krawchuk) in Canada. As a result, by the end of the 1970s the special field of Ukrainian-Canadian studies had been created in Soviet Ukraine, which had no equivalent in Canadian studies in Moscow. To some extent the new field of Ukrainian-Canadian studies eventually contributed to the formation of Ukrainian academic identity in the Soviet field of American studies.[34]

A rise of national patriotic movement in Ukraine and numerous mistakes made by the central Soviet administration in Kremlin discredited Moscow authoritative discourse and made it irrelevant for the Ukrainian intellectuals after 1988. As a result of these developments, even the Russia-orienting and Russian-speaking Americanists from Ukraine began to associate themselves more with the local interests and expressed their frustration with unpredictable politics of Moscow by distancing themselves from Moscow control. Organizational structures of scholarship in Ukraine played an important role in this process. Leadership of Ukrainian academic institutions, including local centers of American studies, strengthened their independent position in research and teaching agenda, rejecting control from Moscow. Many of them used this situation as an opportunity to re-create their own power structures in Ukrainian scholarship without Moscow's control. Now they replaced all union agendas in research and teaching with the regional, national ideas which justified their own (regional/Ukrainian) control over American studies in Ukraine.[35] Many of these scholars, who before 1987 blindly followed the suggestions of their Moscow colleagues, became explicitly anti-Russian leaders of Ukrainian centers for American studies. Paradoxically, these scholars like L. Leshchenko, A. Shlepakov, and V. Yevtukh joined the ruling political elite of post-Soviet Ukraine and built their careers in international diplomacy and politics rather than in academic spheres. These changes were related directly to the diminishing role of Moscow as a center of Soviet scholarly discourse of modernity during perestroika. By 1991, Moscow had already lost its symbolic role for Soviet authoritative discourse and became completely irrelevant for a professional discourse of American studies in the Soviet provinces, especially in non-Russian republics.[36] This created a vacuum which was filled eventually with a new discourse of modernity, this time it was its nation-based version, a regional/Ukrainian discourse that rejected the "universalist" all-union

model of the Soviet socialist modernity, and now, it used both Canada
and the United States as its model.

THREE GENERATIONS OF SOVIET
AMERICANISTS AND GEOPOLITICS

All these changes in identity formation and discursive strategies of Soviet
Americanists were directly connected to a geopolitical situation, and to
new developments in Soviet-American relations. The changes in geopolitical situation of the Cold War after Stalin involved intense Westernization of both Soviet political and popular culture. To some extent the
development and institutionalization of American studies became indicative of Westernization of Soviet intellectuals not only in Moscow, but also
in the provinces.[37] Approximately three different generations of Soviet
Americanists grew up after Stalin. These generations were shaped by
four different geopolitical phenomena. The first generation of Soviet experts in American studies created the first schools of Soviet students who
became interested in the studies of North American countries. These
scholars like Georgi Arbatov and Nikolai Bolkhovitinov contributed to
founding and developing the first official centers for studies of the United States and Canada in Moscow. According to their memoirs and observations of contemporaries, the most important influence for their choice
of studying the United States came from World War II and their aware-
ness of the important role of the United States as the main ally of the
Soviet Union. For many Soviet intellectuals, not only for those who
fought in the war, but also for those who grew up during the war, during
the 1940s, the United States symbolized a great friendship of two great
nations and their victory over fascism and "international reaction."[38] Unfortunately, the depth of understanding of the United States among the
first post-war generation of Soviet Americanists remained very shallow.
A majority of these first professional Soviet Americanists were burdened
by the Marxist belief system, image structures, and categories of analysis.
They suffered from a great deal of cognitive dissonance and simply
looked for evidence to confirm their preconceived images of how the
United States functioned.[39]

The second geopolitical influence came from Khrushchev's Thaw and
the first official attempt to open the Soviet Union to the West and to begin
the first round of relaxation of international tensions with the United
States after 1956. The Youth International Festival in Moscow, the academic exchanges between Soviet and American scholars, the re-organiza-
tion of international tourism and the creation of international travel agencies in the USSR opened new cultural and ideological horizons for a new
generation of Soviet intellectuals known as "*shestidesiatniki*." Future ideological architects of perestroika such as Aleksandr Yakovlev visited and

studied in the United States. The founding fathers of Soviet American studies, the first post-war generation, scholars like Nikolai Bolkhovitinov, Nikolai Sivachev in Moscow and Arnold Shlepakov in Kyiv defended their first dissertations during this period of time.

The third geopolitical influence came from the détente of the 1970s. A new round of relaxation of international tensions (especially between the Soviet Union and the United States) contributed not only to an improvement in US-Soviet relations and increase in scholarly and cultural exchange, but also to the growing consumption of Western cultural products, especially music and films, and, as a result, to mass Westernization of Soviet youth culture.[40] Following the needs of a new diplomacy, the Soviet government created the first Soviet centers for American studies in Moscow and Kyiv. The 1970s was a time of an official institutionalization of American studies in the Soviet Union. The most popular organizers (although, in some cases, the unofficial leaders) of these institutions became the prominent scholars, representatives of the first Soviet post-war generation, such as Arbatov, Bolkhovitinov and Shlepakov. At the same time a new generation of the Brezhnev era (I would call them "*semidesiatniki*") grew up under the new influences of détente and the Westernization of cultural life. Many of them, including V. Tishkov, V. Sogrin, B. Shpotov, S. Appatov, and V. Kalashnikov, would become leaders in American studies in Russia and Ukraine during the 1980s, defending their doctoral dissertations and struggling for their academic career promotions.

The representatives of the last Soviet generation of Soviet Americanists, including Marina Vlasova, Vladislav Zubok, and Andrey Znamenskii, who joined the new centers of American studies later, during the 1980s, were influenced and trained by "*semidesiatniki.*" Although a majority of these scholars grew up during the 1970s, their intellectual trajectory was shaped mainly by the events of the 1980s. That is why I call them "*vosmidesiatniki.*" The period of the late 1980s was the beginning of the last, and the most crucial, geopolitical influence for American studies in the Soviet Union. During this period known as perestroika, not only a development of the entire country, but also the direction and themes of Soviet American studies, had changed. With a new opening of Soviet society to various foreign influences, the new young generation accepted these influences, especially new approaches in methodology, and became the most active participants in restructuring thematic orthodoxy in Soviet American studies, challenging the conservatism of the older generation of "*semidesiatniki,*" scholars like Sogrin and Kalashnikov.

According to some scholars, tensions among the younger and older generations of Soviet Americanists in the 1980s reflected a basic tenet of cognitive dissonance, namely, that after the age of about thirty one tends to look for evidence confirming one's core beliefs and rejects contradictory evidence, because dissonance was psychologically uncomfortable.[41]

At the same time this period witnessed a growing distancing of the Ukrainian scholars from Moscow, and an increase of tensions between Muscovites and provincial scholars. National and regional identity now shaped a research agenda in both Russia and Ukraine. The last generation of Soviet Americanists, *"vosmidesiatniki,"* became shaped by these new controversial developments. They tried to link the old traditions of the founders of the Soviet *Amerikanistika*, scholars like Arbatov and Bolkhovitinov, with the new demands of research and new scholarship from the West. The representatives of this perestroika generation, together with *"semidesiatniki,"* would become leaders in American studies in post-Soviet Russia and Ukraine, trying to re-create he significant role of their field not only in college education, but also in shaping the international and domestic policy of their states.[42]

As we see, using various discursive strategies in their research and publications, Soviet Americanists tried to adjust their intellectual discoveries to the changing realities of Soviet ideological discourse and political life. They not only reflected these realities, but also tried to adjust their personalities and their intellectual interests to these changes. Simultaneously, they also built their own identity, transforming their own Soviet intellectual self, based on various interpretations of American modernity. Eventually, they infused these interpretations of modernity with very different elements of regional/national identity, which under certain political circumstances, became a core for the new post-Soviet national authoritative discourse among both Russian and Ukrainian intellectuals.

NOTES

1. Interview with Arnold M. Shlepakov, April 4, 1991, Kyiv.
2. Interview with Nikolai N. Bolkhovitinov, May 21, 2001, Moscow.
3. Christopher Simpson, "Introduction," *Universities and Empire: Money and Politics in the Social Sciences during the Cold War,* edited and introduced by Christopher Simpson (New York: the New Press, 1998), xvi.
4. Op. cit., xx.
5. See such documents in a correspondence between the CPSU Central Committee and *pervyi otdel* of various institutes of the USSR Academy of Sciences between May and November 1967 in Arkhiv Rossiiskoi Akademii Nauk [Moscow, Russia], Fond 1900, Institut vseobshchei istorii (IVI) Akademii nauk SSSR, 1969–1985, Opis 1: Upravlencheskaia dokumentatsiia IVI, folder for 1969, correspondence; Fond 2021, Institut Soedinennykh Shtatov Ameriki i Kanady (ISKAN) RAN, 1968–1995, Opis 1: Upravlencheskaia dokumentatsia ISKAN, folder for 1968, ll. 1–18; Georgi Arbatov, *The System: An Insider's Life in Soviet Politics* (New York: Random House, 1992), 295–98. About the direct connections of Arbatov (whose KGB codename was Vasilii) see Christopher Andrew and Vasili Mitrokhin, *The Sword and the Shield: The Mitrokhin Archive and the Secret History of the KGB* (New York: Basic Books, 1999), 211–12, 213.
6. Calculations were made according data from *Russian-American Dialogue on the American Revolution,* ed. by Gordon S. Wood and Louise G. Wood (Columbia: University of Missouri Press, 1995), 7; Barbara L. Dash, *A Defector Reports: The Institute of the USA and Canada* (Falls Church, VA: Delphic Associates, 1982), 7; my interview with Nikolai N. Bolkhovitinov, May 21, 2001, Moscow, and my interview with Arnold

Shlepakov, Kyiv, April 4, 1991. See also David Shambaugh, *Beautiful Imperialist: China Perceives America, 1972–1990* (Princeton, NJ: Princeton University Press, 1991), 277–78.

7. *Amerikanskii ezhegodnik. 1971,* (hereafter—*AE. 1971*), 354–58; *AE. 1972,* 303, 331–39, Interview with Shlepakov. In the All-Union list of publications on US history, the most prominent Ukrainian authors were S. I. Appatov, A. A. Mkrtchian and G. N. Tsvetkov.

8. *AE. 1986,* 256–23; Marcus Rediker, "The Old Guard, the New Guard, and the People at the Gates: New Approaches to the Study of American History in the USSR," *William and Mary Quarterly,* 3rd Ser., 1991 (October), vol. 48, 580–97; *AE. 1993,* 201, 202.

9. Interview with Volodymyr B. Yevtukh, December 15, 1995, Kyiv.

10. Vladislav Zubok, *Zhivago's Children: The Last Russian Intelligentsia* (Cambridge, MA: The Belknap Press of Harvard University Press, 2009).

11. See in detail about this in Sergei I. Zhuk, *Rock and Roll in the Rocket City: The West, Identity, and Ideology in Soviet Dniepropetrovsk, 1960–1985* (Baltimore, MD: the Johns Hopkins University Press and Washington, DC: Woodrow Wilson Center Press, 2010).

12. I quote a letter of Nikolai Bolkhovitinov to me, December 12, 1988.

13. See about a lack of historical erudition among communist party's historians in a letter of Nikolai Bolkhovitinov to me, December 12, 1988, and in various interviews, including my interview with Sergei N. Burin, September 5, 1999, Moscow.

14. See interview with I. Beliavskaia in *AE. 1995,* 16.

15. Compare B. M. Shpotov, "Fermerskoie vosstanie Danielia Shaysa," *SShA: ekonomika politika ideologiia* (hereafter—*SEPI*), February 1987, no. 2(206): 46–54, with A. A. Fursenko, "Konstitutsionnyi convent," ibid., July 1987, no. 7 (211): 64–72.

16. M. I. Lapitskii, "Rasprava nad Sakko i Vantsetti," *SEPI,* August 1987, no. 8(212): 43–52, and essay about John Reed and his description of the Russian Revolution in B. A. Gilenson, "On videl rozhdenie novogo mira," *SEPI,* October 1987, no. 10 (214): 45–55. The major articles of *SEPI* November issue were devoted to a theme of the Russian Revolution: see *SEPI,* November 1987 11 (215): 3–49.

17. A. Yu. Mel'vil', "'Obraz vraga' i novoe politicheskoe myshlenie," *SEPI,* January 1988, no. 1(217): 29–39, Lenin citation on p. 38; S. M. Rogov, "O vzaimodeistvii interesov SSSR I SShA," *SEPI,* August 1988, no. 8 (224): 3–13, "classics" citation on p. 3; I. V. Bushmarin, "Obrazovatel'nyi uroven' rabochei sily SShA," *SEPI,* September 1988, no. 9 (225): 72–78, citation p. 72; A. B. Koriev, "Mirnoe sosucshchestvovanie: obshchesotsial'nyi podkhod," *SEPI,* November 1988, no. 11 (227): 46–52, citation on pp. 48, 50, 51, 52; Yu. A. Zamoshkin, "Ob ispol'zovanii kategorii klassovogo antagonizma pri rasmotrenii sovetsko-amerikanskikh otnoshenii," ibid., 53–59.

18. Compare S. B. Stankevich, "'Novaia ekonomicheskaia politika' administratsii R. Niksona v 1971–1974 gg.," *AE* 1986, (Moscow: Nauka, 1986), 5–23, with V. M. Kalashnikov, "Anglo-ispanskoe kolonial'noe sopernichestvo vo Floride (1670–1763 gg.)," ibid., 221–34, and mine: S. I. Zhuk, "Piratstvo: istochnik pervonachal'nogo nakoplenia i forma sotsial'nogo protesta (na primere kolonii New York)," ibid., 235–45.

19. *AE* 1989 was publishes a year later in 1990.

20. See V. B. Yevtukh, *Kontseptsii etnosotsial'nogo razvitia SShA i Kanady: Tipologia, traditsii, evoliutsia* (Kiev: Naukova dumka, 1991), with ritualistic referral to Marx on p. 162.

21. This was a result of the new turn of the entire Soviet historiography as early as the 1980s. To some extent it was a result of publications of the research by Aron Ya. Gurevich, who popularized the ideas of the French Annales among the Soviet reading audience. See about the popularity of cultural history in the late Soviet Union in Laura Engelstein, "Culture, Culture Everywhere: Interpretations of Modern Russia, across the 1991 Divide," *Kritika: Explorations in Russian and Eurasian History,* Spring 2001, 2(2): 363–93; Roger D. Markwick, "Cultural History under Khrushchev and Brezhnev: From Social Psychology to *Mentalités,*" *The Russian Review,* April 2006, 65: 283–301.

22. See *AE 1992: Novyi vzgliad na istoriu SShA* (Moscow: Nauka, 1993), 38–61, 85–115, 136–51, 209–18.

100   *Sergei Zhuk*

23. See in Marcus Rediker, Op. cit., and an American article by Andrei A. Snamenski, "In Black or White, or through Marxist Glasses: The Image of the Indian in the Soviet Press and Scholarship," *American Indian Culture and Research Journal*, 16, no. 1(1992): 119–36.

24. B. M. Shpotov, "Byla li na Yuge i Zapade SShA promyshlennaia revoliutsia? Postanovka problem," *AE 1990*, (Moscow, 1991), 126–41; V. V. Sogrin, "Liberalizm i konservatizm—tsentral'nye ideino-politicheskie traditsii SShA," *AE 1992*, 62–85; S. I. Zhuk, "Max Weber i sotsial'naia istoria," *Voprosy istorii*, 1992, no. 2–3, 172–77; idem, "Ranniaia Amerika: sotsiokul'turnaia preemstvennost' i "proryv v utopiu"," *AE 1992*, 16–38; idem, "'Effekt zerkala': (Zhurnal "*William and Mary Quarterly*" i sovremennaia amerikanskaia istoriografia)," *AE 1994*, (Moscow, 1995), 208–22; idem, Sovremennaia istoriografia rannei Ameriki: put' k "istoricheskomu sintezu"," *Voprosi istorii*, no. 2 (1994): 175–78. All these "perestroika" ideas were summarized in my book: Sergei I. Zhuk, *Traditisionalizm protiv kapitalizma: Sotsial'naia istoria rannei Ameriki* (Dniepropetrovsk: Dniepropetrovsk University Press, 1992).

25. Mark B. Adams, "Science, Ideology, and Structure: The Kol'tsov Institute, 1900–1970," *The Social Context of Soviet Science*, eds. Linda L. Lubarno and Susan Gross Solomon (Boulder, CO: Westview Press, 1980), 198.

26. See about Bolkhovitinov's influence on my research interests in a colonial period of the US history in N. N. Bolkhovitinov, "Izuchenie rannei istorii SShA," *AE 2004*, (Moscow, 2006), 10; and Sergei I. Zhuk, "Colonial America, the Independence of the Ukraine, and Soviet Historiography: The Personal Experience of a Former Soviet Americanist," *Pennsylvania History*, 62, no. 4 (1995): 468–90.

27. Slava Gerovitch, "Writing History in the Present Tense," *Universities and Empire*, 217–18.

28. See Sergei I. Zhuk, *Rock and Roll in the Rocket City*, 210–11, 278–79.

29. Interview with Sergei N. Burin, September 5, 1999, Moscow. Burin referred to a famous short novel by the Soviet Russian writer, published in 1927. See its English translation: Yurii Olesha, *Envy*, translated by Marian Schwartz (New York, 2004).

30. See about a domination of Muscovites in the centers of American studies in the USSR in Barbara L. Dash, Op.cit, 7ff. More than 90 percent of my interviewees from both Russian and Ukrainian provincial universities shared these notions. See especially, a late A. Shlepakov from Kyiv, V. Kalashnikov from Dnipropetrovsk and A. Belonozhko from Zaporizhie.

31. Interview with Viktor M. Kalashnikov, March 3, 1986, Dniepropetrovsk.

32. Interview with Arnold M. Shlepakov, April 4, 1991, Kyiv, Ukraine.

33. Interview with Aleksei B., an Appatov's graduate student, May 15, 1990, Odesa.

34. All major figures in American studies in Soviet Ukraine, like Shlepakov, Appatov, Leonid Leshchenko and Yevtukh, became the experts in a history of Ukrainian Diaspora in Canada. See about their connections with Canadian Communists and formation of Ukrainian academic identity in the Soviet field of American studies in a book by a Ukrainian Canadian: Peter Krawchuk, *Our History: The Ukrainian labour-Farmer Movement in Canada, 1907–1991*, Edited by John Boyd (Toronto: Lugus, 1996).

35. See a description of this process in Kyiv in Leonid Leshchenko and Ihor Chernikov, "Vsesvitnio vidomyi vitchyznianyi uchenyi: Istoryk-miznarodnyk, organizator nauky i diplomat. Do 80-litia vid dnia narodzhennia akademika NAN Ukrainy Arnol'da Mykolaivycha Shlepakova (1930–1996 rr.)" in *Mizhnarodni zv'iazky Ukrainy: naukovi poshuky i znakhidky. Vypusk 19: Mizhvidomchyi zbirnyk naukovykh prats*, edited by S. V. Vidnians'kyi (Kyiv: Institut istorii NAN Ukrainy, 2010), 27–28.

36. See my explanation of this process in Sergei I. Zhuk, "Leveling of the Extremes: Soviet and Post-Soviet Historiography of Early American History," *Images of America: Through the European Looking Glass*, ed. William L. Chew III (Brussels: Free University of Brussels Press, 1997), 63–78.

37. See about Westernization of the Soviet provincial youth in Sergei I. Zhuk, *Rock and Roll in the Rocket City* .

38. See Nikolai N. Bolkhovitinov's writings, especially his "The Study of United States History in the Soviet Union," *American Historical Review*, 74, no. 4 (1969): 1221–42; idem, "How I Became a Historian," *Journal of American Studies*, 14, no. 1 (1980): 103–14; Georgi Arbatov, *The System*; Leonid Leshchenko and Ihor Chernikov, Op. cit., 27.
39. Compare with the similar developments among Chinese Americanists in David Shambaugh, Op. cit., 283.
40. See Sergei I. Zhuk, *Rock and Roll in the Rocket City*, chapters 4–10.
41. David Shambaugh, Op. cit., 284–85.
42. It is obvious in the publication of the symposium papers and proceedings of the post-Soviet Russian Americanists, who represented this combination of generations, and who became leaders of the new local centers of American studies in Russia. See the materials of this meeting (November 26–27, 2009, in Moscow) in *Amerikanskii ezhegodnik. 2008/2009* (Moscow, 2010), see especially pp. 201–13.

BIBLIOGRAPHY

Amerikanskii ezhegodnik. Moscow: Nauka, 1971–2010.
Arbatov, Georgiy. *The System: An Insider's Life in Soviet Politics.* New York: Random House, 1992.
Ball, Alan M. *Imagining America: Influence and Images in Twentieth-Century Russia.* Lanham, MD: Rowman & Litlefield, 2003.
Bolkhovitinov, Nikolai N. "American History in Russia: Retrospect and Prospect," *Journal of American History*, 79, no. 2 (1992): 524–29.
———. "New Thinking and the Study of the History of the United States in the Soviet Union," *Reviews in American History*, 19, no. 2 (1991): 155–65.
———. "How I Became a Historian," *Journal of American Studies*, 14, no. 1 (1980): 103–14.
———. "V arkhivakh i bibliotekakh SSHA: nakhodki, vstrechi, vpechatlenia," *Amerikanskii Ezhegodnik. 1971*, (Moscow: Nauka, 1971), 329–40.
———. "The Study of United States History in the Soviet Union," *American Historical Review*, 74, no. 4 (1969): 1221–42.
Byrnes, Robert F. *Soviet-American Academic Exchanges, 1958–1975.* Bloomington, IN: Indiana University Press, 1976.
Cherkasov, Piotr. *IMEMO. Institut Mirovoi Ekonomiki i Mezhdunarodnykh Otnoshenii. Portret na fone epokhi.* Moscow: Ves' mir, 2004.
Dash, Barbara L. *A Defector Reports: The Institute of the USA and Canada.* Washington, DC: Delphic Associates, 1982.
Denisova, Tamara, and Natalia Vysotska. "American Literary Studies in Ukraine: Yesterday, Today and Tomorrow," *American Studies International*, 41, no. 1/2 (2003): 220–33.
Engerman, David C. *Know Your Enemy: The Rise and Fall of America's Soviet Experts.* New York: Oxford University Press, 2009.
English, Robert D. *Russia and the Idea of the West: Gorbachev, Intellectuals, and the End of the Cold War.* New York: Columbia University Press, 2000.
Gurevich, Aron. *Istoria istorika.* Moscow: ROSSPEN, 2004.
Gutnova, Evgenia V. *Perezhitoe.* Moscow: ROSSPEN, 2001.
Kurilla, Ivan I., and Victoria I. Zhuravleva. "Teaching U.S. History in Russia: Issues, Challenges, and Prospects," *Journal of American History*, 96, no. 4 (2010): 1138–44.
Markwick, Roger D. *Rewriting History in Soviet Russia: The Politics of Revisionist Historiography, 1956–1974*, foreword by Donald J. Raleigh. New York: PALGRAVE, 2001.
Mizhnarodni zv'iazky Ukrainy: naukovi poshuky i znakhidky. Vypusk 19, ed. by S. V. Vidnians'kyi. Kyiv: Institut istorii NAN Ukrainy, 2010.

Nekrich, Aleksandr. *Forsake Fear: Memoirs of an Historian*, trans. by Donald Lineburgh. Boston: Unwin Hyman, 1991 (1st edition: 1979).

Portrety istorikov: vremia i sud'by, ed. by G. Sevostianov, vols. 1–5. Moscow: Nauka, 2000–2010.

Potts, Louis W. "'Who is to Blame? What is to be Done?' Joint Ventures with Russian Americanists in the 1990s," *American Studies International*, 41, no. 1/2 (2003): 41–63.

Pozner, Vladimir V. *Proshchanie s illiuziiami*. Moscow: AST, 2013.

Richmond, Yale. *U.S.-Soviet Cultural Exchanges, 1958–1986*. Boulder, CO: Westview, 1987.

Rossiia i SShA na stranitsakh uchebnikov: opyt vzaimnykh reprezentatsii, ed. by V. Zhuravleva and I. Kurilla. Volgograd: Izd-vo VolGU, 2009.

Russian-American Dialogue on the American Revolution, ed. by Gordon S. Wood and Louise G. Wood. Columbia: University of Missouri Press, 1995.

Shambaugh, David L. *Beautiful Imperialist: China Perceives America, 1972–1990*. Princeton, NJ: Princeton University Press, 1991.

Universities and Empire: Money and Politics in the Social Sciences during the Cold War, ed. by Christopher Simpson. New York: the New Press, 1998.

Zhuk, Sergei I. "Hollywood's Insidious Charms: The Impact of American Cinema and Television on the Soviet Union during the Cold War," *Cold War History*, 14, no. 4 (2014): 1–24.

———. "'Academic Détente': IREX Files, Academic Reports, and 'American' Adventures of Soviet Americanists during the Brezhnev Era," *Cahiers du monde russe*, 54, no. 1–2 (Janvier –juin 2013): 297–328.

———. "Inventing America on the Borders of Socialist Imagination: Movies and Music from the USA and the Origins of American Studies in the USSR," *REGION: Regional Studies of Russia, Eastern Europe, and Central Asia*, 2, no. 2 (2013): 249–88.

———. "Closing and Opening Soviet Society (Introduction to the Forum *Closed City, Closed Economy, Closed Society: The Utopian Normalization of Autarky*)," *Ab Imperio*, no. 2 (2011): 123–58.

———. *Rock and Roll in the Rocket City: The West, Identity, and Ideology in Soviet Dniepropetrovsk, 1960–1985*. Baltimore, MD: the Johns Hopkins University Press and Washington, DC: Woodrow Wilson Center Press, 2010.

———. "Leveling of the Extremes: Soviet and Post-Soviet Historiography of Early American History," *Images of America: Through the European Looking Glass*, ed. by William L. Chew III, 63–78. Brussels: Free University of Brussels Press, 1997.

———. "Colonial America, the Independence of the Ukraine, and Soviet Historiography: The Personal Experience of a Former Soviet Americanist," *Pennsylvania History*, 62, no. 4 (1995): 468–90.

Zubok, Vladislav. "Sowjetische Westexperten," in *Macht und Geist im Kalten Krieg*, ed. by Bernd Greiner, Tim Müller, Claudia Weber, 108–35. Hamburg: Hamburger Edition, 2011.

———. *Zhivago's Children: The Last Russian Intelligentsia*. Cambridge, MA: The Belknap Press of Harvard University Press, 2009.

SEVEN

Zbigniew Brzezinski's Appraisal of the Systemic Inadequacies of Soviet-Style Communism

Bureaucratization, Degeneration, and the Failed Quest for Transformation

Mark Kramer

This chapter critically assesses Zbigniew Brzezinski's writings on Soviet-style Communism from the mid-1960s through the end of the 1980s, a period punctuated by Brzezinski's four years as national security adviser to President Jimmy Carter (1977–1981). In numerous books and essays during this period, Brzezinski moved away from the totalitarian model he had developed earlier in conjunction with Carl Friedrich and focused instead on empirical analyses of the systemic inadequacies of Communist rule in the USSR and Eastern Europe. Although some of Brzezinski's writings included predictions of specific events (events that were ultimately shaped in part by the conscious actions of individuals and groups and in part by aleatory circumstances), my main focus here is on his assessment of the underlying processes and trends in Soviet-style systems that potentially could lead to momentous political change or, instead, to enervating decline.

THE TRANSFORMATION-OR-DEGENERATION PARADIGM

Whatever utility the totalitarian ideal-type may have had in understanding Josef Stalin's dictatorship, the model proved inadequate when applied to the post-Stalin era. Although Brzezinski initially tried to salvage the basic framework with slight modifications, he shifted course in the 1960s and early 1970s and replaced much of the old paradigm with a more viable framework that captured essential features of the Soviet system as it had evolved throughout its history. Brzezinski's new conception preserved a few elements of the totalitarian model and used them to explain how the USSR had metamorphosed into a bureaucratized, ossified polity. Looking ahead, he argued that the key question was whether the Soviet Union would undergo "transformation" and revitalization or would instead gradually succumb to "degeneration" and decay.

Brzezinski first propounded the notion that the Soviet Union was faced with two alternative paths in the future—"transformation or degeneration"—in a landmark article he published in early 1966 in the journal *Problems of Communism*.[1] The article touched off a long series of articles in the same journal that responded to his essay and assessed the prospects for far-reaching change in the Soviet political system. Brzezinski took an active part in these exchanges and gathered his original article (in slightly updated form), thirteen of the responses, and his "concluding reflections" for a book, *Dilemmas of Change in Soviet Politics*.[2]

Comparing the political situation under Stalin with developments after Stalin's death, Brzezinski emphasized the stifling role of Soviet bureaucracy. The Bolsheviks had come to power with an ideology that envisaged the withering away of the state, but in reality the Soviet regime from its earliest days had built up an elaborate bureaucracy. After Stalin's death the USSR no longer had an all-powerful, charismatic figure who could impose his will on the country. Brzezinski argued that the "new generation of clerks" who displaced Nikita Khrushchev in October 1964—nearly all of whom had risen in the hierarchy in the 1930s and 1940s as beneficiaries of Stalin's purges—regarded "bureaucratic stability" as "the only solid foundation for effective government." According to Brzezinski, the Soviet Union was "unique" in being "led by a bureaucratic leadership from the very top to the bottom," resulting in an "extremely centralized and rigidly hierarchical bureaucratic organization" that was "increasingly set in its ways, politically corrupted by years of unchallenged power, and made even more confined in its outlook than is normally the case with a ruling body by its lingering and increasingly ritualized doctrinaire tradition." This lack of flexibility, Brzezinski contended, would "pose a long-range danger to the vitality of any political system" because "decay is bound to set in, while the stability of the political system may be endangered." In particular, "the effort to maintain a doctrinaire dictatorship over an increasingly modern and industrial society" would lead to the "degeneration" of the entire system—a fate that, in Brzezinski's view, could be avoided only if "the bureaucratic Communist dictatorship [were gradually transformed] into a more pluralistic and institutionalized political system" that would "confront major domestic issues" and accommodate the demands of "key groups" whose "growing assertiveness" would otherwise debilitate the regime.[3]

Five points are worth noting about Brzezinski's argument. First, he depicted the "degeneration" of the Soviet system as an exclusively political phenomenon. The process of decay, he believed, would stem not from economic inefficiency or a projected slowdown in economic growth (which he did not even mention in his initial article), but from the smothering impact of an oppressive bureaucracy that wanted to keep ordinary citizens from having any meaningful say in the political arena. Brzezinski's view about the relative weight of political and economic factors in the decline of the USSR changed in later years, but when he first devised his notion of "transformation or degeneration" in the Soviet Union, he was focusing solely on the political dimension of the problem, especially the Soviet "system's growing incapacity" to deal with a multitude of pressing political and social issues, the dearth of top-notch individuals who wanted to ascend to leadership positions in the Communist Party of the Soviet Union (CPSU), and the increasing gap between the stagnant, inflexible Soviet political system and the ever more restless and dynamic Soviet society.

Second, among the "key groups" in the Soviet Union whose "growing assertiveness" Brzezinski believed would pose a long-term challenge to the regime were "the non-Russian nationalities." Few Western analysts at the time ascribed much political importance to Soviet nationalities and ethnic groups, but Brzezinski raised the issue (albeit briefly) in his initial article and then addressed it much more directly in his concluding essay, where he criticized "the inclination of many Western scholars of Soviet affairs to minimize what I fear may be potentially a very explosive issue in the Soviet polity." He elaborated:

> We still live in the age of nationalism, and my own highly generalized feeling is that it is going to be exceedingly difficult for the Soviet Union to avoid having some of its many nationalities go through a phase of assertive nationalism. . . . [The nationalities] can claim such things as political autonomy, constitutional reform, a greater share of the national economic pie, [and] more investment, without it appearing that they wish to secede from the Soviet Union. History teaches us, be it in Algeria or in Indonesia or in Africa, that these demands will grow rather than decline. If they are not met or are suppressed, it is likely that the demands will become sharper and more self-assertive. If they are satisfied, they will grow with the eating. I frankly do not see how the central authorities in the Soviet Union will be able to avoid having a

prolonged period of fairly difficult relations with the non-Russian nationalities.[4]

Although the problem did not become acute until twenty years later, when the political liberalization under Mikhail Gorbachev permitted nationalist discontent to come to the surface, Brzezinski was right to stress the potential volatility of the issue. He came back to the nationalities question numerous times in his later writings.

Third, Brzezinski went astray in his assessment of Soviet leadership dynamics in the wake of Khrushchev's ouster. Arguing that "Khrushchev's fall provides . . . an important precedent for the future," Brzezinski underestimated the extent to which the Soviet system still permitted the leader of the CPSU to consolidate individual power, achieving a status as something more than simply *primus inter pares*. Although a form of "collective leadership" did exist for the first several years after Khrushchev's ouster, Leonid Brezhnev as the CPSU general secretary was always the preeminent leader and gradually removed his chief rivals, establishing a dominant position and dying in office after eighteen years. As Myron Rush pointed out at the time and later, the highly centralized nature of the Soviet polity and the lack of institutionalized succession procedures gave Brezhnev and those who came after him the ability to take steps to forestall any repetition of the conspiracy that resulted in Khrushchev's downfall.[5] Because Brzezinski (in generalizing from Khrushchev's dismissal) mistakenly viewed the leadership contest in Moscow in the early post-Khrushchev era as nothing more than "a protracted bureaucratic struggle" and a "depersonalized political conflict," he neglected the aspects of the system that still allowed power to be concentrated in the hands of a single leader. Brzezinski argued that the emergence of "an increasingly secure 'counter-elite' is likely to make it more difficult for a leader to consolidate his power," but events during the Brezhnev years contravened this assertion. The "counter-elite" were not actually as "secure" as Brzezinski had claimed, and the consolidation of power by a single leader, far from being "more difficult" than it had been for Khrushchev, was in many ways easier. After seeing what had happened to Khrushchev, Brezhnev and his successors knew they must be on their guard and must head off any similar challenges to their own power.

Fourth, Brzezinski's analysis reflected and built on an eclectic mix of academic currents. His emphasis on the emerging divide between Soviet society and the Soviet regime reflected the approach to political order devised in the mid-1960s by Samuel Huntington, who subsequently brought together many of his ideas in his 1968 book, *Political Order in Changing Societies*. (Brzezinski and Huntington were close friends and had coauthored a book comparing the US and Soviet political systems.) Huntington argued that modernizing societies, as measured by higher rates of literacy, education, urbanization, industrialization, economic growth, mass media coverage, and other indicators, were apt to be plagued by political instability and violence unless strong political institutions were in place to maintain order. Brzezinski's argument about the Soviet Union reflected precisely this dynamic—the emergence of what he saw as a dangerous gulf between the Soviet regime and Soviet society. Brzezinski's thesis was also consonant with the work being done by scholars who sought to elucidate the de-radicalization of erstwhile revolutionary regimes. Because China at the time was immersed in its chaotically violent Cultural Revolution, the contrast between Mao Zedong's revolutionary upheavals and the relative conservatism of the Soviet regime was striking. Some scholars such as Richard Löwenthal argued that unless a Soviet-style regime was willing to impose repeated "revolutions from above" (as Mao was doing in China), new social stratifications resulting from economic development would induce key individuals and groups to try to solidify their advantages, causing a gradual move away from proclaimed utopian goals.[6] Brzezinski's analysis was compatible with Löwenthal's, although Brzezinski went further in pointing out that the entrenchment of these new centers of social power (especially within the CPSU's highest organs and central apparatus) was one of the greatest barriers to political modernization and economic flexibility in the USSR.

Fifth, much of what Brzezinski wrote about the Soviet Union in the late 1960s and afterward, including his emphasis on the political and ideological stagnation of the Soviet system, the elimination of mass terror, the growing inability of Soviet leaders to contend with Soviet society, and the changing nature of Soviet leadership dynamics, eliminated core elements of the totalitarian model, essentially marking the de facto abandonment of that model except as an ideal-type of the brutal dictatorship fashioned by Stalin. Robert Tucker in a 1965 article argued that the changes in Soviet politics after Stalin's death meant that the system "should be pronounced, at least provisionally, post-totalitarian."[7] Brzezinski by that time clearly agreed with this sentiment. As he later explained, he had come to see totalitarianism as "a particular phase in the system-society relationship in which the society is in almost complete subordination to the state. That phase may or may not persist for too long, depending on circumstances."[8] In the case of the USSR, he specifically dated this totalitarian period from 1929 to 1953. After Stalin's death, the "limited retraction of political control over society and the surfacing of societal pressures from below" had, he argued, moved the Soviet Union into a post-totalitarian phase.[9] Thus, long before the so-called revisionist critiques of the totalitarian model appeared in the late 1970s and 1980s, the proponents of totalitarianism had acknowledged that the model, even as an ideal-type, was unsuitable for analyzing the post-Stalin Soviet Union.

THE OBSTACLES TO CHANGE IN THE USSR

Brzezinski returned to many of these issues in a lengthy chapter in his 1970 book, *Between Two Ages*. The book, building on an article he published in *Encounter* two years earlier, explored the nature of the "technetronic" age (an age in which society "is shaped culturally, psychologically, socially, and economically by the impact of technology and electronics, particularly in the area of computers and communications"), the role of the United States in the world, the changing nature of political beliefs and ideologies, and the major challenges facing the United States.[10] Foremost among these challenges overseas was the Cold War competition with the Soviet bloc, and Brzezinski therefore devoted seventy pages to an assessment of the USSR and other Communist countries in the aftermath of the August 1968 invasion of Czechoslovakia.

His diagnosis of the fundamental problems confronting the Soviet regime was largely along the lines of his earlier critique, but in addition to analyzing trends in Soviet power, he provided a comparison with Western countries (a comparison distinctly unfavorable for the USSR) and laid out several scenarios of where the Soviet Union might be heading.[11] Brzezinski credited the CPSU with the "unique achievement" of "transforming the most revolutionary doctrine of our age into dull social and political orthodoxy." He contended that the Soviet political system, being both "highly centralized but arrested in its development," had come to be perceived within the USSR as "increasingly irrelevant to the needs of Soviet society [and] frozen in an ideological posture that was a response to an altogether different age." The polity, he argued, had "become the principal impediment to the country's further evolution," causing "the relationship between the political system and the society [to] become dysfunctional." He predicted that the Soviet regime would find it "ideologically more and more difficult to justify" the "continued subordination [of Soviet society] to a political system embodying increasingly sterile nineteenth-century doctrines."

Brzezinski stressed what he saw as the increasingly adverse position of the Soviet Union relative to the United States, especially in overall economic strength. The "absolute gap between the two countries," he argued, "will widen even further." Soviet economic advances, he believed, would be "insufficient to satisfy the ideological ambitions of the political elite" or "to satisfy rising social aspirations" — aspirations that were "certain to escalate as comparison with the West makes it more and more apparent that major sectors of Soviet society have remained extraordinarily antiquated." Brzezinski averred that "Soviet backwardness is particularly evident in agriculture" and other areas suitable for the technetronic age. The Soviet Union, he pointed out, "has not been able to produce technologically advanced products capable of penetrating economically rewarding world markets in the face of Western competition" or to sate "more than the rudimentary needs of domestic consumption." He emphasized the shortcomings of Soviet scientific research outside the military sphere: "The Soviet lag is unmistakable in computers, transistors, lasers, pulsars, and plastics, as well as in the equally important areas of management techniques, labor relations, psychology, sociology, economic theory, and systems analysis." Brzezinski concluded that the "ideological-political centralization" of the Soviet system, which stifled innovation and resulted in a high degree of intellectual conformity, had produced science polices that were at best "capricious" and at worst "catastrophic."

After highlighting the deep-rooted problems facing the Soviet Union, Brzezinski laid out five "alternative paths" or "developmental variants" of the USSR's future course:

1. Oligarchic Petrification: The CPSU's highest organs would retain their dominant "political control over society without attempting to impose major innovations." This "conservative policy [would likely be] masked by revolutionary slogans," but essentially it would amount to a continuation of the status quo.
2. Pluralist Evolution: The CPSU would become a "less monolithic body" and would be "willing to tolerate within its own ranks an open ideological dialogue, even ferment." The party "would cease to view its own ideological pronouncements as infallible" and would instead be a "source of innovation and change."
3. Technological Adaptation: The CPSU would become "a party of technocrats," with a premium on "scientific expertise, efficiency, and discipline." The party would use "cybernetics and computers for social control" and rely on "scientific innovation for the preservation of Soviet security and industrial growth."
4. Militant Fundamentalism: The CPSU would revert to Marxist-Leninist orthodoxy and embark on policies analogous to Mao's Cultural Revolution in China. Even though the Soviet Union might not fall back into Stalinist mass terror or be engulfed by chaotic violence as in China, the hardline reorientation of the Soviet system "in all probability . . . would necessitate the application of force to overcome both actual resistance and sheer social inertia."
5. Political Disintegration: The CPSU would increasingly lose its influence over society in the face of "internal paralysis in the ruling elite, the rising self-assertiveness of various key groups within it, splits in the armed forces, restiveness among the young people and the intellectuals, and open disaffection among the non-Russian nationalities." Having lost faith in the "petrified ideology" of Marxism-Leninism, Soviet leaders would be unable to devise "a coherent set of values for concerted action" to avert a systemic crisis.[12]

Brzezinski averred that "the Soviet leadership will seek to strike a balance between the first and the third variants"—that is, the CPSU Polit-buro would try to maintain the political status quo overall but would integrate larger numbers of technical experts into key positions in the party apparatus, creating "a novel kind of 'technetronic communism.'" Brzezinski did not venture to surmise the long-term future of the Soviet Union, focusing instead on "the near future," "the 1970s," and "approxi-mately a decade ahead." He asserted that "in the short run, development toward a pluralist, ideologically more tolerant system [in the USSR] does not seem likely," in part because the Soviet "political system is not in the near future likely to elevate to leadership a man with the will and the power to democratize Soviet society," and in part because Soviet "society lacks the cohesion and the group pressures necessary to effect democrat-ization from below." In Brzezinski's view, "the Soviet problem with non-Russian nationalities" was a further crucial impediment to democratiza-tion because "the Great Russian majority would inevitably fear that de-mocratization might stimulate the desire of the non-Russian peoples first for more autonomy and then for independence."

In predicting that "the thrust of Soviet social development and the interests of the present ruling elite" made it "unlikely that an effective democratizing coalition could emerge," Brzezinski indicated that he was talking only about "the 1970s." He hinted that a modicum of liberaliza-tion might be feasible in the 1980s after the leaders of Brezhnev's genera-tion passed from the scene. "It is quite possible," he wrote, "that the emerging political elite will be less committed to the notion that social development requires intense concentration of political power." Howev-er, he did not expect liberalization to proceed very far because "evolution into a pluralist system is likely to be resisted by the entrenched political oligarchy." He concluded that unless a Soviet leader came along who was truly committed to "a major transformation of the system as a whole"—something Brzezinski regarded as highly unlikely—"the more probable pattern for the 1980s is a marginal shift toward [a] combination of the second (pluralist evolution) and third (technological adaptation) variants: limited economic-political pluralism and intense emphasis on technologi-cal competence, within the context of a still authoritarian government." Whether this limited shift would be enough to keep the system from being permanently mired in "oligarchic petrification" was doubtful.

Brzezinski saw a reversion to "militant fundamentalism under a one-man dictatorship" as "somewhat more probable than a pluralist evolu-tion," but he did not regard it as especially likely because a dictator attempting to consolidate a militantly ideological regime "would have to overcome enormous inertia and the collective stake of the party oligarchs in preventing the reappearance of one-man rule." Although Brzezinski believed that "the fundamentalist alternative should not be dismissed out of hand, especially if it becomes the only alternative to political disintegration resulting from the petrification of the system" or if a Sino-Soviet war erupted (a scenario adumbrated by the armed clashes along the Sino-Soviet border in 1969), he did not expect a militant fundamentalist regime to be able to gain ascendance in the absence of such extreme circumstances. His bottom line was that with "the conditions prevailing in the early 1970s," the most likely outcome was "oligarchic petrification" combined with some degree of a "'technologization' of the Soviet political system," which would not alter the basic political contours of the USSR.

The broad thrust of Brzezinski's analysis was borne out in the 1970s and early 1980s when the Soviet polity seemed stuck in an ossified, gerontocratic mold, particularly during the final years under Leonid Brezhnev and the brief period under Konstantin Chernenko. Brzezinski accurately highlighted the formidable obstacles to far-reaching change. He did not anticipate the eventual emergence of Gorbachev and the dramatic changes that resulted, but *Between Two Ages* did not wholly foreclose that outcome. Although Brzezinski believed that the advent of genuine democratization and of "a domestic phase of open intellectual creativity and experimentation" was unlikely at best, he never ruled out the possibility. Moreover, he correctly specified the consequences that would ensue from "a transformation of the [Soviet] system."

Brzezinski was less astute, however, in foreseeing the way meaningful political change in the USSR might come about. He argued that change would be spurred by social unrest, including student protests akin to those in many countries around the world in the late 1960s and early 1970s. Brzezinski claimed that "the 1970s will witness the spread to the Soviet Union of convulsions similar to those that Spain, Yugoslavia, Mexico, and Poland began to undergo in the late 1960s." He believed that "more visible social and political tensions," especially "student unrest," would be the only thing that could spur the country's leaders to embark on a truly different course. None of this actually happened, however. No significant student protests occurred in the Soviet Union prior to the Gorbachev era, and in general Soviet society remained surprisingly quiescent throughout the 1970s and early 1980s. Even during the heyday of Solidarity in Poland in 1980–1981, the unrest did not spill over into the Soviet Union more than a very limited amount. Stephen Kotkin has aptly noted that when Gorbachev took office in March 1985, "the Soviet Union was not in turmoil. Nationalist separatism existed, but it did not remotely threaten the Soviet order. The KGB [had] crushed the small dissident movement. The enormous intelligentsia griped incessantly, but it enjoyed massive state subsidies manipulated to promote overall loyalty."[13] Brzezinski's contention that major change in the Soviet Union would come only in response to growing social pressure had the causal arrow pointing in the wrong direction. What actually happened is that far-reaching liberalization during the Gorbachev years paved the way for protests and mass unrest, not the other way around.

One final small point about the analysis in *Between Two Ages* is worth noting. Brzezinski's proposition that Russian concerns about maintaining control over Soviet nationalities militated against democratization in the Soviet Union was a striking foreshadow of the view expressed in the late 1970s and 1980s by Jerry Hough, who repeatedly argued that "the multinational character of the Soviet Union" would preclude "any evolution toward constitutional democracy" in the USSR. In a textbook published in 1979, Hough asserted that Soviet leaders necessarily feared that sweeping liberalization would stimulate the rise of separatist movements in the non-Russian republics and that this in turn would provoke a Russian nationalist backlash. The mere threat of such a development, Hough insisted, deterred Soviet officials from considering the option of genuine democratization. "Even if a Russian prefers democratization for himself, he must know—perhaps unconsciously—that such a development might well produce a major decline in the world position of Russia. . . . [One] can well imagine the normal Russian reaction to the thought of the loss of so much of the country." [14] This line of reasoning essentially reiterated what Brzezinski had argued nearly a decade earlier. The emergence of mass separatist movements in several Soviet republics in the late 1980s after Gorbachev introduced far-reaching political liberalization bore out much of Brzezinski's assessment, with the main exception that he had overestimated the potential for a "Great Russian majority" backlash.

The fact that mass separatist movements emerged in Lithuania, Latvia, Estonia, Moldova, and Georgia does not necessarily mean that the Soviet Union could not have survived genuine democratization. Timely concessions, deal-cutting, and side-payments by Gorbachev might have altered the dynamic in his favor. The Soviet state would have ended up slightly smaller with the loss of several small republics but would still have existed. Instead of responding in this way, however, Gorbachev declined to grant independence to any republic. His unwillingness to brook the loss of even the smallest Soviet republics constrained his leeway for action and was perhaps a reflection of the sentiment to which Brzezinski was alluding.

ASSESSING THE FAILURE OF COMMUNISM

In the latter half of the 1980s, after Brzezinski had served four years as national security adviser in the Carter administration and had written an illuminating memoir of that period, he returned to his longstanding interest in analyzing Soviet-style regimes. The tenor of his assessments of the Soviet political system in the 1980s reflected the important events that were under way but also hewed closely to the themes he had developed in the late 1960s and early 1970s. The advent of Gorbachev and the dramatic changes that followed gave Brzezinski an opportunity to reflect anew on the innate deficiencies of Leninist systems.

The publication of Brzezinski's *The Grand Failure* in 1989 brought him full circle to where he had begun in 1960 with his landmark book *The Soviet Bloc*.[15] In that earlier work, which remains a classic more than half a century after its appearance, Brzezinski traced the shift away from a relatively monolithic Soviet bloc toward a diverse and increasingly fractious Communist world.[16] Not only did he explore the Soviet rift with Yugoslavia during the Stalin era and (in the revised 1967 edition) the bitter splits between the USSR and China and Albania under Khrushchev, he also traced the process of "de-satellitization" whereby the East European countries moved from a position of near-total subordination to Soviet power during the Stalin era to a less subservient and at times refractory posture vis-à-vis the USSR after Stalin's death.

By the time Brzezinski was working on *The Grand Failure*, relations between the Soviet Union and the rest of the Soviet bloc were undergoing momentous change. Events that had seemed inconceivable when he wrote *The Soviet Bloc* had suddenly become routine. The bounds of Soviet tolerance had not yet been fully tested, but the leeway for political liberalization and even democratization in Eastern Europe and the USSR had expanded so much that it gave Brzezinski freer rein to talk about the utter failure of Marxism-Leninism. The book, completed in August 1988, predicted that "by the next century communism's irreversible historical decline will have made its practice and its dogma largely irrelevant to the human condition" and "communism will be remembered largely as the twentieth century's most extraordinary political and intellectual aberration."[17] One of the major themes in the book, developed especially in the first several chapters and the final several chapters (sometimes with considerable repetition, which an editor should have weeded out), is that "the key to communism's historic tragedy is the political and socioeconomic failure of the Soviet system." Brzezinski's analysis of this issue echoed his earlier writings on the subject from the mid-1960s on, supplemented by some crisp judgments about events connected with Gorbachev's reforms and the changes that ensued. Brzezinski traced the origins of Soviet Communism's decline back through Soviet history, showing how the extreme concentration of power under ruthless Bolshevik leaders, especially Stalin, had spawned a political system that long defied any attempts at genuine, lasting liberalization, much less wholesale transformation. "The terminal crisis of contemporary communism," he wrote, "is thus all the more historically dramatic for the very suddenness of its onset."

Brzezinski's assessment of Gorbachev's prospects touched on the economic and social dimensions of the crisis, but above all he stressed the multiethnic configuration of the Soviet Union, an issue he had been highlighting since the 1960s. Describing the "national problem" as the

"Achilles' heel of perestroika," Brzezinski argued that the longstanding dominance of the "Great Russian majority" in the USSR had created an intractable situation. "Genuine decentralization," he maintained, "would inevitably breed demands" in non-Russian republics for equitable treatment, but "central Russian control is so deeply embedded in existing arrangements that the needed corrective would require a massive upheaval." The result, in his view, was a "vicious circle," whereby the "lack of reforms breeds national resentments, but reforms would probably nourish an even greater appetite among the non-Russians for more power." In particular, he expected that "separatist attitudes" would surface promptly "among the Balts and the Soviet Moslems, the latter stimulated by the worldwide resurgence of Islam and the Soviet military failure in Afghanistan." Overtly separatist movements did indeed arise in the Baltic republics early on (in fact, they were already surfacing when Brzezinski was writing), but his prediction that Soviet Muslims would be at the forefront of the independence movements was unfounded. No separatist movements arose at any point in the USSR's Central Asian republics, all of which sought to remain part of the Soviet Union until the very end.

Brzezinski surmised that the intractability of the nationalities question would most likely doom the larger program undertaken by Gorbachev:

> Great Russian fears of growing nationalist conflicts, by impeding the needed reforms, enhance the likelihood that the real prospect for Soviet communism is debilitating decay and not constructive evolution. A truly renovating success — one that results in a creative, innovative, and self-energizing Soviet society — could only happen through the dilution of doctrine, the dispersal of the party's power, and the gradual emancipation of the non-Russians from Moscow's centralized control. It is highly improbable that the party leadership and the ruling elite, no matter how eager for an economic revival, will be prepared to risk going politically that far.

Because public expectations in the Soviet Union had been steadily rising during the Gorbachev period, Brzezinski averred that a possible attempt to clamp down would create an "inherently explosive" and "potentially revolutionary situation." This in turn led him to expect "a progressive breakdown of order [that] could lead eventually to a coup at the center, undertaken by the military, with KGB backing" — a scenario that materialized largely along these lines with the abortive coup d'état in the USSR in August 1991.

Brzezinski also looked in some detail at the changing status of Communism in Eastern Europe and China. Following up on the text of his Hugh Seton-Watson Memorial Lecture at the Centre for Policy Studies in January 1988,[18] he rightly characterized "Marxism-Leninism [as] an alien doctrine imposed on the region by an imperial power whose rule is culturally repugnant to the dominated peoples."[19] Brzezinski argued that changes under way in the Soviet bloc amounted to "the organic rejection by the social system of an alien transplant. . . . The alien system, grafted on by force from outside, is being repudiated by the social organism." This process, Brzezinski argued, was potentially destabilizing because the region was undergoing "both political liberalization and economic retrogression, a classic formula . . . for revolution." In his memorial lecture, Brzezinski claimed that five of the six East European Warsaw Pact countries (East Germany was the exception) were "ripe for revolutionary explosion." [20] He expressed concern that Soviet troops would intervene if "a massive social explosion" occurred in one or more East European countries, and he therefore underscored the importance of seeking "gradual change" in Eastern Europe that would avert a violent upheaval:

> I do not believe for a minute that a massive revolutionary upheaval in the region is in our interest. Were that to occur in the foreseeable future, I still believe, despite what [Alexander] Dubček has said in his recent interview, that the Soviet Union would have no choice but to intervene. It is almost equally certain that the West would impotently stand by, and that reform in the region and perestroika in the Soviet Union would be the victims. Thus, I do not believe that an explosion is something which we should be fomenting, or simply waiting for, or welcoming. Gradual change, I think, is desirable. It should be encouraged. It should be facilitated, and it is feasible. [21]

In the lecture (though not subsequently in *The Grand Failure*), Brzezinski urged a cautious Western strategy that would avoid the impression of trying to bring the East European countries into the Western camp. "Our strategic and historical goal should not be the absorption of what was once called Eastern Europe into what is still called Western Europe." Instead, he called for "the progressive emergence of a truly independent, culturally authentic, perhaps *de facto* neutral Central Europe." He emphasized that he was not proposing the elimination of the Warsaw Pact or the removal of Soviet troops: "When I say *de facto* neutral, I mean mainly neutral in substance but not neutral in form. This would emerge in the context of the continued existence of the alliance systems that define the geo-political reality of contemporary Europe." [22]

Brzezinski's proposed course of action for US policy toward the Soviet bloc in his January 1988 lecture was similar to what some other observers were contemplating at the time. As late as January 1989, when Henry Kissinger met in an unofficial capacity with Soviet leaders in Moscow, he tactfully broached the possibility of a superpower accord regarding the neutralization of Eastern Europe, implying that the incoming administration of George H. W. Bush might be interested. [23] (Gorbachev, however, declined to pursue the matter.) Nonetheless, events in the region were moving so fast that Brzezinski did not include a similar strategy in *The Grand Failure*, a decision that proved wise. By refraining from offering

policy recommendations, Brzezinski kept the book from being immediately overtaken by events. Even though he underestimated how rapidly
and decisively Communism would collapse in Eastern Europe, his diagnosis of the emerging crisis in the region and its connection with the
fundamental crisis in the USSR held up well overall.

Similarly, Brzezinski was largely accurate in predicting that the economic reforms undertaken in China, unlike those in the Soviet Union,
were "probably fated to be successful."[24] In four brief chapters, which are
the most innovative part of the book, he gave a cogent assessment of the
changes unfolding in China under Deng Xiaoping. Brzezinski claimed
that Deng's willingness to dismantle China's collective farms and to allow peasants to grow their own products "carried profound ideological
consequences" in a country like China, which was overwhelmingly
agrarian when the reforms began. Brzezinski went so far as to claim that
the agricultural reform was so important that it "meant that the overwhelming majority of the Chinese people [i.e., peasants] had ceased to
live within a communist framework." This particular assertion may be
problematic, but Brzezinski was on solid ground in pointing out that
Deng's economic "reforms went further than those of the Soviet Union"
not only in agriculture but also in "urban and rural industry, in foreign
trade, in foreign investment, in consumer goods, and in private enterprise. . . . Last but not least, unlike the Soviet Union, China made significant cuts in the size of the army and in defense expenditures."

The Grand Failure appeared before mass protests began in China in the
spring of 1989 and before the brutal crackdown in Beijing in early June
1989. The latter event belied Brzezinski's contention that "centralized political control" would steadily diminish "as China's overall economic
power expanded." In fact, what has happened in China from 1980 to the
present has defied all expectations, combining rapid economic growth
sustained over three-and-a-half decades with a political system that remains tightly under the control of the Communist Party founded by Mao
Zedong. Institutional modernization theory would indeed have led one
to expect in the late 1980s that a burgeoning middle class in China would
eventually push for democratization, but so far that has not happened in
the wake of the Tiananmen Square massacre. Even though Brzezinski
(like almost everyone else) underestimated the Communist regime's ability to preserve tight political control in China, other aspects of Brzezinski's assessment have been borne out remarkably well.

The chief prediction in *The Grand Failure*—that Communism was in its
"final agony" and would be gone by the end of the twentieth century—
was largely, though not wholly, correct. The Soviet regime and all Communist regimes in Europe, including the Albanian and Yugoslavian, collapsed, as did the Mongolian regime. Elsewhere, however, Communist
systems survived. North Korea, Cuba, China, Vietnam, and Laos remain
Communist to this day. One can debate the extent to which China and

Vietnam remain truly Communist in light of their adoption of important capitalist reforms and institutions (a few of which are now also being slowly adopted in Cuba), but there is no denying that they remain repressive, one-party dictatorships headed by Communist rulers. Hence, even though Communism in most parts of the world, especially Europe, has been thoroughly discredited and will not be revived, the system does remain extant in five countries containing roughly one-quarter of the world's population, far more people than in the more numerous countries in which Communist regimes once held power but ceased to exist after the events of 1989 to 1991.

CONCLUSION

When Zbigniew Brzezinski began studying the Soviet Union in the early 1950s, the Soviet regime seemed destined to stay in power indefinitely. The USSR enjoyed substantial prestige from its major role in the victory over Germany in World War II. Under Soviet auspices, Communist rule had spread into Eastern Europe and East Asia, bringing nearly one-third of the world's population under the sway of Soviet-style regimes loyal to Moscow. Many newly independent countries in the developing world looked to the Soviet Union as a natural ally against the West, and the leaders of those countries were often attracted by the Soviet state-led model of development. The USSR seemed to be increasingly on a par with the United States in overall power.

After Stalin's death, however, fissures began to emerge within the Communist bloc, and by the end of the 1950s a bitter rift had opened between the Soviet Union and China. Internally as well, the challenges facing the Soviet regime multiplied. As Brzezinski observed these shifts in the 1960s, he focused on the stultifying impact of the Soviet bureaucracy, which seemed to be depriving Soviet Marxist-Leninist ideology of all its vitality. The theme Brzezinski developed in his 1966 "Problems of Communism" article and his companion book, *Dilemmas of Change in Soviet Politics*—that the Soviet Union would undergo either transformation or degeneration—remained at the heart of his inquiries over the next two-and-a-half decades.

Brzezinski's publications analyzing the Soviet political system from the mid-1960s through the late 1980s, especially the work he produced before he served as national security adviser, were perspicacious and nuanced, reflecting an impressive grasp of Soviet and Russian history and culture and the nature of Communist regimes elsewhere in the world. Although Brzezinski only rarely made explicit use of political science techniques that could shed light on the Soviet system, he took account of some theoretical discussions and incorporated their assumptions into his work. Brzezinski's basic ideas and arguments remained consistent over time, though he suitably adapted them as conditions markedly changed. He pinpointed the systemic weaknesses of the Soviet Union and Soviet-style regimes early on, and this helped him in the late 1980s to understand the depth of the crisis facing Soviet-style Communism. His books and essays after he had served as national security adviser were intended for popular audiences, but most of these writings, especially *The Grand Failure*, also contained insights useful for experts. Brzezinski's analyses over time cogently explained how the Soviet Union's fortunes had deteriorated so sharply from the 1950s, when the USSR seemed to be the major ascendant power in the world with a chance of eclipsing the United States, to the early 1990s, when Gorbachev's efforts to prevent the Soviet Union from falling into a steep decline proved counterproductive and hastened the final crisis and disintegration of the Soviet system.

Even though some aspects of Brzezinski's writings about the USSR were not borne out in the end, his assessments of Soviet history and politics were (and are) convincing on many key points. Brzezinski nowadays is well known mostly for his governmental service and public commentary on US foreign policy and international affairs, and his appraisals of the Soviet political system in the 1960s and early 1970s have been largely forgotten. That is a shame because anyone who takes the time to re-read (or read for the first time) Brzezinski's analyses of the Soviet system will find them a rich, provocative, stimulating source.

NOTES

1. Zbigniew Brzezinski, "The Soviet Political System: Transformation or Degeneration," *Problems of Communism*, vol. XV, no. 1 (January-February 1966): 1–15.
2. Zbigniew Brzezinski, ed., *Dilemmas of Change in Soviet Politics* (New York: Columbia University Press, 1969).
3. All quotations here are from Brzezinski's essays in ibid.
4. Brzezinski, "Concluding Reflections," 160–61.
5. Myron Rush, *Political Succession in the USSR* (New York: Columbia University Press, 1965); Myron Rush, *How Communist States Change Their Rulers* (Ithaca, NY: Cornell University Press, 1974); and Myron Rush, "The Soviet Military Buildup and the Coming Succession," *International Security*, vol. 5, no. 4 (Spring 1981): 169–185.
6. Richard Löwenthal, "Development vs. Utopia in Communist Policy," in Chalmers A. Johnson, ed., *Change in Communist Systems* (Stanford, CA: Stanford University Press, 1970), 33–116.
7. Robert C. Tucker, "The Dictator and Totalitarianism," *World Politics*, vol. 17, no. 4 (July 1965): 555–83.
8. Zbigniew Brzezinski, "Soviet Politics: From the Future to the Past," in Paul Cocks, Robert V. Daniels, and Nancy Whittier Heer, eds., *The Dynamics of Soviet Politics* (Cambridge, MA: Harvard University Press, 1976), 341.
9. Ibid., 341–42.
10. Zbigniew Brzezinski, *Between Two Ages: America's Role in the Technetronic Era* (New York: The Viking Press, 1970). For the earlier article, see Zbigniew Brzezinski, "America in the Technetronic Age," *Encounter*, vol. XXX, no. 1 (January 1968): 16–26.

11. Unless otherwise indicated, quotations here are from Brzezinski, *Between Two Ages*.

12. Ibid., 164–66.

13. Stephen Kotkin, *Armageddon Averted: The Soviet Collapse, 1970–2000* (New York: Oxford University Press, 2001), 27.

14. Jerry F. Hough and Merle Fainsod, *How the Soviet Union Is Governed* (Cambridge, MA: Harvard University Press, 1979).

15. Zbigniew Brzezinski, *The Grand Failure: The Birth and Death of Communism in the Twentieth Century* (New York: Charles Scribner's Sons, 1989).

16. Zbigniew Brzezinski, *The Soviet Bloc: Unity and Conflict* (Cambridge, MA: Harvard University Press, 1960). A revised and expanded edition was published in 1967.

17. Unless otherwise indicated, all quotations here are from Brzezinski, *The Grand Failure*.

18. Zbigniew Brzezinski, "From Eastern Europe back to Central Europe," in Centre for Policy Studies, *A Year in the Life of Glasnost: The Hugh Seton-Watson Memorial Lecture and Other Essays*, Policy Study no. 94 (London: CPS, 1988): 6–18.

19. Brzezinski, *The Grand Failure*, 105.

20. Brzezinski, "From Eastern Europe back to Central Europe," 14.

21. Ibid., 15.

22. Ibid., 15–16.

23. On this episode, see Mark Kramer, "The Demise of the Soviet Bloc," *Journal of Modern History*, vol. 83, no. 4 (December 2011): 816–17.

24. All quotations here are from Brzezinski, *The Grand Failure*.

BIBLIOGRAPHY

Brzezinski, Zbigniew. *The Grand Failure: The Birth and Death of Communism in the Twentieth Century*. New York: Charles Scribner's Sons, 1989.

———. "From Eastern Europe back to Central Europe." In Centre for Policy Studies, *A Year in the Life of Glasnost: The Hugh Seton-Watson Memorial Lecture and Other Essays*, Policy Study no. 94 (London: CPS, 1988): 6–18.

———. "Soviet Politics: From the Future to the Past." In Paul Cocks, Robert V. Daniels, and Nancy Whittier Heer, eds., *The Dynamics of Soviet Politics*, Cambridge, MA: Harvard University Press, 1976, 337–54.

———. *Between Two Ages: America's Role in the Technetronic Era*. New York: The Viking Press, 1970.

———, ed. *Dilemmas of Change in Soviet Politics*. New York: Columbia University Press, 1969.

———. "America in the Technetronic Age," *Encounter*, vol. XXX, no. 1 (January 1968): 16–26.

———. "The Soviet Political System: Transformation or Degeneration," *Problems of Communism*, vol. XV, no. 1 (January-February 1966): 1–15.

———. *The Soviet Bloc: Unity and Conflict*. Cambridge, MA: Harvard University Press, 1960.

Hough, Jerry F., and Merle Fainsod. *How the Soviet Union Is Governed*. Cambridge, MA: Harvard University Press, 1979.

Kotkin, Stephen. *Armageddon Averted: The Soviet Collapse, 1970–2000*. New York: Oxford University Press, 2001.

Kramer, Mark. "The Demise of the Soviet Bloc," *Journal of Modern History*, vol. 83, no. 4 (December 2011), 786–854.

Löwenthal, Richard. "Development vs. Utopia in Communist Policy." In Chalmers A. Johnson, ed., *Change in Communist Systems*, 33–116. Stanford, CA: Stanford University Press, 1970.

Rush, Myron. "The Soviet Military Buildup and the Coming Succession," *International Security*, vol. 5, no. 4 (Spring 1981): 169–85.

———. *How Communist States Change Their Rulers*. Ithaca, NY: Cornell University Press, 1974.

———. *Political Succession in the USSR*. New York: Columbia University Press, 1965.

Tucker, Robert C. "The Dictator and Totalitarianism," *World Politics*, vol. 17, no. 4 (July 1965): 555–83.

EIGHT

The Pedagogy of Patriotism

America and Americans in Soviet Children's Literature

Milla Fedorova

The famous Soviet utopic project, the creation of the new man, primarily targeted children and youth. As one of the characters in Andrei Platonov's *Foundation Pit* explains to an orphaned girl, "there's no knowing what will become of you—but it's clear that nothing's going to become of us has-beens."[1] In order to shape young people, this project required a definition of the new Soviet identity. However, the set of desired qualities, while featuring a distinctive core—commitment to the working collective—was not set in stone immediately after the October Revolution and the Civil War, but rather underwent substantial changes over the Soviet state's history. A dynamic relationship between the concepts of internationalism and patriotism provides the most noticeable example of the changing Soviet values.

In the 1920s promoting the spirit of internationalism was considered one of the Soviet Union's major educational tasks. In his speech at the Third Congress of Komsomol, Lenin named collectivism, internationalism, and new solidarity as the guiding principles for the upbringing of Soviet youth.[2] In the 1930s, however, a major ideological turn took place: as the dream of world revolution subsided, replaced by the theory of building socialism in one separate country, the accent was shifted from internationalism to patriotism. As Catriona Kelly notes, Soviet media in the 1930s represented the Soviet Union as a model of the world in miniature, reorienting the idea of internationalism inward and positing it as a friendship of different nations inside the Soviet Union.[3] Internationalism

121

in a broad sense returned to the stage after World War II when, subordinated to patriotism, it took paradoxical forms in the political context of the Cold War.

The concept of America and Americans played a significant role as the point of departure in the Soviet construction of its new self-identity: in order to define what the new man was, the ideologists had to delineate what he was not.[4] After the revolution, Soviet attitude regarding the United States exhibited a complex combination of inferiority and superiority complexes, reflected in the famous motto "to catch up with and surpass America."[5] While the admittance of temporary inferiority was based on America's technological advancement and high standards of daily life, the ethical and historical superiority of the socialist country over a capitalist one was universal: the superiority of the future over the past. The 1920s, the era of internationalism, demonstrated "Soviet romance" with America and the readiness to borrow and learn from her in multiple spheres, from mass culture to methods of factory organization. However, in the "patriotic" 1930s, despite the fact that the Soviet Union and the United States finally established diplomatic relations (in 1933), the image of America as the ideological adversary, the epitome of capitalism, solidified. Since then, except for a short period of collaboration in the struggle against Nazi Germany, Soviet patriotism included a strong anti-American aspect. Anti-Americanism as a flipside of patriotism became especially evident during the Cold War.

School and literature became the main venues for promoting the complex of Soviet values among youth and shaping the new Soviet man. As scholars of Soviet children's culture often pointed out, shaping the correct ideology (*vospitanie*) was considered more important than education per se (*obrazovanie*); the former was oriented toward a certain norm, and literature played the leading role in this process. According to Evgenii Dobrenko, Russian Association of Proletarian Writers (RAPP) ideologists claimed that the roles of school and literature in the educational process had much in common: "school should teach how to use a work of literature as an ideological weapon, and the school front should be considered as one of the fronts of the literary politics."[6] However, it would be inaccurate to conflate these roles. While the didactic (*vospitatel'naia*) role of the Soviet school was recognized very early, the necessity of ideological content in children's literature changed over time: in the 1920s a group of scholars fought for the relative independence of literature from the necessity to react immediately to the demands of the party and the historical moment. In the 1930s, together with shifting patriotism to the forefront of educational values and enhancing the anti-American aspect of this concept, children's literature was recognized as an important promoter of socialist ideology. Patriotism was supposed to embrace all age groups, although, of course, its role varied depending on the targeted age group, becoming more aggressive the older a child was. Only in the 1960s did the public demand for non-ideological literature for younger children lead to some changes in book publishing policies.[7] However, it is the era of late 1950s–1960s that witnesses mass emergence of Russian fiction targeted at American racism and the general injustice of the capitalist socialist system.

As we see, a scholar of America's literary image in the context of Soviet patriotic education should take into account the dynamics of the relationship between internationalism and patriotism, the complexity of the image of America and its dependence on the Soviet-American political relationship, as well as the developing pedagogical thought and changing role of children's literature in shaping the "correct" ideology. In any case, establishing the "anti-Americanism" of Soviet literature for youth does not even nearly exhaust the problem. The situation is additionally complicated by the fact that for some writers, the texts' compulsory ideological agenda was merely a cover-up for elaborate personal artistic tasks, as it was, for example, for Nikolai Nosov.[8] In other cases the ambiguity of America's image could emerge in the process of perception, since many texts, as it will be shown later, conveyed more than the authors intended. This article will briefly discuss the specificity of the American theme in literature for youth and in education in each of the abovementioned periods. Then, it will focus on the strategies of shaping America's image during the Cold War, since this period accumulated and refined the existing tendencies.

In the 1920s, young people's reading circles underwent significant transformations, as literature for youth came under the authorities' scrutiny. While in 1921 only thirty-three children's books were published, in 1927 their number reached 475.[9] In 1924 Nadezhda Krupskaia, who curated Soviet library science and education, demanded "the reevaluation of all books kept in public libraries, especially the children's sections."[10] The Americanization of young people's reading, especially young people's obsession with Pinkerton-like spy stories caused serious concerns for ideologists. Although some specialists, such as Anna Kalmykova, Nikolai Chekhov and Elizaveta Beketova questioned the necessity of a direct ideological agenda in children's books, Krupskaia called for the Sovietization of books for children and youth and for the combination of entertainment with educational tasks. Several strategies addressed this demand. Popular American genres were adapted to the needs of the Soviet state: for example, Marietta Shaginian's *Mess-Mend* (1924), a famous example of Red Pinkertonism, recruits the devices of detective stories, cinema, and science fiction to condemn American capitalism and glorify "the creative power of the working class of all countries and nations." In *Mess-Mend*, Shaginian portrays the industrial city of Middletown suffocated by numerous factories belonging to a billionaire named Kressling—a mortal enemy of the young Soviet state, who has to employ various cunning deceits in order to resist the growing power of the workers' magical organization. Shaginian contrasts the polluted American Middletown, from which trees have been banished, and the futuristic utopian Soviet Petrograd, where the chimneys are clean because the factories' smoke is clean, and where industry exists in harmony with nature. Although Shaginian did not posit her novel as children's reading, it gradually migrated to this category.[11] Many texts about America intended for an adult audience were recruited for young readers, such as Gorky's "City of the Yellow Devil," which became part of schools' reading programs. Mayakovsky's American poems underwent a similar transformation: his poem "Black and White" was even adapted by Ivanov-Vano and Amalrik into the eponymous animated film (1932).

Other strategies of resisting the influence of American culture involved control over public libraries. According to a study of readers' interests conducted by libraries for Glavpolitprosvet in 1926–1927, translations of American literature constituted a significant portion of Soviet children's reading: boys listed Thomas Mayne Reid, James Fenimore Cooper, and Mark Twain (together with Jules Verne, Sergei Auslender, and Sergei Grigor'ev) among their favorite authors, and named adventure and journey literature as their reading of choice. Girls preferred sentimental stories; among them such American women authors as Louisa Alcott and Mary Dodge. The most popular books read by both genders included Harriet Beecher Stowe's *Uncle Tom's Cabin*, Twain's *The Prince and the Pauper* and *The Adventures of Tom Sawyer*, as well as Cooper's *Leatherstocking Tales*. Young people of a more mature age preferred Jack London's *Martin Eden* and Upton Sinclair's novels.[12] It is easy to see that most of these titles contained the necessary elements of social criticism combined with entertaining plot, which directly addressed Krupskaia's demands. Libraries tried to weed out undesirable, purely entertaining or excessively sentimental titles. Additionally, librarians worked with readers individually: by providing targeted reading recommendations and through plot "clarification," they made sure that books' social messages would not be missed.

Although, as Evgenii Dobrenko notes, the circle of children's reading was formed by a complex of intertwined factors—the state's censorship ambitions, home reading, personal reading preferences, school programs, and so on—the influence of the state through public libraries and, most importantly, the system of public education, was growing. "School integrated literature for the purposes of the communist upbringing of the rising generation."[13] For a while, pedagogical experimentation with school programs left only a subordinate role to literature: fiction merely illustrated key topics of socioeconomic disciplines. For example, Gorky's "City of the Yellow Devil" (1906) (together with Verhaeren's "City-Octopus" and Pushkin's "Bronze Horseman") illustrated the topic of the city, revealing the class struggle in the bourgeois metropolis.[14]

The internationalism of 1920s directed young Soviet citizens' attention to the plight of youth and the growth of revolutionary consciousness in various countries. Distinctions between different capitalist countries almost disappeared. Thus, the compulsory condemnation of American capitalism did not overshadow the idea of united workers of different nations fighting hand in hand for the victory of global revolution. While the inhuman America of the past was supposed to be left behind, the future utopian America would be indistinguishable from Russia in a victorious, communist world. This is why the lists of texts recommended for study at school included both "The City of the Yellow Devil" and Sergei Budantsev's *The Escadrille of the World Commune* (1925). In Gorky's sketch, New York, the epitome of American urbanism, clearly resembles hell. In Sergei Budantsev's novella, the center of the socialist movement is London, and a joint air fleet of Russian and American plane attacks Madagascar, the last refuge of the world's capitalists: Mussolini and Rockefeller. In less utopian works, the Soviet Union becomes the safe refuge for oppressed workers from foreign countries, including former Russian emigrants. In Rustam Bek Tageev's novel *A Russian American* (1926), the protagonist, a boy from a Russian emigrant family, returns to his native land, where he finds new hope after his father's death from exhaustion at Ford's factory.

By the 1930s the vulgar sociological approach was abandoned, and school programs recognized literature not merely as an illustration of social processes but also as a primary force in transmitting desired social values and norms. In 1933, the publishing house *Detskaia literatura* began its work under full control of the state. Since patriotism had replaced internationalism as an educational task, readers' attentions were refocused on the native land. The stories about young people's lives abroad lost their prominence. The data about children's reading preferences available from the 1930s lacked diversity: according to Dobrenko, it became prescriptive rather than descriptive and presented the image of a pioneer interested primarily in books about his own country.

Soviet ideologists distracted young readers from the exotic wonders of America using strategies similar to those employed in late imperial Russia. As Arustamova notes, some national authors in the second half of the nineteenth century tried to break with the image of America as a dreamland of freedom and the chief destination of flights from home.[15] They tried to attract young readers' attention to the motif of exploring their native land, encouraging them to focus on its beauties and natural wonders.[16] Even in Chekhov's story "The Boys" (1887) the dream about America is associated with guilt, sin, and betrayal of one's family (one might even interpret the name of the seducer who persuades the main hero to flee to America—Chechevitsyn (derived from "lentil")—as an intertextual hint at the motif of selling one's birthright).[17]

Marshak's famous children's poem "Mister Twister" (1933), a satirical account of an American millionaire's journey to Soviet Russia, clearly manifests the ideological transition from internationalism to patriotism. As in Tageev's *A Russian American*, in "Mister Twister" the Soviet Union replaces America as the desirable destination for exploited working people; however, while in the former the narrative focuses on American life, in the latter the main events take place in the Soviet Union. The common folk's paradise turns out to be a personal hell for the racist millionaire. Mister Twister, who at first refuses to stay in the same hotel with people of color, cannot find any place to stay in the Soviet Union and, at the same time, cannot break his vicious circular trajectory and escape it: in his dream, there is "no vacancy" for him, even in America. Unintentionally and ironically, the author portrays the Soviet Union as an isolated, claustrophobic world which has no place for the foreign protagonist. Explicitly contrasting American racism with Soviet internationalism, the poem also subliminally juxtaposes the universe opened to an American traveler by Cook's travel company and the Soviet model of the multinational world on a tiny scale—a hotel crammed with representatives of all nations.

During the Cold War, Marshak reworked "Mister Twister," making the poem less playful and the Soviet world more hostile to his hero. This unintentionally made the Soviet Union more frightening to the reader, who is pulled into Twister's point of view.[18]

After the joint victory in World War II, the image of America as the former ally was recast into the image of the enemy. From 1946 to 1947, the party demanded that Soviet writers produce texts "that would denounce bowing to the West, condemn American imperialism, and glorify the image of a true Russian patriot."[19] As a result, international topics reemerged in children's reading, but the new internationalism hinged on the polarization between socialist and capitalist countries and on the recognition of the Soviet Union's superiority, especially its leading role in

Table 8.1.

If	In the room on the right
You	There is a Chinese,
Are worn out	In the room on the left
With boredom	There is a Malay,
And would like	In the suite above you
To see the world—	There is a Mongol,
The Island of Tahiti,	In the one under you—
Paris and Pamir	A Mulatto and a Creole.[a]
Mountains and mines,	
North and South,	
Palms and cedars	
Will be shown to you by Cook.	

[a] This translation was kindly supplied by Larissa and Richard Pevear.

the "fight for peace." "American texts" by Soviet children's writers usually demonstrated that the value of childhood was not recognized in the capitalist world—by contrast, placing the Soviet Union in the first ranks of modernized countries.[20] While in reality Russia struggled hard to drop children's death rates, improve their living conditions, and reach the level of European countries, in literature it presented itself as the main country where children thrived.[21] The stark contrast between the inhumanly oppressive life of poor American children and the happy childhood of Soviet youth was supposed to make Soviet children feel blessed that they were born in the "right place."

The texts about America and Americans of the Cold War period include novellas and stories written in a realistic manner about the suffering of American youth in America (by Sever Gansovskii, N. Kalma and Gertsel Novogrudskii) and about young Americans' visits to the Soviet Union, usually to pioneer camps like Artek (Mark Efetov's *A Letter on the Turtle's Shell*, Yurii Yakovlev's *Samantha*), along with grotesque fantasies such as sci-fi travelogues locating the capitalist world on an isolated planet (Nosov's *Neznaika on the Moon*), and spy stories (Lev Davydychev's *Hands Up, or the Enemy No. 1*). Grotesque spy stories, apparently influenced by Shaginian's *Mess-Mend*, revived the tradition of Red Pinkertonism of the 1920s.

There were no strict borders between these two stylistic trends. For example, Sever Gansovskii, who is best known as a sci-fi writer, in 1952 published a collection of stories *In the Ranks of Fighters* about the oppression and social struggle of children in America. In these stories he presents America as an inhuman alien world—a technique he later uses in "proper" sci-fi to describe fantastic alien worlds. Contrastingly, Nikolai Nosov is famous as a creator of the new psychological, non-ideological children's prose, but in his *Neznaika* series, he turns to satirical social parable in the form of sci-fi travelogue. In *Neznaika on the Moon* (1965), the young Neznaika and his friends embark on a journey to the America-like moon. After experiencing the injustices of capitalism, they assist in launching the moon revolution. This travelogue, locating the dying capitalist world on an isolated planet, harkens back to the tradition of Aleksei Tolstoy's *Aelita*.[22] Like Tolstoy, Nosov portrays the earth as the default land of socialism—while the Western capitalist civilization exists elsewhere, far from our planet. Later authors of Soviet sci-fi, such as Ivan Efremov in *Bull's Hour* (1968), or the Strugatsky brothers in their "Progressors" cycle, often used this technique, describing a journey of earthlings living in the land of victorious socialism/communism to a socially backward society in the condition of wild capitalism. But while Efremov portrays an abstract society living according to capitalist principles, Nosov's Moon demonstrates easily recognizable American features: it is inhabited by distinctly American capitalists with their cigars, top hats and huge automobiles, just as the satirical magazine *Krokodil* represented them. Ilia Kukulin, analyzing Nosov's tale, comes to conclusion that the author uses the ideological discourse only superficially and subordinates it to his private intricate literary game—creating a motley intertextual patchwork of literary travelogues and sci-fi stories. After all, Nosov's parables investigating socialist and communist towns (the "Flower City" and the "Sun City," respectively) also incorporate numerous satirical, nonpolitically correct details.

Among the subtexts of Nosov's *Neznaika on the Moon* Kukulin lists Ilf and Petrov's picaresque Ostap Bender travelogue (*The Twelve Chairs* and *The Golden Calf*). We can also add to this list Ilf and Petrov's *One-Storied America*: after reading their autobiographical travelogue about the journey to America, many readers suggested that Ilf and Petrov should write about Bender's adventures in *One-Storied America*.[23] Nosov fulfills this request in his own book, making his picaro hero embark on a journey to the American moon. In general, the less-than-human civilizations in Soviet sci-fi and the capitalist American world in "realistic" Soviet literature for children prove to be very similar.

Contrasting the rich and the poor, a technique compulsory for early Soviet children's literature, remained prominent in children's literature about America in the 1950s through the 1970s. Often, American children themselves are associated with the poor, working, and oppressed social elements, while adults figure as oppressors. Gansovskii and N. Kalma portray the social class of poor children as a natural reason for the rising class struggle against the corrupt adults who indulge in drinking and debauchery.[24] By the 1950s, the potential of children-activists' images, so popular in Soviet literature of the 1920s (for instance, in Arkadii Gaidar's and Lev Kassil's texts), was almost exhausted, and young activists "were replaced by happy children gratefully accepting the benefits of the advanced Soviet society" as early as in the "high" Stalin era.[25] However, such images thrived in literature about the capitalist countries, and especially about America: the title of Gansovskii's collection *In the Ranks of Fighters* speaks for itself. For instance, in the story "The Mexicans" from this collection, an Irish boy teaches a Mexican family how to escape from the mighty farmer exploiting seasonal workers. In the end, the boy attacks the farmer who chases the runaways and leads a mini-rebellion of the unemployed.

These courageous and resourceful children suffer from unbearable living conditions. In Gansovskii's stories, most of them are homeless: they wander along hot dusty roads or live under bridges. In N. Kalma's *Black Sally* (1939), poor New York families live in houses constructed of large wooden boxes. But it is not merely the children's poverty that is so striking in these stories. The main propagandistic device the writers use is the appeal to their young readers' acute feelings of justice. Unlike isolated cases of injustice that might occur in family life in Soviet children's literature, the scale of injustice—both personal and social—demonstrated in American texts is outrageous. Usually, an act of injustice becomes the pivotal event in the story or novel. Instead of happy endings or catharsis, children's literature about America systematically presents antimiracle and anticatharsis, constructing the image of a hellish world where it is impossible to exist. When it seems that the protagonist has finally found luck and his or her family's life starts improving, the reader can be sure that it will turn out to be a deception: these children rise from their suffering only to be pushed into deeper misfortune.

In another one of Gansovskii's stories, "The Federal Highway 66," little Tommy, whose family is traveling on foot from Texas to California, walks alone at night from the unemployed camp to a rich farmer's house to beg for a few potatoes (on their way to the camp, the family passed huge heaps of potatoes harvested in the fields). The angry farmer reluctantly wakes up, but, to the boy's surprise, gives him a full sack of potatoes. Exhausted but happy, Tommy, whose body is aching for the weight of the sack, drags the potatoes back to the camp and falls asleep. To his despair, in the morning he finds out that the miraculously gained potatoes were poisoned and have already disintegrated, turning into a blue mush. He learns from other unemployed people that rich farmers often destroy the crops this way if prices go down.

N. Kalma's short story "The Red Shoes" (1952) provides an interesting example of an ambiguous happy ending. A poor black mother takes her daughter to the shoe store after the girl's old shoes fall apart. In the store, the girl tries on a pair of beautiful red shoes but they do not fit. The storeowner, however, demands that they pay for the shoes, since no one will agree to put them on after a person of color. The family feels desperate but a white man who happens to be in the store saves the day buying the shoes for his daughter. The happy mother chooses the size they need and in the evening enthusiastically tells her neighbors: "What a kind, generous person I met today! It is not true that good white people do not exist!" However, she is unaware of what the reader knows by that time: the kind man was a visitor from the Soviet Union. While the sufferings of this particular family are relieved, the story assumes that it indeed was a miracle: if one does find any good white people in America, they turn out to be Soviet Russians.

Portraying the regrettable condition of American youth, Soviet authors often employ the motifs of nineteenth-century classical Russian literature, adjusting the theme of "poor people" to new surroundings. For example, in "The Red Shoes" the reader recognizes a motif of Gogol's *Overcoat*: the girl's old shoes have become so decrepit that even the skillful shoe-repairer refuses to fix them, and the mother goes through unbelievable hardship to save money to buy the new ones. In Gansovskii's "Niagara" one easily identifies the plot of Turgenev's "Mumu": a boy who serves a whimsical cruel master secretly keeps a pet, the master's former fighting dog, which the owner has ordered to be drowned. Unlike

Turgenev's Gerasim, at the last moment Gansovskii's protagonist refuses to drown the dog and instead, hides it from his master. Eventually, when his disobedience is revealed, he leaves together with the dog. Thus, the plots of classical stories about social injustice become handy as material for constructing a new narrative, where the Russian past is projected onto American present. Therefore, these texts hint that the Russian present—the glorious Soviet life—may become the American future.

Indeed, glimpses of the distant Soviet Union and the activities of the local Communist party inspired by Soviet example provide the only sources of hope for the suffering characters locked in their isolated capitalist world. In the end of "The Federal Highway 66," an unemployed worker raises his fist and suggests that workers should pay a visit to the capitalists someday, but not at night and not as beggars; this promise replaces the absent catharsis. Each story in the collection finishes with an anticipation of a future struggle that, closer to the book's end, becomes more and more sound: the collection progresses from the personal rebellion of a boy against his master in "Niagara" to a mass protest of unemployed workers in "The Mexicans."

Only the collective effort of numerous working people, children and adults alike, led by American communists makes possible a happy ending in Gertsel Novogrudskii's novella *Dik from the Lower 12th Street* (1958). The young protagonist, Dick, who lives in a poor neighborhood in New York injures his eye, and his family lacks the money to pay for the necessary treatment. Therefore, the doctors suggest that for a smaller amount they can remove one eye, so that the boy does not lose sight in both eyes. The author stresses that the tragic situation does not come as a result of someone's evil will: most of the people in the hospital personally sympathize with Dick, but the capitalist system of health care is simple, clear, and merciless. Although the doctors can save the eye, without the payment they would have to remove it. In the end, Dick's friend Bronze (note the nickname's contrast with gold—an attribute of the rich) and a Communist sailor Tom with the help of newspaper boys, benevolent editors of the paper *The Workers' Voice*, and, of course, conscientious and compassionate workers of New York who buy a special philanthropic issue of the newspaper about Dick's case, manage to raise the necessary sum for the boy's treatment. The characters' adventures keep the reader in suspense until the last pages. Even after the money is raised, numerous dangers of New York life—drug dealers, street gangs, corrupted police—delay the check's delivery to the hospital. Novogrudskii masterfully crafts his novel, subtly incorporating into his narrative specific details of American daily life, such as latchkey kids or the Barnum circus, as well as recurrent motifs of early American texts written by Soviet writers—primarily, New York's resemblance to hell. Novogrudskii draws the reader into the boys' point of view: he emulates children's simple speech and their clear but naïve worldviews. At the same time, he constructs a gap between Dick's and the reader's perceptions. While Dick mocks his mother for comparing New York with hell, the reader fully understands that the city is indeed hellish. The novella repeatedly stresses the disparity between the rich who can afford several cars, decent medical care, life in comfortable and beautiful neighborhoods, and the poor who have to live in constant fear for their jobs', apartments', and children's security. The story sends a clear message: only socialist methods can defeat the capitalist system, but the victory remains local, as long as the system exists.

Exposing American racism remained and important didactic strategy during the Cold War, so children's texts portrayed young African Americans as the most insulted and humiliated members of society. They are double-oppressed—as people of color and as children. If the action takes place in the past, the young protagonist fighting for the rights of black people of color may be white, like Hattie and Morris in Sergienko's *Pegasus, Take Us Away* (1979), set on the eve of the American Civil War. When a slave owner, a former general under Napoleon, who had immigrated to America, wants to sell his slaves breaking the families apart, his teenage daughter Hattie and a young steam locomotive engineer Morris who love each other, help their African American servants escape, becoming part of the "underground railroad." Sacrificing their own lives, they organize a train crash in order to stop the search party. Through this heroic act they achieve a symbolic union—perhaps, the only one possible for young lovers in Soviet teen literature. Sergienko mostly portrays African Americans as abused victims: they are kind and naive, and even Morris treats them condescendingly; however, their creative spirit and wisdom reflect in their tales—masterful stylizations of Uncle Remus's tales of Brother Fox and Brother Rabbit.

As Valentin Kiparsky notes, in texts where the action involving African Americans takes place in modern times, the black teenager usually becomes an active party; he is often smarter, stronger, and more active than his white peers.[26] Such new characters as Snowflake in Vera Liubimova's play *Snowflake* (1948) and Charlie in N. Kalma's novel *Children of the Mustard Paradise* (1950) are full of dignity and refuse to be humiliated. The best student in his class both in studies and in sports, Charlie wins the heart of the white beauty queen of his class, who eventually turns out to be a coward. As in *Pegasus, Take Us Away*, the motifs of love, death, technology, and the problem of color tightly intertwine here: when Charlie participates in a car race, he nearly dies in a car crash because his jealous white classmates, offended by his successes, tampered with his car. In the final chapter, strongly resembling the ending of Alexei Tolstoy's *Buratino* as well as of Tageev's *A Russian American*, Charlie and his uncle, a singer whose image is apparently based on Paul Robson, sail away to the happy land free of racism—the Soviet Union.

Soviet texts about the friendship of children of all nationalities provided a contrast to the outrageous pictures of racial discrimination in

America. In children's literature, pioneer camps, especially Artek, served as a new model of the multinational world, since they brought together young people from Soviet republics, as well as foreigners. The presence of foreigners gave authors another opportunity to juxtapose Soviet and Western values and conditions. Like visiting foreign specialists in the production novels of 1930s, young guests exposed to the virtues of Soviet life learned to appreciate its social justice, superior ethical norms, and the happiness of belonging to the family of working people. The visitor usually played the role of a pupil, while Soviet pioneers functioned as guides to the Soviet world and exemplars of Soviet ethics. For instance, in Agnia Barto's poem "The Redskins" (1958), pioneers teach an American boy visiting their school to smoke the peace pipe and forbid him to demonstrate racist prejudices. They use collective judgment as their educational tool. Mark Efetov's novella about Artek, *A Letter on the Turtle Shell* (1976), invokes and transforms the motifs of *Dick from the Lower 12th Street*: Garry, a guest "from the other side of the world,"[27] learns that one of his new Soviet friends, Vitia, has appendicitis, and suggests that they should raise money for his surgery. Vitia's surprised Russian peers explain that medical care in the Soviet Union is free.

Perhaps, the most famous Artek visitor is Samantha Smith, a child-ambassador of peace and the heroine of Yurii Yakovlev's novella-fantasy *Samantha* (1987), as well as of his theatrical novella *Mistery-Play: Four Girls' Passions* (1992). As the latter title suggests, Samantha's image falls into the category of children-martyrs, pioneer heroes who sacrificed their lives for the common good, even though in reality she was an American girl who died in a plane crash. Upon her arrival in Russia, Yakovlev's Samantha visits major Soviet landmarks, which gives the reader an impression of the main elements composing late Soviet patriotism. Those elements include Lenin's Mausoleum, the cruiser *Aurora* to recall the revolution, the Piskarevskoe Memorial Cemetery as the tribute to the siege of Leningrad and to the Great Patriotic War at large, the space programs (Samantha meets with Valentina Tereshkova), and Artek. A meeting with a famous animal trainer Natalia Durova, perhaps surprising on this list, opens a discussion of America's ecological problems and the extermination of Native American culture. But it is in Artek where Samantha meets and befriends Soviet children, becomes used to their openness and generosity, and makes decisive progress in her search for truth and peace. This quest ends in Leningrad where she finally understands that a country that greatly suffered in the previous war would try its best to prevent the next one, and thus realizes that war mongers descend from her own country.

Besides American texts written by Soviet children's writers, young readers' perceptions of America and Americans continued to be informed by translations of American literature. The Soviet state reprinted works exposing oppression of African Americans and extermination of

Native Americans, such as Cooper's *Leatherstocking* series, Twain's *The Adventures of Tom Sawyer* and *Huckleberry Finn*, and Beecher Stowe's *Uncle Tom's Cabin*. In the 1950s and 1960s, new titles appeared, including Harper Lee's *To Kill a Mockingbird* and Howard Fast's *Tony and the Wonderful Door*, a story of a school boy's time travel from contemporary New York to the time when Manhattan ceased to belong to Native Americans. Some translations appeared in children's journals, which did not always stress what period the texts referred to: for instance, a respondent of Linor Goralik's study "America's Perception by the Last Generation of Soviet Children," recalls reading Irene Hunt's historical novella *No Promises in the Wind* (1970) about children's sufferings during the Great Depression as an account of contemporary America.[28]

However, despite their explicit ideological agenda, many of these texts, both the translated ones and those written by Russian writers in the 1960–1970s, went beyond their social message and allowed glimpses of various American characters, including brave and compassionate protagonists, and of the details of American daily life, as Olga Bukhina aptly notes.[29] One of the most attractive American texts with the minimum amount of social criticism, was Ray Bradbury's *Dandelion Wine*. Apparently, it influenced Sergienko's *Pegasus, Take Us Away*. The Russian author lyrically portrays a beautiful southern town with its fragrant gardens and sounds of flute in the evening, creating an image of an exotic, nostalgic America. Thereby, children's literature contributed to the neurotic perception of America by the last Soviet generation of children. Discussing this phenomenon, Goralik compares the nature of youth's attitude to America to the texture of erotic dream: dangerous and forbidden, yet magically attractive.

NOTES

1. Andrei Platonov, *Foundation Pit*. Transl. by Robert Chandler, Elizabeth Chandler, Olga Meerson (New York: New York Review of Books, 2009), 58.
2. Vladimir I. Lenin, *Zadachi soiuza molodezhi: Rech' na III vserossiiskom s'ezde komsomola*. (Moscow: Politizdat, 1946). Quoted in Marina Balina, *To Kill Charskaia: Paradoxes of Soviet Literature for Children, 1920s–1930s* (St. Petersburg: Aleteiia, 2012), 5.
3. Catriona Kelly, "Malen'kie grazhdane bol'shoi strany: Internatsionalizm, deti i sovetskaia propaganda," *NLO*, N 60 (2003): 218–51.
4. Of course, the old, prerevolutionary Russia, also served as such point of departure. Hence, many American travelogues of Soviet writers point out America's paradoxical backwardness and provide numerous comparisons between American and "archaic" Russian realities (Esenin, Mayakovsky). See Milla Fedorova, *Yankees in Petrograd, Bolsheviks in New York* (DeKalb: NIU Press, 2013), 69–70.
5. The inferiority complex, for obvious reasons, did not occupy any prominent place in official literature; however, we can find its signs in Esenin's travelogue "The Iron Mirgorod" where the traveling narrator refuses to find words to describe the overwhelming grandeur of Western technology. Contrastingly, the superiority complex is ubiquitous in American travelogues: Mayakovsky famously expressed the condescending attitude of the Soviet citizen "looking from above" at the bourgeoisie in

his poem "Broadway." For the analysis of the Soviet superiority complex in the international relations during the Stalin era, see David Michael-Fox "Rise of the Stalinist Superiority Complex" in *Showcasing the Great Experiment: Cultural Diplomacy and Western Visitors to the Soviet Union, 1921–1941(* Oxford, New York: Oxford University Press, 2012), 285–311.

6. Evgenii Dobrenko, *Formovka sovetskogo chitatelia. Sotsial'nye i esteticheskiepredposylki retseptsii sovetskoi literatury* (St. Petersburg: Gumanitarnoe agenstvo, "Akademicheskii proekt," 1997), 138.

7. On the political climate and children's publications of the Thaw era, see Maria Maiofis, "Milyi, milyi trikster," in Ilia Kukulin, Mark Lipovetskii, Maria Maiofis, eds., *Veselye chelovechki: Kul'turnye geroi sovetskogo detstva* (Moscow: NLO, 2008): 241–75.

8. See Ilia Kukulin, "Igra v satiru, ili Neveroiatnye prikliucheniia bezrabotnykh meksikantsev na Lune," in Ilia Kukulin, Mark Lipovetskii, Maria Maiofis, eds., *Veselye chelovechki: Kul'turnye geroi sovetskogo detstva* (Moscow: NLO, 2008): 224–40.

9. Dobrenko, *Formovka sovetskogo chitatelia*, 67: for preschool age, one hundred books; for the seven to ten year old age group, seventy-five books; for children ten to thirteen years old, three hundred books.

10. Balina, *To Kill Charskaia*, 7.

11. Soviet pedagogy paid special attention to the problem of migration of "adult" texts into the sphere of children's literature. According to Maria Rybnikova, mass literature for adults can be easily digested by young readers, while the classical texts require adaptation and explanation of context; therefore, the process of their integration into children's reading often requires more time. Maria A. Rybnikova, "Klassiki v detskom chtenii v proshlom i nastoiashchem" in *Izbrannye Trudy* (Moscow: Pedagogika, 1985).

12. Dobrenko, *Formovka sovetskogo chitatelia*, 69.

13. Ibid, 139.

14. *Gorod v proizvedeniiakh khudozhestvennoi literatury: posobie dlia shkol'noi I politprosvet. raboty.* Comp. by I. V. Vladislavlev, O.S. Leitnekker, B. E. Luk'ianovskii (Moscow: Gos. izd-vo, 1926). More on America in early Soviet education, see in Anna A. Arustamova, "Goriashchaia planeta: SShA v sovetskikh uchebnikakh 1920-kh godov. Gefter.ru http://gefter.ru/archive/5230 (Accessed May 1, 2015). On the transformation of school programs in 1920s–1930s, see Dobrenko, *Formovka sovetskogo chitatelia*, 143.

15. For instance, in Mikhail A. Osorgin, "We did not need any America: we had our own America nearby." *Memuarnaia proza* (Perm': Knizhnoe izdatel'stvo, 1992), 136.

16. Anna A. Arustamova, "Amerika v detskoi literature kontsa XIX veka v Rossii," *Vestnik Permskogo Universiteta,* no. 4 (2009): 76–80.

17. For a detailed discussion, see Fedorova, *Yankees in Petrograd, Bolsheviks in New York*.

18. For a detailed analysis of the poem and its transformations, see Fedorova, *Yankees in Petrograd, Bolsheviks in New York*, 217.

19. Violetta Gudkova, "Mnogikh etim vozdukhom i proskvozilo . . . : Antiamerikanskiie motivy v sovetskoi dramaturgii (1946–1954), *NLO,* no. 95 (2009): 196.

20. As Catriona Kelly notes, in the twentieth century, recognition of the value of childhood was part of the global process of modernization: Catriona Kelly, "Malen'kie grazhdane bol'shoi strany: Internatsionalizm, deti i sovetskaia propaganda," *NLO,* no. 60 (2003): 221.

21. On children's death rates in Russia in comparison with Western countries, see Kvasha, E. A. "Mladencheskaia smertnost' v Rossii v XX veke," *Sotsiologicheskie issledovaniia,* 6 (2003): 47–55.

22. Perhaps, the children's version of such a journey was inspired by Dziga Vertov's animation "Interplanetary Revolution" included into Protazanov's film *Aelita* (1924), loosely based on Tolstoy's novel.

23. Letters of the readers to Evgenii Petrov. RGALI. F. 1821, op. 1, ed. khr. 168.

24. Note the contrast with Sergei Mikhalkov's fairy tale *The Feast of Disobedience* (1971) warning against the grave consequences of children's disobedience to adults.

Addressing his cautionary tale to both children and adults, Mikhalkov makes a clear political statement: in a just society it is necessary to be obedient to authorities in order to prevent anarchy.

25. Catriona Kelly, "Malen'kie grazhdane bol'shoi strany: Internatsionalizm, deti i sovetskaia propaganda," 221.

26. Valentin Kiparsky. *English and American Characters in Russian Fiction* (Berlin: In Kommission bei O. Harrassowitz, Wiesbaden, 1964), 160–61.

27. Although it has never been openly said that Garry is an American, many details point to this fact. The very formulation "from the other side of the world" reinforces the contrast between the Soviet Union and the United States. Typically for the Cold War era, the idea of "America" embraces the capitalist West, contributing to the bipolar picture of the world.

28. Linor Goralik, "Plius na minus . . . : Vospriiatie Ameriki poslednim pokoleniiem sovetskikh detei," *NLO*, no. 95(2009): 240.

29. Olga Bukhina made this observation about translations but it can be extended to the Russian texts as well. See Olga Bukhina, "A Young American: a Portrait in Translation." *Detstvo v nauchnykh, obrazovatel'nykh i khudozhestvennykh tekstakh: Opyt prochteniia i interpretatsii.* Kazan': Izdatel'stvo Kazanskogo universiteta, 2011): 104–8.

BIBLIOGRAPHY

Arustamova, Anna A. "Amerika v detskoi literature kontsa XIX veka v Rossii," *Vestnik Permskogo Universiteta*, no. 4 (2009): 76–80.

———. "Goriashchaia planeta: SShA v sovetskikh uchebnikakh 1920-kh godov." Gefter.ru http://gefter.ru/archive/5230 (Accessed May 1, 2015).

Balina, Marina. "Creativity through Restraint: The Beginnings of Soviet Children's Literature," in Marina Balina, Larissa Rudova, eds., *Russian Children's Literature and Culture.* New York, London: Routledge, 2008, 3–17.

Bukhina, Olga. "Malen'kii amerikanets: Portret v perevode," in A. A. Sal'nikova, ed., *Detstvo v nauchnykh, obrazovatel'nykh i khudozhestvennykh tekstakh: Opyt prochteniia i interpretatsii.* Kazan': Kazanskii un-t, 2011, 104–8.

David-Fox, Michael. "Rise of the Stalinist Superiority Complex" in *Showcasing the Great Experiment: Cultural Diplomacy and Western Visitors to the Soviet Union, 1921–1941.* Oxford, New York: Oxford University Press, 2012.

Dobrenko, Evgenii. *Formovka sovetskogo chitatelia. Sotsial'nye i esteticheskiepredposylki retseptsii sovetskoi literatury.* St. Petersburg: Gumanitarnoe agenstvo, "Akademicheskii proekt," 1997.

Fedorova, Milla. *Yankees in Petrograd, Bolsheviks in New York.* DeKalb: Northern Illinois University Press, 2013.

Goralik, Linor. "Plius na minus . . . : Vospriiatie Ameriki poslednim pokoleniiem sovetskikh detei," *NLO*, N 95 (2009): 229–41.

Gorod v proizvedeniiakh khudozhestvennoi literatury: posobie dlia shkol'noi I politprosvet. raboty. Comp. by I. V. Vladislavlev, O.S. Leitnekker, B. E. Luk'ianovskii. Moscow: Gos. izd-vo, 1926.

Gudkova, Violetta. "Mnogikh etim vozdukhom i proskvozilo. . . : Antiamerikanskiie motivy v sovetskoi dramaturgii (1946–1954)," *NLO*, N 95 (2009): 187–216.

Kelly, Catriona. "Malen'kie grazhdane bol'shoi strany: Internatsionalizm, deti i sovetskaia propaganda," *NLO*, N 60 (2003): 218–51.

Kiparsky, Valentin. *English and American Characters in Russian Fiction.* Berlin: In Kommission bei O. Harrassowitz, Wiesbaden, 1964.

Kukulin, Ilia. "Igra v satiru, ili Neveroiatnye prikliucheniia bezrabotnykh meksikantsev na Lune," in Ilia Kukulin, Mark Lipovetskii, Maria Maiofis, eds., *Veselye chelovechki: Kul'turnye geroi sovetskogo detstva.* Moscow: NLO, 2008, 224–40.

Kvasha, Ekaterina A. "Detskaia smertnost' v Rossii v XX veke," *Sotsiologicheskie issledovaniia*, Vol. 6 (2003): 47–55.

Maiofis, Maria. "Milyi, milyi trikster," in Ilia Kukulin, Mark Lipovetskii, Maria Maio-
   fis , eds., *Veselye chelovechki: Kul'turnye geroi sovetskogo detstva.* Moscow: NLO, 2008,
   241–75.
Osorgin, Mikhail A. "We did not need any America: we had our own America near-
   by." *Memuarnaia proza.* Perm': Knizhnoe izdatel'stvo, 1992, 136.
Platonov, Andrei. *Foundation Pit.* Transl. by Robert Chandler, Elizabeth Chandler,
   Olga Meerson. New York: New York Review of Books, 2009.
Rybnikova, Maria A. "Klassiki v detskom chtenii v proshlom i nastoiashchem," in
   Izbrannye Trudy. Moscow: Pedagogika, 1985.

NINE

American Literary Canons in the Soviet Union and Post-Soviet Russia

Olga Yu. Antsyferova

In his book on the Western canon Harold Bloom observes:

> The Canon, a word religious in its origin, has become a choice among texts struggling with one another for survival, whether you interpret the choice as being made by dominant social groups, institutions of education, tradition of criticism or, as I do, by late-coming authors who feel themselves chosen by particular ancestral figures. Some recent partisans of what regards itself as academic radicalism go so far as to suggest that works join the Canon because of successful advertising and propaganda campaigns.[1]

This citation would be a good starting point for my further discussion of American literary canons in the Soviet Union and Post-Soviet Russia. As a post-Soviet scholar of American literature I would definitely assign myself to those who, in Bloom's sarcastic terms, "worship the composite god of historical process."[2] Analyzing the making of American literary canon(s) in Russia make us think that canon formation *is* the enterprise of dominant social groups, traditions of criticism, institutions of education, and that the canon *is* the fruit of propaganda campaigns.

The "war of canons" seems to be one of the most prominent features of American culture in the 1980s and 1990s. As a scholar I found these drastic changes in teaching American literature quite fascinating. At the same time the powerful foregrounding of such ideological issues as class, race and gender did not strike me as a complete novelty. It could not but occur to me that the canon formation and the development of American literary studies in the Soviet Union, some time ago, had passed through a

137

very similar stage, under a different cultural situation, though, and, probably, with different results. This putative analogy will be the focus of the first part of this chapter.

Interest in American literature, both general and specifically academic, has always existed in Russia, with its own ups and downs. After the revolution of 1917, Soviet literary criticism carried on with the problems touched upon by pre-revolutionary critics—ideologically emphasizing or, on the contrary, abating issues raised up before. Those were problems of contraposition and juxtaposition of Russian and American literatures; reflections upon the advantages of the rapidly developing country; questions about what *Americanism* as a political, economic, ideological, and sociocultural phenomenon is. The initial stage of these reflections in the 1920s makes an impression of a free and practically unrestricted controversy. Thus, in 1922 the almanac "Zapad" ("The West") published "American Impressions" by Vladimir Krymov (1878–1968), a Russian writer and editor. In the section on American literature Krymov reiterates customary clichés about the cult of the dollar and its pernicious influence upon literature, about the domination of "yellow press," dime novels, and so forth. However, the conclusion, perhaps slightly ironical, is rather unexpected: "Read a hundred of novels—you'll find the same everywhere: sine qua non prosperity, happy end, triumph of virtue, vice punished. This is the way the nation is brought up. Why, isn't it really the best way to do it? Where are we now with our dostoevschina and chekhovschina? Gloomy, dreary, dull—and there you always have a happy ending and a healthy disposition."[3]

Almost at the same time, in 1923, Mikhail Levidov (1891–1942), a famous literary critic, publicized in the journal *LEF* his highly ideologized and stylistically avant-gardish stance on American culture—absolutely debunking it and obviously keeping in line with the social command:

> Imagine only: this Americanism is admired. Admired by the whining intelligentsia. Impressed by powerful strength. Muscularity of the soul (fictitious). Cursed by the intelligentsia of a mystical trend. The living spirit is murdered. The soul is crucified on the cross-like footwear advertisement. Love in the elevator. . . . Flowers of life crushed by the mechanical boot. American danger. Psychic contagion. The end is coming. The earth is degrading. . . . This is not just a tragic farce of Americanism. This is a tragic farce of the capitalist culture *en masse*.[4]

These two early responses, different as they may seem, give a striking example of the exclusively (or predominantly) ideological reception of American literature in the Soviet Union. In both cases American literature is judged by its sociocultural effect. Krymov welcomes its optimistic message and assumes that it is an operational instrument for nation development; Levidov apocalyptically connects the end of the earth with the technological progress America epitomizes. Not a word about aesthetic techniques or, for that matter, artistic methods which make this sociocultural work so efficient.

It is absolutely true that "the evolution of the twentieth-century US literature critical reception went hand in hand with the formation of the new Soviet ideology."[5] In the 1920s, during New Economic Policy (NEP), editing houses, both private and state, flooded the Soviet reading market with various samples of contemporary American fiction. According to Deming Brown, American books made up one third of the whole body of translations, coming second only after the French. During seven years of NEP, works by ninety-one American authors were published, eighty of whom were completely new to Soviet readers.[6] The situation favored the onset of literary criticism focused upon American authors; genres of a critical survey and a foreword were most widespread at the time. In the mid-1920s we can speak about the formation of the Soviet school of American literary studies as a separate branch of foreign literature studies. Early Soviet Americanists (Sergey Dinamov, Ivan Kashkin, Anna Elistratova, Evgenii Lann, Abel Startsev) saw their main task as classifying contemporary American authors on purely ideological and sociological bases, originating in the school of Vladimir Friche (1870–1929)—one of the leading Marxist literary scholars. As it was written in one of the booklets, the aim was to find "the overall scheme of demarcation among American authors. We do not base it on so called 'schools' or 'trends,' but on the definite class layers of the literary process. This is the only correct approach to literature."[7]

Sergey Dinamov (Oglodkov) (1901–1939) became the official leader of this school of American literary studies occupying several influential positions—director of the Academic Institute of Language and Literature, director of the Institute of Red Professorate, chief editor of *International Literature* journal, and working at the same time in the apparatus of the Central Committee of Vsesouznaya Kommunisticheskaya Partiya (bolshevikov)—All-Union Communist Part (Bolsheviks)—VKP (b). Coming from a working class family, Dinamov was a postgraduate student of Vladimir Friche— and made a rapid and successful career which was terminated by his arrest on accusations of counter-revolutionary activities, which led to his execution in 1939. In one of his first surveys entitled "Contemporary American Literature" (1926) Dinamov divides modern American fiction into two branches: "entertaining literature" and "literature of protest"—connecting the origin of the latter with the World War I. Naturally enough paying more attention to the second branch, Dinamov defines the 1920s as the "American literary Renaissance." For him this renaissance is represented by the names of Theodore Dreiser, Sherwood Anderson, Sinclair Lewis, Joseph Hergesheimer. All of them are highly acclaimed for carrying on realistic traditions of Frank Norris and Ambrose Bierce. Dreiser seemed to be the leading figure on the American literary horizon. The name of Upton Sinclair seemed to be losing prominence. "He is not so much an artist as a publicist who resorts to the simplistic language of billboards." However, this does not prevent the critic from insisting that "Sinclair is the most progressive writer of the United States and, consequently, the most important for us (though we shouldn't forget that he is for *evolution*, not for *revolution*)."[8] The concessive-adversative syntactic and rhetoric structures are very typical for the early Soviet literary discourse about US literature—they manifest the complicated inner process of negotiations and searches for an American literary phenomenon which would fit the Procrustean bed of communist ideology.

In 1929 survey Dinamov dwells upon the roots of today's American literature and implacably divides the writers of the late nineteenth century into two groups—"genteel realism" and "more consistent realists" (Hamlin Garland, Stephen Crane, and Frank Norris). Here the critic sounds unexpectedly furious about O. Henry ("a typical artist of the American petty bourgeoisie") and Jack London ("an artist of the workers' aristocracy"), which runs counter to the commonly favorable critical reception of both authors, to speak nothing of their popularity among the readers at grass-roots level. *Realism* seems to be the measuring rod for evaluating authors (as opposed to *idealism* which stood for romantic, fantastic, and adventure literature and stemmed, for Dinamov, from the ideology of "decaying aristocracy under capitalist conditions"). Realism is far from homogeneous, though, and differs in quality: "The petty bourgeoisie under modern American conditions can produce only *relatively* realistic literature, because the truly realistic method of rendering reality is available only for an artist with proletarian psycho-ideology."[9] And even this *relative* realism is for the critic far from homogeneity and is subdivided into "quasi-realists" (Edith Wharton, Booth Tarkington, Jack London as the author of *Hearts of Three*)—and "petty-bourgeois realists" (Sinclair Lewis, Sherwood Anderson, John Dos Passos, Floyd Dell). In the spirit of dogmatic Marxism, Dinamov coins the formula: "Writers-idealists escape from reality; quasi-realists distort reality; relative realists reflect the reality unilaterally."[10]

Soviet critics were eager to find an appropriate author who would absolutely conform with communist ideology and who could be "appointed" as the "Number-One American Author." Logically enough, the searches went on in the proletarian literary milieu which proved to be relatively bare of literary talents. Joe Hill with his propaganda poetry, the life-long communist Michael Gold, and Joseph Freeman, an editor of *The New Masses* journal, were among candidates to an ideologically correct creator, but even they always lacked something: "The communist Joseph Freeman after his trip to the USSR stopped writing romantic verses, but he has not yet produced truly proletarian one; he must be going through an inner crisis which is unavoidable for any idealist poet joining the Communist activism."[11] Needless to say, Soviet literary critics unavoidably have to tackle the problem of insufficient ideological *podkovannost'* (efficiency) of American authors. But the psychological naiveté of the 1920s critic ascribing this insufficiency to an inner crisis would later be replaced by violent attacks on political apostasy (as, in the most striking case, with Howard Fast in the late 1950s[12]). The figure of an exemplary proletarian writer proved to be a political and ideological myth.

Along with Dinamov's dogmatic attempts at a purely ideological canon-formation, mention should be made of the brilliant work by Boris Eikhenbaum "O. Henry and the Theory of the Short Story" where the "formalist" critic gives an overview of American literary history from the point of view of its genre and briefly accounts for the enormous success of American literature among the Soviet readers.[13] In 1931 a famous poet (coming from the Acmeist "Guild of poets"), translator and literary journalist Mikhail Zenkevich, made one of the most successful attempts at singling out what the secret of the popularity of American books in Russia might be:

> It is true—in average, the American literature is aesthetically inferior to French. It is true—it lacks a powerful wing of proletariat writers that German literature can boast of. But in American literature we find huge, often formless content—as contrasted to French decorating a boring adultery or petty skepticism with filigree trimming. . . . American literature is of kindred spirit to us due to its grandeur: it reflects the ebullient life of a vast continent, motley variety of races and nationalities, huge industrial cities and primeval deserts, contrasts of effluence and poverty, ripening social conflicts ready to blaze up into violent class struggle. . . . There is no stagnation, and it is constantly replenished with fresh and new names.[14]

The central place in the Soviet American literary canon was definitely prepared for proletarian literature—literature expressing the interests of the "hegemon" class. Teodor Levit (1904–1943), a Soviet poet and translator who was very active as a literary critic in the 1930s, wrote an extensive article on proletarian literature in the United States,[15] studying its genesis, searching for its "true representatives," "allies," and "fellow-travelers." Among the "predecessors" an honorable place is given to Upton Sinclair with his novel *King Coal* (1917). Olga Nesmelova acutely remarks that dealing with *King Coal*, T. Levit lays down the foundation for methodology to be used by Soviet Americanists later on: the critic reveals what is missing (and what is absolutely necessary for him) in Sinclair's novel and how it might be improved in accordance with the "social command."[16] Bravely enough, T. Levit mentions John Reed as one of the founding fathers of proletarian literature (Reed's name was backlisted by Stalin after Vladimir Lenin's death). The foremost among the "allies" is John Dos Passos whose way is that "of the intelligent who consciously, honestly and impetuously moves to the left, to the proletariat."[17] "Fellow-travelers" (U. Sinclair and S. Lewis, among others) are generally treated with sympathy, but are charged with insufficiency of revolutionary spirit and a propensity toward reforms instead of revolutionary struggle. The last section of the article "Biases and Prospects" dwells upon the limitations of the contemporary proletarian literature in the United States: absence of Marxist literary theory, risks of formal experimentation, low theoretical level of the authors, and such.

As time went on, it was becoming evident that the canon of "fellow-travelers" was more promising than that of wholehearted partisans of the proletarian cause. Two years later Abel' Startsev in his article "Universal Crisis of Capitalism and the New Wave of Allies of Proletariat in American Literature" formulated the main task of the proletarian movement in literature—"to clasp the ever-growing wave of fellow-travelers and reshape them into true allies of the working class, to win the best part of intelligentsia over from the bourgeois world."[18] In this more-embracing canon, still formed on a purely class basis, Theodore Dreiser, John Dos Passos, and Ernest Hemingway would find a place, which was far from secure, though, depending on alterations in the authors' attitude toward the USSR and communism.

Whereas in the United States the Afro-American literary canon became a reality only as a result of "culture wars," in the Soviet Union,"black literature" gained access into the official ideological canon as early as the 1920s. During the publishing boom such novels as *Fire in the Flint* (1924, two Russian translations in 1926) and *Flight* (1926, translated in 1928) by Walter F. White, *There is a Confusion* (1924) by Jessie Fauset (translated in 1927 as *Black Skin. An American Novel*), novels by Claude McKay, Langston Hues, and others were presented to Soviet readers.[19]

Deep sympathy for Afro-American writing had something to do with the identification of the former "oppressed class" (proletariat) with the oppressed position of the former slaves in the United States. The similarity was conceptualized in the term "capitalist slavery."[20] Sergey Dinamov was the first to introduce the term "the black renaissance" into Soviet literary criticism and correlate it with the abovementioned "American renaissance"—the cultural boom of the 1920s. He aptly underlines the role of William Dubois with his *Souls of Black Folk* (1903) and his novel *The Quest of the Silver Fleece* (1911) in the rise of Afro-American racial self-consciousness. Interestingly enough, Dinamov was the first in the Soviet Union to mark the uneasy negotiations between class and race in the black artistic consciousness: "It is clear that the race in the black literature comes *before* the class, that *national* canon steps in for *international*."[21] However, in 1934 Dinamov resorts to purely class discourse, racial issue suppressed by it: "The black proletariat under the leadership of the Communist party and in the alliance with the best layers of the black intelligentsia is sure to come to the complete victory, to the complete annihilation of the 'free slavery' of the Negroes in the United States."[22]

With class values prevailing over racial ones, Soviet criticism characteristically pays special attention to such a borderline phenomenon as the image of a Negro in white literature. Strictly speaking, it was quite normal for critics to include in their surveys of Afro-American literature works by white authors about blacks. Thus, Ivan Kashkin in his survey "Novelties in the Negro Literature" includes Michael Gold as "vitally perceiving both social aspects of the Negro issue and the main peculiarity of the Negro art—its musicality."[23] Some of the reviews are marked with exposed, though unconscious racism: "White writers frequently turn to the life of the blacks as their material. Some of them, hostile to the blacks, maliciously distort it; others treat a Negro as an object for mockery; still others address the Negro theme as an exoticism which would satisfy the taste of the American mass reader for something strange."[24]

In 1928 Evgenii Lann reviewed the novel *Nigger Heaven* by Carl Van Vechten, which had been translated into Russian twice by that time. Lann regrets that a gifted and original author is introduced to Soviet readers by his very uncharacteristic and weak work. The critic highly appreciates the aesthetic qualities of the novel—its "well-made plot" and "nearly impeccable composition," but he finds essential flaws with the ideological content. Lann avers that the current situation with the blacks in the United States considerably influenced the plot of the novel and its motivation:

> Making his hero—a negro-intelligent—suffer in the unbearable conditions, suggesting that his companions should tirelessly discuss "the negro problem," the author forced everybody blow hot and cold about the receipts of Booker Washington and Dubois. The former, thinking that prosperity would put the blacks on the same level with the whites, preached assiduity and laboriousness to his fellow tribesmen; the latter—Dubois—picked up the gauntlet of the racial hatred.[25]

Evgenii Lann concludes with the regular recommendations to the author: "If Van Vechten preferred to remain a Master he could not but have noticed those intelligents who desiccate the problem of the Negroes' new Mecca not vertically (between Booker Washington and William Dubois), but in the horizontal plane of class, and not racial struggle."[26]

In the 1930s literary criticism of black literature obtained more and more sociological bias. On the eve of the World War II, Richard Wright's works got considerable ideological support. Fragments from his *Uncle Tom's Children* were translated into Russian in 1938—the same year the book was published in the United States. In 1941–1942 *International Literature* journal published his *Native Son* and several other works, which collected about a dozen immediate reviews under such telling titles as "American Tragedy" (A. Startsev) and "The Black Stepson" (M. Mendelson). Time for Wright's new publications came only in twenty years, in the early 1960s when the Civil Rights movement reminded of the importance of the Afro-American literature. Vladimir Prozorov recapitulates:

> Martin Luther King, Jr. became a popular figure in the Soviet media mostly only after his assassination. Malcolm X and the black nationalist movement were seen as contrary to the doctrine of the proletarian internationalism. Accordingly, books by Leroi Jones (Amiri Baraka), Eldridge Cleaver, or even *Roots* by Alex Haley were not published. Tony Morrison's *Song of Solomon* was translated in the early 1980s, but didn't attract much attention, maybe because of the absence of the necessary historical background (the most widely read novel on Afro-American issue remained *Uncle Tom's Cabin*).[27]

As for the gender issue, it did not seem to be as hot as the two previous ones in the Soviet ideological field. After the 1917 revolution, Soviet women were granted suffrage. Abortion was legalized in 1920, making the Soviet Union the first country legalize it; however, it was banned again between 1936 and 1955. A national network of centers was established. The country's (1918) recognized the equal rights of women. The country's first constitution (1918) recognized the equal rights of women. It accounts for the striking fact that in the authoritative bibliographical reference book *American Literature in Russia: Translations and Criticism (1776–1975)*[28] among 235 personal entries only less than 30 refer to female authors. They are too few not to mention their names. In the 1930s Pearl Buck, the 1938 the Nobel Prize Laureate, was widely published and reviewed in the USSR. The contradictory perception of her famous novel *The Good Earth* reviewed, among other critics, by Vladimir Lenin's wife Nadezhda Krupskaia, is reflected in the title of Anna Elistratova's review—"Talented Apologetics of *Kulak* [wealthy peasant] Illusions."[29] It gives us a clear idea of the predominance of class issue over others. Mention should be made of Mary Heathon Vorse with her book *Strike!* (translated in 1931) and the popularity of Agness Smedley with her Chinese theme. The list would be incomplete without Edna Ferber with her Pulitzer Prize winning novel *So Big* (1924, translated in 1926). Another member of the Algonquin Round Table Group Dorothy Parker appears in 1940s with her *Soldiers of the Republic* (translated in 1942) and *Clothe the Naked* (translated in 1946).

These, now mostly obscure, names excluded, for instance, Gertrude Stein who in her lifetime was honored with only one review in the Soviet press under the title "Primitivism and Simplicity."[30] Margaret Mitchell with her *Gone with the Wind* (1936) is characteristically missing from the list. No translations, only one brief anonymous response in *Literary Review* journal in 1937.

As for other female names, Lillian Hellman started gaining popularity as a publicist and later as a playwright at the end of the World War II.

After the 1960s, works by Shirley A. Grau, Harper Lee, Carson McCullers, Flannery O'Connor, Joyce Carol Oates were introduced to Soviet readers, more for the sake of exposing capitalism and racial prejudices than for the sake of gender issue.

In the second section of the article we shall proceed from the understanding of the literary canon as "list of books for required study."[31] Thus, another aspect of the canon-formation is a selective process performed by a reader/student and stipulated by certain ideological activities of social and teaching institutions.

The 1940s and 1950s were marked by a definite *historical turn* in literary studies in this country. Whether it can be ascribed to the sociopolitical consequences of the World War II and the necessity to know the literature and culture of political allies and enemies, or to some inner processes in the Soviet Academy of Sciences, by late 1940s Soviet literary studies were considered ideologically mature enough to produce academic histories of foreign literatures. At approximately the same period of time, Soviet academician-philologists started working on histories of English Literature (three volumes, 1953–1956), French literature (four volumes, 1946–1963), German Literature (five volumes, 1962–1976). Academic project connected with the history of American literature was the most ill-starred. After the first volume went out in 1947[32] the edition was terminated, and the authors prosecuted. This tragic and absurd event had to do with the anti-cosmopolitanism campaign 1948–1953. One of the authors of this *History* Abel' Startsev reminisces: "I worked for the Academic Institute of the World Literature. The plan was to write a two-volume history of American Literature. At the time the USSR was on friendly terms with the USA. But when the first volume was published, the Cold War broke out, and many books where the USA and American culture were treated favorably became a target of harsh criticism." Startsev was found guilty because "one could hear dollars' tinkling while paging the book. Critics seemed highly annoyed at our high appreciation of American literature in the context of the World literature. I was accused of West-obsequiousness, of misestimating the bourgeois culture and of getting under it pernicious influence."[33] As a result Abel' Startsev was sent to the camp in Karaganda for ten years to be released only after Stalin's death. He was never again admitted to the Academic Institute he used to work for.

Anyhow, it was the first attempt at the Russian-language history of American literature which secured the position of American literary studies as a separate and self-sufficient branch of the Soviet literary studies. The first volume presented the history of American Literature from the first English settlers through "the victory of the bourgeois revolution" to the Civil War. The last section of the book was devoted to the literature of abolitionism. The detailed plan of the volume was worked out by A. Startzev who, together with A. Elistratova and T. Silman, wrote all the chapters of the book. It is noteworthy that, since then, the scheme of the Russian-language histories of American literature remains the same, even into the twenty-first century: large chronological sections start with general surveys of the historical, political, economic, cultural, and other contexts, this initial survey followed by chapters expanding on specific writers.

Characteristically, the first *History* has no footnotes or bibliographical list. One can find only four footnotes on the first pages which refer to F. Engels's and I. Stalin's works. The authors of the *History* do not normally allude to American literary scholars, though a few times, Vernon L. Parrington and Perry G. E. Miller are mentioned in the text. The authors of the *History* welcome realistic trends in Washington Irving, place Edgar Alan Poe in-between "conservative romanticism" and decadence, define the genre of *Mobi Dick* as a "whaler's mystery," and lament about the pervasive pessimism of "bourgeois authors." However, ideological simplifications are not the whole *History*, and the edition still maintains some of its value due to its circumstantiality and the spirit of discovery which must have inspired the pioneering researchers.

After Stalin's death the idea of antagonistic class struggle gradually was supplanted by the concept of peaceful coexistence of the former class enemies, though *ideological* struggle remained most uncompromising. In literary criticism the methodological focus shifted from radical class characteristics to more mediated contraposition of literary schools and trends. The mainstream literary development of the twentieth century started to be understood in terms of struggle between realism and modernism. Realism was considered more expedient for the socialist society, because realistic literature represented the life *as it was* (ideally—in its revolutionary development), and therefore the realistic art *a priori* was more valuable than modernism. Serious studies in modernism began only in 1960s, the term *modernism* replacing *decadence* which had been in use in 1920–1950s. However, up to 1990s modernism evoked only negative connotations and was associated with formal superfluity and deep ideological crisis—"dehumanization."

Not to oversimplify the situation in literary studies after the 1960s, it should be pointed out that the term *realism* became a subject of violent controversy. As a result, such a term as *bourgeois realism* was rejected, the term *critical realism* lost a great part of its universality and, eventually, retained its pertinence only to nineteenth-century literature. A new term was introduced in 1960s—the *twentieth-century realism*[34] —which was much more inclusive and, therefore, allowed for expansion of the American literary canon. Realism stopped being just an ideologically evaluative category; now it was sporadically considered a unique aesthetic system which "reflected the reality in all its complexity" (Dmitrii Zatonsky), as an aesthetic expression of humanism (Alexander Nikoliukin), as an aesthetic phenomenon far from homogeneous and embracing elements of other literary trends (see "social realism" vs. "romantic realism" in Tamara Denisova's works or Vasilii Tolmachov's concept of the romantic, which was dominant in modern literature). New taxonomies of modern American literature were made on the basis of immanent features of the American cultural consciousness. Thus, in 1980 Alexei Zverev suggested taking the American Dream as a key concept for organizing twentieth-century American literary history and, correspondingly, lined up T. Dreiser (*Trilogy of Desire, An American Tragedy, The Bulwark*), F. Scott Fitzgerald (*The Great Gatsby*), Robert Penn Warren (*All the King's Men*), Norman Mailer (*An American Dream*), and Gore Vidal (*Burr*).

Strong sociological bias was still present, but very often class and sociological criticism was more of a compromise made to allow a new author into the canon. Vladimir Prozorov explains: "Book publication in the USSR was completely controlled by government agencies and looked upon as a part of the 'national security.' The question of what was 'acceptable' and what was 'unacceptable' was sometimes decided on a very high level."[35] Besides, one cannot but have a kind word for the authors of prefaces to American books. Making an American author an object of harsh sociological critique might be a compromise necessary to make this author available for the Soviet reading audience.

In this situation new attempts at writing other Russian-language histories of American literature were predictable. In 1971 a two-volume textbook on *History of American Literature*[36] edited by Nikolai Samokhvalov was published. It was written by eleven authors (Samokhvalov included). The *History* definitely has some merits, the main of which is its unprecedented completeness. The first volume includes chapters on American folklore, it takes as its starting point nonfiction narratives of William Bradford and John Smith, the second volume finishes with chapters on Carson McCullers and Phillip Bonosky, which means that the *History* follows the development of American literature up to the latest novelty books. It deals with an impressive quantity of names, alternating surveys with chapters dealing with individual authors. Among its drawbacks one cannot but mention the over-ideologized approach to the material. Thus, the large section on Romanticism is concluded with the chapter about the rather obscure authors Sylvester Judd and George Lippard whose presence here was supposed to offer "connections of the advanced American romanticists with the socialist movement."[37] Rebecca Harding Davis is reproached with limited knowledge of the true proletariat's conditions.[38] Realism is considered the main achievement of world literature, therefore Henry James is said to be "of greater use to realism as a literary critic, not as an artist."[39] His *Turn of the Screw* is not even mentioned, and a few lines given to his late novels deserve citing:

> In *The Wings of the Dove* Kate Croy forces her lover (with whom she is secretly engaged) to marry the deadly ill heiress of an American mil-

lionaire, to take advantage of her riches after her death. Her plan never works out. Densher and Kate quarrel and separate. In *The Golden Bowl* an impoverished Italian aristocrat marries into money Maggie, the daughter of an American millionaire, while his mistress Charlotte marries Maggie's widowed father. The deception is exposed, Maggy saves herself and her father from disgrace, restores harmony in both families making Charlotte leave with her father to America. [40]

Isn't it a nice piece of paraphrase heresy?

In the conclusion to the first volume the authors resort to usual concessive-adversative rhetoric: "Though realism developed in the United States three decades later than in Europe. . . , it greatly contributed to the world realism. It happened so mainly due to the heroic struggle of the American working people, white and black, against slavery and monopolies".[41] The conclusion to the second volume sounds similarly primitive: " Twentieth-century American literature presents such a rich and complex picture, there are so many multidirectional forces acting, that one can make it out only with the help of Lenin's doctrine of two cultures existing within every national culture."[42] It sounded too dogmatic even for the 1970s. I remember how my academic advisor, the famous Leningrad university professor Alexandra Savuryonok, in reading my graduate paper on Henry James, cautiously warned me against relying upon Samokhvalov's *History*. Frankly speaking, as a student, I never read it. It turned out to be too superficial and "vulgarly sociological" to be truly scientific.

It is not by chance that in late 1970s *Literary History of the United States* edited by Robert Spiller was translated into Russian and published in the USSR.[43] There was something slightly ironic about it, though, because during "zastoi years" the last word on the history of American literature available for Soviet readers was spoken in 1948 when Spiller and his group of authors wrote their *Literary History*.

The textbook on American literature of the twentieth century was published in 1984 by Yassen Zasursky in Moscow University Publishing House.[44] This late-Soviet book can be seen as a sample of uneasy ideological negotiations that American literary studies were constantly going through in the USSR. On the one hand, the very titles of some chapters had not seemed to change since early Soviet times: "The October and the First Steps of the Revolutionary Literature," "Critical Realism in 1920s," "Crisis and the Proletarian Literature in 1930s," "Anticommunism and the Literature of the USA," "Socialist Realism in the US Literature: Theory and Practice" and such. However, the scope of the study seems to widen and to embrace some aesthetical issues along with non-Marxist cultural contexts: "Freud and the US Literature," "European School of American Modernism," "Ernest Hemingway Subtexts," "Stream of Consciousness: William Faulkner's *Sound and Fury*," and such.

The figure of Yassen Zassurskii is one of the most influential in the American literary canon-formation in Russia due to another reason. The year 1974 should be mentioned as a special landmark in Soviet/post-Soviet American studies history. In that year, the first conference of Soviet literary scholars was held at Moscow State University, organized by the dean of the School of Journalism, Professor Zasurskii. Since then and up to now, on a permanent basis, these annual conferences have been gathering numerous scholars in American literature from the Soviet and post-Soviet space, putting them in contact with their colleagues from American universities. The proceedings of these academic events, published annually from 1974 to 2014, give a fairly accurate and complete picture of what is going on in Russian studies of American literature and culture and of canon transformations. The themes of the Moscow conferences have varied depending on the sociopolitical situation in the country: from "October and the Literature of the USA. The Impact of the Great October Socialist Revolution on American Literature and Journalism" (1987) through "Mass Culture: an American Experience" (2002) and "Freedom of Choice in the American Civilization" (2004) to "American Culture: From Making a Nation to Transnationalism" (2014). After the breakdown of the USSR, the annual conference of the Russian Society of American Culture Studies remains the central and the most regular event of American studies activities in Russia and an important factor in canon-formation.

The most recent textbook on American literature was issued in 2003 by the veteran of Soviet/post-Soviet American literary studies, Boris Gilenson.[45] This all-embracing textbook traces the history of American literature from 1600 up to 2000, the main focus of the project is its proclaimed concordance with the acting university syllabi in History of Foreign Literature. The thing is, though, that new educational standards introduced into Russian universities in the early 2000s provide for unprecedented flexibility, and a university professor now is actually free to teach the authors of his choice (within reason, of course). That is actually what Gilenson does: his comprehensive textbook is of enormous help for students of American literature, and the choice of names is representative and impressive indeed. However one cannot but notice that the degree of thoroughness in treating this or that literary phenomenon greatly depends upon the sphere of interests of the textbook author.

Recently, a group of scholars studying American literature at the Department of Contemporary Literatures of Europe and America at the Gorky Institute of World Literature of the Russian Academy of Sciences (Moscow) together with some professors from Russian and Ukrainian universities, with Yassen Zasurskii, Maya Koreneva, and Ekaterina Stetsenko at the head have made a very successful attempt—the second since 1947—at writing an academic history of American literature in six volumes.[46] This fundamental and comprehensive edition preserves circumstantiality so characteristic of the Russian school of thinking and its fruitful adherence to studying and teaching literature in wide historical and sociocultural contexts. The new *History* is free from ideological pressing, it minutely describes and interprets many new names and phenomena; it combines academic validity with fresh insights and is of great help to those interested in American literature. However, its main drawback is that the *History* ends on the eve of World War II.

One of the signs of the deeply changed situation in Russian-American sociocultural and academic relations, with its increased freedom and flexibility, is the foundation of what became the Fulbright Summer Schools in the Humanities. They have been held annually since 1997. The schools are the joint initiative of Moscow University and the American Studies Association of Russia, supported and co-organized by the Fulbright Program in Russia. They were founded by Professor MGU Tatiana Venediktova who is the Director of the project. The themes of the Summer Schools vary from year to year but continuous emphasis is maintained on American cultural studies as a comparative discipline. In 2015 the School focused upon various mechanisms of canon formation, upon "great books and critical readings."

Generally speaking, in post-Soviet times conferences, international exchanges, inter-university summer and winter schools and seminars became main factors of canon-formation. The scene of American studies in Russia now is in a state of flux, seeking reasonable balance between traditional academic borderlines of research and fresh interdisciplinary approaches. It might be termed an inter-paradigmatic period. But it is also a time of great intellectual excitement—of experimentation, exploration, critical ferment, and lively debate. If asked what the American literary canon in Russia is like today, I would answer: we have none. And a university professor becomes the key-figure in the canon-formation. Several years ago I built up a special course "American culture as reflected in literary styles." In this interdisciplinary course equal attention is paid to historical background and to aesthetic issues; literature is placed into the broad context of arts. This course can be called a "transformer" because it is changed every year according to students' demands and in correlation with the hottest issues of the moment. So my idea is a deliberate (perhaps, somewhat constrained) rejection of a canon.

While Russian literary *Americanists* are following the latest novelties in US literature and are trying to apply the latest theoretical approaches to the American classics, students' reading preferences, to say nothing of their cultural background and knowledge of American literature, become narrower. Todays' university beginners know practically nothing about American literature. Not even *Uncle Tom's Cabin*. *The Catcher in the Rye* remains student's permanent favorite from year to year. Students like to read Nicholas Sparks and George R. R. Martin.

However, our former and present students sometimes ask us for advice—what to read, for a sort of orientation in boundless ocean of literature. Nostalgia for a canon?

NOTES

1. Harold Bloom, *The Western Canon: The Books and School of Ages* (New York: Riverhead Books, 1995), 19.
2. Ibid., 20.
3. Vladimir P. Krymov, "Amerikanskie vpechatleniia," *Zapad*, no. 4 (1922): 31.
4. Mikhail Yu. Levidov, "Amerikanizma tragifars," *LEF*, no. 2 (1923): 45–46.
5. Olga O. Nesmelova, *Puti razvitiia otechestvennoi amerikanisitki XX veka* (Moscow: Knizhnyi dom, 1998), 13.
6. Glenora W. Brown and Deming B. Brown, *A Guide to Soviet Russian Translation of American Literature* (New York: Columbia University press, 1954), 8, 16.
7. Ivan I. Anisimov, Sergey S. Dinamov, *Perevodnaia belletristika v biblioteke. Avantyurnaia i nauchno-fantasticheskaia literatura (Zaochnye kursy po perepodgotovke bibliotechnykh rabotnikov profsouznykh bibliotek. Urok 15)* (Moscow: Knigoizdatel'stvo VTZSPS, 1929), 1.
8. Serguey S. Dinamov, "Sovremennaia amerikanskaia literatura" *Krasnoe studenchestvo*, no. 3 (1926): 85–87.
9. Sergey Dinamov, "Predislovie," in Upton B. Sinclair, *Den'gi pishut* (Moscow; Leningrad: Gosudarstvennoe izdatel'stvo, 1927), 22.
10. Ibid., 23.
11. Ibid., 25.
12. See: Rossen Djagalov, "'I Don't Boast about it, but I'm the Most Widely Read Author of this Century': Howard Fast and International Leftist Literary Culture, ca. Mid-Twentieth Century," *Anthropology of East Europe Review*, no. 27 (2) (2009): 40–55. https://scholarworks.iu.edu/journals/index.php/aeer/article/viewFile/167/260   (accessed May 5, 2015).
13. Boris M. Eikhenbaum, *O. Henry and the Theory of the Short Story*, transl., with notes and postscript of Irwin R. Titunik (Ann Arbor: Dept. of Slavic Languages and Literatures, University of Michigan, 1968).
14. Mikhail A. Zenkevich, "O novinkakh angliiskoi i amerikanskoi literatury," *Novyi Mir*, no. 12 (1934): 171.
15. Teodor M. Levit, "Proletliteratura SASSh," *Vestnik inostrannoi literatury*, no. 6 (1930): 89.
16. Olga O. Nesmelova, *Puti razvitiya otechestvennoi amerikanisitki XX veka* (Moscow: Knizhnyi dom, 1998), 32.
17. Teodor M. Levit, "Proletliteratura SASSh," *Vestnik inostrannoi literatury*, no. 6 (1930): 90.
18. Abel I. Startsev, "Vseobshchii krizis kapitalizma i novaia volna soiuznikov proletariata v literature Ameriki," *Marksistsko-leninskoe iskusstvoznanie*, no. 5–6 (1932): 61.
19. Liumila V. Filatova, "Negrityanskaia literatura," in Vladimir M. Friche, ed., *Literaturnaia entsiklopediia* (Moscow; Izdatel'stvo Kommunisticheskoi akademii, 1929–1939), in 11 vols. http://feb-web.ru/feb/litenc/encyclop/le7/le7-6491.htm (accessed May 5, 2015).
20. Ivan I. Anisimov, Sergey S. Dinamov, *Litso kapitalisticheskogo rabstva v inostrannoi khudozhestvennoi literature* (Moscow; Leningrad: Gossotzekiz, 1931).
21. Sergey S. Dinamov, "Sovremennaia amerikanskaia literature," *Krasnoe studenchestvo*, no. 3 (1926): 87–88. See also: Olga O. Nesmelova, "Perception of Afro-American Writers by Soviet Literary Criticism of the 1920–30s" http://kpfu.ru//staff_files/F18500529/Perception.of.Afro_American.pdf (accessed May 15, 2015).

22. Ivan I. Anisimov, Sergey S. Dinamov, *Litso kapitalisticheskogo rabstva v inostrannoi khudozhestvennoi literature* (Moscow; Leningrad: Gossotzekiz, 1931), 65.

23. Ivan A. Kashkin, "Novoe v negrityanskoi literature," *Vestnik inostrannoi literatury*, no. 10 (1928): 146.

24. [s.s.], "Negrityanskaia literatura v Amerike," *Na literaturnom postu*, no. 13–14 (1928): 80.

25. Evgenii L. Lann, "Retsenziia na knigu *Negrityanskii rai*. Leningrad: Biblioteka Vsemirnoi literatury, 1928]," *Pechat' i revolutsia*, no.6 (1928): 218.

26. Ibid., 219.

27. Vladimir G. Prozorov, "The Ills of Limitation and the Evils of Disorientation: Perceptions of Post-War II American Literature in the USSR/Russia," *American Studies International*, October 2001, vol. 39, no. 3 (2001): 47.

28. Valentina A. Libman, *Amerikanskaia literatura v russkikh perevodakh i kritike. Bibliografiia 1776–1975* (Moscow: Nauka, 1977).

29. Anna A. Elistratova, "Talantlivaia apologetika kulatskikh illiuzii," *Khudozhestvennaia literatura*, no. 6 (1934): 32–36.

30. Nadezhda M. Aishiskina, "Primitivizm i prostota," *Literaturnyi kritik*, no.1 (1936): 172–84.

31. Harold Bloom, *The Western Canon. The Books and School of Ages* (New York: Riverhead Books, 1995): 17.

32. Anna A. Elistratova, Tamara I. Silman, Abel' I. Startsev, *Istoriia amerikanskoi literatury* (Moscow; Leningrad: Izdatel'stvo akademii nauk SSSR, 1947).

33. Michael Buzukashvili, "Interview s Abelem Startsevym. Abel Startsev: konzlager' za Jacka Londona i Marka Twaina," *Seagull Magazine*, March 1, 2002, no. 5 (21) (2002). http://www.chayka.org/oarticle.php?id=434 (Accessed May 5, 2015).

34. See: Olga O. Nesmelova, *Puti razvitiia otechestvennoi amerikanisitki XX veka*, (Moscow: Knizhnyi dom, 1998), 140–45.

35. Vladimir G. Prozorov, "The Ills of Limitation and the Evils of Disorientation: Perceptions of Post-War II American Literature in the USSR/Russia," *American Studies International*, October 2001, vol. 39, no. 3 (2001): 42.

36. Nikolai I. Samokhvalov, ed., *Istoriia amerikanskoi literatury*, in 2 vols (Moscow: Prosveshchenie, 1971).

37. Ibid., vol. 1, 155.

38. Ibid., vol. 1, 274.

39. Ibid., vol. 1, 227.

40. Ibid., vol. 1, 226–27.

41. Ibid., vol. 1, 340.

42. Ibid., vol. 2, 316.

43. Robert E. Spiller et al., ed., *Literaturnaia istoriia Soedinennykh Shtatov Ameriki*, in 3 vols., (Moscow: Progress, 1977–1979).

44. Yassen N. Zasursky, *Amerikanskaia literatura XX veka* (Moscow: Izdatel'stvo MGU, 1984).

45. Boris A. Gilenson, *Istoriia literatury SShA. Uchebnoe posobie dlia studentov vysshikh uchebnykh zavedenii* (Moscow: Izdatel'skii Tsentr "Akademiia," 2003).

46. Yassen N. Zasursky, Maya M. Koreneva, Ekaterina A. Stetsenko, ed., *Istoriia literatury SShA*, in 6 vols. (Moscow: IMLI RAN, 1997–2013).

BIBLIOGRAPHY

Aishiskina, Nadezhda M. "Primitivizm i prostota," *Literaturnyi kritik*, no. 1 (1936): 172–84.

Anisimov, Ivan I. and Dinamov, Sergey S. *Litso kapitalisticheskogo rabstva v inostrannoi khudozhestvennoi literature*. Moscow; Leningrad: Gossotzekiz, 1931.

————. *Perevodnaia belletristika v biblioteke. Avantyurnaia i nauchno-fantasticheskaia litera-tura (Zaochnye kursy po perepodgotovke bibliotechnykh rabotnikov profsouznykh bibliotek. Urok 15)*. Moscow: Knigoizdatel'stvo VTZSPS, 1929.

Bloom, Harold. *The Western Canon: The Books and School of Ages*. New York: Riverhead Books, 1995.

Brown, Glenora W. and Brown Deming B. *A Guide to Soviet Russian Translation of American Literature*. New York: Columbia University press, 1954.

Buzukashvili, Michael, "Interview s Abelem Startzevym. Abel' Startzev: kontslager' za Jacka Londona i Marka Twaina,," *Seagull Magazine*, March 1, 2002, no. 5 (21) (2002). http://www.chayka.org/oarticle.php?id=434 (Accessed May 5, 2015).

Dinamov, Sergey S. "Predislovie,," in Sinclair, Upton B. *Den'gi pishut*. Moscow; Lenin-grad: Gosudarstvennoe izdatel'stvo, 1927, 3–26.

————. "Sovremennaia amerikanskaia literatura," *Krasnoe studenchestvo*, no. 3 (1926): 85–88.

Djagalov, Rossen. "'I Don't Boast about it, but I'm the Most Widely Read Author of this Century': Howard Fast and International Leftist Literary Culture, ca. Mid-Twentieth Century," *Anthropology of East Europe Review*, vol. 2, no. 27 (2009): 40–55.

Eikhenbaum, Boris M. *O. Henry and the Theory of the Short Story*. Transl., with Notes and Postscript of Irwin R. Titunik. Ann Arbor: Dept. of Slavic Languages and Liter-atures, University of Michigan, 1968.

Elistratova, Anna A. "Talantlivaia apologetika kulatskikh illiuzii," *Khudozhestvennaia literatura*, no. 6 (1934): 32–36.

Elistratova, Anna A., Silman, Tamara I., and Startzev Abel I. *Istoriia amerikanskoi litera-tury*. Moscow; Leningrad: Izdatel'stvo akademii nauk SSSR, 1947.

Filatova, Liudmila V. "Negrityanskaia literatura," in Vladimir M. Friche, ed., *Literatur-naia entsiklopediia*. Moscow: Izdatel'stvo Kommunisticheskoi akademii, 1929–1939, http://feb-web.ru/feb/litenc/encyclop/le7/le7-6491.htm (accessed May 5, 2015).

Gilenson, Boris A. *Istoriia literatury SShA. Uchebnoe posobie dlia studentov vysshikh ucheb-nykh zavedenii*. Moscow: Izdatel'skii Tsentr "Akademiia," 2003.

Kashkin, Ivan A. "Novoe v negrityanskoi literature," *Vestnik inostrannoi literatury*, no. 10 (1928): 143–46.

Krymov, Vladimir P. "Amerikanskie vpechatleniia," *Zapad*, no. 4 (1922): 28–31.

Lann, Evgenii L., "[Retsenziia na knigu *Negrityanskii rai* (Leningrad: Biblioteka Vse-mirnoi literatury, 1928)]," *Pechat' i revolutsiia*, no. 6 (1928): 217–19.

Levidov, Mikhail Yu. "Amerikanizma tragifars," *LEF*, no. 2 (1923): 45–46.

Levit, Teodor M, "Proletliteratura SAShS," *Vestnik inostrannoi literatury*, no. 6 (1930): 74–98.

Libman, Valentina A. *Amerikanskaia literatura v russkikh perevodakh i kritike. Bibliografiia 1776–1975*. Moscow: Nauka, 1977.

Nesmelova, Olga O. "Perception of Afro-American Writers by Soviet Literary Criti-cism of the 1920–30s" http://kpfu.ru//staff_files/F18500529/Perception.of.Afro_American.pdf (Acessed May 5, 2015).

————. *Puti razvitiia otechestvennoi amerikanisitki XX veka*. Moscow: Knizhnyi dom, 1998.

Prozorov, Vladimir G., "The Ills of Limitation and the Evils of Disorientation: Percep-tions of Post-War II American Literature in the USSR/ Russia," *American Studies International*. vol. 39, no. 3 (October 2001): 41–50.

Samokhvalov Nikolay I., ed. *Istoriia amerikanskoi literatury*, in 2 vols. Moscow: Prosveshchenie, 1971.

Spiller, Robert E. et al., eds. *Literaturnaia istoriia Soedinennykh Shtatov Ameriki*, in 3 vols. Moscow: Progress, 1977–1979.

Startsev, Abel I. "Vseobshchii krizis kapitalizma i novaia volna soiuznikov proletaria-ta v literature Ameriki," *Marksistsko-leninskoe iskusstvoznanie*, no. 5–6 (1932): 39–62.

[s.s.]. "Negrityanskaia literatura v Amerike," *Na literaturnom postu*, no. 13–14 (1928): 79–80.

Zasursky, Yassen N., *Amerikanskaia literatura XX veka*. Moscow: Izdatel'stvo MGU, 1984.

Zasursky Yassen N., Koreneva Maya M., Stetsenko Ekaterina A., eds. *Istoriia literatury SShA*, in 6 vols. Moscow: IMLI RAN, 1997–2013.

Zenkevich, Mikhail A. "O novinkakh angliiskoi i amerikanskoi literatury," *Novyi Mir*, no. 12 (1934): 163–76.

Zhuravleva, Victoria I., Kurilla, Ivan I., eds. *Rossiia i SShA na stranitsakh uchebnikov: opyt vzaimnykh reprezentatsii [Russia and the United States: Mutual Representations in the Textbooks]*. Volgograd: Izd-vo VolGU, 2009.

Part II

Disciplines and Area Studies Centers in the Context of Foreign Policy Making and Societal Demand

TEN

Russia in the Representations of the Council on Foreign Relations during the Period of Nonrecognition

Alexander B. Okun and Iana V. Shchetinskaia

At the time of World War I and especially during the Paris Peace Conference, a remarkable situation had come about in the relations between political power and the expert community. It never really had happened before that experts like economists, historians, diplomats, political scientists, and journalists played such an important role in formulating political ideology. Due to this situation, a demand emerged for the institutionalization of expert resources, which at that time meant creating a system of foreign policy research institutes. In 1921 one of the first international research institutions, the Council on Foreign Relations (CFR), was founded and headquartered in New York City.

Originally, the CFR was a nonpartisan organization. Among its founders were Elihu Root, a Republican, a secretary of war, who also served as a secretary of state, and the council's president, John W. Davis, a Democrat, who had used to be a US ambassador to Great Britain and in 1924 was a presidential candidate. The early council members included highly qualified lawyers, economists, scholars, and diplomats, as well as high-ranking government officials.[1] This diverse membership was meant to provide the council with independence in producing and promoting ideas and a range of commercial resources. Producing high quality analysis was stated as a primary purpose of the organization: "The Council on Foreign Relations aims to provide a continuous conference on the international aspects of America's political, economic, and financial problems . . . spreading a knowledge of international relations, and, in particular, in developing reasoned American foreign policy."[2]

The activity of the council developed in three main directions. Discussions on the most vital problems of international relations with a participation of special guests—prominent American or foreign politicians, diplomats, and other public figures (the first guest was G. Clemenceau on November 21, 1922)—were the first one. These conferences were not open to the general public and their proceedings were not published, with very few exceptions.[3]

The second form of the council's activity was the creation of special "study groups" to investigate the problems of the postwar world: the domestic basis of foreign policy, the Russian revolution, and international finance. These groups issued reports intended for American political and business elite.

One of the most important measures to achieve the council's goals was the publication of *Foreign Affairs* which first appeared in September 1922. *Foreign Affairs* is a journal, which provides profound foreign policy analysis as well as a platform for discussing widely diverging viewpoints. Its first editor-in-chief was a professor of history at Harvard College, Archibald C. Coolidge. The journal's first issue contained a statement setting out the editorial policy and its goals:

1. To promote the discussion of current questions of international interest.
2. To provide competent American and European experts with the opportunity to express their opinions on major international issues.
3. To represent diverse views and to remain tolerant to wide differences of opinion.[4]

Over the first decade of the journal's existence these principles remained constant and helped its members to carry out effective analysis. Later this approach helped to transform the journal into an important source which could influence political debate. The initial issue of the journal included articles by E. Root, C. W. Eliott, J. F. Dulles, E. Beneš, and A. Tardieu. The list of prominent thinkers, who published their articles on the pages of *Foreign Affairs*, has been quite impressive ever since.

Since the creation of *Foreign Affairs*, it has been important for its founders to perform in-depth analysis of international problems dealing with Russia for several reasons, both global and subjective. The first reason was Russia's complex and contradictory role in international affairs, the second was interest in Russia within the United States. Furthermore, the journal's editor, A. C. Coolidge, was one of the most outstanding experts in Russian studies. He visited Russia many times, collected a huge library of Russian books and books on Russia. According to the managing editor H. F. Armstrong, who, after the death of A. Coolidge in

1928, became the editor, it was highly important to focus on the Russian topic.[5] As a result, thirty-eight articles about Russia were published over the first eleven years and forty-five issues of *Foreign Affairs*. One of these articles was published in issue number one under the title "Russia after Genoa and the Hague" under the initial "K" and this was the article by A. Coolidge himself. This article attracted a lot of interest, partly because it was the only one published under the pen-name, partly because it was the longest of all articles in the issue. In this article Coolidge gave a profound analysis of Russian domestic and foreign policy problems and made an attempt to predict Russia's further political and economic development. The author touched upon the question of whether it would be rational to recognize the Soviet Russia, and he gave arguments for and against this possible decision. He stressed that Russia played a crucial role in world economy due to its resources and rapid economic development. For Coolidge these factors were far too important to be ignored by other countries, thus, international recognition of Russia was just the matter of time. He emphasized that the United States could recognize Soviet Russia without damaging its political image. "To recognize the government of a country does not imply that we admire it, it is merely to take note of an existing fact."[6]

Coolidge's article was intended mostly for American readers; however, it received a lot of unexpected attention. In November 1922 Frank Golder, who was a student of Coolidge at Harvard, and one of the pioneers in Russian studies in the United States wrote Coolidge a letter in which he informed him that K. Radek got interested in the journal and published a review in the *Pravda* newspaper. Golder stressed that Radek was especially interested in the Coolidge's article and highly praised it as he claimed that this article was the best one dealing with Russia recently. More than that, Radek gave the article to V. Lenin, who studied it and marked it up. Golder and Radek exchanged their journal issues, so, an issue of *Foreign Affairs* containing commentaries and marks made by Lenin and Radek is in the CFR archive.[7]

The analytical approach toward representations of Russia in the first article published in *Foreign Affairs* remained practically the same in later articles. In further publications authors also expressed sustainable interest in Russian studies and they focused their attention on both domestic policy and foreign policy issues of Soviet Russia and later the USSR. Another principle was providing objective research by publishing articles by authors of different backgrounds and sometimes opposing viewpoints. Analysis of *Foreign Affairs* publications is presented in the tables below.

Authors of these articles can be divided into three groups according to their positions and backgrounds:

Table 10.1.   Number of articles about Russia per year

1922	1923	1924	1925	1926	1927	1928	1929	1930	1931	1932	1933
2	3	3	3	3	4	3	5	6	2	2	1

1. Representatives of various Russian emigration movements (V. Chernov, V. Zenzinov, B. Bakhmeteff, Y. Danilov, and P. Haensel).
2. Soviet government officials (K. Radek, C. Rakovsky, and N. Liubimov).
3. American and foreign experts (A. C. Coolidge, M. Florinsky, N. Roosevelt, H. Laski, P. Scheffer, W. Miller, C. Sforza, K. Kawakami, W. H. Chamberlin, E. Vandervelde, B. Hopper, J. E. Spurr, R. Kelley, P. Cravath, and M. Davis).

At that time the CFR lacked scholars who were engaged in Russian studies and this problem was a serious obstacle for producing relevant research. According to David Engermann, "There was no field of Russian Studies, just a handful of scholars, varying widely in interest, energy, training, and talents, spread thinly across American universities."[8] In this regard, analysis was mostly provided not by scholars, but by journalists, who used to work in Russia (P. Scheffer, W. H. Chamberlin, M. Davis, and K. Kawakami), as well as politicians (C. Sforza, E. Vandervelde, and H. Laski), lawyers (P. Cravath), and diplomats (N. Roosevelt and R. F. Kelley). Only a few scholars paid attention to developing research concerning Russian problems: A. C. Coolidge, M. Florinsky, and B. Hopper. However, they represented different political positions, ranging from extreme anti-communism (R. F. Kelley) to Marxism and left-wing views (E. Vandervelde, H. Laski, W. H. Chamberlin, and K. Kawakami).

Russian immigrants, who published their works, such as V. Chernov and B. Bakhmeteff and others, occupied a special place among experts. V. Chernov, the leader of the Social-Revolutionaries Party worked as a specialist in the sphere of USSR domestic policy. From 1923 to 1930, *Foreign Affairs* published five articles dealing with different aspects of internal policy, all written by Chernov. He was particularly interested in the intra-party struggle of the 1920s, which started after Lenin's death. In terms of this infighting Chernov managed to provide analysis of many Soviet political leaders, as he knew most of them personally. In his article from 1924, dedicated to Lenin's personality, Chernov describes him as a great man, who was extraordinarily masterful in working out tactics, in dealing with political rivals as well as allies. Moreover, the author stressed that Lenin could always sense the needs of his audience. Along with that, he had no respect for the convictions of anyone else and was absolutely ruthless with his political opponents. Chernov anticipated that Lenin's death would have led to a sort of split and political in-fighting within the

Table 10.2.   Categorizing articles according to the topic

Domestic policy	Foreign policy	Economy	Social issues	The problem of nonrecognition
10	10	11	4	3

party.[9] In his subsequent articles, Chernov also provided insight into Lenin's personality, describing him as Bolshevism's embodiment:

> Lenin was the two-faced Janus of Bolshevism. On one side there showed the face of a fanatic, a cold theoretician and drafter of dogmas, a compiler of a catechism of social philosophy which tolerates no deviations—the face of an old-time religious sectarian, except that he took Marx's *Capital* for his Bible. The other side showed the face of a crafty practical politician, who gives little consideration to his own dogmas in his choice of tactics for the immediate present.

In actuality, political struggle within the party reflected this contradiction and conflict between the two sides inevitably resulted in the triumph of a partisan bureaucracy controlled by Stalin. The consequence of Russian domestic policy development during that period was the establishment of the absolute proletarian dictatorship and the confluence of partisan organization and institutional power.[10] In the article, published in 1930, Chernov stated that his earlier estimates happened to prove true and made new negative forecasts, anticipating new crises: "But the scale of the balance has decidedly turned in favor not of the smooth, evolutionary course, but of a course rich in cataclysms and perturbations."[11]

Boris Bakhmeteff, the former ambassador from the Russian Provisional Government in Washington, DC, published two articles devoted to Russian internal policy in *Foreign Affairs*. In 1924 he noted some contradictions between Bolshevism theory and practices and "democratic forces of life." Bakhmeteff wrote that "autocracy of the state, economic collectivism, and internationalism are the bases of the system on which the country is governed today." However, at the same time, he remained hopeful that "the present, no matter how overwhelming it appears to the outside observer, is but a point in the great process of transformation from the old regime to the future democracy."[12]

His next article "Ten Years of Bolshevism," was published in 1928. In it, Bakhmeteff tried to summarize the first decade of Soviet Russia. The most important result for him was that "Russia became a gigantic structure of economic etatism."[13] Later that year Bakhmeteff discussed the situation in Soviet Russia with J. Dewey and P. Cravath at a CFR dinner.[14] The year 1928 marked the beginning of a new upsurge of interest in Russia. P. N. Milyukov, minister of foreign relations in the Russian Provisional Government, was a speaker at another CFR dinner in May. H. F. Armstrong visited Moscow and met with M. Litvinov, acting commissar for foreign relations in Soviet government, and discussed with him the future of Russian-American relations in the context of the coming American presidential elections.[15]

V. Zenzinov, another leader of Social-Revolutionaries Party, acted as an expert on Bolshevik's agrarian policy[16] and General Y. Danilov analyzed the Soviet military forces.[17] Paul Haensel (Pavel Petrovich Gensel), Russian and American financier, economist, and scholar, who from 1921 to 1928 was a consultant for the Soviet finance ministry and a chief of the financial department of the Institute of Economic Studies in Moscow—he emigrated from Russia only in 1928—wrote an article for *Foreign Affairs* on Soviet labor policy. He particularly stressed different methods used for government economic program fulfillment. Enthusiasm of workers in the state factories was the first one, "But the chief cause of what progress has been made is to be found in the drastic exploitation of the working class and in the pressure which has been put on all other classes. The methods applied by the Soviet Government in dealing with labor would be impossible in normal times in any civilized democratic country." The main conclusion of the article was that "the whole economic system of Soviet Russia today is based on pressure and forced labor."[18]

These very critical views written by Russian political opponents of Soviet power were balanced by giving Soviet government officials the opportunity to publish their work on the pages of *Foreign Affairs*. Karl Radek and Christian Rakovsky published articles devoted to the foreign policy of Soviet Russia and tried to convince Americans of its peaceful character. One of the most important aims of Rakovsky's article was to express the aspiration of Soviet government to establish diplomatic relations with the United States.[19] N. Liubimov, a leading Russian economist and expert in international economic relations (he also had translated John Maynard Keynes into Russian), analyzed economic relations between Russia and Western world. He concluded that foreign concessions didn't play any important role in the Soviet economic system. Though, "the effective employment of foreign technical methods, especially in industries admitting of high standardization of the American type, presents for us so urgent a problem that the Government has embarked on a program of still more energetic measures to encourage closer relations between our economic organs and reliable firms in America and Europe."[20]

Publication of the articles of Soviet officials and Western leftist intellectuals enabled accusations against the CFR of supporting the Bolsheviks. This charge became part of conspiracy theory on the connections between Wall Street and Russian Revolution.[21] In fact, however, those publications absolutely matched the principles of independent and objective expertise which were proclaimed by the CFR according to Latin rule "Audiatur et altera pars." In the future, the council also followed this rule by providing pages of *Foreign Affairs* for L. Trotsky, N. Khrushchev, and so on.

In 1923 the study group on Russia and Central Europe was created with Coolidge and the director of the CFR I. Bowman as co-chairs. The tasks of this group were to investigate the international consequences of the Russian revolution and the perspectives of American-Russian relations. Another important issue was the economic situation and especially the New Economic Policy (NEP) of the Soviet government. According to R. Schulzinger's analysis, based on the CFR archive, the first meetings of the Soviet study group "presented a mixed picture of a Bolshevik government securely in power but not likely to expand beyond its own borders." So, Soviet Russia was not an immediate threat and the question of economic cooperation with it became part of the agenda. This was particularly important for firms and banks which invested in Russia before the revolution. The NEP of the Soviet government could be regarded as an opportunity to return on the Russian market. That is why the NEP took a significant place in council's research and on the pages of *Foreign Affairs*. The report of the Soviet study group of March 23 said that the NEP is a return to sanity and sound business practice, but it represented only a temporary truce with the concessionaries.[22] At the same time *Foreign Affairs* published Arthur Bullard's reviews on several books about recent Russian economic development in which he stated that the NEP was not "a return to capitalism," because it had not changed "the political structure of the Soviets," and was a victory of those willing to face reality over the orthodox Communists. So, the future of the NEP was uncertain.[23] That realistic analysis was the basis for recommendations for American business to get into Russia, make money, and get out as quickly as possible.[24] These recommendations were taken into consideration, at least the business career of A. Hammer or W. A. Harriman (he was a member of the CFR) in Russia developed in accordance with them.

Interest in Soviet economic policy and the NEP was sustained through the 1920s and reality confirmed the predictions. In the January 1929 issue of *Foreign Affairs*, Paul Scheffer (a journalist, who worked in Soviet Union for seven years and after that published several books on his Russian experience) published an article under title "The Crisis of the 'NEP' in Soviet Russia." He considered that crisis as a consequence of the conflict between the socialistic and private forms of economics, and concluded that it was the objective result of the evolution of Soviet economic system.[25]

Different aspects of that system were the subjects of articles published by Harvard Professor B. Hopper and journalist W. H. Chamberlin. The attitude of both of them toward Russia could be regarded as quite sympathetic, but their texts differed a lot. Hopper analyzed the process of Soviet industrialization. He believed that "the Russian people have no alternative to industrialization but continued economic backwardness" though the price of it might be exorbitant because "the Soviet Government is consciously sacrificing the welfare of the present generation to that of the next" which could become a collective society of dehumanized robots.[26] In a 1932 article, he focused on the fact that Soviet society avoided this danger and made two conclusions:

> The first is that regimentation has enabled Soviet Russia to weather the depression with fewer apparent economic dislocations than those which have shaken the capitalist world. The second is that the Bolsheviks are taking advantage of the breathing spell to shift their emphasis from the machine to the human beings who operate the machine . . . and they feel free to take definite steps to improve the welfare of their people and to advance 'world revolution' not, as they have threatened in the past, by open aggression, but by example.[27]

That positive image of a great and successful social experiment in Soviet Russia was very popular among Western leftist intellectuals both in academia and mass media. W. H. Chamberlin's articles in *Foreign Affairs* confirmed this observation.[28]

The Council on Foreign Relations could not stay away from the discussion on American recognition of the Soviet government. This problem had been touched upon in the first issue of *Foreign Affairs* in Coolidge's article. After that, in almost every article or discussion connected with Russia the theme of recognition was present. This issue became particularly important at the end of the 1920s through the beginning of the 1930s, in the time of Soviet industrialization and the expansion of US-Russian economic relations. M. Davis, an American journalist and international relations specialist, executive for the Carnegie Endowment for International Peace, who had been working in Russia for several years, underlined the economic basis of prospective American recognition of Soviet Union in 1927. He traced the history of political and diplomatic relations between Soviet Russia and foreign countries and found that "there is a tendency to throw business to nations from whom the Soviet Government desires and expects recognition. . . . But with the United States, under present circumstances, the Soviet Government can have slight hope of establishing diplomatic relations." So, Russian-American economic relations were based on pragmatic "internal economic needs of the government."[29]

P. Scheffer argued that the political aspect of the American recognition was far more important than the commercial one. He criticized the idea of recognition as a wrong American policy toward Soviet Russia:

> For some eleven years now the American Republic has refused recognition on ethical grounds. Moscow would infer from a change in the American attitude that economic considerations had forced the United States to give up its opposition to the Soviet Government; for no one knows better than the people at Moscow that the ethical argument

against recognition is as well substantiated and valid as ever. They would promptly attribute the change of policy to America's economic weakness.

Therefore, American recognition would be the victory of Bolsheviks and "under these circumstances recognition by America could only provoke Communist Russia to greater aggressiveness and enterprise in its attacks on the bourgeois European countries and their colonial points of weakness." More than that, "turning to the direct effects which American recognition might have within the Soviet sphere itself, we may say that it would be regarded as a personal victory for Stalin, and just the sort of victory he needs." Scheffer thought that negative consequences of recognition would be much more significant than any possible benefits. [30]

The article by vice president of the CFR, lawyer P. D. Cravath became a sort of summary of the discussion mentioned above. Cravath also stressed the importance of the problem: "the question of recognition of the Soviet Government of Russia by the United States is one of the most vital international problems confronting the American people." As a result, he formulated the following basic theses:

1. "Usually the primary motive of a government in recognizing the government of another state is self interest. It simply seeks to establish relations which will enable it to protect the life, liberty and property of its citizens and to promote their interests, and reciprocally to establish a basis for dealing with the other country and its citizens."
2. "Our government has frequently established cordial diplomatic relations with governments that were notoriously autocratic and vicious. Usually the sole test that our government seeks to apply is whether the new government is sufficiently entrenched in power effectively to govern within its own borders and to perform its international obligations."

Based on this, Cravath tried to determine the pros and cons of the solution. He could see only few arguments for the continuation of the policy of nonrecognition. The most important among them was that the Soviet government's policy didn't meet certain conditions and its recognition would mean "a surrender of 'cherished rights of humanity' or of American principles." At the same time, he asked "is it wise diplomacy to insist upon a definitive agreement as a condition of recognition?" His answer was negative and he offered to use the experience of normalization of American relations with the revolutionary government in Mexico where the US diplomatic mission was sent to "ascertain by negotiation with the Mexican Government whether there could be found a promising basis for the ultimate recognition and determination of those claims" as a precedent. "Upon receiving a satisfactory report from its mission, the

American Government entered into diplomatic relations with the revolutionary government in Mexico and after prolonged negotiations the American Ambassador brought about a settlement of most of the questions at issue between the two nations." Besides, recognition didn't include approval of Soviet principles and methods. In fact, Cravath repeated the argument published in the Coolidge' 1922 article.

The benefits for America of recognition of the Soviet Union would be much more numerous:

1. "Our government would be in a position through its diplomatic representatives to protect the life, liberty and property of Americans visiting, or sojourning in, Russia."
2. "Our government would be able by the usual diplomatic methods to encourage and protect American trade with Russia."
3. "Only by the establishment of diplomatic relations can outstanding differences between the United States and Russia, such as those in relation to dumping and convict labor, be dealt with adequately."
4. "With an Ambassador at Moscow and consuls in the principal trading centers of Russia our government would be able to assemble reliable information for the guidance of our merchants, manufacturers and bankers."
5. "Finally, it seems a great pity that the United States should be the only one of the Great Powers which has deliberately excluded itself from exercising any influence through the usual diplomatic channels in the development of the institutions of the most populous nation in Europe, whose return to economic, social and political stability is essential for the peace and prosperity of the civilized world."[31]

Actually, Cravath (and we may say the CFR itself) formulated and grounded the strategy of American government in the problem of recognition of the Soviet Union which was implemented two years later.

To sum up, one can conclude that the Russian question was among the most important issues of the activity of the CFR. The Council of Foreign Relations reviewed different aspects of this question and reflected the full range of positions and opinions. The result was the development of recommendations for the government in addressing one of the most important problems of US foreign policy.

Research dealing with Soviet Russia problems was crucial for shaping principles and methods of foreign policy analysis within the CFR in the future. First, the idea of gathering and processing the opinions from various people with different backgrounds and working in different professional fields made the boundaries between different spheres of knowledge blurry, and introduced a multidisciplinary approach. At the same time, this pluralism of opinions could not but lead to presenting one problem from many different sides, which, benefited for the quality and depth of the research, and encouraged further collaboration among scholars and discussion in the public sphere. Furthermore, this diversity of opinions as well as the CFR seeking publicity facilitated cooperation among members of a certain discussion and attracted new members. This fact is very important as open collaboration in research is a specific feature which distinguishes think tanks from a lot of other kinds of research organizations, study groups, advocacy groups, and. Actively seeking a variety of specialists involved in Russian studies led to all-round, independent analysis, which was monitored not by one person, but by many experts. All these features were important steps for creating a system of profound analysis. It also should be mentioned, that analyzing American relations with Soviet Russia was a part of a long and successful process of rethinking and rebuilding relations among journalists, scholars, and policymakers, which now makes the United States the world leader in effective policy research.

NOTES

1. Peter Grose, *Continuing the Inquiry: The Council on Foreign Relations from 1921 to 1996* (New York: A Council on Foreign Relations Book, 2006), 9.

2. Laurence H. Shope and William Minter, *Imperial Brain Trust: The Council on Foreign Relations and United States Foreign Policy* (New York and London: Monthly Review Press, 1977), 16.

3. Hamilton F. Armstrong, *Peace and Counterpeace: From Wilson to Hitler* (New York: Harpers and Row Publishers, 1971), 198–203; Peter Grose, *Continuing the Inquiry*, 10–11.

4. Editorial, *Foreign Affairs*, September 15, 1922, vol. 1, no. 1:1–2.

5. Armstrong, *Peace and Counterpeace*, 192.

6. K, "Russia after Genoa and the Hague," *Foreign Affairs*, September 15, 1922, vol. 1, no. 1: 154.

7. Harold J. Coolidge and Robert H. Lord, *Archibald Cary Coolidge: Life and Letters* (Boston and New York: Houghton Mifflin Company, 1932), 314–15; Armstrong*Peace and Counterpeace*, 193–94.

8. David C. Engerman, *Know Your Enemy: The Rise and Fall of America's Soviet Experts* (Oxford: Oxford University Press, 2009), 2.

9. Victor Chernov, "Lenin," *Foreign Affairs*, March, 15, 1924, vol. 2, no. 3: 369–70, 372.

10. Victor Chernov "Bolshevik Romance and Reality," *Foreign Affairs*, January, 27, vol. 5, no. 2: 308, 319–20.

11. Victor Chernov, "Russia's Two Parties," *Foreign Affairs*, October, 30, 1930, vol. 9, no. 1: 94.

12. Boris Bakhmeteff, "Russia at the Cross-Roads," *Foreign Affairs*, March, 15, 1924, vol. 2, no. 3: 421, 435.

13. Boris Bakhmeteff, "Ten Years of Bolshevism," *Foreign Affairs*, July, 1928, vol. 6, no. 4: 591.

14. "Discuss Russia of Today," *New York Times*, December, 6, 1928: 59.

15. Armstrong, *Peace and Counterpeace*, 412–13.

16. Vladimir Zenzinov, "The Bolsheviks and the Peasant," *Foreign Affairs*, October, 1925, vol. 4, no. 1: 134–43.

17. Yuri Danilov, "The Red Army," *Foreign Affairs*, October, 1928, vol. 7, no. 1: 96–109

18. Paul Haensel, "Labor under the Soviets," *Foreign Affairs*, April, 1931, vol. 9, no. 3: 397.

19. Karl Radek, "The War in the Far East: A Soviet View," *Foreign Affairs*, July, 1932, vol. 10, no. 4: 541–57; Karl Radek, "The Bases of Soviet Foreign Policy," *Foreign Affairs*, January, 1934, vol. 12, no. 2: 193–206; Christian Rakovsky, "The Foreign Policy of Soviet Russia," *Foreign Affairs*, vol. 4, no. 4: 574–84.

20. Nikolai Liubimov, "The Soviets and Foreign Concessions," *Foreign Affairs*, October, 1930, vol. 9, no. 1: 105.

21. James Perloff, *The Shadows of Power: The Council on Foreign Relations and the American Decline* (Appleton, WI: Western Islands, 1988), 38–42.

22. Robert D. Schulzinger, *The Wise Men of Foreign Affairs: The History of the Council on Foreign Relations* (New York: Columbia University Press, 1984), 20–21.

23. Arthur Bullard, "The New Russian Economic Policy," *Foreign Affairs*, March, 15, 1923, vol. 1, no. 3: 142–43.

24. Schulzinger, *The Wise Men of Foreign Affairs*, 21.

25. Scheffer, "The Crisis of the "NEP" in Soviet Russia," 234–41.

26. Bruce C. Hopper, "The Soviet Touchstone: Industrialization," *Foreign Affairs*, April, 1930, vol. 8, no. 3: 397–98.

27. Bruce C. Hopper, "Soviet Economy in a New Phase," *Foreign Affairs*, April, 1932, vol. 10, no. 3: 464.

28. William Henry Chamberlin "The Russian Peasant Sphinx," *Foreign Affairs*, April, 1929, vol. 7, no. 3: 477–87; William Henry Chamberlin, "Making the Collective Man in Soviet Russia," *Foreign Affairs*, January, 1932, vol. 10, no. 2: 280–92; William Henry Chamberlin, "The Balance Sheet of the Five Year Plan," *Foreign Affairs*, April, 1933, vol. 11, no. 3: 458–69.

29. Malcolm W. Davis, "Soviet Recognition and Trade," *Foreign Affairs*, July, 1927, vol. 5, no. 4: 659.

30. Paul Scheffer, "American Recognition of Russia: What It Would Mean to Europe," *Foreign Affairs*, October, 1930, vol. 9, no. 1: 39–41.

31. Paul D. Cravath, "The Pros and Cons of Soviet Recognition," *Foreign Affairs*, January, 1931, vol. 9, no. 2: 266–76.

BIBLIOGRAPHY

Armstrong, Hamilton F. *Peace and Counterpeace: From Wilson to Hitler*. New York: Harpers and Row Publishers, 1971.

Bakhmeteff, Boris. "Ten Years of Bolshevism," *Foreign Affairs*, July, 1928, vol. 6, no. 4.

———. "Russia at the Cross-Roads," *Foreign Affairs*, March, 15, 1924, vol. 2, no. 3.

Bullard, Arthur. "The New Russian Economic Policy," *Foreign Affairs*, March, 15, 1923, vol. 1, no. 3.

Chamberlin, William Henry. "The Balance Sheet of the Five Year Plan," *Foreign Affairs*, April, 1933, vol. 11, no. 3.

———. "Making the Collective Man in Soviet Russia," *Foreign Affairs*, January, 1932, vol. 10, no. 2.

———. "The Russian Peasant Sphinx," *Foreign Affairs*, April, 1929, vol. 7, no. 3.

Chernov, Victor. "Russia's Two Parties," *Foreign Affairs*, October, 30, 1930, vol. 9, no. 1.

———. "Lenin," *Foreign Affairs*, March, 15, 1924, vol. 2, no. 3.

———. "Bolshevik Romance and Reality," *Foreign Affairs*, January, 27, 1927, vol. 5, no. 2.

Coolidge, Harold J., and Robert H. Lord. *Archibald Cary Coolidge:Life and Letters*. Boston and New York: Houghton Mifflin Company, 1932.

Cravath, Paul D. "The Pros and Cons of Soviet Recognition," *Foreign Affairs*, January, 1931, vol. 9, no. 2.

Danilov, Yuri. "The Red Army," *Foreign Affairs*, October, 1928, vol. 7, no. 1.

Davis, Malcolm W. "Soviet Recognition and Trade," *Foreign Affairs*, July, 1927, vol. 5, no. 4.

"Discuss Russia of Today," *New York Times*, December, 6, 1928.

Engerman, David C. *Know Your Enemy. The Rise and Fall of America's Soviet Experts.* Oxford: Oxford University Press, 2009.

Foreign Affairs, 1922–1933.

Grose, Peter. *Continuing the Inquiry: The Council on Foreign Relations from 1921 to 1996.* New York: A Council on Foreign Relations Book, 2006.

Hopper, Bruce C. "Soviet Economy in a New Phase," *Foreign Affairs*, April, 1932, vol. 10, no. 3.

———. "The Soviet Touchstone: Industrialization," *Foreign Affairs*, April, 1930, vol. 8, no. 3.

Liubimov, Nikolai. "The Soviets and Foreign Concessions," *Foreign Affairs*, October, 1930, vol. 9, no. 1.

Perloff, James. *The Shadows of Power. The Council on Foreign Relations and the American Decline.* Appleton, WI: Western Islands, 1988.

Radek, Karl. "The Bases of Soviet Foreign Policy," *Foreign Affairs*, January, 1934, vol. 12, no. 2.

———. "The War in the Far East: A Soviet View," *Foreign Affairs*, July, 1932, vol. 10, no. 4.

Rakovsky, Christian "The Foreign Policy of Soviet Russia," *Foreign Affairs*, vol. 4, no. 4.

Scheffer, Paul. "American Recognition of Russia: What It Would Mean to Europe," *Foreign Affairs*, October, 1930, vol. 9, no. 1.

———. "The Crisis of the "NEP" in Soviet Russia," *Foreign Affairs*, January, 1929, vol. 7, no. 2.

Schulzinger, Robert D. *The Wise Men of Foreign Affairs: The History of the Council on Foreign Relations.* New York: Columbia University Press, 1984.

Shope, Laurence H., and William Minter. *Imperial Brain Trust: The Council on Foreign Relations and United States Foreign Policy.* New York and London: Monthly Review Press, 1977.

Zenzinov, Vladimir. "The Bolsheviks and the Peasant," *Foreign Affairs*, October, 1925, vol. 4, no. 1.

ELEVEN

Knowing Allies and Enemies

The World War II Origins of
Soviet Studies in American Universities

David C. Engerman

Area studies, which grew alongside Soviet-American global tensions in the late 1940s and early 1950s, were in fact a product of a very different age. They owed their institutional structures and sources of funding not just to the Cold War—as recent scholarship takes for granted—but more importantly to World War II. The exploration of the full gamut of area studies is a book-long project and a sprawling one at that. This chapter traces the genealogy of area studies programs in the United States by focusing on the evolution of Soviet studies—one of the first area programs to reach fruition, and the one most obviously related to Cold War geopolitics. This chapter will show how the assumptions of World War II were embedded in early area studies programs, and also how the programs' founders had multiple aims in mind. Soviet studies programs—like those that emerged to study Asia, the Middle East, Africa, and Latin America—clearly had the "Cold War" connections to national security that have been the source of recent criticism. But they also served intellectual and pedagogical agendas usually left out of critical accounts of the so-called "Cold War social sciences."[1]

Those few observers who identify the World War II origins of area studies in American universities often point to the transplantation of the Office of Strategic Services (OSS, the wartime predecessor to the CIA) into the ivory tower. Sovietology's critics and fans alike often attribute the field's early character—usually meaning its connections to national security and its emphasis on the social sciences—to the institutions of World War II. For instance, presidential advisor and one-time Harvard dean McGeorge Bundy celebrated the "curious fact" that "the first great center of area studies" was the OSS's Research and Analysis Branch.[2]

The OSS did house an impressive array of scholars, divided up according to world region: Latin America, Europe/Africa, Far East, and the USSR. The scholars were selected on the basis of expertise amid a wartime attitude of total mobilization. As a result, political heterodoxy ran rampant in the OSS ranks: the head of the USSR division, Geroid Tanquary Robinson, was a onetime Greenwich Village radical, while his staff included many with close connections to radical politics in the 1930s; the OSS also employed a contingent of the Frankfurt School, including Herbert Marcuse. Just as the group mixed politics, they also mixed disciplines, as the regionally organized divisions brought together political scientists, sociologists, historians, and economists focused on a given region.[3] The research aims—estimates of military and economic capabilities and predictions of political stability—placed a premium on social-scientific research of current events. The applied nature of the OSS work, which was read by policymakers not fellow scholars, called for an interdisciplinary approach; as one analyst put it, the consumers of OSS reports were "not interested in the production of principles of social sciences, neatly departmentalized," but in analyses that "involved all the disciplines" to answer pressing tactical and strategic questions. The result was an interdisciplinary research program—first created for the study of the USSR—that one historian aptly termed "social science in one country."[4] According to the oft-told tale, OSS veterans returned to their old universities and departments at the conclusion of the war and transplanted that successful experience into educational institutions.[5] Tracing the field's origins to wartime intelligence serves both to emphasize the applied nature of the work as well as the close connections to national security organs.

This tale of origins—that area studies were directly descended from intelligence organs—is, however, misleading in many ways. There were significant differences between the intelligence model and the university programs that soon emerged. The universities expanded the definition of area studies to include not just research, but also training for a new generation of area experts.[6] With their focus on training, university area studies programs—including Soviet studies—looked very different from the OSS.

Indeed, other wartime programs—those related to training—served as models for early Soviet studies as much as, if not more than, the OSS. Three related endeavors bequeathed a great deal of the form, content, and personnel that would define Soviet studies (and area studies in general) during the decade after the war: the armed services, the Rockefeller Foundation, and Rockefeller Foundation beneficiaries. All three of these programs, furthermore, differed from OSS by building on interwar academic experiments.

Two of the wartime efforts in area studies training were run by the armed services but located on university campuses. Both the Army and the Navy established language-and-area programs at American universities during the war. The Army, in fact, had two distinct enterprises: the Army Specialized Training Program (ASTP) enrolled enlisted personnel while the Civilian Affairs Training Program (CATP) trained officers. ASTP was far larger and broader; its 150-plus programs taught some sixty thousand personnel everything from medicine to engineering to psychology. Nineteen American universities hosted ASTP programs in foreign language and area studies; each employed its own faculty members as well as large cohorts of émigrés as teachers. In the Slavic programs, as in those for other world regions, language training accounted for about half of the instructional hours, with the remaining hours divided between literature, history, culture, and current economic and political events. A similar mix of language and area training prevailed at the CATP programs.[7]

The Navy's Oriental Languages School (OLS), housed at the landlocked University of Colorado, trained about two hundred officers in its few short years of existence. In spite of the small size of its Russian School, it taught Russian to at least three future scholars: historian Martin Malia, literature scholar Hugh McLean, and psychologist Raymond Bauer. (Another OLS student had a more troubling and troubled career: William Remington stood accused of espionage by the "Red Spy Queen" Elizabeth Bentley, went to prison on perjury charges, and was murdered by other inmates.) The Navy program's language instruction did not differ markedly from that in ASTP, though OLS did not devote as much time to broader area studies subjects.[8]

Language and literature scholars played important roles in designing and implementing the Army and Navy programs. They also employed similar techniques in language instruction—techniques still dominant in introductory language teaching in the United States. Instructors with graduate training gave lectures on grammar and syntax twice per week; these were supplemented by daily drill sections with a much smaller class size by native speakers. The oral drill instructor required no training, according to early enthusiasts; after all, the instructor was "not a teacher, but an animated phonograph record." This approach built on experiments in intensive language instruction conducted at Berkeley, Harvard, and Columbia in the 1930s. Funded by the Rockefeller Foundation, these experiments sought to improve instructional techniques for foreign languages in general, and to emphasize oral and aural skills rather than writing skills and grammar. The new approach was in keeping with recent trends in linguistics scholarship that emphasized actual usage rather than abstract grammar, but served other purposes as well.

Oral communication would be especially important for Army officers and enlisted personnel serving as occupation forces overseas — much as it would for naval officers working as liaisons with foreign counterparts. Just as important was the efficiency of this lecture-plus-drill approach: it allowed a relatively small number of university faculty members to teach a large number of students. In the words of one official, the drill instructors provided "better instruction at lower unit cost" than conventional approaches. After the war, various educational commissions evaluated the ASTP and OLS programs and endorsed that pedagogical approach for peacetime instruction; indeed, one termed the approach "a revelation to us and to the country."[9]

Among the groups promoting new forms of language instruction in the context of an area studies program was the Rockefeller Foundation, which was a driving force behind area studies, and especially Slavic studies, during World War II. Through direct grants as well as an alphabet soup of other organizations, the Rockefeller Foundation played the single largest role in the evolution of area studies. Grants to the American Council of Learned Societies (ACLS) and the Social Science Research Council (SSRC) supported conferences to outline an intellectual agenda for "world area studies." And its own staff members convened meetings and supported early programs for research and especially training in Slavic studies, which they saw as a model for future area studies. Only months after the American entry into the war; the foundation's director for the humanities, David H. Stevens, said, that "The face of the future is not hard to read — demands for people who can handle languages and cultures of the Far East is bound to increase." (It is worth noting here that Rockefeller officials included Russia within the "Far East" in its grants to universities and freestanding organizations like the Institute for Pacific Relations.) Stevens thought that regional programs were not merely responses to the present emergency but "food for the present and future." The Rockefeller Foundation's vision was almost an antithesis of the "know your enemy" approach that critics assign to Cold War area studies; on the contrary, the foundation had an inclusive and humanistic notion of the content and purposes of area studies programs.[10]

In 1943, the Rockefeller Foundation hosted a small conference on Slavic studies that brought together a dozen leading Slavic experts, many of whom were active in campus-based training programs for the military. They wanted to know what lessons from the military training programs might apply to postwar programs in the Slavic field. Contemporary politics was far from a major concern. Philip Mosely, a Rockefeller official who later joined the Columbia faculty, believed that the principal aim of Slavic studies should be to study and disseminate knowledge about the importance of the "Slavic peoples" in the world's culture, politics, and economics. The discussions frequently cited the USSR's role in the postwar economy, and the opportunities for expanding US-Soviet trade relations after the war.[11] The focus was on building American-Soviet ties, both cultural and economic, not on knowing the enemy. This inclusive approach would carry over into the first postwar years of Soviet studies.

Where Rockefeller officials themselves left off (with a focus on the humanistic aspects of areas studies), the SSRC picked up. Again, interest during the war was on the intellectual outcomes of area studies. One influential report, by University of Chicago sociologist and dean, Robert Redfield, hoped that area studies would help social scientists overcome their "European and American cultural provincialism." Harvard sociologist Talcott Parsons also celebrated area studies for the possibility that it could bring about the integration of the social sciences. At stake was scholarship, not foreign policy.[12] Most of those involved in wartime discussions of area studies took as a given that the programs would be in the national interest. One important ACLS report set priorities that reveal wartime interests; top billing went to embattled allies Britain and France as well as Axis powers Germany and Italy—along with Spain and Portugal reflecting fears that the Iberian Peninsula might become another front in the war.[13] Taken together, scholars and foundation officials envisioned a program of postwar area studies that focused on whole civilizations, that had a broad humanistic component, and that would offer intellectual benefits for a wide range of scholars. These aims did not disappear as the uneasy wartime alliance between the United States and the Soviet Union turned into Cold War antagonisms in the years after 1945.

The Rockefeller Foundation's programs on Slavic studies, discussed during the last years of the war and coming to fruition in 1945 and 1946, had three goals. First, they sought to establish an exchange program, bringing Soviet scholars to the United States to teach Americans about Soviet life.[14] These attempts, half-hearted at best, quickly came to nothing. More serious was the foundation's support for Far Eastern-Slavic studies at a handful of universities in the American west. Long a supporter of Asian studies—especially at universities in the American west—the foundation expanded these efforts to incorporate the study of Russia in 1944 and 1945. Program brochures celebrated the ways in which "The Far West Looks to the Far East" and included Russia as part of the Far East with no explanation or clarification. The third Rockefeller effort in Slavic studies was the largest and would be the most enduring: the establishment of the Russian Institute at Columbia University. The impact of these grants, rooted in wartime discussions about Slavic studies, varied widely. The variations came about because of institutional and individual idiosyncrasies, especially as universities coped with a changing of the guard among scholars active in Slavic studies. The University of California–Berkeley (which was among the first American universities to teach the Russian language) suffered the death of one leader, émigré George Z. Patrick, just as World War II ended. Next in line was historian Robert F. Kerner, yet foundation officials did not want him in charge; even the university president admitted that Kerner's "rough edges" might cause some trouble.[15] Similarly, individual quirks hindered the growth of Rockefeller Foundation–supported programs at other institutions. But in all of the western grants, Slavic studies programs were add-ons, both administratively and intellectually, to its well-established Asian programs; Slavic programs suffered for these circumstances.

Stanford University, home to the Hoover Institute and Library on War, Revolution, and Peace, seemed like a natural site for a major center in Slavic studies. The Hoover had an extraordinary collection of documents related to the Russian Revolution as well as international Communism. Like the Rockefeller Foundation, the Hoover Institute leaders looked at Slavic studies very much in the mode of the wartime Grand Alliance—much to the chagrin of its namesake and benefactor, whose anti-communism grew more virulent and vociferous after World War II. Hoover officials, in spite of their differences with their sponsor, shared a great deal with Rockefeller Foundation personnel; both groups, for instance, emphasized pedagogical lessons from the campus-based military programs. The political goals, too, emphasized wartime internationalism. One goal of regional studies, according to Hoover Institute Chairman Harold H. Fisher, was to "build up a consciousness of our common humanity"; in his publications and lectures of the mid-1940s, he emphasized the possibility of America and Russia together leading a "world community." (A battle royal over the political orientation of the Hoover programs lasted through the 1950s, ultimately ending with the purge of left-wingers like Fisher.)[16] In spite of obvious political affinities, though, the Rockefeller Foundation steered clear of major grants to Stanford. The death of its capable Russian teacher, George Lentz, left it without a leader. More distressing to the Rockefeller staff was the Hoover Institute itself, which seemed promiscuous in the projects it sponsored, working well outside of its areas of expertise. The lack of integration between Hoover and the Stanford faculty also caused concern.[17] Only the University of Washington built an effective Slavic studies institute with the Rockefeller funds; its Far East and Slavic Institute was a small but productive program, thanks in large part to its impresario, Donald Treadgold.[18]

All of these postwar programs drew explicitly upon wartime models of organization and instruction as well as personnel active in military, intelligence, or diplomatic work. All of them, furthermore, carried on a wartime view of the world, in which the Soviet Union was an ally (if an unreliable one), not an implacable enemy. What was true for the smaller programs out west also applied to the first successful Slavic program, at Columbia University.

Those who trace the origins of Soviet studies to the OSS typically use Columbia University as its exhibit A. Columbia's Russian Institute, founded in 1946, does seem like a direct successor of the OSS. The Russian Institutes's founding director was Geroid Tanquary Robinson, a historian who had taken leave from Columbia to run the OSS's USSR division; economist Abram Bergson (who had led Robinson's economics branch) was also on the founding staff of the Russian Institute. Other key Russian Institute faculty (legal scholar John Hazard and historian Philip Mosely) had served in the State Department during the war.

This collective experience in wartime intelligence shaped the future direction of the Russian Institute, but not necessarily in predictable ways. From its beginnings, the Columbia program emphasized training over research, the production of experts over the production of knowledge. In 1944, while Robinson was still leading the OSS's USSR division, he argued that Columbia could perform a useful "national service" by "doing all that an academic program can do to prepare a limited number of American specialists to understand Russia and Russians." The Russian Institutes's founding document reiterated this claim. Recognizing the expansion of instruction on Soviet topics, Robinson insisted that the most urgent task was "to raise the standard of existing instruction in this field and to promote research interests among those who carry on instruction." Yet the focus on instruction constantly won out over research at Columbia; much to Robinson's continuing dismay, the Russian Institute's research program never reached the same level as Harvard's. Its training program, however, was a great success. Its MA degree program, in particular, aimed to train Russia experts for work in government agencies.[19] In the institute's first decade, close to half (45 percent) of those receiving MA degrees went to work for the US government.[20]

Even if the Russian Institute never became a research organization like the OSS, lessons from the wartime period shaped both its structure and attitudes. There was a direct organizational continuity between wartime programs and postwar ones. And the Columbia program inherited much the same sentiment about the Soviet Union as Rockefeller Foundation officials had expressed during the war. One of the best indicators of this attitude was the effort on the part of Columbia faculty—with Rockefeller Foundation support—to create a permanent slot for visiting scholars from the USSR, each of whom would come for a year. One Columbia professor called it "one of the most important things that we can do." Though Soviet higher-education officials eventually vetoed the effort, Columbia faculty had already devoted substantial time and energy to discussing appropriate personnel, and had already garnered approval in principle from the US Department of State.[21] The faculty at Columbia were themselves on the left of the American political spectrum—another sign, perhaps, of the ways in which the Cold War was slow to take shape in Russian studies. Ernest Simmons, hired away from Cornell to teach Slavic languages and literatures, had the longest and most leftist of resumes, including leadership of the New York State Labor Party and activities in the Henry Wallace's presidential campaign in 1948. While none of the other core faculty had records like Simmons's, most had spent at least part of the 1930s (a deadly decade in Soviet history) not just studying but celebrating one or another aspect of Soviet life: Hazard earned a law degree from the Moscow Juridical Institute while Mosely praised collectivization as a means to "tremendous economic improvement."[22] Wartime organization and wartime attitudes shaped Columbia's Russian Institute before and after its founding in 1946, even as American-Soviet relations grew more antagonistic.

Indeed, the institutional structure that housed the Russian Institute was itself an outgrowth of World War II. At its founding in 1946, the Russian Institute was to be the first component of Columbia's new School of International Affairs (SIA, now known as the School of International and Public Affairs), which was built on the literal and figurative foundations of the wartime Naval School of Military Government and Administration at Columbia University. The Naval School, which began by teaching officers about the cultures of the Pacific Islands, soon became what a founding faculty member called a "frankly experimental" effort to organize research and teaching around world areas rather than disciplines. While the Naval School was still operating during the war, Columbia faculty and administrators planned for its peacetime conversion into SIA. There was strong support for the wartime area approach. One important faculty report called area studies "important, necessary, even indispensable" for Columbia: "no American in the future," it exhorted, "can be called educated who is ignorant about his world neighbors." The SIA would maintain the Naval School's "federal" and geographic organization; the Russian Institute was the first to come into being, followed by institutes focused on East Asia, Europe, the Near East, and Middle East. Enemies and friends alike would be subjects of area institutes.[23]

The rise of Soviet area studies at Harvard was a more complicated affair, but one that also demonstrates the shadows cast by the World War II experience. Harvard divided research and training into separate organs. An interdisciplinary MA in Soviet Regional Studies emerged under the aegis of a new International and Regional Studies Program in 1945. That program, devoted exclusively to teaching, incorporated a range of disciplines; the founders hoped to "make use of the lessons learned during the war in the intensive teaching of foreign languages as well as the techniques of a joint attack of social sciences and humanities on a given civilization." Much as Columbia's area studies training complex (at SIA) built upon wartime foundations, so too did Harvard's. Indeed, the new International and Regional Studies Program was a direct descendent of Harvard's School for Overseas Administration, which had housed wartime training programs. As perhaps befit Harvard, it hosted the Army's Civil Affairs Training Program, which was for officers what ASTP's language/area programs were for enlisted personnel.[24]

Area-oriented research at Harvard was administratively distinct from its teaching programs; the new Russian Research Center (RRC) took responsibility for conducting research on the USSR. The Center followed up on a different wartime agenda than the training programs; it sought to remake the social sciences in the ways adumbrated by Redfield and Parsons during the war. Social scientists had poured into Washington bureaucracies during the war, with each discipline carving out its own strongholds and claims to centrality. While a young and brash Paul Samuelson called World War II "the economists' war," anthropologists and sociologists begged to differ. Harvard faculty had special prominence: sociologist Samuel Stouffer served in the US Army's Research Branch, producing the four-volume study of *The American Soldier*. Clyde Kluckhohn joined fellow anthropologists Ruth Benedict and Margaret Mead at the Foreign Morale Analysis Division of the Office of War Information, where they produced (among other things) Benedict's famous analysis of Japanese culture "from afar," *The Chrysanthemum and the Sword*. As the war ended, these scholars were energized by their discoveries and their sense that they had helped steer the ship of state—a much exaggerated, if not entirely fictional, influence. They sought to apply their techniques of modes of research to world affairs in peacetime.[25]

In 1947, the Carnegie Corporation was searching for a program that would demonstrate the possibilities of the behavioral sciences—an ill-defined but eventually very well-funded amalgam of the social sciences, with sociology returning to its original role as the "mother of the social sciences." The Carnegie Corporation's aim, as one official put it, was to turn a center for the study of Russian behavior "from a free-floating idea into a working program with a roof (presumably ivy-covered) over its head and identifiable figures scurrying around it, and one or more men of sense and wisdom to lead it gently by the hand."[26]

This interest in behavioral science led the Carnegie Corporation naturally to Harvard's Talcott Parsons, who was in large part responsible for the grant that created the Russian Research Center. Parsons was the behavioral sciences' leading impresario. He believed that they would unify the social sciences; his interest in area studies was part of his grandiose scheme for a unified theory of society. Thus the center was as much focused on technique as on region. Indeed, internal Carnegie memoranda refer to the RRC as Harvard's "research on problems of Russian behavior." Its mission was to "develop a program of research upon those aspects of the field of Russian studies which lie peculiarly within the professional competence of social psychologists, sociologists, and cultural anthropologists."

The paradigmatic example of the behavioral science approach to understanding the USSR was the Refugee Interview Project (RIP), for which the Air Force's Human Relations Research Institute paid the Russian Research Center roughly $1 million (over $10 million in 2015 terms).

The project's proponents within the Air Force had been trained in the behavioral sciences at Harvard and elsewhere; along with RRC faculty, they believed that the project could yield both scholarly innovation and useful information for the military. That dual aims could be easily met is evident in the great similarity between the final report to the Air Force and the academic version published by Harvard University Press; only minor changes in organization were required to turn a military report into an academic document. The report must have been a grave disappointment to air force brass, rightly considered the most assertively anti-Soviet branch of the American military during the Cold War. The final report, published as *How the Soviet System Works*, stressed the common ground between the United States and the USSR as complex industrial societies; it also insisted that the USSR was a stable industrial society, not one teetering on the brink of collapse, or atomized along the lines of Hannah Arendt's notion of totalitarianism. In short, the project was hardly in agreement with the official Air Force line on the USSR. Instead, it offered training—and sources—that contributed handily to the growing field of Soviet Studies.[27] The Interview Project was, however, the last gasp for behavioral science in Soviet studies. After its completion of the Refugee Interview Project—Harvard's largest research endeavor in the 1950s—the Russian Research Center focused almost exclusively on conventional political and economic topics.[28]

This social-scientific focus helps explain one remarkable fact about the center's leadership: the members of the founding executive committee may have been "men of sense and wisdom," but none had studied Soviet affairs or knew the Russian language. The center's first director, Clyde Kluckhohn, was a specialist in Navaho culture who had spent the war analyzing the "culture and personality" of the Japanese for the Office of War Information.[29] Kluckhohn had any number of skills to contribute to the RRC—administrative, methodological, and personal (he was well-connected in the wartime and postwar intelligence community)—that, in a way, compensated for his near-total ignorance of the regional focus of the Russian Research Center.[30] While the Harvard faculty contained many Russia experts in the late 1940s—some émigré, some American born—none were part of the Russian Research Center in its initial phase. Social-scientific expertise mattered more than specific knowledge about the Slavic world or for that matter about communism. Harvard's main contributions, according to its founders, would be the demonstration of a new, unified approach to the social sciences.

The trajectory of Harvard's area studies programs as they moved from war to peace was shaped by institutional and personal particularities—as were those at Columbia and Stanford. Yet some general trends are visible in the very first years of modern Soviet Studies—that is, in the years up to 1950. The major Soviet studies programs all drew on the experiences of the recent world war: graduate-level programs at Harvard, Columbia, and elsewhere all took their inspiration, organization, personnel, and pedagogy from wartime military programs. Research programs, like those at Hoover and Harvard, did model themselves to some degree on the OSS. The OSS approach of interdisciplinary scholarship for direct application, and of close ties to government carried over into the Cold War, as did the attitude of total intellectual mobilization.

These common trends were not simply the result of a *Zeitgeist* that haunted each institution. Philanthropic foundations fostered this environment as they applied their funds to meet their own intellectual and political goals. These organizations, and particularly the Rockefeller Foundation, helped develop a common method and message for area studies through carefully planned and well-organized work in area studies and especially in Slavic studies. Rockefeller Foundation officials brought together scholars from different universities to discuss common problems. They provided funding to meet their own vision of area studies as promoting inclusion and incorporation—not exclusion and enmity—and did so successfully enough to shape the first years of area studies, even in the most fraught of circumstances and even about America's newest enemy.

One measure of the tardiness of Soviet Studies in toeing a Cold War line is a perverse one: the extent to which its leading individuals and institutions came under attack in the heyday of anti-Communism. Two of the five core faculty at Columbia had their names named by Senator McCarthy himself. Major "Cold Warriors" like Merle Fainsod and Philip Mosely were denied the security clearances necessary for them to continue their consulting work with military and intelligence agencies. Even Harvard's Refugee Interview Project came under fire for supporting radicals. Herbert Hoover spearheaded an effort to rid his namesake institute of those he considered traitorous leftists.[31] Without lending credence to any accusations of treason, though, it is worth noting that many of the accused scholars had long questioned the growing public fear of an ineluctable conflict between the United States and the USSR.

It is here that tensions between two legacies—intellectual and institutional—of World War II became visible conflicts. The war's intellectual legacy in area studies was to promote inclusion and intercultural understanding, and to do so by bringing together scholars with varying disciplinary and political perspectives. The institutional legacy, meanwhile, emphasized the interlocking world of scholarship, training, and national security, as scholars served as bureaucrats and analysts as well as authors and teachers. It was this government service that put some of the early Sovietologists under the purview of the Senate's Government Operations Subcommittee—chaired after 1953 by none other than Joseph McCarthy. By promoting close collaboration with government—while at the same time holding a wide range of political viewpoints—the creators of Cold

War area studies helped lay the groundwork for the attacks that they faced in the anti-Communist inquisitions of the early 1950s.

NOTES

1. For critics of early area studies, see Sigmund Diamond, *Compromised Campus: The Collaboration of Universities with the Intelligence Community, 1945–1955* (Oxford: Oxford University Press, 1992); Bruce Cumings, "Boundary Displacement: Area Studies and International Studies during and After the Cold War," in *Universities and Empire: Money and Politics in the Social Sciences during the Cold War*, ed., Christopher Simpson (New York: New Press, 1998); and Immanuel Wallerstein, "The Unintended Consequences of Cold War Area Studies," in *The Cold War and the University: Toward an Intellectual History of the Postwar Years* (New York: New Press, 1997).

2. McGeorge Bundy, "The Battlefields of Power and the Searchlights of the Academy," in *The Dimensions of Diplomacy*, ed., E. A. J. Johnson (Baltimore: Johns Hopkins University Press, 1964), 2.

3. For an excellent overview of the OSS, see Barry Katz, *Foreign Intelligence: Research and Intelligence in the OSS, 1942–1945* (Cambridge, MA: Harvard University Press, 1989). On Robinson life as a Greenwich Village radical in the aftermath of World War I, see Engerman, *Modernization from the Other Shore: American Intellectuals and the Romance of Russian Development* (Cambridge, MA: Harvard University Press, 2003), 142–47. On Marcuse, see Tim B. Müller, *Krieger und Gelehrte: Herbert Marcuse und die Denksysteme im Kalten Krieg* (Hamburg: Hamburger Edition, 2010).

4. Katz, *Foreign Intelligence*, chap. 5.; Betty Abrahamsen Dessants, "The American Academic Community and United States-Soviet Relations: The Research and Analysis Branch and Its Legacy, 1941–1947" (PhD diss., University of California-Berkeley, 1995), quoting Richard Hartshorne's 1942 memorandum on pp. 49–50.

5. Philip E. Mosely, "The Growth of Russian Studies," in *American Research on Russia*, ed. Harold H. Fisher (Bloomington: Indiana University Press, 1959), 7–8; and the items listed in note 1.

6. The training imperative was, of course, not limited to area studies programs. A very suggestive article by David Kaiser argues that the intellectual content of postwar physics was shaped by the conceptualization of Physics Departments' "products" as physicists, not physical knowledge. See David Kaiser, "Cold War Requisitions, Scientific Manpower, and the Production of American Physicists after World War II," *Historical Studies in the Physical and Biological Sciences* 33 (2002): 131–59.

7. Oleg A. Maslenikov, "Slavic Studies in America, 1939–1946," *Slavonic and East European Studies* 25 (April 1947): 531–32; A. E. Sokol, "The Army Language Program," *Journal of Higher Education* 17 (January 1946): 9–16; Lawrence G. Thomas, "Can the Social Sciences Learn from the Army Program?" *Journal of Higher Education* 17 (January 1946): 17–25; William N. Fenton, Reports *on Area Studies in American Universities* (Washington, DC: Smithsonian Institution Ethnogeographic Board, 1945).

8. On the Oriental Language School, see A. E. Hindmarsh, *The Navy School of Oriental Languages: History, Organization, and Administration* (c. May 1945), appendixes 36–37—in University of Colorado Archives. See also William Nelson Fenton for the Commission on Implications of Armed Services Educational Programs, *Area Studies in American Universities* (Washington, DC: American Council on Education, 1947). On Remington, see Gary May, *Un-American Activities: The Trials of William Remington* (Oxford: Oxford University Press, 1994).

9. Harry Kurz, "The Future of Modern Language Teaching," *Modern Language Journal* 27:7 (November 1943), 463; David H. Stevens, "Proposal for National Plan of Work on Foreign Languages, Institutions, and Customs," 7 June 1944, Rockefeller Foundation Records (Rockefeller Archive Center), Record Group 3.2, Series 900, Box 31, Folder 165. Graves to Stevens, 1 February 1944, in RF Records, Record Group 1.1,

Series, 200R, Box 225, Folder 2688. Revelation from Horatio Smith (Columbia) in letter to Chilton, 18 August 1944, Army Services Forces Records (US National Archives, Record Group 160), Entry 12, Box 12, Book II, p. 11. For postwar evaluations, see for instance, Paul F. Angiolillo, *Armed Forces' Foreign Language Teaching: Critical Evaluation and Implications* (New York: S.F. Vanni, 1947); Alonzo G. Grace, *Educational Lessons from Wartime Training: The General Report of the Commission on Implications of Armed Services Educational Programs* (Washington, DC: American Council on Education, 1948); and Robert John Matthew, *Language and Area Studies in the Armed Services: Their Future Significance* (Washington, DC: American Council on Education, 1947).

10. Conference on "Analysis of Program in Relation to Changing World Conditions," fall 1942—in RF Records, Record Group 3.1, Series 900, Box 23, Folder 173.

11. Mosely to Stevens, 9 March 1943, RF Records, Record Group 1.1, Series 200R, Box 208, Folder 3338. *Conference on Slavic Studies* (New York: Rockefeller Foundation, 1943): 25–26.

12. Robert Redfield, "Social Science Considerations in the Planning of Regional Specialization in Higher Education and Research," 10 March 1944, in RF Records, Record Group 3.2, Series 900, Box 31, Folder 165. Talcott Parsons, "Notes for Panel Discussion on the Objectives of Area Study" (28 November 1947), in Records of the Graduate School of Public Administration (Harvard University Archives), Series UAV 715.17, Box P-R.

13. *Conference on Area and Language Programs in American Universities* (New York: Rockefeller Foundation, 1944): 93.

14. Roger F. Evans interview with George E. Taylor, 9 February 1945, RF Records, Record Group 2, Series 785, Box 311, Folder 2108. John Gardner interview with Ernest J. Simmons, 30 August 1946, Carnegie Corporation of New York (CCNY) Records (Columbia University Library), Series III.A, Box 113, Folder 11.

15. The grants were offered to the Claremont Colleges, Stanford University, and the Universities of California, Colorado, and Washington—see "The Far West Looks to the Far East," in RF Records, Record Group 1.1, Series 253R, Box 3, Folder 22. Joseph H. Willets to Stevens, 16 September 1947, RF Records, Record Group 1.2, Series 205R, Box 9, Folder 66; and the correspondence between Stevens and Robert Sproul in Office of the President, (University Archives, Bancroft Library), Series 4, Box 27, Folders 7–8.

16. Harold H. Fisher, "Memorandum on the Study of Foreign Affairs," 6 January 1945, in RF Records, Record Group 1.1, Series 205R, Box 8, Folder 58; Fisher, *America and Russia in the World Community* (Claremont, CA: Three Associated Colleges, 1946). For conservatives' distaste of the Hoover Institution in the 1950s, see George Nash, *Herbert Hoover and Stanford University* (Palo Alto, CA: Hoover Institution Press, 1982), chaps. 8–9.

17. Report of Interview with Merrill Bennett (1948), RF Records, Record Group 1.2, Series 205R, Box 9, Folder 59; Charles Fahs Interview Report with John Gardner, 15 September 1947, RF Records Record Group 2, Series 200, Box 366, Folder 2480; Charles Fahs Diary, 18-22 September 1949, in RF Records, Record Group 1.1, Series 205R, Box 17, Folder 258.

18. Robert F. Byrnes, "Donald W. Treadgold: A Life of Intellectual Curiosity and Service," *Modern Greek Studies Yearbook* (1997): 109–47.

19. Robinson, "The Russian Institute," appendix to "The Report of the Committee on the Proposed Graduate School of Foreign Affairs" (27 November 1944), Columbia University Central Files [hereafter CUCF] (Columbia University Archives), Personal Subseries: Schuyler Wallace. Geroid Robinson, "A Program of Advanced Training and Research in Russian Studies," 24 April 1947, in CUCF, Personal Subseries: Philip Mosely.

20. Cyril E. Black and John M. Thompson, "Graduate Study of Russia," in *American Teaching about Russia*, ed. Black and Thompson (Bloomington: Indiana University Press, 1957): 65.

21. See the correspondence between Abram Bergson, Geroid Robinson, and Ernest Simmons in fall 1945—all in Geroid Tanquary Robinson Papers (Columbia University Archives), Box 50 (quoting Simmons letter of 8 October 1945).

22. On Mosely's enthusiastic reports from Moscow in 1931, see Philip Edward Mosely Papers (University of Illinois), box 1 (quoting from letter of 5 June 1931); on Hazard, see his *Reflections of a Pioneering Sovietologist* (New York: Oceana Publications, 1984), chaps. 3–6. Simmons's connections activities in the American Labor Party are obsessively traced in his massive FBI file, 100-263405.

23. "History of the NSMGA" (1944), in Bureau of Naval Personnel Records (U.S. National Archives, Record Group 24), Entry 470, Box 6; *A History of the School of International Affairs and Its Associated Area Institutes*, ed., Gray L. Cowan (New York: Columbia University Press, 1954), 19; Horatio Smith, "Preliminary Report on a Committee on Area Studies," 13 July 1943, CUCF, Personal Subseries: Smith. "Report of the Committee on the Proposed Graduate School of Foreign Affairs," 27 November 1944, in CUCF, Personal Subseries: Wallace.

24. *Report of the President of Harvard College, 1945–46* (Cambridge MA: Harvard College, 1946), 37. There is no suitable history of the School for Overseas Administration, directed by Carl Friedrich. Harvard hosted CATP programs on Europe and the "Far East," which included some work on the USSR—see *Report of the President of Harvard College, 1943–44* (Cambridge MA: Harvard College, 1944): 27–29.

25. Paul Samuelson, "Unemployment Ahead," *New Republic* 111 (11 September 1944): 298. Ellen Herman, *The Romance of American Psychology: Political Culture in an Age of Experts* (Berkeley: University of California Press, 1995); Peter Buck, "Adjusting to Military Life: The Social Sciences Go to War, 1941–1950)," in *Military Enterprise and Technological Change: Perspectives on the American Experience*, ed., Merritt Roe Smith (Cambridge, MA: MIT Press, 1985).

26. John Gardner to Clyde Kluckhohn, 28 July 1947, in CCNY Records, Series III.A, Box 164.

27. Clyde Kluckhohn, Alex Inkeles, and Raymond Bauer, *How the Soviet System Works: Cultural, Psychological, and Social Themes* (Cambridge, MA: Harvard University Press, 1956). For more details, see Engerman, *Know Your Enemy: The Rise and Fall of America's Soviet Experts* (Oxford: Oxford University Press, 2009), chap. 2.

28. [John Gardner,] "Russian Studies" (15 July 1947), in RRC Correspondence (Harvard University Archives), Series UAV 759.10, Box 1. Devereux Josephs to Clyde Kluckhohn, 20 January 1948, CCNY Records, Series III.A, Box 164, Folder 4. See also Ron Robin, *Making of the Cold War Enemy: Culture and Politics in the Military-Intellectual Complex* (Princeton: Princeton University Press, 2001), chap. 1.

29. Virginia Yans-McLaughlin, "Science, Democracy and Ethics: Mobilizing Culture and Personality for World War II," in *Malinowski, Rivers, Benedict and Others: Essays on Culture and Personality*, ed., George W. Stocking (Madison: University of Wisconsin Press, 1986). For a critical view, see Christopher Shannon, "A World Made Safe for Differences: Ruth Benedict's 'The Chrysanthemum and the Sword," *American Quarterly* 47 (December 1995): 659–80.

30. For a more generous assessment, see Alex Inkeles, "Clyde Kluckhohn's Contribution to Studies of Russia and the Soviet Union," in *Culture and Life: Essays in Memory of Clyde Kluckhohn*, ed., Walter W. Taylor, *et al.* (Carbondale: Southern Illinois University Press, 1973).

31. *The Lamont Case: History of a Congressional Investigation*, ed. Philip Wittenberg (New York: Horizon, 1957): 31–55, *passim*; on Fainsod, see Adam B. Ulam, *Understanding the Cold War: A Historian's Personal Reflections*, second edition (New Brunswick, NJ: Transaction, 2002), 107. On Mosely, see the extensive rebuttal and detailed correspondence in Mosely Papers, Box 12. On the Refugee Interview Project, see George W. Croker, "Some Principles Regarding the Utilization of Social Science Research within the Military," in *Case Studies in Bringing Behavioral Science into Use* (Stanford: Stanford Institute for Communication Research, 1961): 122–24.

BIBLIOGRAPHY

Angliolillo, Paul F. *Armed Forces' Foreign Language Teaching: Critical Evaluation and Implications*. New York: S. F. Vanni, 1947.

Black, Cyril E., and John M. Thompson. "Graduate Study of Russia." In *American Teaching about Russia*, eds. Cyril E. Black and John M. Thompson. Bloomington: Indiana University Press, 1957.

Buck, Peter. "Adjusting to Military Life: The Social Sciences Go to War, 1941–1950." In *Military Enterprise and Technological Change: Perspectives on the American Experience*, ed. Merritt Roe Smith. Cambridge, MA: MIT Press, 1985.

Bundy, McGeorge. "The Battlefields of Power and the Searchlights of the Academy." In *The Dimensions of Diplomacy*, ed. E. A. J. Johnson. Baltimore: Johns Hopkins University Press, 1964.

Byrnes, Robert F. "Donald W. Treadgold: A Life of Intellectual Curiosity and Service," *Modern Greek Studies Yearbook* (1997): 109–47.

Conference on Area and Language Programs in American Universities. New York: Rockefeller Foundation, 1944.

Conference on Slavic Studies. New York: Rockefeller Foundation, 1943.

Cowan, Gray L., ed. *A History of the School of International Affairs and Its Associated Area Institutes*. New York: Columbia University Press, 1954.

Croker, George W. "Some Principles Regarding the Utilization of Social Science Research within the Military." In *Case Studies in Bringing Behavioral Science into Use*. Stanford, CA: Stanford Institute for Communication Research, 1961.

Cumings, Bruce. "Boundary Displacement: Area Studies and International Studies during and After the Cold War." In *Universities and Empire: Money and Politics in the Social Sciences during the Cold War*, ed. Christopher Simpson. New York: New Press, 1998.

Dessants, Betty Abrahamsen. "The American Academic Community and United States-Soviet Relations: The Research and Analysis Branch and Its Legacy, 1941–1947." PhD diss., University of California-Berkeley, 1995.

Diamond, Sigmund. *Compromised Campus: The Collaboration of Universities with the Intelligence Community, 1945–1955*. Oxford: Oxford University Press, 1992.

Engerman, David C. *Know Your Enemy: The Rise and Fall of America's Soviet Experts*. Oxford: Oxford University Press, 2009.

———. *Modernization from the Other Shore: American Intellectuals and the Romance of Russian Development*. Cambridge, MA: Harvard University Press, 2003.

Fenton. William N. *Area Studies in American Universities*. Washington, DC: American Council on Education, 1947.

———. *Reports on Area Studies in American Universities*. Washington, DC: Smithsonian Institution Ethnogeographic Board, 1945.

Fisher, Harold H. *America and Russia in the World Community*. Claremont, CA: Three Associated Colleges, 1946.

Grace, Alonzo G. *Educational Lessons from Wartime Training: The General Report of the Commission on Implications of Armed Services Educational Programs*. Washington, DC: American Council on Education, 1948.

Hazard, John. *Reflections of a Pioneering Sovietologist*. New York: Oceana Publications, 1984.

Herman, Ellen. *The Romance of American Psychology: Political Culture in an Age of Experts*. Berkeley: University of California Press, 1995.

Inkeles, Alex. "Clyde Kluckhohn's Contribution to Studies of Russia and the Soviet Union." In *Culture and Life: Essays in Memory of Clyde Kluckhohn*, ed. Walter W. Taylor, et al. Carbondale: Southern Illinois University Press, 1973.

Kaiser, David. "Cold War Requisitions, Scientific Manpower, and the Production of American Physicists after World War II," *Historical Studies in the Physical and Biological Sciences* 33 (2002): 131–59.

Katz, Barry. *Foreign Intelligence: Research and Intelligence in the OSS, 1942–1945.* Cambridge, MA: Harvard University Press, 1989.

Kluckhohn, Clyde, Alex Inkeles, and Raymond Bauer. *How the Soviet System Works: Cultural, Psychological, and Social Themes.* Cambridge, MA: Harvard University Press, 1956.

Kurz, Harry. "The Future of Modern Language Teaching," *Modern Language Journal* 27:7 (November 1943).

Maslenikov, Oleg A. "Slavic Studies in America, 1939–1946," *Slavonic and East European Studies* 25 (April 1947): 531–32.

Mathew, Robert John. *Language and Area Studies in the Armed Services: Their Future Significance.* Washington, DC: American Council on Education, 1947.

May, Gary. *Un-American Activities: The Trials of William Remington.* Oxford: Oxford University Press, 1994.

Mosely, Philip E. "The Growth of Russian Studies," in *American Research on Russia,* ed. Harold H. Fisher. Bloomington: Indiana University Press, 1959.

Müller, Tim B. *Krieger und Gelehrte: Herbert Marcuse und die Denksysteme im Kalten Krieg.* Hamburg: Hamburger Edition, 2010.

Nash, George. *Herbert Hoover and Stanford University.* Palo Alto, CA: Hoover Institution Press, 1982.

Report of the President of Harvard College. Cambridge, MA: Harvard College, various years.

Robin, Ron. *Making of the Cold War Enemy: Culture and Politics in the Military-Intellectual Complex.* Princeton, NJ: Princeton University Press, 2001.

Samuelson, Paul A. "Unemployment Ahead," *New Republic* 111 (11 September 1944): 298.

Shannon, Christopher. "A World Made Safe for Differences: Ruth Benedict's 'The Chrysanthemum and the Sword,'" *American Quarterly* 47 (December 1995): 659–80.

Sokol, A. E. "The Army Language Program," *Journal of Higher Education* 17 (January 1946): 9–16.

Thomas, Lawrence G. "Can the Social Sciences Learn from the Army Program?" *Journal of Higher Education* 17 (January 1946): 17–25.

Ulam, Adam B. *Understanding the Cold War: A Historian's Personal Reflections,* second edition. New Brunswick, NJ: Transaction, 2002.

Wallerstein, Immanuel. "The Unintended Consequences of Cold War Area Studies." In *The Cold War and the University: Toward an Intellectual History of the Postwar Years.* New York: New Press, 1997.

Wittenberg, Philip, ed. *The Lamont Case: History of a Congressional Investigation.* New York: Horizon, 1957.

Yans-McLaughlin, Virginia. "Science, Democracy and Ethics: Mobilizing Culture and Personality for World War II." In *Malinowski, Rivers, Benedict and Others: Essays on Culture and Personality,* ed. George W. Stocking. Madison: University of Wisconsin Press, 1986.

Archival Collections Cited

Columbia University Rare Book and Manuscript Library

  Carnegie Corporation of New York Records
  Columbia University Central Files
  Geroid Tanquary Robinson Papers

Harvard University Archives

  Graduate School of Public Administration Records
  Russian Research Center Records

Rockefeller Archive Center; Rockefeller Foundation Records

US National Archives

    Army Services Forces Records
    Bureau of Naval Personnel Records

University of California at Berkeley Bancroft Library: Office of the President
University of Colorado Archives: General Collections
University of Illinois Library: Philip Edward Mosely Papers

TWELVE

Slavic and Soviet Area Studies at the University of Kansas

Richard T. De George

The history or the story of Slavic and Soviet Area Studies (SSAS), Soviet and East European Studies (SEES), Russian and East European Studies (REES), and Russian, East European, and Eurasian Studies (REES)—the four names that the Program and Center at the University of Kansas (KU) have had—can be told in many ways and from many different perspectives. The successive designations indicate the change in the field over the last fifty or so years. I will tell the story from my perspective, that is, from the perspective not of one of the administrators of the program, but from the perspective of someone who was involved with the program from the start or almost from the start—depending on where one considers the start. If I were to choose a theme, it would be improbability and the Cold War.

For me, the first improbability is that I became part of the program at all. The story of my appointment at KU might help set the stage for understanding what KU was like in 1959. I was a New Yorker, had spent two years studying in Europe and two years in the army, and I was finishing my PhD in philosophy at Yale. I applied to KU because a friend of mine from Yale was there and encouraged me to do so. The Philosophy Department at the time had only three faculty members. But KU had a great chancellor, Franklin Murphy (who, unfortunately for us, left in 1960 to become chancellor at University of California, Los Angeles (UCLA) and then publisher of the *L.A. Times*), and a dynamic dean of the college, George Waggoner. Two of us showed up from Yale for philosophy interviews, and although there was only one position announced, after the interviews the dean decided to hire us both—an enormously improbable event for anyone who knows KU today. The dean also decided to give the Philosophy Department an office and a part-time secretary, a typewriter, and a supplies-and-expenses budget—all of which it hitherto lacked. What was true of the Philosophy Department was true of other departments as well. Philip Griffin, who wrote a history of the university for the KU centennial (it offered its first classes in 1866) described KU at the time as a third-rate university seeking to become second rate. The description was not appreciated by many at KU, but it was probably true that the university was third tier (but not third rate), seeking to become second tier (a goal which by all national objective measures it has achieved).[1]

Being adventurous, my wife and I and our one-year-old daughter decided to come to KU for a few years. We arrived in August 1959. I was a freshly minted PhD. In 1959, Lawrence (where the University of Kansas is located) had a population of about thirty thousand. It was hardly a cosmopolitan town. Kansas was dry by local option and one could buy liquor by the drink, including wine, only at private clubs. KU had about eight hundred faculty members and 10,188 students. The teaching load was three courses a semester for all ranks. My beginning salary for nine months was $5,400. There was no air conditioning and teaching summer school—until Summerfield Hall (the first air-conditioned building on campus) was finished—was no fun. Tuition was $70 a semester. (Contrast these facts with facts of the current situation: population of Lawrence [which is now cosmopolitan], over ninety thousand; number of faculty, over 2,600; number of students, approximately thirty thousand.)

World War II had ended only fourteen years earlier and we had all lived through it, as well as through the McCarthy era. The Cold War was on, and in 1957 the Soviets had launched *Sputnik*, which was taken as a signal that the United States was falling behind in science and education, and perhaps in the Cold War.

In November 1957 Chancellor Murphy had established a Chancellor's Committee on Foreign Language Study. The committee's report appeared in September 1959. The "Conclusions and Recommendations" section of the committee's report read in part "As soon as practicable, add area programs for Russia, Germany, and the Far East. Financial support for these should be sought either from the Federal government or from interested private foundations." There already was a Latin American area program and major. It is noteworthy that Roy Laird,[2] an assistant professor of political science and a specialist in Soviet agriculture, was on the committee. The report had taken note of the fact that in September 1958, Congress passed the National Defense Education Act (NDEA), which included funding foreign language study and area studies centers.

To some, the recommendation that there should be a Russian area program must have sounded like pie in the sky—the height of improbability. In 1959, Slavic languages and literatures at KU were part of the German Department, and had a faculty of two—an instructor, Sam Anderson, and an assistant professor, George Ivask. The History Department had one faculty member in the area, Oswald (Ozzie) Backus,[3] who had been promoted to professor the previous spring. Geography and political science each had one assistant professor in the area—for a total of five faculty members in the area—all but one of them junior in rank.

Despite the implausibility of the recommendation, a Slavic and Soviet Area Studies (SSAS) Committee was formed with Ozzie Backus as the chair. It boldly issued a document, "Future Development of Russian Language and Area Studies," in which it announced plans to become a National Defense Education Act (NDEA) Center. Ozzie was the moving force in bringing that plan to reality.

You may have noticed that when I listed five faculty members who might be considered in the Slavic and Soviet area, I did not include myself, even though I had arrived on campus in the fall of 1959. Nor did I include Harry Shafer who was an assistant professor in economics, but who did not join the program until several years later. How did I become a member? I will go into that part of the story because I think it illustrates a lot about the period and the early beginnings of SSAS.

In 1959, there was a small faculty club in the white building opposite the Kansas Student Union Building. It was the place where many faculty members went to eat lunch. Many brought their own in brown bags, and we sat at long tables, where one quickly met colleagues in other departments. It didn't take long before one had met at least half the faculty in the college, and a number from the other schools. I don't remember exactly where or when I met Ozzie Backus—but there were many opportunities for doing so. Nor do I know how he came to know that I knew Russian, although it would not have been surprising that I might have mentioned it when I learned he was in Russian history. In any event it was not long before Ozzie came to see me and said that KU was planning on starting a Soviet area program and he felt that in order to do so it needed someone who could offer a course or courses in Marxism and Soviet thought, since so much in the Soviet Union was driven by ideology. Would I do it? In 1959 the probability of having a philosopher on the faculty who knew Russian or who could teach Soviet Marxism or who would agree to such a proposal was too small to calculate. That I happened to be on campus was certainly not something anyone could have reasonably expected.

For me, his request came out of the blue. I was teaching three courses a semester, and had never taught before. So each course was a new preparation. In addition, I told him, I knew almost nothing about Marxism, I had never had a course in it, and I knew even less about Soviet philosophy. My only qualification was that I could read Russian. But that was enough for Ozzie. He suggested that I apply for an Elizabeth Watkins Summer Faculty Scholarship from KU, and that I spend the summer reading Marx and whatever else I needed to teach the course. That sounded more interesting than teaching summer school. Perhaps I had also mentioned to him that I had almost become a Foreign Service Officer and turned down the appointment so I could finish my dissertation. Because of my Russian I had served two years as an army intelligence officer—even if it was during peacetime. I surprised myself—but evidently not Ozzie—by agreeing, if I got the summer grant. I was officially made a member of the committee in the fall of 1960—over fifty years ago. In the summer of 1961 I received the Watkins Scholarship, and in the fall of 1961 I offered a course in Marxism, Leninism, and Soviet philosophy. Little did I imagine at the time that this apparently simple decision would change my career and research for the next thirty years.

How does one learn enough to teach a course in Marxism, Leninism, and Soviet philosophy? In 1960 there were no textbooks in English on the subject and so far as I knew no one was teaching a similar course. So I set about reading Marx, Engels, Lenin, and Stalin. Ozzie Backus suggested I get *Novye Knigi* (*New Books*), which listed books forthcoming from the Soviet Union three months hence. He tipped me off that books published in printings of two thousand copies or less were scholarly. So I started ordering scholarly books and subscribed to *Voprosy Filosofii* (*Problems of Philosophy*). Between them I began to learn who was doing what in Soviet philosophy. We were all conscious that the John Birch Society—an active anti-communist group in Wichita, Kansas—was on the lookout for any communist. Harassment by that group was a risk we all worked under.

By sheer accident (another improbability), in 1960, Professor J. M. Bochenski, a well-known historian of logic and of the history of philosophy, visited KU for a semester as the Rose Morgan Professor in the Philosophy Department. It turned out that he was also the head of the Institute for Soviet Studies at the University of Fribourg in Switzerland, the only center in the West to specialize in Soviet and East European Marxism. He invited me to join his institute for a year. The Ford Foundation had recently started a program in Soviet Area Training Fellowships. In 1961–1962, I applied and received one of the fellowships. So in 1962 I took my wife and family off to Switzerland for a year. In looking back on the list of fellows for that year, I was surprised by how many were later to be well-known names in the field. Included in the list was also Jarek Piekalkeiciwz,[4] who came to KU in the Political Science Department in 1963. Looking at the list helped me remember that in 1960 there were very few people trained in Soviet area programs. Most of us had PhDs in our discipline and had to learn the area. Several years later when we set up the requirement for a Masters in the area, with required courses in various fields, none of the faculty had had the required range of courses, and so in a sense none of us could qualify for a Master's degree from KU in area studies.

While in Switzerland I came to realize that I needed more than book learning, and I asked the Ford Foundation to fund a month-long trip to the USSR, which to my surprise, they did. I visited Moscow, Leningrad, Odessa, Kiev, and Kharkov, and in each city met with professors of Marxism-Leninism, especially ethics, since that was to be my specialty.[5] The month was instructive in many ways. On the flight from Bern to Moscow I was the only American, and when we changed planes in Prague, I was left in the waiting room without my passport, watched over by a guard with a submachine gun until the last possible minute before the plane took off, when I was finally allowed to board. We arrived in Moscow and I noticed five or six portly men in black suits who looked official. I figured they knew their way around and I followed them, expecting they would lead me to passport control and customs. They opened one door after another and I followed closely behind. When we went through the last door, I found myself on a Moscow street without my luggage, and without having gone through immigration or customs—an illegal alien. I went to the exit from which passengers were emerging and was stopped by an armed guard who told me that was an exit not an entrance. It took some time to convince him that I had innocently taken the wrong door and that my luggage was inside and that I had still to go through passport control and customs. I guess he found my story so unusual that instead of calling his superior, he finally just let me back in. The next day, when I registered at the American embassy I met for the first time Zbigniew Brzezinski, Urie Bronfenbrenner, and Lewis Feuer—all notables in the field of Soviet studies, who, like me, had arrived in Moscow in time for the May Day parade.

In 1991 I learned that the KGB had a dossier on me and that my activities during that month, as well as during later visits, had been reported on by the guides I was assigned and by others. One guide, a woman graduate student from the Institute of Philosophy in Moscow, was almost expelled from the Institute because her reports on me contained nothing detrimental or suspicious. I met her again in a receiving line at the institute in 1988 by which time she was a professor. I failed to recognize her (it was twenty-five years later), which I later learned caused her embarrassment, because she had told her colleagues I would surely remember her even though she had given me no hint about having been my guide. I assume other KU SSAS members who went to the Soviet Union had comparable KGB dossiers.

It was almost unbelievable that although Marxism-Leninism was taught in over one half of the world, and served as the ideology that informed and helped guide Soviet and Chinese practice, it was little studied in the United States. Philosophy departments didn't think it was real philosophy and Daniel Bell's book *The End of Ideology* was widely accepted despite all the evidence to the contrary in the communist world. Those at KU in SSAS knew better.

The SSAS committee achieved what sounds like the miraculous. In 1960 Heinrich Stammler[6] was hired as an associate professor in Slavic languages and literatures. In the fall of 1961 Slavic languages and literatures was separated from the German Department to form an independent department on its own with five faculty members. In the same year the SSAS Program was officially launched, had a budget, and appeared in the catalogue as offering an undergraduate co-major. In 1962 Herbert Ellison[7] was hired as an associate professor in the History Department and became chairman of the Slavic and Soviet Area Studies Committee, with responsibility for internal matters; Ozzie Backus became Director of Off-Campus Activities. The listed faculty members were Anderson, Backus, De George, Ellison, Knos, Laird, and Stammler.

The program was small, but developing. Roy Laird ran a conference on Soviet agricultural and peasant affairs at KU on September 20–22, 1962, and the papers were published as the first volume of the newly established Slavic Studies Series.[8] Ozzie Backus established library exchanges with a host of libraries in the USSR and Eastern Europe.

I already mentioned that I spent 1962–1963 in Switzerland at the Institute for East European Studies. It was the height of the Cold War and while we were there the Cuban missile crisis took place. We were tempted to return to the United States to be there in case war broke out. The American embassy sent US citizens a warning that the Swiss borders would be closed in case of war and that we should stock up on a list of food supplies they sent us, since those items were imported and would not be available. Fortunately, before we could do much, Khrushchev blinked and war was averted. But the Cold War dominated events and all other international conflicts and activities—from Vietnam to Korea to foreign aid to African nations—were played out in terms of the overarching conflict between the United States and its allies and the USSR and its communist bloc. That in turn gave special importance and meaning to SSAS. Being part of it was being part of the massive worldwide struggle. One of the reports concerning the start of SSAS raised the question of what the area program could offer faculty to induce them to become affiliated with it. It did not consider the attraction of being part of something that had relevance beyond that which most academic research has. In retrospect that was an attraction that none of us ever articulated but one that was probably the greatest motive we had for taking on new courses, teaching overloads, and devoting time to an activity outside some of our specialties, and one which many of our disciplinary departments saw as a distraction from their core concerns.

Fortunately for SSAS, the 1960s were a period of rapid growth for KU. By 1965 the SSAS faculty numbered seventeen. It had more than tripled in five years. Although the first application by SSAS for NDEA Center status and grant money was turned down, in 1964 SSAS introduced a certificate of proficiency on the graduate level, and that helped our next application. In 1965 KU was designated a National Resource Center and given a two-year grant of $36,000. The SSAS program was now officially housed in the center. Herb Ellison was the first director, with Backus as associate director. An executive committee of eleven members was formed with at least one representative from each of the eight departments. History and political science usually had two members. As the only one in the area in philosophy, I was a continuing member. The committee met monthly at the home of the director at 7:30 in the evening. It was not unusual to have coffee and some goodies — and sometimes beer — and for some of the members to smoke cigars. The semi-social setting of the meeting carried over into receptions in various members' homes after SSAS lectures, and we all got to know each other socially as well as professionally. Anna Cienciala,[9] joined the History Department in 1965, John Alexander[10] in 1966. Gerald Mikkelson[11] and Steve Parker[12] were appointed in the Slavic Department in 1967. Leslie Dienes[13] came to KU in geography in 1968, and Norman Saul[14] in history in 1970. (By way of a footnote, Norman and I had both been in the same military intelligence unit at Fort Bragg, North Carolina, during our period in the army.)

KU was not the only one growing. Many other colleges and universities were similarly expanding. In 1960 college enrollments stood at 3.6 million nation-wide. By 1970 they had more than doubled to 7.5 million students. The growth of the faculties across the country made for something of a seller's market for faculty and the turnover was considerable, with schools raiding faculty from other schools. One result was the relatively short terms of the newly hired directors of the KU center. Ellison left at the end of the 1967–1968 school year. Roy Laird served as acting director for a year, until we hired James Scanlan[15] in philosophy as the new director starting in the fall of 1969. In the same year S. V. Utechin[16] joined the faculty as a Visiting Professor of History and he became a permanent faculty member in fall 1970. For a short period KU had the strongest concentration of faculty in Russian and Soviet thought in the United States — four of us: Scanlon, Stammler, Utechin, and De George. But it was short lived. From the point of view of the faculty Scanlan was a good director. But he felt the fit was not a good one for him, and he left for Ohio State University after three years. In November 1970, William Fletcher[17] (with an appointment in Religion) became director, and at last we had a long-term director. He stayed on until December 1992.

Funds from the grant were used primarily for speakers, library, scholarly travel, visitors, and office needs. The faculty traveled frequently and often took leave. In 1965–1966 I was a senior fellow and visiting professor at the Russian Institute at Columbia. Zbigniew Brzezinski was the director. He met weekly with the center fellows for lunch, at which he held forth on the area issues of the week. While at Columbia, I wrote *Soviet*

Ethics and Morality and also gave a lecture with Isaiah Berlin as my commentator. Through that contact I invited him to KU for a lecture, which he gave under SSAS auspices—one of the many illustrious speakers the faculty invited with center funds

In 1967 I took a trip through Poland, Czechoslovakia, and Hungary to meet philosophers whose work I had read. It served as the basis for my book *The New Marxism*,[18] which is what I called the humanistic Marxism coming out of Eastern Europe. After the Soviet invasion of Czechoslovakia in 1968, one after the other of the New Marxists was either silenced or forced to leave. When Leszak Kolakowski went to Canada, I was able to invite him to KU for a lecture with the support of SSAS, and KU offered him a faculty position. Unfortunately for us, Berkeley did the same and he chose Berkeley. SSAS funds enabled us to invite a dozen or so of the New Marxists from Eastern Europe, and Svetozar Stojanovic,[19] from Yugoslavia, came as a visiting professor every fall semester for seven years.

In 1968 the Slavic Department, with a faculty of twelve, started its PhD program. In the same year SSAS introduced an MA program in the area. It also started a Polish subspecialty and negotiated a Poznan-Kansas exchange, with the first actual exchange of faculty and students taking place in 1970. Yugoslavia was the second such area of concentration SSAS adopted, and on February 1, 1975 we added East Germany as the third. But Germany was not a Slavic country, and so in September 1976 the faculty agreed to change our name from Slavic and Soviet Area Studies (SSAS) to Soviet and East European Studies (SEES). It was officially approved by the Kansas Board of Regents in November 1977. In March 1976, we took a hint from the NDEA suggestions for centers, and adopted plans for our first outreach program, which was still a new concept at that time. It involved reaching out and offering our individual and collective expertise to the community outside the university—grade schools and high schools, smaller colleges in the region, civic organizations, and the general public.

Much of the growth of the program was due to the support of the college dean. Alas, in August 1980, the college adopted a more decentralized approach to hiring. Thenceforth, the departments decided on new appointments. It became much more difficult to get departments to make hires in the SEES area. Had that policy been in force twenty years earlier, it is doubtful the program could have grown as it did.

The KU library deserves special mention. The 1983 SEES Program Review cited the Slavic collection in the library as one of strongest in country. With relatively little money from KU, the collection had grown from 9,000 volumes in 1960, to 84,893 volumes in 1970, to 200,000 volumes in 1974, to an impressive 310,000 volumes in 1983, with exchanges with thirty institutions in six Slavic and East European countries.

Staffing the team-taught, year-long seminar, which was required for MA students, had been a continuing and unresolved difficulty, since it was taught on an overload basis and not all the pogram faculty shared in the load in any systematic fashion. Finally, in September 1984, Bill Fletcher suggested he would conduct the seminar alone, and call on others to mentor students on an individual basis. There was nary a dissenting vote.

Then, in 1985, the unimaginable happened. The Title VI office of the Department of Education did not recommended KU for NDEA Center funding. It was a shock to all of us. The following years were touch and go without Title VI money. The college office took up a little of the slack so we could keep most of our staff. But all the extras—travel, library, visiting lecturers, visiting faculty—disappeared, and the supplies-and-expenses allocation was cut in half. We realized in practice what we had been well aware of—namely, the importance of NDEA money for the success of the program. Fortunately, in the next competition we were successful and in 1988 we regained our status as a National Research Center.

In1985, Mikhail Gorbachev took over as head of the Soviet Union. The next year he introduced his program of *glasnost'* and *perestroika*, which signaled a loosening of the reins by the government on a variety of policies. In 1989, Poland, Hungary, East Germany Bulgaria, Czechoslovakia, and Romania all threw over their communist governments. Gorbachev did nothing. No one predicted that in 1991 the Soviet Union would collapse—another improbability. All of the specialists in Soviet and East European Area Studies were as surprised as anyone else. But it happened, and of course it marked the end of Soviet and East European Studies as we had known it for thirty years. The Cold War had ended. I changed the name of my course from "Marxism, Leninism, and Soviet Philosophy" to "Marxism," since then there was no new work in philosophy worth mentioning or studying coming out of Russia or Eastern Europe that was appropriate to the course. However, the mindset of those brought up thinking in Marxist categories did not change overnight, so the course was still relevant to those interested in the area, and Marxism still had an appeal in the West, which it had lost in the East.

In the spring of 1992, with the Soviet Union gone, the name of the program was again changed from Soviet and East European Studies (SEES) to Russian and East European Studies (REES). The program had to reinvent itself in many ways. In September, 1992, at Bill Fletcher's suggestion, we embarked on a new Ukrainian initiative. On December 31, 1992, Bill Fletcher stepped down as director of REES. The program had thirty-eight faculty members and fifty-five candidates for a MA degrees. It was ranked as number two in the country for an MA by the US Department of Education. We had come a long way since the bold initiation of a program with few faculty and little funding. Bill Fletcher's letter of resignation noted that "All of our previous assumptions, our models and our paradigms, are now history." He served twenty-two years. During his last year Maria Carlson[20] was appointed associate director of the center, and she took over as director on January 1, 1993.

That is the program as it was for thirty-three years. They were interesting, sometimes exciting years, to live through. But in many ways, the best was yet to come. As the center continued to grow its reach expanded and it was again renamed, this time to Russian, East European, and Eurasian Studies.

Jumping ahead, the Center and Program today has sixty-two core teaching faculty (including fifteen language specialists, nineteen humanists, and eighteen social scientists), from fifteen departments in the College of Arts and Sciences and four of the university's professional schools. The library collection in the area has grown to 460,000 volumes and is the major such collection in the United States in the geographical area between the University of Illinois and the University of California, Berkeley. CREES, as the center is known, is a thriving research, education, and outreach center. It serves as a resource for K–12 teachers, post-secondary educators, business, media, government, and the military. Its faculty, in their research and teaching, cover the entire region from the new European Union members in the west to the Russian Far East and from the indigenous peoples of the Arctic to the traditionally Islamic societies of the South Caucasus and Central Asia. Students can study not only Russian, Ukrainian, Bosnian/Croatian/Serbian, Czech, Polish, and Slovene, but also Turkish, and Uyghur among others.

In 1960, when the program was established, no one could have foreseen how it would grow and thrive. In the beginning it was in some ways a baby of the Cold War. But in its maturity it has grown well beyond that and is an important part of a major university in the Midwest portion of the United States.

NOTES

This chapter is based on a presentation I made on the occasion of the fiftieth anniversary of the program on August 27, 2010 at the University of Kansas. The presentation was one of three, and covers only the period from 1960 to 1993. Two other presenters continued the history and brought it up to the present. In this chapter, I have added some facts about the current status of the center, but I have not given the detailed account that they did. At the suggestion of the editor, I have retained the informal tone of the original presentation. The chapter is as much a story of my involvement in the program as it is a history of the program. I was brought into Soviet studies from the outside. Most of my colleagues in the program were trained and did their graduate work in one or more of the disciplines the field covers, especially history, political science, geography, and, of course, Russian and East European languages and literatures. To give some indication of the research interests of the early members I have noted in footnotes one or a few of their books. I have not mentioned articles, honors, or other information. The information about the present members of the center is available at the center's Web site:http://crees.ku.edu/faculty.

1. In some ways it is first tier. Some of its schools and departments are ranked first in the United States; many are in the top ten; and it is a member of the prestigious Association of American Universities. But it does rank below the Ivy League schools and of some of the larger state universities.

2. Roy D. Laird, *Collective Farming in Russia; a Political Study of the Soviet Kolkhozy* (Lawrence: University of Kansas Publications, Social Science Studies, 1958); *The Politburo: Demographic Trends, Gorbachev, and the Future* (Boulder, CO; London: Westview Press, 1986); *The Soviet Legacy* (Westport, CT: Praeger, 1993).

3. Oswald P. Backus, *Motives of West Russian Nobles in Deserting Lithuania for Moscow, 1377–1514* (Lawrence: University of Kansas Press, 1957).

4. Jaroslaw Piekalkiewicz, *Communist Local Government: A Study of Poland* (Athens: Ohio University Press, 1975); *Public Opinion Polling in Czechoslovakia, 1968–69* (New York: Praeger Publishers, 1972).

5. Among other works, see my *Soviet Ethics and Morality* (Ann Arbor: University of Michigan Press, 1969), and *Patterns of Soviet Thought: The Origins and Development of Dialectical and Historical Materialism* (Ann Arbor: University of Michigan Press, 1966).

6. Heinrich A. Stammler, *Teodor Trajanov als Wortfu͏̈hrer des bulgarischen Symbolismus; Nietzsche und Teodor Trajanov: "das hohe Lied" (Pel "sen na pel͏„snitel")* (Mu͏̈nchen: Bulgarische Akademische Gesellschaft "Dr. Peter Beron," 1991); *What is the national character of the Macedonian Slavs?* (Sofia, Bulgaria: JMRO, 1991).

7. Herbert J. Ellison, *History of Russia* (New York: Holt, Rinehart and Winston, 1964.

8. Roy D. Laird, ed., *Agricultural and Peasant Affairs* (Lawrence: University of Kansas Press, 1963).

9. Anna M. Cienciala, *Poland and the Western Powers 1938–1939: A Study in the Interdependence of Eastern and Western Europe* (London: Routledge & K. Paul, Toronto: University of Toronto Press, 1968).

10. John T. Alexander, *Catherine the Great: Life and Legend* (New York: Oxford University Press, 1989).

11. Valentin Rasputin, *Siberia on Fire: Stories and Essays*, selected, translated, and with an introduction by Gerald Mikkelson and Margaret Winchell (DeKalb: Northern Illinois University Press, 1989).

12. Stephen Jan Parker, *Understanding Vladimir Nabokov* (Columbia: University of South Carolina Press, 1987).

13. Leslie Dienes, *Soviet Asia: Economic Development and National Policy* (Boulder, CO: Westview Press, 1987).

14. Norman E. Saul, *Russia and the Mediterranean, 1797–1807* (Chicago: University of Chicago Press, 1970); *Distant Friends : the United States and Russia, 1763–1867* (Lawrence: University Press of Kansas, 1990); *Concord and Conflict: the United States and Russia, 1867–1914* (Lawrence: University Press of Kansas, 1996); *War and Revolution: the United States and Russia, 1914–1921* (Lawrence: University Press of Kansas, 2001); *Friends or Foes?: the United States and Soviet Russia, 1921–1941* (Lawrence: University Press of Kansas, 2006).

15. James P. Scanlan, *Marxism in the USSR: A Critical Survey of Current Soviet Thought* (Ithaca, NY: Cornell University Press, 1985).

16. S. V. Utechin, *Bolsheviks and Their Allies After1917: the Ideological Pattern* (Abingdon, UK: Carfax Publishing Co., 1958); *Russian Political Thought; a Concise History* (New York: Praeger, 1964).

17. William C. Fletcher, *Religion and Soviet Foreign Policy, 1945–1970* (London: Oxford University Press for the Royal Institute of International Affairs, 1973); *The Russian Orthodox Church Underground, 1917–1970* (London, New York: Oxford University Press, 1971); *Soviet Believers: the Religious Sector of the Population* (Lawrence: Regents Press of Kansas, 1981); *Soviet Charismatics: the Pentecostals in the USSR* (New York: P. Lang, 1985); *A Study in Survival; the Church in Russia, 1927–1943* (London: SPCK, 1965).

18. *The New Marxism* (New York: Pegasus, 1968).

19. Svetozar Stojanović, *Between Ideals and Reality; a Critique of Socialism and Its Future*, translated by Gerson S. Sher (New York: Oxford University Press, 1973); *In Search of Democracy in Socialism: History and Party Consciousness*, translated by Gerson S. Sher (Buffalo: Prometheus Books, 1981); *Serbia: the Democratic Revolution* (Amherst, NY: Humanity Books, 2003).

20. Maria Carlson, *No Religion Higher Than Truth: A History of the Theosophical Movement in Russia, 1875–1922* (Princeton, NJ: Princeton University Press, 1993).

BIBLIOGRAPHY

Alexander, John T. *Catherine the Great: Life and Legend.* New York: Oxford University Press, 1989.

Backus, Oswald P. *Motives of West Russian Nobles in Deserting Lithuania for Moscow, 1377–1514.* Lawrence: University of Kansas Press, 1957.

Carlson, Maria. *No Religion Higher Than Truth: a History of the Theosophical Movement in Russia, 1875–1922.* Princeton, NJ: Princeton University Press, 1993.

Cienciala, Anna M. *Poland and the Western Powers 1938–1939: A Study in the Interdependence of Eastern and Western Europe.* London: Routledge & K. Paul, Toronto: University of Toronto Press, 1968.

De George, Richard T. *Soviet Ethics and Morality.* Ann Arbor: University of Michigan Press, 1969.

———. *The New Marxism.* New York: Pegasus, 1968.

———. *Patterns of Soviet Thought: The Origins and Development of Dialectical and Historical Materialism.* Ann Arbor: University of Michigan Press, 1966.

Dienes, Leslie. *Soviet Asia: Economic Development and National Policy.* Boulder, CO: Westview Press, 1987.

Ellison, Herbert J. *History of Russia.* New York: Holt, Rinehart and Winston, 1964.

Fletcher, William C. *Soviet Charismatics: the Pentecostals in the USSR.* New York: P. Lang, 1985.

———. *Soviet Believers: the Religious Sector of the Population.* Lawrence: Regents Press of Kansas, 1981.

———. *Religion and Soviet Foreign Policy, 1945–1970.* London: Oxford University Press for the Royal Institute of International Affairs, 1973.

———. *The Russian Orthodox Church Underground, 1917–1970.* London, New York: Oxford University Press, 1971.

———. *A Study in Survival; the Church in Russia, 1927–1943.* London: SPCK, 1965.

Laird, Roy D. *The Politburo: Demographic Trends, Gorbachev, and the Future.* Boulder, CO; London: Westview Press, 1986.

———. *The Soviet Legacy* (Westport: Praeger, 1993).

———, ed. *Agricultural and Peasant Affairs* (Lawrence: University of Kansas Press, 1963).

———. *Collective Farming in Russia; a Political Study of the Soviet Kolkhozy.* Lawrence: University of Kansas Publications, Social Science Studies, 1958.

Parker, Stephen Jan. *Understanding Vladimir Nabokov.* Columbia: University of South Carolina Press, 1987.

Piekalkiewicz, Jaroslaw. *Communist Local Government: A Study of Poland.* Athens: Ohio University Press, 1975.

———. *Public Opinion Polling in Czechoslovakia, 1968–69.* New York: Praeger Publishers, 1972.

Rasputin, Valentin. *Siberia on Fire: Stories and Essays,* selected, translated, and with an introduction by Gerald Mikkelson and Margaret Winchell. DeKalb: Northern Illinois University Press, 1989.

Stammler, Heinrich A. *Teodor Trajanov als Wortfuĭhrer des bulgarischen Symbolismus; Nietzsche und Teodor Trajanov: "das hohe Lied" (Peĭ„sen na peĭ„siteĭ).* München: Bulgarische Akademische Gesellschaft "Dr. Peter Beron," 1991.

————. *What is the national character of the Macedonian Slavs?* Sofia, Bulgaria: JMRO, 1991.

Saul, Norman E. *Friends or Foes?: The United States and Soviet Russia, 1921–1941*. Lawrence: University Press of Kansas, 2006.

————. *War and Revolution: the United States and Russia, 1914–1921*. Lawrence: University Press of Kansas, 2001.

————. *Concord and Conflict: the United States and Russia, 1867–1914*. Lawrence: University Press of Kansas, 1996.

————. *Distant Friends: The United States and Russia, 1763–1867*. Lawrence: University Press of Kansas, 1990.

————. *Russia and the Mediterranean, 1797–1807*. Chicago: University of Chicago Press, 1970.

Scanlan, James P. *Marxism in the USSR: A Critical Survey of Current Soviet Thought*. Ithaca, NY: Cornell University Press, 1985.

Stojanović, Svetozar. *Serbia: The Democratic Revolution*. Amherst, NY: Humanity Books, 2003.

————. *In Search of Democracy in Socialism: History and Party Consciousness*, translated by Gerson S. Sher. Buffalo: Prometheus Books, 1981.

————. *Between Ideals and Reality; a Critique of Socialism and Its Future*, translated by Gerson S. Sher. New York: Oxford University Press, 1973.

Utechin, S. V. *Russian Political Thought; a Concise History*. New York: Praeger, 1964.

————. *Bolsheviks and Their Allies After 1917: The Ideological Pattern*. Abingdon, UK: Carfax Publishing Co., 1958.

THIRTEEN

The Politics of Knowledge

Teaching Russian Studies at an
American Community College

William Benton Whisenhunt

American higher education consists of many different levels of educational institutions. High profile and highly selective American colleges and universities will often provide the best opportunities for hosting a research institute on Russian studies. These institutes and study centers play an invaluable role in the promotion of Russian studies for students, scholars, and the public in the United States. They are especially important for educating the next generation of scholars to advance the field. However, nearly half of American college and university students begin their higher education at community colleges. The primary purpose of such colleges is to provide the first two years of a bachelor's degree (BA) and professional training for immediate employment. Yet, Russian studies at such institutions is underrepresented.

At College of DuPage (a community college in suburban Chicago), I have taught a traditional Russian/Soviet history class to one hundred students per year for eighteen years. I have also team-taught a course twice on Russian history and geography. In addition, my geography colleague and I have brought more than fifteen speakers on Russia to our campus over the past ten years. Lastly, I have taken forty-five students to Russia for short tours of major historical sites in St. Petersburg, Novgorod, and Moscow in 2008, 2010, and 2012. While the major research centers are essential to the promotion of Russian studies in the United States, community colleges should not be overlooked considering this is where so many American undergraduate students begin their collegiate studies today.

The emergence of modern American community colleges began more than a century ago. At the end of the nineteenth century, the presidents of four major American universities (Michigan, Stanford, Minnesota, and Chicago) promoted the idea of creating what they called junior colleges. Junior colleges, the predecessor of community colleges, were designed to provide the first two years of a traditional bachelor's degree (BA) at locations that were more convenient for more students. These university presidents believed that greater access to higher education for more Americans was a worthwhile goal. They generally believed that an educated society was a solid foundation for a democratic society.[1]

William Rainey Harper, President of the University of Chicago, encouraged the local school system in Joliet, Illinois (approximately forty miles southwest of Chicago) to create a junior college to function as the bridge between high school and university education. In 1901, Joliet Junior College opened and is now the oldest such institution in continuous operation in the United States. In 1907, the state of California established a system of junior colleges throughout the state. Throughout the twentieth century, junior colleges continued to expand in nearly every state. After World War II, the Baby Boom Generation created a pressing need for more educational opportunities. By the 1960s, this inspired a new generation of educational leaders to create what we know now as community colleges.[2]

A community college is different from a junior college. Even though both offer the first two years of a traditional bachelor's degree, a community college embraces a wider mission. As the name implies, a community college sets out to educate the entire community in whatever way it can. First, a community college offers programs related to technical or vocational fields such as welding, heating and air conditioning, nursing, and many others. Often these programs will lead directly to employment while receiving an associate's degree or a certificate. Second, many students attend for self-enrichment. They are not working in a program that will result in employment and they are not necessarily working toward a formal degree. Rather, they simply want to take a college level class for their own academic fulfillment. Third, students attend to receive their first two years of university education before moving to a university for the traditional bachelor's degree. Fourth, students at community colleges cover many generations. While most students are eighteen to twenty-four years old, I often have students in their thirties and forties. The youngest student I have had was sixteen and the oldest was ninety-one years old.

Today, the majority of students at community colleges are pursuing a bachelor's degree. However, a large percentage of students, perhaps as many as 40 percent in some community colleges, are pursuing technical or vocational training. There are over 1,200 community colleges in the

United States today. California has the most with 125. My home state, Illinois, has fifty-three. My college, College of DuPage, is one of the largest in the United States with about thirty thousand students. Of all students pursuing higher education in the United States today, nearly half are attending community colleges. Yet, in preliminary research of the curricula of American community colleges, less than 10 percent of these colleges have any course offerings directly related to Russia. In this research, I searched for courses in key areas: language, history, geography, political science, literature, and business. Additionally, of the fifty US states, at least thirteen states had no specific course offerings related to Russia.[3]

My main argument here is that the lack of course offerings on Russia at American community colleges presents a serious gap in American higher education. With so many Americans beginning their higher education at community colleges, this curricular void needs to be filled. Since students lack the opportunity to learn about Russia at this level, they will rarely have time to take such courses in their last two years of university education. By the time students reach the university level, they have determined a major and will focus most of their studies on that area. Yet, without even the opportunity to learn about Russia, they do not know what they are missing. Beyond this issue, though, Russia falls between two worlds in the American education system. Since Russia does not fit neatly into the Western or non-Western worlds, students often fail to learn about Russia at all. About ten years ago, I had a student take the Russian history course from me during a summer term. He was a high school social studies teacher at a local private high school. He told me that he was taking the class because he did not know anything about Russia. That is not surprising, but he also revealed that he had skipped the Russia unit in his curriculum for ten years because he just did not know enough to teach it. I hope this is not the norm, but it was rather disturbing since a decade of students passing through that school had no exposure to Russia. This does not help students' academic preparation. It also does not help in continuing to foster better Russian-American relations.

I am fortunate though. I am a Russian historian, specializing in Russian-American relations, who is able to teach Russian history at a community college. The primary reason why I am able to do this is because my college is large, well-funded, and in suburban Chicago. More remote community colleges are not able to offer these kinds of courses. At my college, we promote Russian studies in four key ways.

First, I teach a traditional survey course on Russian history every term. Over the past eighteen years, I have taught this course to approximately 1,800 students. This course focuses on Russia's history from the 900s to the 1990s. Even though it covers one thousand years of history, I focus the course on the period from Ivan IV (the Terrible) to the collapse of the Soviet Union. In this course, I have used many different textbooks over the years.[4] I also enhance the course by having students read some examples of Russian literature and memoirs. Some of the literature I have had students read include works by Pushkin, Turgenev, Bulgakov, Chukovskaya, Grossman, Solzhenitsyn, and many more.[5] Some of the memoirs I have had students read include works by Anna Labzina, Savva Purlevskii, Anna Bek, John Scott, Marguerite Harrison, and many others.[6] At the conference in Moscow in 2011 where I first presented a brief version of this chapter, Professor Ivan Kurilla asked me how many of those nearly two thousand students who have taken Russian history from me have become specialists. I told him that I did not know, but the reality is that none of them have. It is really not the reason most students at my college would take a class like mine.

Students take this class for many reasons. For most students, they have some interest in Russia, but this course also satisfies a degree requirement. I often have students who know someone who is Russian (or from another part of the former Soviet Union) or they have an ancestor who was from Russia. More recently, I have young students from different parts of the former Soviet Union (mostly Lithuania) who immigrated to the United States in the 1990s, but they do not know much about their birthplace. Most students seem to enjoy the course and are always fascinated by the things about Russia they did not know.

In a recent survey of seventy students taking my history course, I found that only about fifteen of them had a significant knowledge of Russia before entering. Most students held superficial and stereotypical views of Russians. Some students did not realize that it was not called the Soviet Union any longer. On the other side of that divide, I had a number of students who did not know it was ever called the Soviet Union. Despite the name issue, I had a significant number who thought it was still a communist country. Some saw Russia simply as a land of vodka and alcoholics. Others saw it simply as a place that was riddled with mafia. As you can see from this rather simple and brief survey of my students, the starting point for my course is rather elementary.[7]

My history course is consistently offered at my college. We do also offer Russian language, but it has only been offered inconsistently over the past eighteen years. Currently, we offer the first year of Russian language to about fifty students annually. We usually have only one part-time faculty member teach Russian. That person has usually been a native speaker. We have also offered Russian literature and Russian geography, but also not on a consistent basis.

Second, my geography colleague and I have taught a course together twice on the history and geography of modern Russia to students in our honors program. It was a small and highly motivated group of students. One barrier to undergraduate students doing serious research on Russian history is, of course, language. Despite that barrier, these students produced some good work on Russia. My colleague developed an electronic book (e-book) that students used for the geography portion of the course. This e-book contained narrative descriptions of certain geographical issues, maps, video clips, articles, and links to Web sites. It was a wonderful resource for our students in their study of Russia. This course provided an examination of Russia through two different perspectives. The students were able to see how Russia's geography and history have played a part in what Russia is today.

Third, in conjunction with these honors courses (which we have offered twice), we have hosted speakers on many topics. Two of the most notable speakers were Dr. Murray Feshbach of the Woodrow Wilson International Center for Scholars and Dr. Blair Ruble of the Kennan Institute for Advanced Russian Studies. These speakers not only spoke to our class, but they also gave presentations to a campus audience. Some of the other speakers who we have hosted include: Dr. Thomas Porter of North Carolina A&T University on political reform, Dr. Joel Ostrow of Benedictine University on the Putin administration and Dr. Uli Schamiloglu of the University of Wisconsin at Madison on Tatars in modern Russia. Unfortunately, because of financial constraints we have not been able to host scholars from Russia.

Fourth, while all of these activities are either through regular courses, special courses, or guest speakers, I have also led three study tours to Russia. In 2008, 2010, and 2012, I led three groups of students to Russia. This program links my traditional history course with a field studies experience. After studying Russia's history in the classroom, students are able to visit many of the places we studied. My study tours focus on St. Petersburg and Moscow. We visit many of the historical sites that most people would expect including the Hermitage, Peter and Paul Fortress, St. Basil's Cathedral, the Kremlin, and many others. However, we also learn about other parts of Russia. I have taken students to paint their own porcelain pieces at the Lomonosov Porcelain Factory in St. Petersburg, visited a wooden architecture museum near Novgorod, descended into Stalin's Cold War bunker near the Taganskaya metro stop in Moscow, and visited an Old Believer community. These study tours are approximately ten to twelve days. The students are exposed to Russia's past and present. Many of our group meals include traditional Russian food and cuisine from some other areas of the former Soviet Union including Ukraine, Georgia, and Azerbaijan. I led some of the tours myself, but I also employed local guides to get a Russian perspective. Remembering that community colleges serve the community, it should not be surprising that of the forty-five students I have taken to Russia they range in age from twenty to eighty years old. On my 2008 study tour, my own parents took part.

The cost of the study tour presents difficulty for younger students even though I did have six students in their twenties on my study tour in

2010. I once had a Russian friend ask me why I focused my study tours on Moscow and St. Petersburg when there are so many other interesting places in Russia. The simple answer came from one of my other students from many years ago. The latter student said that most Americans go to Russia once or never. So, for an American making that one trip, it makes sense to focus on those two cities. In March of 2010, I spent a week in Siberia (Irkutsk, Lake Baikal, and Ulan-Ude) with the idea that I would take students there. In 2014, I offered a trip to Siberia, but it was cancelled due to lack of interest and the expense of the trip. In addition, it was very difficult to promote the trip considering the events starting in November of 2013 with protests in Kiev, the coverage of the 2014 Winter Olympics in Sochi, the annexation of the Crimea, and the war in eastern Ukraine.

Since the fall of 2013, the mainstream media in the United States has been focusing more attention on Russia and the region. This attention began with protests in Ukraine over a potential agreement with the European Union. This tension continued into 2014, and it was overtaken in the mind of the public by the events surrounding the 2014 Winter Olympics in Sochi. The news stories focused on the lack of preparation, packs of dogs, and Vladimir Putin running the Olympics as his own private festival. About three days after the Olympics concluded, the crisis over Crimea erupted eventually leading to a swift vote for annexation of the territory into Russia and then military tensions erupting in eastern Ukraine that lasted the rest of 2014 and into 2015. Along the way, the United States inserted itself into this crisis by working with European countries to impose economic sanctions on Russia.[8]

So, how do these events relate to the study of Russia and the broader region at a community college? First, in the Spring of 2014, I was interviewed ten times by local radio, newspapers, and college newspapers about the events in Russia. In one sense, this makes some sense since I have published on the history of Russian-American relations. In another sense, it does not. I am not an expert on current issues in Russia and so my perspective is quite historical and not necessarily the most up to date. Interestingly, one of the media outlets told me that I was the only person they could find when they simply searched the Internet for some kind of local (Chicago area) expertise. While this is clearly not true, it was distressing in a couple of ways. First, is this how the media searches for subject experts? Second, there are many great colleges and universities in the Chicago area with experts in this area. Another media member told me that I was one of a few people who responded to them. Both realities present problems for the public perception of Russia.

This new crisis also creates an interesting interaction in my classes. Some students bring outlandish media accounts of events in Russia and Ukraine. When I challenge the source and the perspective of the author, students have a difficult time reconciling very different views. In addition, President Putin as a caricature of himself is often a distraction from the complicated relations between Russia and Ukraine. Most of my students desire a simple answer. Most want to know if it is time to start a new cold war with Russia. I try to tell them that the relationship is far more complicated than that. Despite the fact that the United States has placed economic sanctions on Russia, Russia is a key player in the nuclear talks between the United States and Iran. In addition, in late March 2015, the United States and Russia collaborated on a year-long space mission with American astronauts and Russian cosmonauts working together. The complicated relationship often confuses my students and the public. I tried to offer another study trip to Russia for May 2015, but it was cancelled for low enrollment mainly because students feared what might be happening in the region. Remember, American community colleges are open admission and so the range of students is quite varied. Some students are struggling to stay in community colleges while others could easily do well at some of the most elite institutions in the United States.

Recently, President Barack Obama proposed free tuition for America's community colleges. While this initiative sounds very exciting, it has some obvious difficulties. First, if tuition is no longer charged for community colleges, then how will they be funded? This is not clear in the proposal as laid out. Most funding for community colleges comes from tuition and local property taxes. In some states, they state governments fund community colleges, but the federal government as a rule is not the primary funding source for community colleges. Second, what will be the purpose of community colleges going forward? Currently, community colleges serve the purpose of the first two years of a bachelor's degree, but they also provide short-term job training through specialized programs. Some in the community college world believe that this offer of free community college will make them more of training centers for jobs rather than the beginning two years of a bachelor's degree. If that happens, then Russian studies might be in some danger. This could lead to curricula at community colleges becoming even more uniform and devoid of more specialized courses. This is a bold proposal from President Obama and unlikely to get much support from a Republican-controlled U.S. Congress any time soon. However, in the Chicago area there are two examples of community colleges where there are limited offers of free tuition. William Rainey Harper College in Palatine, Illinois, and the City Colleges of Chicago offer limited forms of free tuition. At both colleges, these offers are limited by student performance. Both require a certain grade point average in high school, academic preparation, public service, and/or future degree and career plans.[9] In some ways, this is designed to put community colleges on a career path much earlier. Some fear that free tuition programs will apply more pressure on community colleges to conform leaving little room for developing specialized courses, like Slavic studies, at this level.

While American research institutes at large and prestigious colleges and universities provide an essential service for the study of Russia, I contend that an expanded curriculum for community colleges is a pressing need. My story is not typical. As noted earlier, most community colleges have no curriculum on Russia at all. The obstacles to this idea are significant, though. First, Russia falls in between the Western and non-Western world according to the American education system so it is hard to classify. Second, some consider the teaching of courses on one country to be too specific for a community college curriculum. Yet, many more community colleges have courses dedicated to Asian, Latin American, and Middle Eastern studies. Third, American community college education often follows trends. During the Cold War, Russia (even at community colleges) was studied much more. Now, with America's economic focus on Asia and its security focus on the Middle East, those areas receive more curricular attention. And fourth, many faculty at community colleges do not have the academic preparation to teach courses on Russia. Even in a difficult academic job market in the United States right now, still less than 25 percent of faculty have doctorates at community colleges. These realities mixed with a view held by many in and out of community colleges, that they should serve what Americans call "general education" as a primary purpose, the battle to include more specialized studies will be difficult.

Since the eruption of the difficulties between Russia and Ukraine (and the United States as a result) over the past year or so, a conversation has reignited over how each side studies the other. The relatively new Web site, Russia Direct, has been at the forefront of the discussion of Russian-American relations (in general) over the past year, but more recently, they are hosting a conference on the future of Russian Studies in America. They have just released a report about the top Russian Studies centers in the United States. The top five institutions are no surprise—Harvard, Wisconsin, Columbia, Illinois, and Stanford. Victoria Zhuravleva illustrates many fine points about the difficulties concerning the decline of Russian studies in the United States from language study and ability to frequency of travel experience in Russia.[10] These five institutions and many others provide outstanding graduate education in Russian studies, but the problem still remains the same. How do American students pursue Russian studies from high school to graduate school? Also, a general knowledge of Russia for more Americans is a pressing need. If a community college is their first step in that higher educational world, then there are many students who will never be exposed to Russia as a possibility for serious study.

In conclusion, the "Politics of Knowledge" is critical concerning how information about Russia reaches a broader audience. While most of my students will never pursue a more serious study of Russia, I feel as though I have served a purpose. Many of my students will be local and state leaders. They will sit on local school boards, run for city councils, and serve as state leaders. These people will make decisions that affect local school district, city, and state decisions. If they are not even exposed to Russian studies at some level of their higher education, it is unlikely that they will be able to make meaningful decisions concerning Russia. This is not only a problem for the academic world, but it is also a problem for the future of Russian-American relations.

NOTES

1. William Benton Whisenhunt, *Learning is the Greatest Adventure: A History of College of DuPage, 1966–2006* (Glen Ellyn, IL: College of DuPage Press, manuscript), 4.
2. Ibid., 4–5.
3. "U.S. Community Colleges," http://www.utexas.edu/world/comcol/state/.
4. Nicholas Riasanovsky and Mark Steinberg, *A History of Russia*, 8th edition, (Oxford: Oxford, 2010); John M. Thompson, *Russia and the Soviet Union: An Historical Introduction from the Kievan State to the Present* (Boulder, CO: Westview, 2008); Paul Bushkovitch *A Concise History of Russia* (Cambridge: Cambridge University Press, 2012).
5. Alexander Pushkin, *The Captain's Daughter and Other Stories* (New York: Vintage, 1968); Ivan Turgenev, *Fathers and Sons* (Oxford: Oxford University Press, 1992); Mikhail Bulgakov, *Heart of a Dog* (New York: Grove Press, 1968); Lydia Chukovskaya, *Sofia Petrovna* (Evanston, IL: Northwestern University Press, 1994); Vasily Grossman, *Everything Flows* (New York: New York Review of Books, 2010); Alexander Solzhenitsyn, *One Day in the Life of Ivan Denisovich* (Oxford: Oxford University Press, 1994).
6. Anna Labzina *Days of a Russian Noblewoman: The Memories of Anna Labzina, 1758–1821,* edited and translated by Gary Marker and Rachel May (DeKalb, IL: Northern Illinois University Press 2001); Savva D. Purlevski, *A Life Under Russian Serfdom: The Memoirs of Savva Dmitrievich Purlevskii, 1800–1868,* edited and translated by Boris Gorshkov, (Budapest: Central European University Press, 2005); Anna Bek, *The Life of a Russian Woman Doctor: A Siberian Memoir, 1869–1954,* edited by Anne D. Rassweiler and Adele Lindenmeyr, (Bloomington: Indiana University Press, 2004); John Scott, *Behind the Urals: An American Worker in Russia's City of Steel,* edited by Stephen Kotkin (Bloomington: Indiana University Press, 1989); Marguerite Harrison, *Marooned in Moscow: The Story of an American Woman Imprisoned in Soviet Russia,* edited and introduced by William Benton Whisenhunt, (Montpelier: Russian Life Books, 2011).
7. "Survey of Incoming Russian History Students," College of DuPage, 2011.
8. Andrew Wilson, *Ukraine Crisis: What it Means for the West* (New Haven, CT: Yale University Press, 2014), 1–95.
9. "Chicago Star Scholarships," http://www.ccc.edu/departments/Pages/chicago-star-scholarship.aspx; "Harper College Announces Free Tuition Scholarships," http://www.chicagotribune.com/suburbs/buffalo-grove/news/ct-harper-college-free-tuition-met-20150330-story.html.
10. "Russia Direct presents its Ranking of Russian Studies Programs in US," http://www.russia-direct.org/russian-media/russia-direct-presents-its-first-ever-ranking-russian-studies-programs-us.

BIBLIOGRAPHY

Bek, Anna. *The Life of a Russian Woman Doctor: A Siberian Memoir, 1869–1954.* Edited by Anne D. Rassweiler and Adele Lindenmeyr. Bloomington: Indiana University Press, 2004.

Bulgakov, Mikhail. *Heart of a Dog*. New York: Grove Press, 1968.
Bushkovitch, Paul. *A Concise History of Russia*. Cambridge: Cambridge University Press, 2012.
"Chicago Star Scholarships," http://www.ccc.edu/departments/Pages/chicago-star-scholarship.aspx.
Chukovskaya, Lydia. *Sofia Petrovna*. Evanston, IL: Northwestern University Press, 1994.
Grossman, Vasily. *Everything Flows*. New York: New York Review of Books, 2010.
"Harper College Announces Free Tuition Scholarships," http://www.chicagotribune.com/suburbs/buffalo-grove/news/ct-harper-college-free-tuition-met-20150330-story.html.
Harrison, Marguerite. *Marooned in Moscow: The Story of an American Woman Imprisoned in Soviet Russia*. Edited and introduced by William Benton Whisenhunt. Montpelier: Russian Life Books, 2011.
Labzina, Anna. *Days of a Russian Noblewoman: The Memories of Anna Labzina, 1758–1821*.Edited and translated by Gary Marker and Rachel May. DeKalb: Northern Illinois University Press, 2001.
Purlevskii, Savva D. *A Life Under Russian Serfdom: The Memoirs of Savva Dmitrievich Purlevskii, 1800–1868*. Edited and translated by Boris Gorshkov. Budapest: Central European University Press, 2005.
Pushkin, Alexander. *The Captain's Daughter and Other Stories*. New York: Vintage, 1968.
Riasanovsky, Nicholas and Mark Steinberg. *A History of Russia*. 8th ed. Oxford: Oxford University Press, 2010.
"Russia Direct presents its Ranking of Russian Studies Programs in US," http://www.russia-direct.org/russian-media/russia-direct-presents-its-first-ever-ranking-russian-studies-programs-us.
Scott, John. *Behind the Urals: An American Worker in Russia's City of Steel*. Edited by Stephen Kotkin. Bloomington: Indiana University Press, 1989.
Solzhenitsyn, Alexander. *One Day in the Life of Ivan Denisovich*. Oxford: Oxford University Press, 1994.
"Survey of Incoming Russian History Students." College of DuPage, 2011.
Thompson, John M. *Russia and the Soviet Union: An Historical Introduction from the Kievan State to the Present*. Boulder, CO: Westview Press, 2008.
Turgenev, Ivan. *Fathers and Sons*. Oxford: Oxford University Press, 1992.
"U.S. Community Colleges," www.utexas.edu/world/comcol/state/.
Whisenhunt, William Benton. *Learning is the Greatest Adventure: A History of College of DuPage, 1966–2006*. Glen Ellyn, IL: Manuscript, 2009.
Wilson, Andrew. *Ukraine Crisis: What It Means for the West*. New Haven, CT: Yale University Press, 2014.

FOURTEEN

American Studies on the Shores of Neva

In the Pursuit of Scholarly Identity

Ivan A. Tsvetkov and Alexander I. Kubyshkin

A period of academic freedom after the end of the Cold War has opened up broad prospects for the St. Petersburg Americanists. At this time, despite quickly multiplying financial and organizational problems, many Russian scholars experienced some euphoria and high hopes for the future. Americanists and, in particular, the St. Petersburg Americanists, had their own special reasons for that.

First, the official communist ideology was finally gone. Due to the specificity of their research, the ideological constraints had been felt more strongly by Americanists than by the representatives of many other social disciplines.

Second, Russians in the 1990s demonstrated keen interest in the experience of American civilization in its various manifestations, from the traditions of businesses and mass culture products, to the development of technologies and the systems of state institutions.

Third, the end of the Cold War coincided with a new phase of the information revolution, which for residents of Russia first manifested itself in the fall of the "Iron Curtain," removing censorship restrictions on the dissemination of Western literature and residents' ability to travel to foreign countries. A few years later, almost simultaneously with the rest of the world, Internet technologies began to spread in Russia. This radically changed information processing and opened up new, previously unseen perspectives of study by the social sciences.

Fourth, the old Soviet academic institutions' loss of the "monopoly" on science and the changing realities in the education system created a unique window of opportunity for the formation of new scientific, educational, and cultural centers, including ones in the field of American studies.

The latter circumstance was particularly important for the St. Petersburg Americanists. Over the last few decades of the Soviet Union, in St. Petersburg, or rather "Leningrad," as it was called from 1924 to 1992, American studies had, using the popular modern term, a "limited sovereignty."

During the Soviet period the academic centralization and concentration of human, financial, and organizational resources in Moscow (where Lenin moved the capital in 1918) inevitably reduced any "non-Moscow" research center to the category of a provincial branch, which was unable to claim a leading role in defining research priorities, book publishing, training, and so on.

The research center's struggle for independence, a right to be original, an ability to create their own school of thought, and to focus studies on specific topics (of course, without departing from the Marxist methodology)—all this became a driving force behind the creation of regional centers of American studies in the Soviet Union.[1] However, the rivalry of Leningrad and Moscow had still another, deeper meaning. As residents of the old imperial capital, the inhabitants of Leningrad always claimed a special status in all spheres of life, and especially in the field of science and education, in which they considered themselves unfairly overlooked and disadvantaged.

In the midst of the Cold War, Moscow authorities began institutionalizing Soviet American studies as a formal scientific discipline, but in fact this was an ideological and propaganda instrument of global confrontation against Washington, DC. They had to start this business virtually from scratch. However, in reality, a serious study of the United States in Russia started long before the revolution of 1917, and it started in St. Petersburg.

By the beginning of the twentieth century, in St. Petersburg, American studies was already a mature scholarly field, with dozens of authors (Maxim Kovalevsky, Alexei Babine, and Pavel Mizhuev, just to name a few) and a long list of published research. Only subsequent, turbulent political events prevented its final emergence as a formal university discipline. The revolution did not only slow down, but it did almost destroy the decade's long tradition of American studies in Russia; many scholars either emigrated or changed their occupations, or even perished under the thumb of the Soviet totalitarianism.

When the Leningrad academic community joined Moscow in the 1960s and participated in a state-sponsored study of the "main rival," the United States, Leningrad researchers retained some independence and sense of historical continuity with their predecessors, the St. Petersburg Americanists of the pre-revolutionary era. According to modern St. Petersburg historian Vladimir Noskov, "the distance from the center of decision-making and preservation of the research culture inherited from the old St. Petersburg school of thought resulted in maintenance of the more creative spirit by Leningrad historians, comparing to their colleagues in the new capital."[2]

It should be noted that, for some reasons, history as a scientific discipline has become a base for the new Soviet American studies. This could be explained by the place that "historical materialism" occupied among the Soviet social sciences, and by the stance held by Soviet leaders, especially Stalin, toward history. From the mid-1930s, Stalin paid great attention to the establishment of the Soviet historical sciences, which he considered an important and indispensable tool of ideological indoctrination.

As a result, most of the Soviet Americanists, both in Moscow and Leningrad, and in other regional centers, were historians. They studied the United States in accordance with the canons of "historical materialism," and wrote articles, monographs, and dissertations on such subjects as the history of class struggle in the United States (working-class movement, the protests of farmers, blacks' struggle against slavery and segregation), the history of the War of Independence and the Civil War (with particular attention to their social consequences), the role of capitalist monopolies in US foreign policy, and the history of Russian-American relations.

In Leningrad, the leading centers of academic study of the United States and training of Americanists were the Faculty of History at Leningrad State University (LGU), the Faculty of History at the Leningrad State Pedagogical Institute (LGPI), and the Leningrad branch of the Institute of History of the Academy of Sciences of the USSR (LOII). Leningrad's Americanists of the first "post-war" generation (Raphail Ganelin, Alexander Fursenko, and Victor Furaev) were graduates of the history department at LGU. Boris Romanov, a well-known Leningrad historian who graduated from St. Petersburg University in 1912, was a great influence on their development as scholars. Romanov transmitted traditions of the St. Petersburg historical school of thought to his students, in particular "zest to work with primary sources."[3]

By the end of the Cold War, Ganelin, Furaev, and Fursenko were the patriarchs of the Leningrad Americanists. Over the course of twenty years (until 1996), Furaev led the Department of World History at LGPI. Due to the nature of the post-graduate program at LGPI, which focused on attracting young teachers from the regions, it was Furaev who became a scientific advisor to many talented researchers from the provinces. They selected the history of the United States as the topic of their PhD theses (called *kandidatskaya dissertatsiya*, in Russian), and after returning to their home cities, these scholars continued to develop that research area. Thus, Furaev in the Soviet times was, in a sense, the translator of the Leningrad (St. Petersburg) traditions of American studies to the entire territory of the USSR.

In 1990, Fursenko was elected to the Academy of Sciences of the USSR with full member status and as a head of the historical branch. His postgraduate students, representatives of the "second generation" of Leningrad Americanists, Victor Pleshkov, Vladimir Noskov, and Sergey Isaev, formed the core of the study group on the history of the United States in the sector of general history of the LOII. Among the Faculty of History at LGU, Boris Shiriaev studied the problems of the early American history, and in 1989 he became a head of the Department of Modern and Contemporary History.

The scholarly results of the Soviet period of St. Petersburg ("Leningrad") American studies were quite impressive, though, of course, the number and variety of publications were far behind that of Moscow. Several works have become classics of the Soviet Amerikanistika and retain a certain scientific value to this day. Among them are monographs: by Alexander Fursenko, *The American Revolution and the Formation of the United States* (1978); Raphail Ganelin, *Soviet-American Relations in late 1917–early 1918* (1975); Victor Furaev, *Soviet-American Relations, 1917–1939* (1964); Boris Shiriaev, *The Political struggle in the United States, 1783–1801* (1981); and Victor Pleshkov, *US Foreign Policy at the End of the XVIII Century (Sketches of Anglo–American Relations)* (1984). After the collapse of the USSR, the collective work *Formation of the United States* (1992) edited by Alexander Fursenko was published, which can be considered as a summation of the efforts of Leningrad Americanists to develop this research theme.

Of course, the works of the Leningrad Americanists were not free from the limitations that were common for Soviet American studies and for Soviet social sciences in general. Choosing subjects predefined by ideology, absolute faith in the Marxist "immutable laws of social development," following the unwritten stylistic canons of the "Soviet" historical narrative that killed the author's individuality—all this, in varying degrees, was typical for the works of the Leningrad Americanists, including those listed.

But the new political situation after 1991 opened up new horizons and opportunities for all scholars, including the "patriarchs," who were still in excellent academic shape.

As individual researchers, Americanists of the first two Soviet generations and scholars of the third generation, who first expressed themselves after the start of a new political era, achieved excellent research results from 1990 to 2015. Even just listing titles of the articles and books devoted to the United States that were published in St. Petersburg in the post-Soviet period would take dozens of pages. In addition, several new centers for the study of the United States were opened in St. Petersburg during this period. If judged only in terms of quantity, American studies in St. Petersburg over the past two decades has been booming.

However, a deeper and more detailed analysis indicates the opposite: the old Russian and the restored Soviet traditions of American studies in St. Petersburg were not strengthened since 1991, but eroded and dissolved without being replaced by something new and original. To ascertain this, let us turn to the institutional history of American studies on the shores of Neva in the post-Soviet period.

The most notable new academic and educational center of American studies that emerged in St. Petersburg after 1991 was the Department of American Studies at the Faculty of International Relations, St. Petersburg State University. Professor Boris Shiriaev, the well-known historian and Americanist, initiated its creation in 1996. Looking back to the circumstances of the creation of the department, one should admit that it was not so much the result of a long progressive development of American studies in St. Petersburg, but rather a consequence of the favorable confluence of the unique circumstances.

The crisis of the social sciences after the collapse of the official Soviet ideology led to a serious reformatting of the old academic and educational centers. At St. Petersburg State University (SPSU), the Faculty of History has always been one of the most "ideological" faculties, and it is natural that in the early 1990s a serious fight broke out between faculty members of different ideological and methodological orientations. Perhaps, that fight would have ended in the simple redistribution of administrative powers, but in the new political realities of St. Petersburg another scenario occurred.

At that time, Anatoly Sobchak was the mayor of St. Petersburg—a prominent liberal politician, one of the heroes of the perestroika, who worked before as a professor of the law faculty of Leningrad State University. When a group of liberal-minded professors, former colleagues and friends of Sobchak (Konstantin Khudoley, Boris Shiriaev, and Vatanyar Yagya), took the initiative to launch the new educational program for World History and International Relations, their idea found understanding and support in the structures of the city government. The chairman of the Foreign Relations Committee of the St. Petersburg mayor's office at this time was Vladimir Putin, the future president of Russia. He was directly involved in the process of creating the new School of International Relations at St. Petersburg State University (1994) headed by Khudoley, and the Department of American (until 2008, "North American,") studies became one of its first structural subdivisions.

A two-tier system of bachelor's and master's degrees was almost immediately established at the new School; a master's program for "American Studies" was created in 1998 and the first postgraduate students entered the department in 1996. The School of International Rela-

218

Ivan A. Tsvetkov and Alexander I. Kubyshkin

tions as a whole, and the Department of American Studies, in particular, quickly turned into one of the most prestigious departments of SPSU, with a steady flow of ambitious applicants.

It should be said that a certain excitement that arose around the new educational programs was a kind of advance payment to teachers and scholars working at the School of International Relations. They sounded like magic words: "International Relations," "American Studies" — these formulas in the minds of Russians in the 1990s were the equivalent of the new, previously forbidden vistas opened before the young generation after the fall of the "Iron Curtain." It is not surprising that among the new students were many children of the political, cultural, and academic elite of St. Petersburg and other Russian regions.

Beginning in the late 1990s, about twenty bachelors of arts and eight to ten masters of arts annually graduated from the Department of American Studies. Thus, the number of graduates specializing in studying of the United States and Canada, (which was also included in the curriculum,) produced by the SPSU has increased several times in comparison with the Soviet period. Of course, only a few of them later entered the graduate school and continued to engage in the scholarly research of America. However, we can say that the new scientific and educational center in the field of American studies had been successfully created, and had become operational by the beginning of the twenty-first century.

Another project in the field of American studies, the Russian-American seminar, was successfully implemented under the leadership of professor Shiriaev at the School of International Relations. This academic forum met annually, usually during the period of the famous "White Nights" in St. Petersburg, gathering representatives of Russian and American universities that specialize in various aspects of the American studies and Russian-American relations. Frequent guests of the seminar were Petersburg politicians and public figures.

Workshop sessions were a week long, and one of the days was traditionally allocated for presentations and discussions in the field of American culture and literature. Professor Elena Apenko, head of the History of Foreign Literatures Department at the Philological Faculty of St. Petersburg State University, usually presided at these meetings. Combining the representatives of the various socio-humanitarian disciplines in one scholarly seminar was one of the first attempts at St. Petersburg to practice an interdisciplinary approach in American studies. During the preceding decades, linguists, historians, and philosophers had virtually no platform for regular meetings and scientific communication on subjects related to the wide field of American studies. At the same time, since the 1950s at the Philological Faculty of Leningrad State University, a strong and quite influential school for the study of American literature was formed, and its achievements were even better known abroad than the works of other St. Petersburg Americanists.

In addition to the Department of American Studies, the organization of a joint educational program with Bard College (1996), which led to the creation of another center of American Studies within St. Petersburg State University, was an important initiative. Subsequently, mainly through the efforts of its director, historian and Americanist Valery Monakhov, the Faculty of Liberal Arts was created based on that program (2011), with the former minister of finance of Russia, Alexei Kudrin, as its first dean. However, despite close cooperation with American partners and the issuance of double diplomas (from St. Petersburg University and Bard College) to graduates, there is no special profile or program in American studies at the Faculty of Liberal Arts, although many of the faculty taught and performed extensive research on topics related to the history and culture of the United States and Russian-American relations.

Some steps toward the creation of educational programs and research projects in American studies were undertaken from 1990 through the 2000s by the representatives of other academic institutions of St. Petersburg. Another meeting place for Russian and foreign Americanists, in addition to the Russian-American seminar, were conferences like Russian-American Links, which have been organized in St. Petersburg since 2003 on the initiative of a linguist Yurii Tretyakov. Several scientific and educational centers (St. Petersburg University of the Russian Academy of Sciences, European University at St. Petersburg, and the St. Petersburg Association for International Cooperation) acted as the co-sponsors of the conference.

In contrast to the Russian-American seminar where philologists were respected, but still considered guests, here they and representatives of other "non-political" disciplines might have felt more confident. Organizers directly stated in the official press release: "We expect the speakers to approach the theme from a multidisciplinary perspective: this would encourage an interdisciplinary discussion, lead to a more profound understanding of issues considered, and suggest avenues for further joint investigations."[4]

The Center for North American Studies and the St. Petersburg branch of the Russian Society for the Study of Canada were established in the St. Petersburg State University of Economics and Finance, mainly due to the efforts of candidate of philological sciences Tatiana Kuzmina. Historian and Americanist Vladimir Noskov, who chaired the Department of General History of the Russian State Pedagogical University (Hertzen University) from 1996 to 2007, acted as the Russian co-chair of the joint Russian-American educational project: "American Studies: New Curricula and New Pedagogies for English and Social Sciences." The project was initiated and co-chaired by David W. McFadden, professor of Fairfield University in Fairfield, Connecticut.

This project, which like many others realized in this period in St. Petersburg, was funded by the US State Department. It can be argued that the programs initiated and funded by the US government made notable contributions to the development of American studies at St. Petersburg after the end of the Cold War. Dozens of St. Petersburg scholars had a chance to visit the United States because of US government grants. The library of the American Cultural Center at the US Consulate General (later transformed into the "American Corner" at one of the city's libraries) helped to fill the lack of scientific literature, especially during the first post-Soviet years. The real "guardian angel" for St. Petersburg Americanists in this period was Tatiana Kosmynina, who worked in the culture department of the US Consulate General's office and was responsible for relations with the academic community. Through her tireless energy and personal charisma, many scholars from St. Petersburg and other cities of the Russian North-West managed to establish contacts with American colleagues and gained invaluable experience from direct acquaintance with the American civilization.

The momentum of the institutional growth of American studies in St. Petersburg, generated by perestroika and the end of the Cold War, began to show signs of slowing somewhere in the mid-2000s. Instead of a new acceleration phase and the transition to a next qualitative level of development, St. Petersburg American studies entered a period of stagnation and uncertainty.

All attempts to consolidate the efforts of various groups of researchers in the field of American studies were futile; they did not find common ground or a base for convergence. The Russian bureaucratic tradition, which implies stiff competition for the attention of the authorities and access to state-controlled resources, defined the behavior of Americanists, both in the new and old centers of American studies, which quickly became covert opponents.

This could have been a healthy competitive environment, if it had come in the form of scientific debate within the professional community. However, because funding in most cases came from the state, the survival and development of research centers (especially as the fiscal capacity of the state increased in the 2000s) depended, mostly, not on the decisions of academic councils and departments, but on the benevolence of bureaucrats. In making financial decisions, bureaucrats had very different motives than promoting the development of the new methodologies and interdisciplinary connections.

Despite the fact that dozens of professional Americanists worked at research centers and universities in St. Petersburg in the 2000s, they have not been able to organize the publication of an academic journal, which could represent their achievements and serve as a platform for scientific dialogue. The publication activity of the St. Petersburg researchers was limited to the publishing of the collections of materials from various kinds of conferences and seminars, as well as monographs and textbooks. On occasion, their articles were published in Moscow academic journals.

An academic journal could become the focal point for the consolidation of the St. Petersburg Americanists and could promote the formation of a regional school of thought, with special themes and methodology. The absence of such a journal can be explained by organizational difficulties (scarcity of money, unwillingness to incur the wrath of administrative structures for the "excessive initiative," which is yet another manifestation of the Russian bureaucratic servility) and objective scientific reasons: the disunity of researchers, who do not see the ground for systematic, cooperative research in common themes and subjects.

Another symptom of the weakness of the new structures of American studies in St. Petersburg was scholars' inability to adequately withstand the onslaught of bureaucratic innovations, the flow of which engulfed Russian science and education at the turn of the first decade of the twenty-first century.

Under the pretext of fighting "ineffective universities" and the implementation of the government regulations to "modernize" the Russian system of science and education (with the final goal to increase its competitiveness in the international arena), the officials of the Ministry of Education and Science started, among other things, to implement the so-called "competence-oriented curricula." It soon became clear that educational programs such as American studies hardly fit into the new matrix. For example, the Department of American Studies at the Faculty of International Relations, SPSU, has been saved through great effort, but instead of taking four consecutive years of classes related to the United States and Canada (from "An Introduction to the American Studies" and "History of the United States" to "The U.S. foreign policy" and "History of American Literature"), undergraduate students are now able to select only a small "American module," taught for one year.

At about the same time, the Department of North American Studies was renamed the Department of American Studies, which outwardly looked like it was being expanded and strengthened by including in the curriculum Latin American issues (political relevance of which for Russia at the turn of the first decades of the twenty-first century has increased significantly). However, in reality this measure had a dual effect on the quality of teaching and research. Further expansion of the research subject, which already suffered from a lack of certainty, led to a final dilution of the scientific guidance for students and teachers. Now any researcher one way or another engaged in the studying of any of the two American continents could be defined as an "Americanist." The identification of American studies as a discipline dealing first and foremost with the study of the United States, its history, and its culture, has become less and less relevant.

Changes in Russian political ideology that led first to the sustained growth of anti-Americanism in Russian society, and then to the absolute demonization of the United States directed by government propaganda also slowed development of American studies in St. Petersburg. The United States, once again, has been declared the main rival of Russia in the international arena. This process had its peaks and valleys, but has accelerated since the beginning of the third term of Putin's presidency in 2012, and reached its culmination in 2014 and 2015 due to the Ukrainian revolution and the subsequent events.

The history of the Soviet "Amerikanistika" during the Cold War shows that an intensity of ideological confrontation can contribute to the development of the scientific areas that are important to political leadership. Following this logic, the current aggravation of the Russian-American relations could also lead to authorities giving ample funding and attention to the centers of American studies. However (and this can be considered one of the unfortunate Russian academic traditions), authorities in Russia often need not a science as such, but the "correct" science, one that serves to justify the decisions made in the government's offices. Scholars who expressed doubts over the wisdom of the approved political strategy or offered an alternative view of events could not rely on attention and support from inside such a system.

The political impartiality and, in some cases, a penchant for expression of "pro-American" positions by the post-Soviet Americanists, including those at St. Petersburg, started to be seen as a problem. The very fact that the financing of the individual researchers, conferences, and trips was provided by the US State Department has already caused suspicions, and forced officials to treat existing centers of the American studies with growing apprehension.

On the other hand, for many St. Petersburg Americanists, especially of the older generation, the return of the image of America as the chief enemy of Russia was not much of an ideological problem. Instead, they saw it as the return of the lost status quo, something that helped found a common ground after decades of disunity and methodological vacillation.

However, the course of events revealed that many Russian politicians of the new "anti-American" formation allowed the feasibility of a more careful study of the "potential enemy" only after performing a "cleaning of the field," to eliminate an old institutional structure that was not well suited to the new challenges it faced. In the beginning of 2015, government agencies began to consider the first steps in this direction, but some of the "bottom-up initiatives" have already manifested themselves in full scale.

The most typical example of this can be seen in the fate of the Russian-American seminar, which survived the different phases of the development of relations between Russia and the United States in the post-Soviet period. It flourished from the late 1990s to the early 2000s, when academicians from leading European and US universities gladly visited St. Petersburg, even despite an impressive participation fee (from which, incidentally, Russian participants were exempt). Then, gradually, the stream began to dry up, and from 2012 to 2014, participants from the United States have been seen as exotic and not very welcome guests. Moreover, in the midst of the Ukrainian crisis in May 2014, the seminar was attended by a large delegation from China, and someone jokingly suggested renaming the Russian-American seminar as the Russian-Chinese seminar.

As the second decade of the 2000s began, the reduced numbers of post-graduates who planned to stay in the field was seen as another symptom of the American studies crisis in St. Petersburg. Despite the steady and even increasing flow of post-graduate students, few young scientists chose topics in US history and planned to continue the academic career after defending their PhD ("candidate of science") dissertation. In some of the older centers of American studies, such as the St. Petersburg Institute of History and the Faculty of History, SPSU, academic self-reproduction has fully stopped; all working scholars there presently came to academia during the Soviet era.

The School of International Relations, wishing to improve the academic standing of the team in the face of the increasing bureaucratic pressure, chose the tactic of inviting well-known experts from other regional centers. In particular, Americanist professors Alexander Sergounin and Alexander Kubyshkin moved to St. Petersburg at that time. However, the lack of a sustained influx of young researchers makes the prospect of American studies in St. Petersburg rather uncertain.

Thus, at the beginning of 2015, American studies in St. Petersburg was similar to the post-Soviet Russian democracy in its institutional design: after a period of euphoria and more or less successful creation of the basic structures, further development stalled and prospects began to look very vague. However, although science lives in the given institutional framework, it continues to develop only through the efforts of its individual creators. Therefore, we turn now to the question of what the St. Petersburg Americanists managed to achieve during the two tumultuous post-Soviet decades.

Perhaps the most serious challenge faced by the St. Petersburg Americanists since 1991 was a crisis of identity, the disappearance of any definite and stable landmarks: where, how, and why to move; and how to justify their interest in a particular topic. Almost limitless creative freedom was unusual and somewhat frightening. The disappearance of ideological constraints, so expected and desired, left researchers alone with the subject of their research and required extraordinary efforts to create a new system of methodological reference points.

It quickly became clear that relying on the experience of foreign colleagues, borrowing themes, subjects, and methods, did not work for of a number of reasons such as the irrelevance of many Western practices in Russian reality and the difficulty of mastering the multilayered and contradictory scientific baggage of Western civilization, which for many decades penetrated the "Iron Curtain" in only a slight trickle.

As a result, the academic achievements of the Russian scholars of the first post-Soviet decade, in the area of American studies and in other social sciences, were the result of a complex combination of individual research strategies, attempts to find a place in the international and Russian methodological context, and opportunistic maneuvering in times of financial and political uncertainty.

When one of the authors of this article entered the post-graduate program in the Department of North American Studies of SPSU in 1996, the only wish their academic supervisor stated about the topic of his future dissertation was to "choose something related to the United States." It should be noted that at that time there were no visible thematic preferences about studying the United States in the Russian academic and political world: everything was new, interesting, and unusual. As a result, a key criterion for selecting the topic proved to be the so-called "blank spots of history" approach, popular since the beginning of perestroika. Because Soviet and Russian literature could boast almost no publications on the Taiwan issue (Taiwan was seen as a part of China, and its special study was considered "inappropriate"), the theme of their thesis was defined as "The US policy towards the Taiwan issue."[5]

Subsequently, the study of US foreign policy in the Asia-Pacific region has become one of the trademarks of the department; many of its members specialized in various aspects of the topic (Yana Leksyutina, Andrei Kovsh, Irina Lantsova, Nikolai Fedorov, and Ivan Tsvetkov). The most significant works were published by Yana Leksyutina; in 2014, she defended her doctoral thesis on US-China Relations.[6] In 2003, the master's program "Pacific Studies" was created; however, the American theme was somewhat overshadowed in this framework by oriental and region-wide courses.

Another feature of the approach characterizing the study of the United States in the Department of American Studies has been special attention to foreign policy with a much weaker interest in the internal political and social processes. Only once every four years, in connection with the presidential campaign in the United States, does domestic policy become the subject of attention, but no fundamental research on these issues has been conducted.

As for the study of US foreign policy, the department had several important achievements. In 2006, Boris Shiriaev published the course of lectures "US Foreign Policy," which went through several editions and became a popular reference book for students.[7] In 2012 and 2014, a team of researchers from the department published two monographs on the latest trends in US foreign policy during the Obama administration.[8]

A particular area of research in the department was the study of the US public diplomacy. The first work on this topic was published by Natalia Tsvetkova in the late 1990s; subsequently she worked fruitfully, examining various aspects of the foreign cultural and information policy of the United States. In 2011, she defended her PhD thesis at the University of Groningen (The Netherlands). She is the author of the fundamental monograph on the Soviet-American rivalry in the universities of East and West Germany during the Cold War, published in English (2013).[9] In collaboration with Alexander Kubyshkin, she also authored a very popular textbook on American public diplomacy.[10]

Most of the works of the Department of American Studies had a political science bias or were formally performed in the methodological framework of political science. This reflects the general trend in the development of American studies at the Faculty of International Relations, which largely has focused on the study of topical issues of contemporary foreign policy. However, the department was able to save a classic, typical Soviet era approach to the American studies as a historical discipline. Good examples of this are the monographs by Yurii Akimov[11] and Nikolai Fedorov,[12] and the textbook *The American Historians*, published by Ivan Tsvetkov in 2008.[13]

However, the pure classical approach to the study of the United States can be found in St. Petersburg only in the old academic centers that existed in the USSR and survived its demise. In the St. Petersburg branch of the Institute of History, Alexander Fursenko, Viktor Pleshkov, Vladimir Noskov, and Sergey Isaev continued to work on a variety of research projects, from the study of the American colonial period, to the questions of the history and historiography of Russian-American relations. Particularly noteworthy are the fundamental monographs by Alexander Fursenko about the Cuban missile crisis,[14] by Sergey Isaev about James Madison,[15] as well as the series of articles by Vladimir Noskov about the life of American diplomats in St. Petersburg.[16]

In the Faculty of History of SPSU, the traditions of American studies were preserved through the research and teaching activities of Professor Vladimir Ushakov. Over the past decades, he has published several books and numerous articles, mostly on the founding fathers of the American state.[17]

Another traditional dimension of American studies in St. Petersburg, the study of the history of American literature, is represented in recent years by names of the researchers of the Philological Faculty of SPSU: Elena Apenko, Elvira Osipova, and Andrei Astvatsaturov.[18]

In summary, let's define some characteristics of the St. Petersburg scholars' approach to American studies that give it a special place in the structure of this academic discipline in Russia and, perhaps, beyond.

First, despite the political turmoil of the twentieth century, the memory of the first pre-revolutionary period of development of American studies in Russia, when St. Petersburg was the capital of the Russian Empire, is still alive. Many of the St. Petersburg Americanists still consider themselves the heirs of this glorious tradition—even more so than the heirs of the Soviet "Amerikanistika," which is associated with Moscow and other regional centers.

Second, a tradition of the so-called "Petersburg historical school of thought" has always had a great influence on the works of the St. Petersburg Americanists. This tradition is associated with the activity of a whole galaxy of St. Petersburg historians of the nineteenth and twentieth centuries, such as Konstantin Bestuzhev-Rumin, Alexander Presnyakov, and Boris Romanov. Its essential features include the categorical rejection of all sorts of sociological dogmatism and a very thorough approach to the analysis of the historical sources.

With regard to American studies, this tradition is reflected in choosing themes and subjects, the study of which would not put Russian researchers in obviously disadvantageous positions compared to their American counterparts because of the unequal opportunities of access to the historical documents. Hence, there is interest among the St. Petersburg Americanists in US-Russian relations, issues related to the "American traces" in the local history. In addition, it can be argued that the cautious attitude to all sorts of the holistic theories in some way helped St. Petersburg Americanists to preserve their academic identity in the period of historical materialism.

After the collapse of the Soviet ideology, the academic community of St. Petersburg was much less enthusiastic about the variety of fashionable Western theories, particularly in the field of international relations. Thus, most of the researchers at the Department of American Studies of SPSU preferred to work in the paradigm of realism, not only because of their inability to learn the nuances of the more recent theoretical currents, but also because from their college years forward they were taught to focus not on theory, but on the sources.

Third, while away from the metropolitan centers of the political decision making, the St. Petersburg Americanists, especially dealing with the modern development of the United States, on the one hand, were relatively autonomous in their choice of research projects, but on the other hand, in the absence of direct and targeted funding, they were often forced to rely on intuition in determining political conjuncture, hoping to attract attention and support from government agencies. Quite often, this led to frustration, because the initiative projects, even if relevant to the political agenda, ended up unnoticed and unclaimed. This has contributed to the formation of psychological complexes, intensified a struggle for scarce resources, and prevented the consolidation of scientists from the different organizations and academic centers.

It can be argued that one of the causes of the American studies crisis in St. Petersburg, which become apparent by the beginning of the 2010s, was an internal contradiction between the great ambitions of the old school of thought and its lack of relevance in the new political environment.

Thus a problem of "provincialism" in American studies in St. Petersburg, that has been well-known since the Soviet era, has not disappeared in a quarter of a century after the collapse of the USSR. In conjunction with the new phase of political anti-Americanism, an economic crisis, and the general decline of the Russian system of science and education, it increases the risk of further erosion of American studies in St. Petersburg as the integral school of thought, and the loss of its special position and status in Russian academia.

The only hope is that the people, the researchers who continue to engage in the American studies in St. Petersburg in spite of the all troubles, still have the ability to see in it meaning, value, and perspective.

NOTES

1. Of course, the content and nature of the discipline had little in common with an interdisciplinary focused American studies that emerged in the United States in the twentieth century.

2. Noskov, V. "Peterburgskaja amerikanistika: osnovnye etapy razvitija" (American Studies in St. Petersburg: the Main Stages of Development), in *Sankt-Peterburg—Soedinennye Shtaty Ameriki. 200 let diplomaticheskih otnoshenij* (St. Petersburg—United States of America. 200 years of Diplomatic Relations). St. Petersburg: OLMA, 2009, 196–97.

3. Ibid., 197.

4. *X-NET. Humanities & Social Sciences Online. (2009). CFP. Conference: Russian-American Links: Leaps Forward and Backward in Academic Cooperation (St.Pete, 2010). Available at* http://h-net.msu.edu/cgi-bin/logbrowse.pl?trx=vx&list=H-Soyuz&month=0910&week=d&msg=BSefPg1y42M1m7rz/7KleA.

5. Tsvetkov, Ivan. "*Politika SShA po otnosheniju k tajvan'skoj probleme, 1949–1999 gg*" (The US policy towards the Taiwan Issue. 1949–1999). Thesis for the degree of candidate of historical sciences (St. Petersburg, 2000). Available at http://www.ushistory.ru/dissertatsii/76-politika-ssha-po-otnosheniju-k-tajvanskoj-probleme-1949-1999-gg.html.

6. Leksyutina, Yana. *SShA i Kitaj: linii sopernichestva i protivorechij* (USA and China: Lines of Rivalry and Contradictions) (St. Petersburg: SPBU Publishing House, 2011).

7. Shiriaev, Boris. *Vneshnjaja politika SShA* (Foreign Policy of the USA) (St. Petersburg: SPBU Publishing House, 2006).

8. Shiriaev, Boris, Tsvetkov, Ivan and Leksyutina Yana (eds.). *Politika SShA v Aziatsko-Tihookeanskom regione v period administracii B. Obamy.* (US Policy in Asia-Pacific during B. Obama Administration) (St. Petersburg: SPBU Publishing House, 2010); Shiriaev, Boris, Leksyutina Yana and Bogdanov Alexei (eds.) *Vyzovy i dilemmy vneshnej politiki SShA v nachale XXI veka* (Challenges and Dilemmas of US Foreign Policy in the beginning of the 21st Century) (St. Petersburg: SPBU Publishing House, 2014).

9. Tsvetkova, Natalia. *Failure of American and Soviet Cultural Imperialism in German Universities, 1945–1990* (Leiden-Boston: Brill, 2013).

10. Kubyshkin, Alexander and Tsvetkova, Natalia. *Publichnaja diplomatija SShA* (The US Public Diplomacy) (Moscow: Aspect Press, 2013).

11. Akimov, Yurii. *Ot mezhkolonial'nyh konfliktov k bitve imperij: anglo-francuzskoe sopernichestvo v Severnoj Amerike v XVII—nachale XVIII v* (From Intercolonial Conflicts to the Empires' Struggle: Anglo-French Rivalry in North America) (St. Petersburg: SPBU Publishing House, 2005); Akimov, Yurii. *Severnaja Amerika i Sibir' v konce XVI—seredine XVIII v. Ocherk sravnitel'noj istorii kolonizaci* (North America and Siberia in the End of

XVI—the Middle of the XVIII Century. Essay on the Comparative History of Colonization) (St. Petersburg: SPBU Publishing House, 2010).

12. Fedorov, Nikolai. *Idei admirala A. T. Mehena i voenno-morskaja politika velikih derzhav v konce XIX—nachale XX veka.* (Ideas of Admiral A.Mahan and Navy Politics of
the Great Powers) (St. Petersburg: SPBU Publishing House, 2010).

13. Tsvetkov, Ivan. *Amerikanskie Istoriki* (The American Historians) (St. Petersburg:
SPBU Publishing House, 2008).

14. Fursenko Alexander, and Timothy Naftali. *"One Hell of a Gamble": Khrushchev,
Castro, and Kennedy, 1958—1964.* (New York and London: W.W. Norton & Co. 1997);
Fursenko A., Naftali T. *Khrushchev's Cold War. The Inside Story of an American Adversary*
(New York and London: W.W. Norton & C°; 2006)

15. Isaev, Sergey. *Dzhejms Medison: Politicheskaja biografija* (James Madison: A Political Biography) (St. Petersburg: Nauka, 2006).

16. Noskov, Vladimir. "Peterburgskaya amerikanistika: osnovnye etapy razvitiya"
(Petersburg Amerikanistika: Main stages of development), in *Sankt-Peterburg—Soedinennye Shtaty Ameriki. 200 let diplomaticheskih otnoshenij* (St. Petersburg: OLMA, 2009);
Noskov, Vladimir. "Amerikanskie diplomaty v revolyutsionnom Petrograde (fevral'—oktyabr' 1917 g." (American diplomats in the Revolutionary Petrograd) in *Politicheskaja Rossija pervoj chetverti HH veka: Pamjati V.I. Starceva* (St. Petersburg: RGPU,
2006).

17. Ushakov, Vladimir. "'Norma' i 'patologiya' v povedenii politika:
Dzh.Vashington v harakteristikah sovremennikov i istorikov" (Norm and pathology
in politician's behavior: G. Washington in the contemporaries' and historians' characteristics), in *Predstavlenija ljudej o "norme" i "patologii" v processe istoricheskogo razvitija:
Materialy XXXI Vserossijskoj nauchnoj konferencii* (St. Petersburg: Poltorak, 2012).

18. Astvatsaturov, Andrei. *Genri Miller i ego "parizhskaja trilogija"* (Henry Miller and
his "Paris trilogy") (Moscow: NLO, 2010); Apenko, Elena. "Ponjatie "afroamerikanec"
v rossijskom/sovetskom soznanii" (Term "Afro-American" in Russian/Soviet mind), in
Rossijsko-amerikanskie svjazi: afroamerikancy i Rossija (St. Petersburg: SPBU, 2009); Osipova, Elvira. "Realizm v spore s romantizmom (Mark Tven, Charl'z Uorner 'Pozolochennyj vek')" (Realism in argument with Romanticism), in *"Amerikanistika: Aktual'nye
podhody i sovremennye issledovanija"* (Kursk: KGU, 2013).

BIBLIOGRAPHY

Akimov, Yurii. *Severnaya Amerika i Sibir' v konce XVI—seredine XVIII v. Ocherk sravnitel'noy istorii kolonizatsii* (North America and Siberia in the End of XVI - the Middle
of the XVIII Century. Essay on the Comparative History of Colonization). St. Petersburg: SPBU Publishing House, 2010.
———. *Ot mezhkolonial'nykh konfliktov k bitve imperiy: anglo-frantsuzskoe sopernichestvo v
Severnoy Amerike v XVII—nachale XVIII v* (From Intercolonial Conflicts to the Em-
pires' Struggle: Anglo-French Rivalry in North America). St. Petersburg: SPBU Publishing House, 2005.
Apenko, Elena. "Ponjatie "afroamerikanets" v rossiyskom/sovetskom soznanii" (Term
"Afro-American" in Russian/Soviet mind). In *Rossiysko-amerikanskie svyazi: afroamer-
ikantsy i Rossiya* St. Petersburg: SPBU, 2009.
Astvatsaturov, Andrei. *Genri Miller i ego "parizhskaja trilogiya"* (Henry Miller and his
"Paris trilogy"). Moscow: NLO, 2010.
Fedorov, Nikolai. *Idei admirala A.T. Mehena i voenno-morskaja politika velikih derzhav v
konce XIX—nachale XX veka* (Ideas of Admiral A.Mahan and Navy Politics of the
Great Powers). St. Petersburg: SPBU Publishing House, 2010.
Fursenko, Alexander, and Timothy Naftali. *Khrushchev's Cold War. The Inside Story of an
American Adversary.* New York and London: W.W. Norton & Co., 2006.
———. *"One Hell of a Gamble": Khrushchev, Castro, and Kennedy, 1958—1964.* New York
and London: W.W. Norton & Co., 1997.

Isaev, Sergey. *Dzhejms Medison: Politicheskaja biografija* (James Madison: A Political Biography). St. Petersburg: Nauka, 2006.
Kubyshkin, Alexander, and Natalia Tsvetkova. *Publichnaja diplomatija SShA* (The US Public Diplomacy). Moscow: Aspect Press, 2013.
Leksyutina, Yana. *SShA i Kitaj: linii sopernichestva i protivorechij.* (USA and China: Lines of Rivalry and Contradictions). St. Petersburg: SPBU Publishing House, 2011.
Noskov, Vladimir. "Peterburgskaya amerikanistika: osnovnye etapy razvitiya" (Petersburg Amerikanistika: Main stages of development). In *Sankt-Peterburg—Soedinennye Shtaty Ameriki. 200 let diplomaticheskih otnoshenij* (St. Petersburg—United States of America. 200 years of Diplomatic Relations). St. Petersburg: OLMA, 2009.
———. "Amerikanskie diplomaty v revolyutsionnom Petrograde (fevral'—oktyabr' 1917 g." (American diplomats in the Revolutionary Petrograd). In *Politicheskaja Rossija pervoj chetverti XX veka: Pamyati V. I. Starceva.* St. Petersburg: RGPU, 2006.
Osipova, Elvira. "Realizm v spore s romantizmom (Mark Tven, Charl'z Uorner 'Pozolochennyj vek')" (Realism in argument with Romanticism). In *"Amerikanistika: Aktual'nye podhody i sovremennye issledovanija."* Kursk: KGU, 2013.
Shiriaev, Boris. *Vneshnjaja politika SShA* (Foreign Policy of the USA). St. Petersburg: SPBU Publishing House, 2006.
Shiriaev, Boris, Yana Leksyutina, and Alexey Bogdanov (eds.). *Vyzovy i dilemmy vneshnej politiki SShA v nachale XXI veka* (Challenges and Dilemmas of US Foreign Policy in the beginning of the 21st Century). St. Petersburg: SPBU Publishing House, 2014.
Shiriaev, Boris, Ivan Tsvetkov, and Yana Leksyutina (eds.). *Politika SShA v Aziatsko-Tikhookeanskom regione v period administratsii B. Obamy* (US Policy in Asia-Pacific during B. Obama Administration). St. Petersburg: SPBU Publishing House, 2010.
Tsvetkov, Ivan. *Amerikanskie Istoriki* (The American Historians). St. Petersburg: SPBU Publishing House, 2008.
———. "Politika SShA po otnosheniju k tayvan'skoy probleme, 1949–1999 gg" (The US policy towards the Taiwan Issue. 1949-1999). Thesis for the degree of candidate of historical sciences. St. Petersburg, 2000.
Tsvetkova, Natalia. *Failure of American and Soviet Cultural Imperialism in German Universities, 1945–1990.* Leiden-Boston: Brill, 2013.
Ushakov, Vladimir. "'Norma' i 'patologiya' v povedenii politika: Dzh.Vashington v harakteristikah sovremennikov i istorikov" (Norm and pathology in politician's behavior: G.Washington in the contemporaries' and historians' characteristics). In *Predstavlenija ljudej o "norme" i "patologii" v processe istoricheskogo razvitija: Materialy XXXI Vserossijskoj nauchnoj konferencii.* St. Petersburg: Poltorak, 2012.

FIFTEEN

Contemporary Dialogue of Russian and American Historiographies

Vladimir V. Sogrin

The relationship of Russian and the US historiographies can be divided into two periods: the Soviet and post-Soviet ones. Between the two periods there is a significant difference. The mainstream of the Soviet period was characterized by the struggle of Russian and American historiographies each claiming the monopoly of historical truth. In the post-Soviet period the dialogue of historiographies became prominent, though confrontation did not disappear. Confrontation is variable and depends much on changes in the domestic political realities in each country, as well as their relationships in the international arena.

In the Soviet period, Russian *Amerikanistika* relied on Marxist–Leninist formation theory and class approach that predetermined its confrontation with American historical scholarship. Also Russian *Amerikanistika* developed in the context of the Cold War, which influenced its attitudes toward the United States. And in addition anti-American recommendations were given from "above" (that is by the USSR Communist Party) and it was dangerous to ignore them. Finally, we should take into account the fact that in Soviet historical scholarship there was a special branch of "Criticism and struggle against bourgeois falsifications of history," which was extremely influential and militant. A great number of internal historiography conferences during the Soviet period were devoted to the struggle against the bourgeois, or, as it was often called, the "anti-Marxist historiography."

In post-Soviet era Russia, *Amerikanistika* of the Soviet period received a lot of criticism. In many respects the criticism was fair. But in this chapter, I would like to call for the balanced assessment of Soviet *Amerikanistika*, which possessed both faults and achievements. As for achievements, I want to mention as an example the study of history of the two-party system of the United States by the laboratory of *Amerikanistika* at the Department of History at Moscow State University (MGU). This center was created in the second half of the 1970s by Professor Nickolai V. Sivachev, one of the brightest historian-*Amerikanists* of the Soviet era. At that time the Soviet ideological cliché concerning the two-party system of the United States was "two parties, one policy." That is, distinctions between the two main parties of the United States were not simply belittled, but denied. Under direction of Sivachev historians of Moscow State University discovered that two-party system at all historical stages represented on one hand the consensus concerning the American fundamental principles, and, on the other hand, alternatives in understanding ways to improve American institutions.[1]

Sivachev was the initiator and main "punching power" of the 1974 introduction of the lecture program of leading American specialists on US history at the history faculty of Moscow State University, which was funded by the Fulbright Program. Every year the "stars" of American historiography such as Eric Foner and Leon Litwack read advanced lecture courses to students of MGU. The interaction of historiographies of the United States and the Soviet Union intensified thanks very much to the politics of détente pursued by the leadership of the two super powers during that decade. At the peak of détente, academic exchanges intensified, the colloquia of historians of the USSR and the United States were held regularly. An important role in the organization of those exchanges and meetings belonged to the Soviet Academy of Sciences and to the Institute of World History of the Russian Academy of Sciences.

There were other positive trends in the evolution of the Soviet *Amerikanistika*. But I will proceed with mentioning its main faults. Using Soviet ideological doctrines as their guide, Soviet scholars determined that capitalist civilization, including the United States, was the "lowest" stage in relation to the communist civilization. According to Soviet social sciences and humanities, after the events of October 1917, world capitalism entered a stage of permanent, general crisis. This "general crisis" was divided into three stages, and it was obviously meant, that the third stage which began in 1960s with anti-colonial revolutions in Africa, would be for capitalism the final one.

The fiasco of Russian socialism was followed by radical changes in all spheres of life, including the social sciences and *Amerikanistika*. American studies were influenced by political transformations, which should be briefly mentioned. During the first stage of his reforms, Soviet reformer Mikhail Gorbachev, who came to power in 1985, tried to implement the great Soviet dream "to catch up and overtake America" on the basis of socialist modernization. In 1987, Gorbachev changed the reformist strategy, intending to combine socialism with the free market economics and democracy. Suddenly, the United States went from USSR enemy number one to Russia's best friend. This shift directly influenced Russian American studies. No less than one half of *Amerikanists* turned into apologists for the United States. The United States began to be considered a middle-class society, a people's democracy, the embodiment of material abundance and spiritual freedom. The climax of Russian love for the United States was reached at the beginning of the Yeltsin era. But from the middle of 1990s the situation again began to change and the United States once again cam to be an enemy of Russia by official ideologists and the majority of public. However, since then, academic freedom has been preserved and scholars have a choice of research approaches to the history of the United States. I myself belong to the school of *Amerikanists* who believe that the research task is to deepen the objective balanced approach to the study of the United States, to oppose propaganda pressures from any side, and to promote creative dialogue of Russian and American historiographies and cultures.

Since the second half of the 1980s there was a real boom in the translation and publication in Russia of works by American historians. Rehabilitation of American Sovietology was surprising: those who were called anti-Soviet, appeared as a reputable and qualified specialists in Russian history. A vivid example is Richard Pipes, before designated in the USSR as anti-Soviet number one. Many of his works were translated into Russian. There were even more translations and publications of books of American specialists on the history of the United States. Within two decades the number of "conservative" works translated into Russian significantly exceeded the number of books by American "leftist" historians published in the USSR in previous seventy years. I will mention only some of best-known historians of United States that were translated into Russian: Daniel J. Boorstin, Arthur M. Schlesinger Jr., Frederick J. Turner, and Louis Hartz.[2]

Russian scholars accepted American social sciences and humanities "invasion" with satisfaction and the majority expressed a willingness to consider the positively theoretical approaches, concepts, and conclusions of the US scholars. Not all but many among them were willing to build further relationships with US social sciences and humanities scholars through dialogue instead of confrontation. The reaction of the American scholars was, in my opinion, somewhat different. They were ready for the role of teachers, but were not prepared for an equal dialogue.

As an example, I consider the publication in the United States in the post-Soviet period of four editions of the works of Russian *Amerikanists* with commentaries by American scholars and responses by Russian authors. The first book, published in 1989, was devoted to the period of the New Deal; the second one, published in 1995, covers the period of the American Revolution; the third book, published in 1997, is dedicated to the Russian-American cultural relations before 1914; finally, the fourth book, published in 2000, includes the entire history of US political parties. The publication as a whole cannot be considered quite satisfactory for the reason that it included the translations into English those works of Russian historians that had been published mainly in 1960–1970s. In the context of the serious transformation of post-Soviet *Amerikanistika* in the 1990s the translations were in many ways outdated. However, they are not the worst works from the Soviet period, and were designed in the spirit of school of Nikolai Sivachev about which I wrote above. I must say that the prefaces in all four books are written in the form of a dialogue, which takes into consideration the spirit of the times. But the comments of American historians regarding specific articles are written in many if not most cases in the spirit of the Cold War, with frank claims to knowledge of an absolute truth.

Let me give two examples relating to my own articles. In the 1995 book, Pauline Maier devoted sixteen pages to my article that was published in Russian in 1978 and dedicated to the comparison of the sociopolitical views of Thomas Jefferson, Thomas Paine, and Benjamin Franklin. Calling me a historian from "another world," Maier refused to think over my conclusions, arguments, and comparisons, and completely concentrated instead on a presentation of her own works and views as well as an enumeration of the works of American authors that came to light after the original release of my article and were not, of course, used by me. In my half-page answer, I stressed that Maier did not eschew a Cold War mentality and that Karl Marx, whose influence on my approach made Maier angry, was no less sophisticated and creative than Maier and that messianism was not the best method of dispute with a foreign opponent.[3] In another book my article about the emergence of political parties in the United States in conjunction with an article of Marina Vlasova on the Democrats and the Whigs was commented on by William G. Shade. Vlasova and I were unanimous on most important points: Shade was guided by the stereotypes of American scholars typical in the perception of foreign, especially Russian studies of the United States.[4] Absolute confidence in the superiority of the American historical profession and a belief that Russian authors at best can only repeat what was written and said by the Americans was the leitmotif of both Maier and Shade.[5]

This attitude, that Russian historians can't say anything that Americans do not already know, influences the essence of present-day cultural and information exchange between Russia and the United States. It's not an exchange of equal cultures but a one-way movement. I already named a number of American scholars who were translated into Russian between 1990 and the 2000s and were published in Moscow. I can name no less than one hundred more American scholars published in those two decades in Russia. And if I ask American colleagues to name at least one or two research monographs of Russian professional historians of the

United States that were published in the same decades in the United States, I am afraid that will put them in a deadlock. And in my soul I don't doubt that the majority of American historians have this response in their minds: what can scholars from Russia tell us that is new? It turns out that American perceptions of Russian historians, taken together, are not worth even one-tenth of one Richard Pipes.

The mentor tone, an indicator of messianic consciousness and sense of national superiority, is also typical of American scholars in their analysis of Russian society today. Edward Batalov, a famous Russian *Amerikanist*, convincingly showed this in one of his last books.[6] As is evident from the study of Batalov, typical American estimates of the Russian political process have a number of methodological shortcomings, chief among which is its "measurement" on the basis of democratic norms of their own country, considered as the universal role model for the world.

The confrontation matrix, unfortunately, still retains a strong position in the relationship of historiographies between the two countries. To lay the blame only on American scholars would, of course, be an obvious exaggeration. The Russian national mentality also preserves confrontational traits which affect the social sciences and humanities of Russia. In the 2000s, Russian attitudes toward the United States began to be more confrontational in comparison with those in the 1990s. This is obviously reflected in books by American authors translated and published in Russia in the recent decade. In the 1990s, books by American scholars that were translated into Russian were predominantly written by liberal and conservative authors presenting a positive image of America. In the 2000s and 2010s, a larger proportion of books written by American scholars that were translated into Russian were harshly critical of the United States. The authors are mainly radical researchers, such as Michael Parenti, Howard Zinn, Gore Vidal,[7] and also those like the conservative traditionalist Patrick J. Buchanan,[8] who severely criticize the domestic and foreign policy of the United States. It is significant that the Russian publishing houses, which publish these books with financial assistance of "Patriotic" national sponsors (and in the 1990s, American authors were published mainly with the financial support of the US Information Agency), edit them, often, in the category "America against America." That is, the reader is expected to say: these are real vices and shortcomings of America, because they are recognized by American intellectuals and not by Russian domestic propaganda.

Domestic propaganda after the year 2000 dramatically increased anti-Americanism. Anti-Americanism was more regularly used in works by professional historians. Here are two examples. Andrei N. Sakharov, the chair of the Institute of Russian history and a corresponding member of the Russian Academy of Sciences came up with the concept that Russia in 1905 could actually win the war against Japan and its loss was a result of the machinations of the USA who forced Russia to give up to Japan southern Sakhalin and the Kurils.[9] The US role in the Russian-Japanese conflict was demonized by Sakharov. In fact as it was long ago shown by both American and Russian historians the United States, under President Theodore Roosevelt, professed a strategy of maintaining a balance of powers and therefore American diplomats in the negotiation process in 1905 demanded concessions from the defeated Russians, but also successfully resisted the excessive claims made by Japan. Sakharov obviously falsified history, writing that Russia in 1905 gave up Kurils to Japan because of US demands. In fact as it was long ago shown by both American and Russian historians the United States, under President Theodore Roosevelt, professed the strategy of maintaining a balance of powers and therefore American diplomats in the negotiation process in 1905 demanded concessions from the defeated Russia but also successfully resisted the excessive claims of Japan. And Kurils belonged to Japan since 1875.

A young historian, Ivan B. Mironov, in his 2011 doctoral dissertation, categorically rejected the traditional conclusions of Russian historians that the sale in 1867 of Alaska to the United States was due to the objective economic and political interests of Russia. He attributes the sale of Alaska to aconspiracy of American "agents of influence" in Russia: "The Sale of Alaska was preceded by many years of the activities of a small group of high officials in the government of the Russian Empire, whose purpose was the creation of artificial prerequisites concessions Russian overseas territories to the United States of America."[10] In fact, he includes the Emperor Alexander II and the famous Minister of Foreign Affairs Alexander M. Gorchakov among the ranks of "American agents."

Anti-Americanism fortunately didn't destroy the academic freedom created during the Gorbachev period. Acadenuc freedom and the idea of dialogue between Russian and world historiography survives. Keep in mind that confrontation, which is preserved in works by such people as Sakhrov and Mironov, means pursuit of a research monopoly, an attempt to discredit and eliminate oppoisng visions and that dialogue means the exchange of research results among different schools of historiography and discussion aiming at joint approach to historical truth. Confrontation is a "zero-sum game," and dialogue is an enrichment of each side through convincing arguments and irrefutable facts exchanged by opponents that enlarge and improve general historical knowledge in the interests of historiography as a whole. It should be recognized that the culture of dialogue in Russian historiography is still not formed but is in development in the post-Soviet period, and positive results have been achieved.

Today the influence of confrontation is slowly diminishing as the struggle against "bourgeois schools" in professional Russian studies of history gives way to dialogue and discussion with all directions and schools of world and American historiographies. The main criterion for the relationship to the findings and concepts on this or that school is its compliance with the historical reality rather than value-ideological preferences. Russian *Amerikanistika*, as well as the whole domestic historiography preserving national characteristics, became more closely integrated into world historiography, which entails recognition and the maximum allowance for a variety of research achievements of foreign schools.

But such an approach to foreign historical schools raises a number of new research challenges. Chief among them stems from the fact that American history schools are in many cases in an antagonistic relationship, and mechanical, non-professional perceptions of their research results can lead to naive eclecticism or adoption of unprincipled position. I will illustrate the seriousness of this problem with the help of two classic fundamental works on the history of the United States that were translated into Russian in the post-soviet period. They belong to prominent leaders of rival historical schools. First the three-volume monograph of Daniel Boorstin on historical experience and the achievements of North American civilization.[11] The second work is a huge monograph by Howard Zinn called *People's History of the United States,*[12] published in the United States for the first time in the early 1980s and after that republished more than ten times. Both works are widely known in the United States, and the names of their authors entered the pantheon of American historical scholarship. But these works are antagonistic in their approach to American history and in their conclusions.

Boorstin's work is the story of an enterprising American people and individuals from social backgrounds other than the white race who achieved success in various spheres, including the material one.. This is the story of those in America who are called "winners," and they, as is evident from the work of Boorstin, comprise the majority of the nation. Zinn's work is chiefly the story of those who at various stages of American history turned out to be in the ranks of "losers," that is the Indians, blacks, Hispanics, poor whites, and the vast majority of women of all races. According to Zinn, "losers" not "winners" form the majority of the nation.

Boorstin and Zinn base their work on a wealth of factual material and both authors pretend to create a satisfactory and impressive synthesis of American history. But because the two in fact come to antagonistic conclusions the reader is posed with a difficult question: whose synthesis corresponds to historical truth? In my opinion, the syntheses of both Boorstin and Zinn are one sided in character, although at the same time, I do not question the authenticity of historical material, as well as many of conclusions and generalizations contained in both works. They comprise a significant part of the historical truth, but not all of it, and if you talk about the whole historical truth, it should be, in my view, recognized that in both works it is seriously impaired. The positions of Boorstin and Zinn reflect not their own personalities but an important feature of American historical scholarship in general. At all times it was divided into rival schools. Objective evaluation of different schools of American historiography is vital in determining Russian *Americanists* independent research position in the study of US history. Here I want to draw attention to one important feature of modern historiography in the United States that clearly indicates that the study of national history by any national historiography consistently experiences a dramatic effect on the part of politics and the public.

At the present stage, American historiography is significantly influenced by so-called political correctness —a worldview shaped in American society, especially in liberal circles, under the influence of sociopolitical processes and changes in the last third of the twentieth century. These changes should be characterized as clearly positive: chief among them is recognition by American society of civil and legal equality of the black race with the white, and the second is the recognition of unconditional equality and equity, in all social spheres, of American women.

These two great truths, endorsed by American society under the influence primarily of broad democratic movements of 1960s through 1980s, accompanied by numerous acts, claiming the equality of blacks and women, had the strongest impact on changes in national mentality and culture. The impact on social sciences and historiography was significant.

In historiography there was the rise of "women" and "black" studies and as a result the picture of American history was seriously diversified and enriched. This is an obvious advantage in the development of American historical scholarship. But the study of historical issues also brought to light some serious distortions, which are in clear contradiction with the principles of historicism. The most important events of the past, such as the US War of Independence, the Civil War, the Progressive era of the early twentieth century and the New Deal of 1930s were judged not so much due to their positive innovations in comparison with previous eras, but in connection with their failure to ensure equal rights for blacks, women, and other oppressed social groups. In all periods of America's past, historians search manifestations of women's work for equality and the role of those manifestations in many cases are exaggerated, and in historical generalizations their influence as well as the influence of African Americans was given to a disproportionate place, which they in fact in many eras didn't occupy. A "politically correct" view of American history produced a great influence on teachings at schools and universities.

The concept of "pros" and "contras" in generalizations about American history may reflect the presence of certain ideological positions in the approach of a historian. If I try to outline my own position, I would prefer the definition *humanistic approach*. The concept of "pros" and "contras" in generalizations on American history may reflect the presence of certain ideological positions in approach of a historian. If I try to out-line my own position, I would prefer the definition humanistic approach. My criterion is improvement of the material conditions and of all compo-nents of quality of life for all classes, groups and members of society. But of course, this approach in professional historical work cannot acquire the character of the imperative for it creates the risk of progression to a position similar to that of political correctness or some other sort of anti-historical vision. The most reliable antidote to that danger again is histor-icism—evaluation of historical changes in the context of the historical conditions and possibilities of the society. Delete the end of the sentence.

Other historians might have different theoretical positions. And those differences are also an important reason why historians will always re-main different, and Russian historiography will not copy American historiography and vice versa. It is important that these differences were not erected in the absolute, not led to the replacement of the dialogue of national historiographies by confrontation. This danger can be neutral-ized through the professional basics and features of historical writings which are in many respects universal.

An important tool for the development of dialogue between two na-tional historiographies is regular contact, particularly through confer-ences. It should be noted that the conferences establishing direct contacts and developing dialogue between Russian and American historians at a certain stage were under threat. In the 1990s they almost ended because of the financial difficulties of Russian science organizations. Exchanges between US and Russian academies of sciences which were regular in the 1970s and 1980s stopped. Round-table discussions of large teams of Rus-sian and American historians which were held once every two years in previous decades also stopped. The situation began to change for the better in the 2000s as a result of independent initiatives of individual scientific-educational centers and institutions both in the United States and in Russia.

An important role was played by the Institute of World History of the Russian Academy of Sciences and by the Russian State University for the Humanities. As a result, a series of Russian-American conferences that contributed to the affirmation of the dialogue form of the relationship of historiographies of the two countries were held. Let me mention some of these conferences.

In the Russian State University for the Humanities a conference dedi-cated to the 200th anniversary of the establishment of diplomatic rela-tions between Russia and the United States was held in February 2007. Historians of the two countries discussed various aspects of the history of Russian-American relations as well as other important topics. The confer-ence materials were published on "equal footing"—all the speeches were printed in two languages and in full.[13] In fall of the same year the confer-ence commemorating two centuries of diplomatic relations between Russia and the United States was held at the Institute of World History of the Russian Academy of Sciences. The conference was attended by many ambassadors of the USSR/Russia in the United States and the United States to the Soviet Union/Russia as well as by "stars" of American historiography. The conference materials were published thematically in several books (in this case as well as publications of the Russian State University for the Humanities) in "parity" format.[14]

The conference dedicated to Abraham Lincoln was held in 2009 in the Russian State University for the Humanities. Interestingly, the reports of the American participants on Lincoln were much more critical than estimations of Russian scholars (that is in my opinion due to the influence of political correctness on Americans). Acquaintance with materials of the conference shows that aggregate reports of Russian and American historians create a more complete and comprehensive view of the heritage Abraham Lincoln.[15]

The Institute of World History of the Russian Academy of Sciences with the support of the US Embassy in Moscow held in November 2013 the international conference under the title "Changing Perceptions of Russia in the United States. Changing Perceptions of the USA in Russia. 1933–2013." The conference was attended by seventy scholars among them leading experts on the subject from the United States and the leading Russian historians.[16] It is qualitatively different from the colloquia of the Soviet and American historians of the 1970s and 1980s. Confrontation was not noticeable at all. Creative dialogue based on the interchange of facts and arguments to examine objective historical truth dominated the proceedings. I hope that the trend of fruitful dialogue between Russian and American historians will only be strengthened in future.

NOTES

1. Among the papers, which summarize the activities of the team, I can single out two: Alexander S. Manykin, Viacheslav A. Nikonov, Yurii N. Rogoulev, Evgenii F. Yaz'kov, " Nekotorye itogi izucheniia istorii dvukhpartiinoi sistemy SShA," *Novaia i noveishaia istoriia* , no. 2 (1988); Il'ia V. Galkin, Alexander S. Manykin, Vladimir O. Pechatnov, "Dvukhpartiinaia sistema v politicheskoi istorii SShA," *Voprosy istorii* , no. 9 (1987).

2. Daniel J. Boorstin, *Amerikantsy: Kolonial'nyi opyt [The Americans: The colonial experience]*, (Moscow: "Progress" and "Litera," 1993); Daniel J. Boorstin, *Amerikantsy: Natsional'nyi opyt [The Americans: The national experience]* (Moscow: "Progress"—"Litera," 1993); Daniel J. Boorstin, *Amerikantsy: Demokraticheskii opyt [The Americans: The democratic experience]* (Moscow: "Progress"—"Litera," 1993); Arthur M. Schlesinger Jr., *Tsikly amerikanskoy istorii [Cycles of American history]* (Moscow: "Progress-Akademiia," 1992); Louis Hartz, *Liberal'naia traditsiia v Amerike [The liberal tradition in America]* (Moscow: "Progress-Akademiia," 1993). Frederick J. Turner, *Frontir v amerikanskoi istorii [The Frontier in American History]* (Moscow: Ves' mir, 2009).

3. Gordon S. Wood and Louise G. Wood, eds., *Russian-American Dialogue on the American Revolution* (Columbia, MO; and London: University of Missouri Press , 1995):105–42.

4. Joel H. Silbey, ed., *Russian-American Dialogue on the History of U.S. Political Parties.* (Columbia, MO; and London: University of Missouri Press, 2000): 75–77.

5. Since those times Professor Shade had probably changed his mind; he invited several Russian scholars to be contributors to the volume of *Encyclopedia of U.S. Political History* that he edited, see *Encyclopedia of U.S. Political History,: Expansion, Division, and Reconstruction, 1841–1877*, volume 3 (CQ Press, 2010).

6. Edward Y. Batalov , *Problema demokratii v amerikanskoi politicheskoi mysli XX veka* [*Problems of Democracy in American Political Thought of the 20th Century]* (Moscow: Progress–Traditsiia, 2010) .

7. Gore Vidal, *Pochemu nas nenavidiat. Vechnaia voina radi vechnogo mira* [Perpetual War for Perpetual Peace, or How We Got to Be Hated] (Moscow: Izdatel'stvo AST, 2006); Howard Zinn, *Narodnaya istoriya SShA: s 1492 goda do nashikh dnei [A people's history of the United States, 1492–present]* (Moscow: Ves' mir, 2006); Michael Parenti, *Vlast' nad mirom. Istinnye tseli amerikanskogo imperializma [Against Empire]* (Moscow: Pokolenie, 2006).

8. Patrick J. Buchanan, *Smert''Zapada [The Death of the West: How Dying Populations and Immigrant Invasions Imperil Our Country and Civilization]* (Moscow and St. Petersburg: AST, 2003); Patrick J. Buchanan , *Pravye i ne-pravye. Kak neokonservatory zastavili nas zabyt' o reiganovskoi revoliutsii i povliiali na prezidenta Busha [Where the Right Went Wrong: How Neoconservatives Subverted the Reagan Revolution and Hijacked the Bush Presidency]* (Moscow: AST, 2006); Patrick J. Buchanan , *Na kraiu gibeli [State of Emergency: The Third World Invasion and Conquest of America]* (Moscow: AST, 2008).

9. Andrei N. Sakharov, "Pravda o neokonchennoi voine. Pozornyi proigrysh Russko-iaponskoi voiny 1905 g. ne bolee chem istoricheskii mif," *Rossiiskaia gazeta* , November 13, 2006.

10. Ivan B. Mironov, *Politika pravitel'stva Rossiiskoi imperii v osvoenii i likvidatsii severo-amerikanskikh kolonii (1799–1867 gg.)*, Avtoreferat dissertatsii na soiskanie uchenoi stepeni kandidata istoricheskikh nauk (Voronezh: Izdatel'stvo Voronezhskogo Universiteta, 2011), 14.

11. Mentioned above books of Daniel J. Boorstin.

12. Mentioned above book of Howard Zinn.

13. Victoria I. Zhuravleva, ed., *Rossiisko-amerikanskie otnosheniia v proshlom i nastoiashchem: obrazy, mify, real'nost''[Russian-American Relations in Past and Present: Images, Myths, and Reality]* (Moscow: Izdatel'stvo RGGU, 2007)

14. Alexander A. Chubarian, ed., *200 let rossiisko-amerikanskikh otnoshenii. Nauka i obrazovanie [200 Years of Russian—American Relations. Science and Education]* (Moscow: Izdatel'stvo Olma, 2007)

15. See Victoria I. Zhuravleva, ed., *Avraam Linkol'n. Uroki istorii i sovremennost' [Abraham Lincoln. Lessons of History and Contemporary World]* (Moscow: Izdatel'stvo RGGU, 2010).

16. See *Meniaiushcheesia vospriiatie Rossii v SShA. Meniaiushcheesia vospriiatie SShA v Rossii, 1933–2013 [Changing Perceptions of Russia in the United State. Changing Perceptions of the United States in Russia, 1933-2013]*, Elektronnyi nauchno— obrazovatel'nyi zhurnal "Istoriia," vol. 30, no. 7 (2014).

BIBLIOGRAPHY

Chubarian, Alexander A., ed. *Rossiia—SShA: politika i diplomatiia v XX-XXI vv [Russia–USA: Politics and Diplomacy in the 20th–21st Centuries]* Moscow: Izdatel'stvo Olma, 2008.
———, ed. *200 let rossiisko-amerikanskikh otnoshenii. Nauka i obrazovanie [200 Years of Russian–American Relations. Science and Education]* Moscow: Izdatel'stvo Olma, 2007.
Graham, Otis L., Jr. *Soviet-American Dialogue on the New Deal.* Columbia, MO;and London: University of Missouri Press, 1989.

Meniaiushcheesia vospriiatie Rossii v SShA. Meniaiushcheesia vospriiatie SShA v Rossii,
1933–2013 [Changing Perceptions of Russia in the United State. Changing Perceptions of
the United States in Russia, 1933–2013] , Elektronnyi nauchno—obrazovatel'nyi zhurnal "Istoriia," vol. 30, no, 7 (2014).

Shade, William, ed. *Encyclopedia of U.S. Political History: Expansion, Division, and Recon-*
struction, 1841–1877, volume 3. Thousand Oaks: CQ Press, 2010.

Silbey, Joel H., ed. *Russian-American Dialogue on the History of U.S. Political Parties.*
Columbia, MO; and London: University of Missouri Press, 2000.

Sogrin, Vladimir V. "Meniaiushcheesia vospriiatie SShA v postsovetskoi Rossii,"
Obshchestvennye nauki, no. 2 (2014): 78–91.

———. "Istoricheskaia mysl' XX veka,"*Obshchestvennye nauki,* no. 2 (2005): 115–23.

Wood, Gordon S., and Louise G. Wood, eds. *Russian-American Dialogue on the American*
Revolution. Columbia, MO; and London: University of Missouri Press , 1995.

Yaz'kov, Evgenii F., ed. *Dvukhpartiinaia sistema SShA: proshloe i nastoiashchee. Vzgliad*
sovetskikh uchenykh [The US Two-Party System: Past and Present. A View of Soviet
Scholars]. Moscow: Progress, 1989.

Zhuravleva, Victoria I., ed. *Avraam Linkol'n. Uroki istorii i sovremennost' [Abraham Lin-*
coln. Lessons of History and Contemporary World] . Moscow: Izdatel'stvo RGGU, 2010.

———, ed. *Rossiisko-amerikanskie otnosheniia v proshlom i nastoiashchem: obrazy, mify,*
real'nost"[Russian-American Relations in Past and Present: Images, Myths, and Reality].
Moscow: Izdatel'stvo RGGU, 2007.

SIXTEEN

Studying Russian Politics After the Cold War

Changes and Challenges

Vladimir Gel'man

The study of politics in various countries and regions of the globe is an indispensable part of political science as a discipline. However, unlike many other political science subfields, its developments are more dependent on current political dynamics, which often affect not only the research agenda but also major academic directions. Thus, it is no wonder that the academic studies of post-communist politics as a whole and of Russian politics in particular underwent dramatic changes over the last quarter century, after the collapse of communism and of the Soviet state and the end of the Cold War. These changes resulted from the process of complex transformation in Eastern Europe and the former Soviet Union in terms of changes of their political regimes, economic systems, and state- and nation-building. Against this background, the developmental logic of disciplinary changes of political science also greatly contributed to major changes in the scholarly landscape of studies in Russian politics. Sovietology as a separate and very peculiar subfield of political science has been replaced by comparative political studies in Russian politics, which reflected general canons of the discipline and fit its theoretical frameworks and methodological approaches. Also, the process of generational changes among scholars changed the very profile of this field: those specialists, whose research agenda was formed during the decades of the Cold War, were gradually replaced by younger counterparts, whose academic trajectories developed after the collapse of communism and the end of the Soviet Union.

The set of research problems in the studies of Russian politics, their theoretical frameworks, information sources, and methods of data mining and analysis tremendously renewed after the Soviet collapse. However, both academic and policy-driven demand for studies of Russian politics after the Soviet collapse—at least, until the Russian annexation of Crimea and the new round of confrontation between Russia and the West in 2014—decreased after the Soviet collapse, at least among those scholars who work outside Russia, and also qualitatively changed.[1] Russia's political developments are rarely considered by political scientists through the lenses of an area studies approach, which considers a given country as a subject matter of research. Rather, Russia is perceived as a case of various political phenomena, which are understood as a substantive focus of academic knowledge in political science. This comparative turn, which was typical for studies of politics in other countries and regions of the globe during the last decades,[2] greatly contributed to major shifts in the very logic and language of research in Russian politics, and to the reframing of its understanding in terms of scholarly conclusions and (if relevant) of policy recommendations. Paradoxically, these major changes in studies of Russian politics occurred nearly simultaneously with dramatic changes in Russian politics, when some analysts either observed its major continuity with regard to the Soviet era[3] or discussed tendencies of "new authoritarianism" in Russia and other post-Soviet countries.[4]

This chapter is devoted to an overview and preliminary analysis of developmental trends in academic studies of Russian politics as a disciplinary subfield in comparative politics (which is, in turn, a major part of the international political science). It is concentrated only on English-language publications, given the fact that English is the lingua franca of contemporary social sciences in general and of political science in particular.[5] The analysis is focused on those publications, which deal with major issues of Russian domestic politics after the collapse of the Soviet Union, such as political regime changes, key actors, and political institutions. Studies of Russian foreign policy (which belong to the subfield of international relations, other part of political science as a discipline), as well as interdisciplinary studies of ethnicity, and economic and social policies in Russia, lies beyond the scope of this chapter, even though they are closely related to its framework. The chapter discusses the substantive achievements and shortcomings of studies in Russian domestic politics in the more than two decades since the end of communist power and of the Soviet Union. To what extent does recent research improved our understanding of post-Soviet politics in Russia? What are the issues which are worth more in-depth analysis? What about the picture of contemporary Russian politics against the background of comparative studies in international political science: is objective, or, rather, biased for various reasons? What are those problems of Russian politics which remain under-investigated by scholars?

THEN AND NOW: FROM SOVIETOLOGY TO STUDIES OF RUSSIAN POLITICS

For a number of decades, studies of Soviet politics in the West (known as "Sovietology") were developed as a separate and very peculiar disciplinary subfield in political science, which had rather semiperipheral academic status at that time.[6] On the one hand, the strategic priorities of American and West European governments and the tense ideological environment of the Cold War raised demands for knowledge in this field and the very claim of "know your enemy"[7] contributed to extensive training of experts on Russian studies, the increase of their numbers, and in-depth studies. On the other hand, the closed nature of the Soviet political system, the limited availability of information sources, and questionable reliability of data not only provoked the rise of interpretive (if not speculative) Kremlinology but also left studies of Soviet politics out of the major developmental of comparative political studies. Yet, Sovietology was not completely out of mainstream of political science: at least since the 1960s, specialists employed the "model fitting" approach for research in Soviet politics: they used various frameworks of analysis of interest groups or political culture, which were elaborated for empirical studies of modern Western democracies and then adjusted to studies of other regions of the world (including communist countries).[8] This period also was marked by extensive debates between scholars of the concept of "totalitarianism" (who considered the Soviet Union a very special type of totalitarian political system in the manner of an "evil empire") and scholars of "revisionism," who believed that the Soviet political system may be perceived as a case of the universal international trend of modernization. The very milieu of Sovietologists was ideologically motivated and views and preferences of many scholars, to a certain extent, were driven by their personal perceptions of the Soviet Union and Russia.[9] The contribution of Soviet scholars to international discussions on Soviet politics at that time was nearly lacking, with some exceptions of representatives from émigré circles.

The end of Sovietology resulted from the turbulent political changes of 1989–1991: Sovietologists often were not only unable to predict these developments but also failed to explain them.[10] Upon the end of communist regimes and the collapse of the Soviet Union, their professional credibility was questioned, while the demand for training of experts on Russian studies in the West decreased during the 1990s, and the number of specialized research centers and educational programs diminished. In the

2000s, the major focus of interests in area studies both in North America and in Europe gradually shifted toward China and the Middle East, but research in Russian and Soviet politics still attract new generations of scholars, and one might expect a new increase of demand for, and expertise in, the field. After almost a quarter century since the Soviet collapse the scholarly profile of studies in Russian politics greatly changed in three different yet interrelated dimensions.

First, the new face of studies of Russian politics (both in Russia and in the West) is presented by representatives of the new generation of scholars: those who are now in their forties and fifties, who emerged as professionals during the collapse of the Soviet system and the development of the new Russia after 1991. One might argue that by and large the international academic community of scholars of Russian and post-Soviet politics now is less affected by ideological motivations, and the format and style of academic discussions (even though very heated with regard to a number of contentious issues) is much more value-neutral than it was during the Cold War period. Second, in contrast with some Sovietologists of the "old school," the younger generation, which specialized in studies of Russian politics, are often "genetical" comparativists of a broader (or non-area-specific) scholarly profile or sometimes trained as experts on other countries and regions.[11] Third, international scholarship in Russian politics has greatly benefited from contributions of Russian scholars themselves: I mean here both those, who are working in Russian universities and other institutions, and Russian-born scholars who are working elsewhere and belong to the Russian academic diaspora. Although the impact of Russian scholars on international academic discussion about issues in Russian politics has not remained very high and the pool of internationally renowned Russian political scientists is rather limited (to put it mildly), one might cautiously expect a gradual increase of this impact over the next ten to fifteen years.[12]

Indeed, the unexpected and often unpredictable trajectory of Russia's political developments provided major incentives for scholars across the globe, who have strived to solve new research puzzles regarding Russian politics, looking on new empirical evidence and datasets. From the 1950s to the 1980s Sovietologists were forced to rely upon incomplete and often unreliable data or to use some substitutes and secondary sources.[13] Post-Soviet Russian politics from the 1990s to 2010s gave birth to a boom of new primary source materials, ranging from mass surveys, elite interviews, and electoral statistics to disclosed police reports on the magnitude of strikes in Russian regions, which were used by Graeme Robertson in his quantitative study of mass protests in Russia in the 1990s.[14] In other words, both methodologically and empirically studies of post-Soviet Russian politics definitely fit contemporary disciplinary standards of political science research. At the same time, the development of advanced information technologies, increasing opportunities of international research collaboration, and the emergence of numerous scholarly networks, projects, and environments opened new horizons for a more in-depth and complex understanding of Russian politics. The question is: how these changes influenced the substantive agenda of research in Russian politics? What about the new knowledge (beyond new facts and figures), which was produced by scholars of Russian politics over more than two decades? How do scholars perceive the present day and future directions of the Russian polity and how has research in Russian politics enriched our understanding of politics across the globe?

UNDERSTANDING RUSSIAN POLITICS: OPTIMISM, PESSIMISM, OR REALISM?

The simplest way of observation of evolutionary trends in studies of Russian politics over the last two decades is just a brief look on titles of books, which were published in the field. Initially, in mid-1990s, these titles sounded very promising, such as *Democracy from Scratch* (M. Steven Fish),[15] or *The Rebirth of Politics in Russia* (Michael Urban).[16] In the 2000s, their message became more skeptical—for example, *Russia's Unfinished Revolution* (Michael McFaul)[17] or *Between Dictatorship and Democracy* (edited by McFaul and others).[18] After that, criticism prevailed in *Democracy Derailed in Russia* (Fish, again, ten years after his first book)[19] and *The Crisis of Russian Democracy* (Richard Sakwa).[20] And now, some titles like *Authoritarian Russia* (Vladimir Gel'man)[21] routinely neighbored with *Putin's Kleptocracy* (Karen Dawisha)[22] or *The Consolidation of Dictatorship in Russia* (Joel Ostrow and others),[23] so the picture looks rather gloomy if not hopeless. The list of troubling features of Russian politics in the 2010s included unfair and fraudulent elections, the coexistence of weak and impotent political parties with a dominant "party of power" (which was also weak and impotent), heavily censored (and often self-censored) media, rubber-stamping legislatures at the national and subnational levels, politically subordinated and shamelessly biased courts, arbitrary use of state economic powers, and widespread corruption. These assessments resonate with numerous critical evaluations of Russia's politics and governance by domestic and international agencies and experts:[24] despite the huge variety of their analytical frameworks and the use of diverse methodologies, techniques, and approaches, almost everybody agrees that the political regime in present-day Russia is genuinely nondemocratic. However, beyond this gloomy consensus on current trends in Russian politics various scholars and experts are widely diverse in their assessments of features of the Russian political regime and, more importantly, in their explanations of Russia's political trajectories (which resemble pendulum-like swings) as well as in their statements about the political future of the country.

The most popular view on Russian political trends considers them through the prism of growing dissatisfaction with the unfulfilled promises of democratization after the end of communist rule. A typical statement of this kind might be summarized in the title of article by Kathryn Stoner-Weiss, "Authoritarianism without Authority."[25] In other words, they perceive the case of Russia and other post-Soviet countries merely as outliers from the ideal model of success stories of EU-driven post-communist democratic transformation in Eastern Europe. However, other scholars explicitly rejected this approach because of its normative bias. They argued that Russia in many ways is a "normal country" with mid-range level of socioeconomic development,[26] which is faced with numerous problems and challenges not so much different from many other states and nations ranging from Latin America to South-East Asia. Thus, according to such an approach, Russia should not be blamed as the deviant case of permanent and irresolvable political troubles but rather as a typical case of poor quality of political institutions under conditions of "crony capitalism"[27] and treated as a laggard rather than outlier on the global political map. Also, a number of scholars pointed out the coexistence of both democratic and authoritarian elements of Russian politicoeconomic order and qualified it as a special type of "hybrid" political regime,[28] which should be studied in a more detailed way because of the need for a nuanced understanding of its features (the assessment of the Russian political regime as a "hybrid" was popular until very recently also because for various reasons some observers hesitated to label it "authoritarian").

Theoretical frameworks for the analysis of Russian politics also differ widely due to scholarly use of explanatory and interpretive schemes borrowed from various disciplines and also because of diverse focuses of research interests. To put it very bluntly, specialists on studies in Russian politics can be divided into "pessimists," "optimists," or "realists," depending upon the conclusions of scholarly analyses and the different logical foundations of their research programs.[29] If one compares political studies with medical diagnostics, then the causes of numerous illnesses of Russian politics are perceived as results of genetically transmitted deceases, or of post-traumatic syndromes, or of poisoning. "Pessimists" believe that the major illnesses of Russian political system are determined by the "legacy of the past" (both Soviet and pre-Soviet) and therefore cannot be cured, at least, in the short-term perspective. They mostly concentrate on the negative influence of Russian history and culture on contemporary political developments, and their explanations of Russian politics are merely path-dependent. Since many troubling symptoms in Russian politics, ranging from post-imperial syndromes to patrimonial political leadership and dominance of subversive informal governance[30] are deeply historically embedded, then the argument of "pessimists," who consider Russian post-Soviet experience as a major "flight from freedom"[31] toward an eternal continuity of autocracy looks rather convincing. Pessimism has found numerous followers.

Unlike "pessimists," "optimists" tend to perceive the large share of numerous pains of Russian politics as side effects of complex and rather traumatic processes of post-Soviet transformation, which include the major redrawing of state boundaries as well as a severe decline of the coercive and distributive capacity of the Russian state in the 1990s and its following contradictory revival in the 2000s.[32] This very painful and protracted post-traumatic syndrome can be overcome only in the relatively long period of time, similarly to recovery of broken bones in the living organism. One might hope that the impact of steady and continuous economic growth, if and when it will successfully contribute to building of a strong modern state, may gradually contribute to the political modernization and democratization of Russia,[33] and its recent authoritarian trends will be eliminated in some decades after the change of political leadership.

Finally, "realists" argue that the major turn of Russia's illnesses from the "growing pains" of the 1990s into the "chronic deceases" of the 2000s and 2010s result from intentional actions of special interest groups, whose behavior is similar to a poisoning of Russia's social organism. The list of poisoners, who aim to maximize their own power and wealth at the expense of political rights and civil liberties in Russia, include various actors and segments of the Russian elite: oligarchs,[34] *siloviki*,[35] "Kremlin's towers,"[36] and presidents—both Boris Yeltsin[37] and Vladimir Putin.[38] Many experts in Russian politics lament the cycling nature of post-Soviet political changes,[39] which may even resemble a "vicious circle." Intentionally imposed barriers to political competition and the attempts of Russia's rulers to stay in power at any cost may diminish the possible impact of any antidotes for Russian society. To what extent the Russian social organism will be able to obtain immunity against authoritarian poisoning after this painful trial-and-error experience, or rather, chronic deceases will put insurmountable obstacles to its political revival,[40] remains to be seen.

COMPARATIVE PERSPECTIVES

A recent trend of analyzing contemporary Russian politics within the broader theoretical and comparative frameworks of political science became the major advantage in the field after the end of communism. During several decades of the Cold War, comparative political studies included Russia mostly as an object of historical research such as classical *Social Origins of Dictatorship and Democracy* by Barrington Moore Jr.,[41] or used it to perform comparative analyses as in *States and Social Revolutions: A Comparative Analysis of France, Russia, and China* by Theda Skocpol.[42] At

the same time, comparative studies of contemporary political developments were rather sporadic despite some notable exceptions.[43] On the
other hand, contemporary studies of post-Soviet politics in Russia are
legitimately, if not routinely, embedded into a three-dimensional comparative perspective: (1) cross-national, (2) cross-temporal, and (3) cross-
regional (comparative within-nation).

First, the Russian case has been included into many large-N cross-
national comparative projects and international datasets, such as studies
of political values and attitudes (such as the *World Values Survey*[44] or
European Social Survey[45]), corruption perceptions (Transparency International index),[46] quality of governance (project by the World Bank[47] and
other agencies) and so on. These research tools and measurements, which
offer contradictory (and often very unpleasant) evidence about Russia's
place on the global political map, are widely used by numerous scholars,
analysts and experts who deal both with global trends and with Russian
politics, economy, and society. Moreover, beyond variable-oriented
quantitative cross-national large-N comparisons some more focused
case-oriented qualitative studies (which were based upon small-N comparisons) include many instances of post-Soviet Russian politics, put into
historical as well as contemporary contexts. The list of parallels with
political developments in post-Soviet Russia include examples of the
emergence of party politics in the United States in the first decades of
nineteenth century (Henry Hale),[48] long-term dominance of the ruling
party, PRI, in twentieth-century Mexico (Ora John Reuter and Thomas
Remington),[49] ideological constellations during the early years of the
Third Republic in France as well as in Weimar Germany (Stephen Hanson),[50] state-business relationships in the United States during Gilded
Age (Vadim Volkov),[51] and the like.

Also, a growing number of research projects were conducted by both
Russian and Western scholars with the use of comparative analyses of
subnational (i.e., regional and local) politics in Russia: political, social,
and economic diversity of its regions and cities provides a number of
advantages for this type of research. Besides numerous monitoring projects, conducted by various (mostly Russian) scholars, systematic cross-
regional comparative political studies had a certain impact on the understanding of logic and dynamics of Russian politics nationwide. The range
of research topics of these studies is broad, from nationalist political mobilization in Russian ethnic-based republics (Dmitry Gorenburg),[52] to the
development of political parties in the regions of Russia (Grigorii V. Golosov),[53] the participation of businessmen in regional legislative elections
(Scott Gehlbach et al.),[54] and so on. These studies (together with many
others) contributed to the major shift in analysis of Russian politics: it is
no longer considered a somewhat isolated and unique object of studies
but more and more understood as a comparatively oriented case in the
changing international picture of various political phenomena.

WHAT HAS BEEN DONE AND WHAT LIES AHEAD?

It is difficult to find meaningful topics of empirical political research, which were not entirely covered in studies of post-Soviet Russian politics in one way or another. Changes in political institutions, patterns of governance, mass political orientations and political behavior, the role of ideas, ethnicity, and nationalism, and many other political phenomena in Russia over the last two decades were not only placed on the global political map but also deeply analyzed according to contemporary disciplinary standards of political science. To summarize, one might say that academic studies of contemporary Russian politics is a legitimate part of mainstream comparative political research. But what about the substantive impact of new knowledge on post-Soviet Russian politics for our understanding of politics around the globe? Do studies of Russian politics matter for political science?

Some studies, which analyze numerous features of Russian and post-Soviet politics, offer us interesting, important, and sometimes counterintuitive conclusions and implications. For example, Graeme Robertson convincingly argues that the mass socioeconomic protests in the Russian regions during the 1990s were nothing but a by-product of contradictions between federal and regional elites, and that the mass public was just a resource used by both sides of these conflicts and was not acting independently.[55] Andrew Wilson, in his perceptive and vivid analysis of "virtual politics" in Russia and other post-Soviet states comes to the conclusion that manipulative political technologies of ruling groups in the 1990s and 2000s served not only as a tool in political struggles but also legitimated the political status quo and effectively countered any alternatives to existing political regimes and their leaders.[56] But, by and large, the theoretical and comparative impact of empirical studies of post-Soviet Russian politics on international political science has remained rather limited even vis-à-vis studies of Soviet politics—at least, as of yet.[57] What are the causes of this state of affairs and should we blame scholars or the academy as a whole?

In essence, studies of politics in contemporary Russia offer new challenges for the research agendas of political science (as well as for other social science disciplines) and also pose some new constraints. On the one hand, present-day Russia might be perceived as an El Dorado for scholars interested in analysis of corruption, clientelism, arbitrary rule, state-run propaganda, or institutional decay—contemporary Russian experience gives them plenty of evidence and empirical data for testing existing approaches as well as for elaborating new theoretical frameworks. But at the same time, numerous subfields of studies in Russian politics have become more and more systematically questioned—not only because of the policy of systematically "tightening the screws" by Russian authorities (who hated independent scholarship), but mostly because of the questionable value of research as such. First and foremost, political constraints are relevant for research in electoral politics: while foundations of competitive elections were undermined if not eliminated in Russia in the 2000s, then the validity of official electoral statistics (as well as of election-related mass surveys) is very much dubious. And if these datasets are relevant only for research on forensic electoral fraud (which has flourished in Russian studies),[58] then to what extent can we rely upon these sources for studies of voting behavior or electoral strategies of political parties? At least, scholarly frameworks and research tools should be more "fine-tuned" for studies of electoral authoritarianism in Russia as well as in other parts of the globe.[59] From this viewpoint one might expect that in the foreseeable future more in-depth studies on Russian politics may enrich our understanding of logic of political developments under authoritarian regimes, which have been a rather peripheral subject matter in political science until very recently.[60]

But should we believe that the time for a new "breakthrough" in studies of Russian politics has not come yet and just expect that the cumulative increasing of our knowledge and the interdisciplinary efforts of the international academic community will, in the end, pave the way to pathbreaking scholarly achievements in political science not only because of new data from Russia but also because of new ideas that will emerge from studies of Russia politics? Despite some "bias for hope" one cannot exclude the reality that these expectations may become groundless. At least one basic distinction between studies of Soviet and post-Soviet Russian politics should be taken into account. Unlike the Soviet Union, present-day Russia is not a global superpower, which claimed (successfully or not) its global leadership. Its very status as a "normal country" is also questioned in many ways.[61] Rather, it is a semi-peripheral state, which is closed to an average global level of economic and human development and which is aimed to be unique but in reality is banal if not dull. And, if so, then the study of politics in such a country has no grounds to result in major research findings beyond area studies: maybe it simply can't offer any new original answers on the key questions of contemporary political science? In any case, the search for answers to these questions will form a substantive agenda for new generations of scholars of Russian politics, both in Russia and in the West.

NOTES

The chapter is a part of "Choices of Russian Modernization," a research project, funded by the Academy of Finland.

    1. See J. Paul Goode, "Redefining Russia: Hybrid Regimes, Fieldwork, and Russian Politics," *Perspectives on Politics*, 8, no. 4 (December 2010): 1055–75.
    2. See Robert H. Bates, "Area Studies and the Discipline: A Useful Controversy?" *PS: Political Science and Politics*, 30, no. 2 (June 1997): 166–69.

3. On continuity of post-Soviet Russian politics, see, for example, Stephen White and Olga Kryshtanovskaya, "The Sovietization of Russian Politics," *Post-Soviet Affairs*, 25, no. 4 (October–December 2009): 283–309; Vladimir Gel'man and Sergei Ryzhenkov, "Local Regimes, 'Sub-National Governance,' and the 'Power Vertical' in Contemporary Russia," *Europe-Asia Studies*, 63, no. 3 (May 2011): 449–65. For a broader discussion on the role of historical legacies in Russia and other post-Communist countries, see *Historical Legacies of Communism in Russia and Eastern Europe*, eds. Mark Beissinger and Stephen Kotkin (Cambridge: Cambridge University Press, 2014).

4. See Steven Levitsky and Lucan Way, *Competitive Authoritarianism: Hybrid Regimes after the Cold War* (Cambridge: Cambridge University Press, 2010); Grigorii V. Golosov, "The Regional Roots of Electoral Authoritarianism in Russia," *Europe-Asia Studies*, 63, no. 4 (June 2011), 623–39; Vladimir Gel'man, "The Rise and Decline of Electoral Authoritarianism in Russia," *Demokratizatsiya: The Journal of Post-Soviet Democratization*, 22, no. 4 (Fall 2014), 503–22; William Zimmerman, *Ruling Russia: Authoritarianism from Lenin to Putin* (Princeton, NJ: Princeton University Press, 2014).

5. Without denying the importance of scholarly products published in any other language than English (including Russian), one should realize that their areal of reading and academic influence are rather limited and, in the end, the most important research pieces that produced in other languages, sooner or later usually appear in English, too.

6. For some assessments, see, for example, George Breslauer, "In Defense of Sovietology," *Post-Soviet Affairs*, 8, no. 3 (July–September 1992): 197–238; Peter Rutland, Sovietology: "Notes for a Post-Mortem," *National Interest*, 31, no. 3 (July 1993), 109–22.

7. See David Engerman, *Know Your Enemy: The Rise and Fall of America's Soviet Experts* (Oxford: Oxford University Press, 2009).

8. See Gabriel Almond and Laura Rosselle, "Model Fitting in Communist Studies," in Gabriel Almond, *A Discipline Divided: Schools and Sects in Political Science* (London: Sage, 1990), 86–116.

9. In this regard, personal biographies of several scholars of Soviet politics, who formed both as scholars and as personalities during and soon after the World War II, such as Richard Pipes and Zbigniew Brzezinski, greatly influenced Sovietologists' approaches to the study of Russia and of the Soviet Union.

10. "The 'Autumn of the People' was a dismal failure of political science," Adam Przeworski, *Democracy and the Market: Political and Economic Reforms in Eastern Europe and Latin America* (Cambridge: Cambridge University Press, 1991), 1.

11. For example, Michael McFaul, one of the most prolific scholars of Russian and post-Soviet politics and later on, an ambassador of the United States in Russia, was initially trained as an expert on Africa. Upon his research visit to Moscow in 1988 McFaul was so deeply impressed by the rise of pro-democratic movement in the Soviet Union that he changed his research field and became a leading expert on Russia. See McFaul, *Russia's Unfinished Revolution*, ix–x.

12. For a critical overview of the state of political science in Russia, see Vladimir Gel'man, "Political Science in Russia: Scholarship without Research?" *European Political Science*, 14, no. 1 (March 2015), 28–36.

13. For example, mass surveys on politically relevant topics were prohibited in the Soviet Union until the end of the 1980s. This is why Western scholars, who were interested in research of political attitudes and orientations of Soviet citizens were forced to rely upon analysis of surveys of former Soviet citizens, who emigrated to the West after the World War II or in the 1970s, so the sampling has been biased nearly by definition See Alex Inkeles and Raymond Bauer, *The Soviet Citizen: A Daily Life in Totalitarian Society* (Cambridge, MA: Harvard University Press, 1959); *Politics, Work and Daily Life in the USSR: A Survey of Former Soviet Citizens*, ed. James R. Millar (Cambridge: Cambridge University Press, 1987).

14. See Graeme Robertson, "Strikes and Labor Organizations in Hybrid Regimes," *American Political Science Review*, 101, no. 4 (November 2007), 781–98.

15. M. Steven Fish, *Democracy from Scratch: Opposition and Regime in the New Russian Revolution* (Princeton, NJ: Princeton University Press, 1995).

16. Michael Urban, with Vyacheslav Igrunov and Sergei Mitrokhin, *The Rebirth of Politics in Russia* (Cambridge: Cambridge University Press, 1997).

17. Michael McFaul, *Russia's Unfinished Revolution: Political Change from Gorbachev to Putin* (Ithaca, NY: Cornell University Press, 2001).

18. *Between Dictatorship and Democracy: Russia's Post-Communist Political Reform*, eds. Michael McFaul, Nikolay Petrov, and Andrei Ryabov (Washington, DC: Carnegie Endowment for International Peace, 2004).

19. M. Steven Fish, *Democracy Derailed in Russia: The Failure of Open Politics* (Cambridge: Cambridge University Press, 2005).

20. Richard Sakwa, *The Crisis of Russian Democracy: The Dual State, Factionalism, and the Medvedev Succession* (Cambridge: Cambridge University Press, 2011).

21. Vladimir Gel'man, *Authoritarian Russia: Analyzing Post-Soviet Regime Changes* (Pittsburgh: University of Pittsburgh Press, 2015).

22. Karen Dawisha, *Putin's Kleptocracy: Who Owns Russia?* (New York: Simon and Schuster, 2014).

23. Joel Ostrow, with Georgii Satarov and Irina Khakamada, *The Consolidation of Dictatorship in Russia: An Inside View of the Demise of Democracy* (New York: Praeger, 2008).

24. A wide range of critical assessments of current developments and trajectories in Russian politics can be found in the annual reports of numerous international NGOs, such as Human Rights Watch (http://www.hrw.org), Amnesty International (http://www.thereport.amnesty.org), and especially *Nations in Transit* by Freedom House (http://www.freedomhouse.org).

25. See Kathryn Stoner-Weiss, "Russia: Authoritarianism without Authority," *Journal of Democracy*, 17, no. 1 (January 2006), 104–18.

26. See Andrei Shleifer and Daniel Treisman, "'A Normal Country," *Foreign Affairs*, 83, no. 2 (April 2004), 20–38.

27. See Gulnaz Sharafutdinova, *The Political Consequences of Crony Capitalism Inside Russia* (Notre Dame, IN: University of Notre Dame Press, 2011).

28. See Nikolay Petrov, Maria Lipman, and Henry E. Hale, "Three Dilemmas of Hybrid Regime Governance: Russia from Putin to Putin," *Post-Soviet Affairs*, 30, no. 1 (January–February 2014), 1–26.

29. See Gel'man, *Authoritarian Russia*, chapter 2.

30. See Alena Ledeneva, *Can Russia Modernise? Sistema, Power Networks, and Informal Governance*, (Cambridge: Cambridge University Press, 2013).

31. See Richard Pipes, "Flight from Freedom: What Russians Think and Want," *Foreign Affairs*, 83, no. 3 (June 2004), 9–15.

32. See Vadim Volkov, *Violent Entrepreneurs: The Use of Force in the Making of Russian Capitalism* (Ithaca, NY: Cornell University Press, 2002).

33. See Andrei Shleifer and Daniel Treisman, "Normal Countries: The East 25 Years after Communism," *Foreign Affairs*, 93, no. 6 (November–December 2014). http://www.foreignaffairs.com/articles/142200/andrei-shleifer-and-daniel-treisman/normal-countries (accessed April 4, 2015); Treisman D., "Income, Democracy, and Leader Turnover," *American Journal of Political Science*, 2014, early view publication, DOI: 10.1111/ajps12135 (accessed April 4, 2015).

34. See David Hoffman, *Oligarchs: The Wealth and Power in the New Russia* (New York: Public Affairs, 2002).

35. See Daniel Treisman, *The Return: Russia's Journey from Gorbachev to Medvedev* (New York: Free Press, 2011).

36. See Nikolay Petrov, "Nomenklatura and the Elite," in *Russia in 2020: Scenarios for the Future*, eds. Maria Lipman and Nikolay Petrov (Washington, DC: Carnegie Endowment for International Peace, 2011), 499–530.

37. For a critical overview, see Lilia Shevtsova, *Yeltsin's Russia: Myths and Reality* (Washington, DC: Carnegie Endowment for International Peace, 1999). For a more

positive assessment of Yeltsin, see Timothy J. Colton, *Yeltsin: A Life* (New York: Basic Books, 2008).

38. See Lilia Shevtsova, *Putin's Russia* (Washington, DC: Carnegie Endowment for International Peace, 2007); Dawisha, *Putin's Kleptocracy*. For a more positive assessment of Putin, see Richard Sakwa, *Putin: Russia's Choice* (London: Routledge, 2004).

39. See Henry E. Hale, *Patronal Politics: Eurasian Regime Dynamics in Comparative Perspective* (Cambridge: Cambridge University Press, 2014).

40. See Gel'man, *Authoritarian Russia*.

41. Barrington Moore Jr., *Social Origins of Dictatorship and Democracy: Lords and Peasants in the Making of the Modern World* (Boston: Beacon Press, 1966).

42. Theda Skocpol, *States and Social Revolutions: A Comparative Analysis of France, Russia and China* (Cambridge: Cambridge University Press, 1979).

43. Samuel Huntington and Zbigniew Brzezinski, *Political Power: USA/USSR* (New York: Viking Press, 1964).

44. See *World Values Survey* http://www.worldvaluessurvey.org/ (accessed April 4, 2015).

45. See *The European Social Survey* http://www.europeansocialsurvey.org/ (accessed April 4, 2015).

46. See *Transparency International Corruption Perception Index* http://www. transparency.org/policy_research/surveys_indices/cpi (accessed April 4, 2015).

47. See *The World Bank. The Worldwide Governance Indicators Project* http://info. worldbank.org/governance/wgi/index.asp (accessed April 4, 2015).

48. See Henry E. Hale, *Why Not Parties in Russia? Democracy, Federalism, and the State* (Cambridge: Cambridge University Press, 2006).

49. See Ora John Reuter and Thomas F. Remington, "Dominant Party Regimes and the Commitment Problem: The Case of United Russia," *Comparative Political Studies*, 42, no. 4 (April 2009), 501–26.

50. See Stephen E. Hanson, *Post-Imperial Democracies: Ideology and Party Formation in Third Republic France, Weimar Germany and Post-Soviet Russia* (Cambridge: Cambridge University Press, 2010).

51. See Vadim Volkov, "Standard Oil and Yukos in the Context of Early Capitalism in the United States and Russia," *Demokratizatsiya: the Journal of Post-Soviet Democratization*, 16, no. 3 (Summer 2008), 240–64.

52. Dmitry Gorenburg, *Minority Ethnic Mobilization in the Russian Federation* (Cambridge: Cambridge University Press, 2003).

53. Grigorii V. Golosov, *Political Parties in the Regions of Russia: Democracy Unclaimed* (Boulder, CO: Lynne Rienner, 2004).

54. Scott Gehlbach, Konstantin Sonin, and Ekaterina Zhuravskaya, "Businessman Candidates," *American Journal of Political Science*, 54, no. 3 (August 2010), 718–36.

55. See Robertson, "Strikes and Labor Organizations in Hybrid Regimes."

56. See Andrew Wilson, *Virtual Politics: Faking Democracy in the Post-Soviet World* (New Haven, CT: Yale University Press, 2005).

57. See David Laitin, Post-Soviet Politics, *Annual Review of Political Science*, 3 (2000): 117–48.

58. See Mikhail Myagkov, Peter Ordeshook, and Dmitry Shakin, *The Forensics of Election Fraud: Russia and Ukraine* (Cambridge: Cambridge University Press, 2009); Walter Mebane and Kirill Kalinin, *Electoral Fraud in Russia: Vote Counts Analysis Using Second-digit Test*, Paper for presentation at the Annual meeting of the Midwest Political Science Association (Chicago, 2010) http://www-personal.umich.edu/~wmebane/ mw10B.pdf (accessed April 4, 2015); Ruben Enikolopov, Vasily Korovkin, Maria Petrova, Konstantin Sonin, and Alexei Zakharov, "Field Experiment Estimate of Electoral Fraud in Russian Parliamentary Elections," *Proceedings of the National Academy of Sciences*, 110, no. 2 (2013), 448–52.

59. See Levitsky and Way, *Competitive Authoritarianism*; Andreas Schedler, *The Politics of Uncertainty: Sustaining and Subverting Electoral Authoritarianism* (Oxford: Oxford University Press, 2013).

60. See, however, Jennifer Gandhi, *Political Institutions under Dictatorship* (Cambridge: Cambridge University Press, 2010); Milan Svolik, *The Politics of Authoritarian Rule* (Cambridge: Cambridge University Press, 2012).

61. See Shliefer and Treisman, "A Normal Country"; for a major criticism of this approach, see Zimmerman, *Ruling Russia*.

BIBLIOGRAPHY

Almond, Gabriel, and Laura Rosselle. "Model Fitting in Communist Studies." In Gabriel Almond, *A Discipline Divided: Schools and Sects in Political Science*, 86–116. London: Sage, 1990.

Bates, Robert H. "Area Studies and the Discipline: A Useful Controversy?" *PS: Political Science and Politics*, 30, no. 2 (June 1997): 166–69.

Beissigner, Mark, and Stephen Kotkin, eds. *Historical Legacies of Communism in Russia and Eastern Europe*. Cambridge: Cambridge University Press, 2014.

Breslauer, George. "In Defense of Sovietology." *Post-Soviet Affairs*, 8, no. 3 (July–September 1992): 197–238.

Colton, Timothy J. *Yeltsin: A Life*. New York: Basic Books, 2008.

Dawisha, Karen. *Putin's Kleptocracy: Who Owns Russia?* New York: Simon and Schuster, 2014.

Engerman, David. *Know Your Enemy: The Rise and Fall of America's Soviet Experts*. Oxford: Oxford University Press, 2009.

Enikolopov, Ruben, Vasily Korovkin, Maria Petrova, Konstantin Sonin, and Alexei Zakharov. "Field Experiment Estimate of Electoral Fraud in Russian Parliamentary Elections." *Proceedings of the National Academy of Sciences*, 110, no. 2 (2013): 448–52.

The European Social Survey http://www.europeansocialsurvey.org/ (accessed April 4, 2015).

Fish, M. Steven. *Democracy Derailed in Russia: The Failure of Open Politics*. Cambridge: Cambridge University Press, 2005.

———. *Democracy from Scratch: Opposition and Regime in the New Russian Revolution*. Princeton, NJ: Princeton University Press, 1995.

Gandhi, Jennifer. *Political Institutions under Dictatorship*. Cambridge: Cambridge University Press, 2010.

Gehlbach, Scott, Konstantin Sonin, and Ekaterina Zhuravskaya. "Businessman Candidates." *American Journal of Political Science*, 54, no. 3 (August 2010): 718–36.

Gel'man, Vladimir. *Authoritarian Russia: Analyzing Post-Soviet Regime Changes*. Pittsburgh: University of Pittsburgh Press, 2015.

———. "Political Science in Russia: Scholarship without Research?" *European Political Science*, 14. no. 1 (March 2015): 28–36.

———. "The Rise and Decline of Electoral Authoritarianism in Russia." *Demokratizatsiya: The Journal of Post-Soviet Democratization*, 22, no.4 (Fall 2014): 503–22.

Gel'man, Vladimir, and Sergei Ryzhenkov. „Local Regimes, 'Sub-National Governance,' and the 'Power Vertical' in Contemporary Russia." *Europe-Asia Studies*, 63, no. 3 (May 2011): 449–65.

Golosov, Grigorii V. "The Regional Roots of Electoral Authoritarianism in Russia." *Europe-Asia Studies*, 63, no. 4 (June 2011): 623–39.

———. *Political Parties in the Regions of Russia: Democracy Unclaimed*. Boulder, CO: Lynne Rienner, 2004.

Goode, J. Paul. "Redefining Russia: Hybrid Regimes, Fieldwork, and Russian Politics." *Perspectives on Politics*, 8, no. 4 (December 2010): 1055–75.

Gorenburg, Dmitry. *Minority Ethnic Mobilization in the Russian Federation*. Cambridge: Cambridge University Press, 2003.

Hale, Henry E. *Patronal Politics: Eurasian Regime Dynamics in Comparative Perspective*. Cambridge: Cambridge University Press, 2014.

———. *Why Not Parties in Russia? Democracy, Federalism, and the State*. Cambridge: Cambridge University Press, 2006.

Hanson, Stephen E. *Post-Imperial Democracies: Ideology and Party Formation in Third Republic France, Weimar Germany and Post-Soviet Russia*. Cambridge: Cambridge University Press, 2010.

Hoffman, David. *Oligarchs: The Wealth and Power in the New Russia*. New York: Public Affairs, 2002.

Huntington, Samuel, and Zbigniew Brzezinski. *Political Power: USA/USSR*. New York: Viking Press, 1964.

Inkeles, Alex, and Raymond Bauer. *The Soviet Citizen: A Daily Life in Totalitarian Society*. Cambridge, MA: Harvard University Press, 1959.

Laitin, David. "Post-Soviet Politics," *Annual Review of Political Science*, 3 (2000): 117–48.

Ledeneva, Alena. *Can Russia Modernise? Sistema, Power Networks, and Informal Governance*. Cambridge: Cambridge University Press, 2013.

Levitsky, Steven, and Lucan Way. *Competitive Authoritarianism: Hybrid Regimes after the Cold War*. Cambridge: Cambridge University Press, 2010.

McFaul, Michael. *Russia's Unfinished Revolution: Political Change from Gorbachev to Putin*. Ithaca, NY: Cornell University Press, 2001.

McFaul, Michael, Nikolay Petrov, and Andrei Ryabov, eds. *Between Dictatorship and Democracy: Russia's Post-Communist Political Reform*. Washington, DC: Carnegie Endowment for International Peace, 2004.

Mebane, Walter, and Kirill Kalinin. *Electoral Fraud in Russia: Vote Counts Analysis Using Second-digit Test*, Paper for presentation at the Annual meeting of the Midwest Political Science Association (Chicago, 2010) http://www-personal.umich.edu/~wmebane/mw10B.pdf (accessed April 4, 2015).

Millar, Jamers R., ed. *Politics, Work and Daily Life in the USSR: A Survey of Former Soviet Citizens*. Cambridge: Cambridge University Press, 1987.

Moore Jr., Barrington. *Social Origins of Dictatorship and Democracy: Lords and Peasants in the Making of the Modern World*. Boston: Beacon Press, 1966.

Myagkov, Mikhail, Peter Ordeshook, and Dmitry Shakin. *The Forensics of Election Fraud: Russia and Ukraine*. Cambridge: Cambridge University Press, 2009.

Ostrow, Joel, with Georgii Satarov and Irina Khakamada. *The Consolidation of Dictatorship in Russia: An Inside View of the Demise of Democracy*. New York: Praeger, 2008.

Petrov, Nikolay. "Nomenklatura and the Elite." In *Russia in 2020: Scenarios for the Future*, eds. Maria Lipman and Nikolay Petrov, 499–530.0 Washington, DC: Carnegie Endowment for International Peace, 2011.

Petrov, Nikolay, Maria Lipman, and Henry E. Hale. "Three Dilemmas of Hybrid Regime Governance: Russia from Putin to Putin." *Post-Soviet Affairs*, 30, no. 1 (January–February 2014): 1–26.

Pipes, Richard. "Flight from Freedom: What Russians Think and Want." *Foreign Affairs*, 83, no. 3 (June 2004): 9–15.

Przeworski, Adam. *Democracy and the Market: Political and Economic Reforms in Eastern Europe and Latin America*. Cambridge: Cambridge University Press, 1991.

Reuter, Ora John, and Thomas F. Remington. "Dominant Party Regimes and the Commitment Problem: The Case of United Russia." *Comparative Political Studies*, 42, no. 4 (April 2009): 501–26.

Robertson, Graeme. "Strikes and Labor Organizations in Hybrid Regimes." *American Political Science Review*, 101, no. 4 (November 2007): 781–98.

Rutland, Peter. "Sovietology: 'Notes for a Post-Mortem.'" *National Interest*, 31, no. 3 (July 1993): 109–22.

Sakwa, Richard. *The Crisis of Russian Democracy: The Dual State, Factionalism, and the Medvedev Succession*. Cambridge: Cambridge University Press, 2011.

———. *Putin: Russia's Choice*. London: Routledge, 2004.

Schedler, Andreas. *The Politics of Uncertainty: Sustaining and Subverting Electoral Authoritarianism*. Oxford: Oxford University Press, 2013.

Sharafutdinova, Gulnaz. *The Political Consequences of Crony Capitalism Inside Russia.* Notre Dame, IN: University of Notre Dame Press, 2011.

Shevtsova, Lilia. *Putin's Russia.* Washington, DC: Carnegie Endowment for International Peace, 2007.

———. *Yeltsin's Russia: Myths and Reality.* Washington, DC: Carnegie Endowment for International Peace, 1999.

Shleifer, Andrei, and Daniel Treisman, "Normal Countries: The East 25 Years after Communism." *Foreign Affairs*, 93, no. 6 (November–December 2014).

———. "A Normal Country." *Foreign Affairs*, 83, no. 2 (April 2004): 20–38.

Skocpol, Theda. *States and Social Revolutions: A Comparative Analysis of France, Russia and China.* Cambridge: Cambridge University Press, 1979.

Stoner-Weiss, Kathryn. "Russia: Authoritarianism without Authority." *Journal of Democracy*, 17, no. 1 (January 2006): 104–18.

Svolik, Milan. *The Politics of Authoritarian Rule.* Cambridge: Cambridge University Press, 2012.

Transparency International Corruption Perception Index http://www.transparency.org/policy_research/surveys_indices/cpi (accessed April 4, 2015.

Treisman Daniel. "Income, Democracy, and Leader Turnover." *American Journal of Political Science*, 2014, early view publication, DOI: 10.1111/ajps12135 (accessed April 4, 2015).

———. *The Return: Russia's Journey from Gorbachev to Medvedev.* New York: Free Press, 2011.

Urban, Michael, with Vyacheslav Igrunov and Sergei Mitrokhin. *The Rebirth of Politics in Russia.* Cambridge: Cambridge University Press, 1997.

Volkov, Vadim. "Standard Oil and Yukos in the Context of Early Capitalism in the United States and Russia." *Demokratizatsiya: the Journal of Post-Soviet Democratization*, 16, no. 3 (Summer 2008): 240–64.

———. *Violent Entrepreneurs: The Use of Force in the Making of Russian Capitalism.* Ithaca, NY: Cornell University Press, 2002.

White, Stephen, and Olga Kryshtanovskaya, "The Sovietization of Russian Politics." *Post-Soviet Affairs*, 25, no. 4 (October–December 2009): 283–309

Wilson, Andrew. *Virtual Politics: Faking Democracy in the Post-Soviet World.* New Haven, CT: Yale University Press, 2005.

The World Bank. The Worldwide Governance Indicators Project http://info.worldbank.org/governance/wgi/index.asp (accessed April 4, 2015).

World Values Survey http://www.worldvaluessurvey.org/ (accessed April 4, 2015).

Zimmerman, William. *Ruling Russia: Authoritarianism from Lenin to Putin.* Princeton, NJ: Princeton University Press, 2014.

Conclusion

Ivan Kurilla and Victoria I. Zhuravleva

On the pages of *Russian/Soviet Studies in the United States, Amerikanistika in Russia,* Russian and American historians, political scientists, and philologists analyze the formation of academic knowledge of the *Other* (American or Russian *Other* respectively).

This collection includes chapters on various key themes, and the *first one* among them is the strong connection between the interest toward the other country, the effort to study it, on the one hand, and the climate of Russian-American relations and the domestic and foreign policy agendas of the two countries, on the other. In this regard, we can conclude that the Russian Studies in the United States and *Amerikanistika* in Russia have the same underlying character as the Russian-American relations as a whole.

The chapters contributed by Ivan Kurilla and Vladimir Noskov describe the 1850s and 1860s as a distinctive departure point, the formation period of "academic pre-knowledge," during which learning about the *Other* drew on European sources and works written by journalists, travelers, and diplomats. This "academic pre-knowledge" was directly related to the national agenda of the observer society: the foreign-policy one (mutually beneficial interactions within the Vienna system of international relations) and the domestic one (that coincided in important parts: territorial expansion, fate of such institutes of unfree labor and personal bondage as slavery and serfdom, policies toward ethnic minorities; the Russian Empire's modernization with American participation was also present in the domestic discussions).

The growth of mutual interest had widened the information pool about the other country and its inhabitants and led to the appearance of the first academic studies about the *Other*. These processes had made discourse about the *Other* more intense and multifaceted, but, instead of eliminating stereotypes, had often catalyzed the creation of myths about the other country. The authors show that the framework of "academic pre-knowledge" gave rise to questions that would draw the researchers' attention for years to come. For the American specialists in Russian and Soviet studies, these questions would revolve around the need for liberal reforms in Russia and its expansionist policies, while the Russian and the

Soviet *Americanists* would analyze the American experience of industrial development and the ingredients of the American prosperity.

The individuals who contributed to the formation of the "academic pre-knowledge" would often become teachers of those who became founders of Russian and American studies as academic disciplines at the turn of the twentieth century. That period of academic history of Russian-American relations is in the focus of Norman Saul's and Victoria Zhuravleva's analysis. Saul draws special attention to the gender aspects of this process and to the role that American women (including those of Russian descent) played in it. Zhuravleva traces the formation of long-term mutual academic interest between Russians and Americans in the context of the new mutual "discovery" of each other and those changes that the international relations system and the domestic political development of the two countries underwent at the turn of the century.

In the Russian Empire, this "academic demand" for American studies was closely linked to the need for political and economic reforms, felt by liberal university professors and advocates of economic rapprochement with the United States. Not surprisingly, these two groups dominated the ranks of American studies specialists in Russia. Meanwhile, in the United States, the need to study Russia more closely arose from America's integration into world politics, the change of its foreign-policy priorities, and also from the professionalization of history as an academic discipline aimed at the study of both the national development model and of those found in other countries and regions of the world. This process of mutual cognition that was mirrored in public and political discourses grew more intense during World War I—the period when growing collaboration and large-scale rapprochement between Russian and the United States placed, for the first time, the need for serious mutual study on the agenda of their bilateral relations.

The inter-war period, the majority of which was a time of nonrecognition, becomes the next rather important phase in the academic history of Russian-American relations. It was a period of rethinking not only of Russian identity and the US image in the USSR but Russia's image in the United States as well. These were the formative years for area studies specialists whose attitudes and research interests defined the tenor of US-USSR relations during the Cold War. In the United States, it was also a foundational time for the creation of expert centers that dedicated their attention to other countries, including Soviet Russia. These developments are analyzed in detail in the second part of our book, but are also mentioned by authors in the first part.

The chapters dedicated to American Sovietology and to Russian *Amerikanistika* show that the Cold War history of these two research disciplines is directly related to the formation of the ideological and geopolitical *Other* (Soviet or American *Other* respectively) in the context of the bipolar US-Soviet confrontation. The authors trace the influence that the changing climate of Soviet-American relations and the domestic political situation in the two countries had on the evolution of the two research disciplines and also on the process of their institutionalization. Thus, in his analysis of area studies at the beginning of the Cold War and of Sovietology as the first successful area studies project, David Engerman emphasizes, on the one hand, the impact of the intellectual and institutional heritage of World War II, and, on the other hand, the tension between the two components of this heritage that arose in the times of McCarthyism.

Richard T. De George, an American Russian studies veteran, tells the story of Slavic and Soviet studies program at the University of Kansas as "a baby of the Cold War" and places special emphasis on the fact that the program caught the attention of the John Birch Society—an active anti-Communist group in Wichita, Kansas. The 1957 *Sputnik* launch in the Soviet Union also left its mark on the development of area studies and Sovietology programs, since it brought to the fore the troubling realization that the United States could lose the Cold War if it lost the scientific and technological competition with the Soviet Union. Thus, it was no accident that in September 1958 the US Congress approved the National Defense Education Act that included funding mechanisms for foreign language study and area studies centers.

Mark Kramer analyzes the research evolution of Zbigniew Brzezinski, who created the theory of totalitarianism together with Carl Friedrich, in the context of changes in Soviet-American relations, events in the Soviet Union, and of the American "revisionist" challenge. Sergei Zhuk focuses his attention on the influences that World War II and the détente period in Soviet-American relations had on the formation of the distinct generations of Soviet *Americanists*. In turn, Olga Antsyferova examines in great detail the role of the American literary canon in the ideological confrontation of the two countries. She relates the tragic fate suffered by the authors of the first Soviet academic edition of the history of American literature at the start of the Cold War and then shows how "Khrushchev's thaw" and the subsequent decrease of international tensions produced a methodological shift in Soviet literary criticism "from radical class characteristics to more mediated contraposition of literary schools and trends" (in the frame of the American literary canon it was the dichotomy realism versus modernism).

The chapters written by Vladimir Gel'man and Vladimir Sogrin and co-authored by Alexander Kubyshkin and Ivan Tsvetkov show, each in its own way, that after the fall of the USSR and the end of the Cold War, the academic study of the *Other* did not lose its direct dependence on the state of bilateral relations and on the national agenda. During the first decade of the twenty-first century, the changes in the political climate of post-Soviet Russia resulted in growing anti-Americanism and the cancellation of American-funded research programs. On the one hand, this was due to the fact that Russian-American relations had worsened in comparison with the preceding decade, and, on the other, to the growing disenchantment that the realities of Putin's Russia produced in the United States and the feeling that America again "lost Russia." The disappearance of the Soviet superpower and the new status that post-Soviet Russia had acquired in the system of international relations had noticeably diminished the interest in the academic research on Russia in the United States. More than a study subject, Russia became an object of cultural and economic diplomacy.

At the same time, the authors draw attention to the clearly positive changes that were occurring in the academic environment. Vladimir Sogrin, Alexander Kubyshkin, and Ivan Tsvetkov describe the diverse manifestations of a broader Russian-American research dialogue, the publications of new American studies texts in Russia, and the newly acquired methodological freedom. Vladimir Gel'man writes about a new phenomenon—the study of post-Soviet Russian politics in a comparative context involving both a new generation of American political scientists and scholars from Russia. It must be noted that the division of the American political scientists into "optimists," "pessimists," and "realists," proposed by Gel'man, correlates with the same sociopolitical discourses about Russia that are described in Zhuravleva's chapter and had emerged at the turn of the twentieth century from a particular text about Russia and from the contemporary American context. However, the authors also note that these positive developments were often accompanied by negative phenomena.[1]

The formation of expert knowledge about the *Other* is the *second recurrent theme* of the present volume and also the main focus of the chapter co-authored by Alexander Okun and Iana V. Shchetinskaia. The authors describe the emergence of the first American expert center—the Council on Foreign Relations—as the reaction to the outcomes of the World War I and to the Paris Peace Conference. The polemic about the issue of political recognition of the USSR took place on the pages of the council's journal, *Foreign Affairs*. The authors analyze how expert knowledge about Soviet Russia was produced at the intersection of political and academic discourses and with the participation of advocates for very diverse ideological currents (from conservative to radical) and for two very distinct political systems (American and Soviet). This wide ideological spectrum created a space for productive dialogue about the essence of Soviet foreign policy and the prospects of Soviet-American relations. Archibald C. Coolidge, first editor-in-chief of Foreign Affairs, is to be thanked for this unique interaction that has not lost its importance in the present day.

David Engerman, Mark Kramer, and Vladimir Gel'man also consider the role of expert knowledge in US policymaking toward USSR and post-Soviet Russia. Engerman investigates the degree of influence that intelligence organs had in the making of Sovietology. He comes to the conclusion that well-established university programs differed from the intelligence model in that, apart from studying Russia academically, they also trained regional experts in general and experts on the Soviet Union in particular. Mark Kramer considers the professional career of Zbigniew Brzezinski, who had served as the director of the Russian Institute at Columbia University and the national security adviser to President Jimmy Carter, to be a characteristic case of the interaction between academic and expert communities, between Sovietology and state policy. The subjects of Vladimir Gel'man's research are the political scientists that combine university professorships with work at the most prominent US think tanks.

In the United States, as in the USSR, political and ideological demand for academic and expert knowledge determined the disciplinary content of university programs in Russian/Soviet studies and *Amerikanistika* and also stimulated the process of institutionalization. All the texts of the present volume refer to this aspect of the academic study of the *Other*.

The *third cross-cutting theme* of this volume is the importance of scientific emigration from Soviet Russia for the development of Russian Studies in the United States. Marina Bulanova focuses her chapter on this theme, as she analyzes the outstanding impact of two Russian emigrant sociologists—Pitirim Sorokin and Nikolai Timasheff—on the formation of the scientific base for Russian/Soviet Studies in America. Bulanova demonstrates that, while the Russian sociologist Maxim Kovalevsky had contributed to the enduring liberal-universalist myth about the Russian revolution, *Sorokin's* universal sociology of revolutions presented a more realistic and better balanced evaluation of this phenomenon, and Timasheff offered a sociologically sound characteristic of the Soviet regime and emphasized that its successes were not due to the Bolshevik experiment as such, but to Russia's return to its proper historical development as an industrial society.

In general, scientists that emigrated from Soviet Russia have contributed to the liberal-universalist approach to the study of Russia in the United State. As Victoria Zhuravleva shows, this conclusion applies not only to sociologists, but also to liberal historians, such as Georgy Vernadskiy, Mikhail Karpovich, and Mikhail Florinskiy. References to this issue, as well as the general study of the academic history of Russian-American relations, point us to the conclusion that both past and present developmenst of Russian studies in the United States and of American studies in Russia has been closely linked to heated sociopolitical debates about the fate of Russian liberalism.

The chapters written by Milla Fedorova and William Whisenhunt introduce *the fourth recurrent theme* of the volume: the problem of the formation and propagation of "common knowledge" about the *Other* that is described in the preface. Milla Fedorova demonstrates that Soviet literature for children and youth used the image of the American *Other* to teach new generations about all that was foreign to the new type of human beings that the Soviet regime tried to form. Fedorova shows that both the Soviet children's and youth literature about America and careful selections from the works of American authors that formed part of the Soviet school program were part of a patriotic pedagogy. She comes to a surprisingly timely conclusion that through this juxtaposition of "us and them," readers could discern not only a variety of American characters, but also an image of America as a dangerous and forbidden, but also luring and attractive, country. Perhaps these readings should be counted among the factors that explain the ambivalent feelings toward America — envy/superiority, love/hate—that are so deeply rooted in the Russian public conscience and have provided the base for the current upsurge of anti-Americanism in Russia.

William Whisenhunt explains the meaning and the purpose of Russian studies programs at American community colleges with references to his own teaching experience. His argument is not about the preparation of Russian studies specialists, but about giving students adequate basic notions about Russia that can destroy myths and stereotypes frequently found in American society. Community college graduates can become political and public figures at local and state levels, become members of school boards, and sit on municipal councils. Thus, as the author justly remarks, their ideas and perceptions about Russia have direct relevance for the development prospects of Russian-American relations in general.

The problem of "common knowledge" formation about the *Other* is also addressed in the chapters by Ivan Kurilla, Vladimir Noskov, Norman Saul, and Victoria Zhuravleva. This thematic focus is due to the nature of their chosen periods of study in the development of academic knowledge about the United States in Russia and about Russia in the United States.

All authors pay special attention to *the fifth* and *final cross-cutting theme*—the role of the "human factor" in the academic study of the *Other*. In this sense, the present volume is a history of individuals—journalists, translators, diplomats, engineers, literary writers, administrators, politicians, and, obviously, researchers—who have made their distinctive contributions to the development of Russian and American studies at different moments of the academic history of Russian-American relations. It is a history of their personal ideas and also a history of research schools. For example, in the case of Russian/Soviet *Amerikanistika*, Kubyshkin and Tsvetkov write about the St Petersburg/Leningrad school, Vladimir Sogrin mentions Nikolai Sivachev's school,[2] Sergei Zhuk analyzes Nikolai N. Bolkhovitionov's academic school, to which both editors of this volume happen to belong,[3] while they in turn cite the school of Moscow State University for International Affairs (MGIMO)[4] and the Institute for USA and Canada Studies (ISKAN).[5]

The "personal dimension" in the academic study of the *Other* becomes especially important, since, until to the mid-twentieth century, Russian studies in the United States and *Amerikanistika* in Russia did not really exist as academic fields.Instead, they were limited to individual researchers and researcher groups that had different thematic interests, were dispersed in different universities, and were very disparate in terms of talent and preparation levels.

The "human factor" analysis also allows us to address the question of how researchers' professional identities were related to their national and regional identities. Sergei Zhuk elaborates on this issue through his comparative analysis of Moscow and Kiev *Amerikanistika* schools, while Kubyshkin and Tsvetkov provide interesting material about the St Petersburg/Leningrad school.

In this volume, we have deliberately brought together "inside" and "outside" evaluations of successes and failures in the academic study of the *Other*. Our "insiders" are authors who have directly participated in the process of shaping Sovietology and Russian studies in the United States or *Amerikanistika* in the USSR and Russia and who have reflected on these professions and their personal roles in them. The "outsider" group is formed by those who observed this process from the viewpoint of the society that was the subject of study and also those who have immigrated to the *Other* country and had to reformat their professional identities in a new academic environment. Generational differences are another relevant variable that we had in mind in designing this collection. We believe the volume is made more interesting by the different approaches and perspectives that we have managed to pool together in this fashion.

The history of Russian/Soviet studies in the United States and *Amerikanistika* in the Russian Empire/the USSR/post-Soviet Russia is the essential part of the history of Russian-American relations as a whole. We suppose that the conclusions and observations of the authors give an opportunity for better understanding both the correlation between the academic, political, and media contexts and the role of specialists on Russian studies in the United States and *Amerikanistika* in post-Soviet Russia in the formation of a pragmatic agenda of bilateral relations that takes into account the lessons of the current crises.

The project that gave rise to this volume could be continued by including among its participants members of the United States and Russian expert communities and also specialists in history and sociology of science from both sides of the Atlantic. This collection makes evident the gaps that exist in American and Russian research with respect to reflections about the heritage of studying the *Other* in light of new methodological developments. In this sense, American specialists in Russian studies are significantly ahead of their Russian counterparts.[6] Among the best examples of this are David C. Engerman's latest book entitled *Know Your*

Enemy and its excellent critical review written by Catriona Kelly who draws on the history of Sovietology and reflects on the prospects of Russian studies in the United States.[7]

Our project could also be inscribed into a broader analysis of how the United States is studied in Europe and in the rest of the world outside the United States. A recent attempt of European historians of the United States to do a systematic analysis of this kind demonstrated both similarities and differences among researchers from different European countries with regard to the choice of research questions and to the approaches to their scholarly study.[8] Our volume offers rich material for the scholars engaged in comparative history, another rapidly advancing discipline.

When it comes to the process of mutual study, Russians and Americans have a lot both to be proud of and to subject to professional critical reflection. What is important is that neither praise, nor critical reflections should be silenced or distorted to serve current political needs and propaganda objectives. We believe that the academic communities of the two countries are able to find the response to this challenge through dialogue.

NOTES

1. The underside of the positive processes described by Vladimir Gel'man is made clear by Angela Stent who demonstrates that comparative politics experts and international relations theorists with no special training on Russia are an ever-growing presence in the faculty of Russian studies programs at US universities. See: Angela Stent, "How Deep is the Russian Studies Bench?" in *Best Russian Studies Programs 2015*. Russia Direct Report, issue 8 (April 2015): 25.

2. About this academic school, see Evgenii F. Iaz'kov, "N. V. Sivachev i razvitie shkoly nauchnykh issledovanii i prepodavaniia istorii Soedinennykh Shtatov Ameriki v Moskovskom universitete," in Alexander C. Manykin., ed., *Pamiati professora N. V. Sivacheva. SShA: evoliutsiia osnovnykh ideino-politicheskikh kontseptsii* (Moscow: Izdatel'stvo Moskovskogo universiteta, 2004): 5–16; Yurii N. Rogoulev, "The Study of US History in Russia," in Cornelis A. van Minnen and Sylvia L. Hilton, eds., *Teaching and Studying U.S. History in Europe. Past, Present and Future* (Amsterdam: VU University Press, 2007): 219–29.

3. About Nikolai N. Bolkhovitinov's role in Soviet and post-Soviet *Amerikanistika*, see Victoria I. Zhuravleva, Ivan I. Kurilla, "Ne razzhigat' vrazhdu, a sposobstvovat' vzaimoponimaniiu mezhdu narodami. Pamiati Nikolaia Nikolaevicha Bolkhovitinova, cheloveka i uchenogo," in Victoria I. Zhuravleva and Ivan I. Kurilla, eds., *Rossiia i SShA na stranitsakh uchebnikov: opyt vzaimnykh reprezentatsii* (Volgograd: Izd-vo VolGU, 2009): 370–400.

4. About *Amerikanistika* in the Moscow Institute of International Relations, see Vladimir O. Pechatnov, "Nauchnaia shkola amerikanistiki," *Vestnik MGIMO-Universiteta*, no. 5 (2014): 131–35.

5. About the Institute for US and Canadian Studies, see, for example, the memoir of its "founding father" Georgii A. Arbatov, *Chelovek sistemy* (Moscow: Izdatel'stvo Vagrius, 2002).

6. This does not mean that there have been no publications on this problem in post-Soviet Russia. However, the majority of the existing publications are anniversary

articles and edited books dedicated to the memory of leading Soviet Americanists. Among the most recent, interesting, and promising publications, see, for example: Vladimir V. Noskov, ed., William G. Rosenberg, co-ed. *Rossiia i SShA: poznavaia drug druga. Sbornik pamiati akademika Aleksandra Aleksandrovicha Fursenko [Russia and the United States: Perceiving Each Other. In memory of the Academician Alexander A. Fursenko]* (Saint-Petersburg: Nestor-Istoriia, 2015).

7. Catriona Kelly, "What Was Soviet Studies and What Came Next?" *The Journal of Modern History*, 85 (March 2013): 109–49.

8. See Ivan Kurilla, "Reflections from Russia," in Nicolas Barreyre, Michael Heale, Stephen Tuck, Cécile Vidal, eds., *Historians across Borders: Writing American History in a Global Age* (Oakland: University of California Press, 2014): 174–80.

Index

Abele, Daniel, xviin1
Adams, Herbert, 52
Adams, John, 8
Adams, Mark B., 100n25
Adrianople Treaty of 1829, 7
African Americans (Negro, Blacks, Black Americans), 9, 10, 33–34, 49, 52, 131, 132, 143, 144, 215, 237, 238
Agrenev (Slavianskii), Dmitri, 29, 40n7
Aishiskina, Nadezhda M., 152, 152n30
Akimov, Yurii, 225, 227n11, 228
Aksakov brothers, 18
Aksakov, Ivan, 20, 22, 26n16, 27
Alaska, Sale of, 236
Alcott, Louisa, 124
Alent'eva, Tatiana V., 69n12, 73
Alexander II, 5, 9, 17, 18, 19–20, 40n6, 236
Alexander III, 17
Alexander Macedon, 19
Alexander, John T., 199n10, 200
Alexeeva, Ekaterina, xix
Allen, Philip J., 82
Allen, Robert V., 68n4, 69n10, 70n39, 71n44, 73
Almond, Gabriel, 253n8, 256
Amalrik, Leonid A., 124
American Civil War, viii, 3, 9, 17, 18, 19, 20, 25, 30, 131, 146, 215, 238
American Constitution, 8, 51, 90
American Cultural Center, 219
American Historical Review, 30
American Indians. *See* Native Americans
American Oriental Society, 30
American Red Cross, 37
American Relief Administration (ARA), 39
American Republic, 6, 7, 51, 164

American Revolution (War of Independence), 53, 58, 215, 233, 238
American-Russian Chamber of Commerce, 45
Amerikanskii ezhegodnik , 90
Anderson, Sam, 17, 194
Anderson, Sherwood, 139–140
Andrew, Christopher, 98n5
Angiolillo, Paul F., 183n10
Anisimov, Ivan I., 151n7, 151n20, 152, 152n22
anti-Americanism, xiii–xiv, 68, 88, 122–123, 221, 222, 227, 231, 235, 236, 261, 264
Antsyferova, Olga Yu., 261, 285
Apenko, Elena, 218, 225, 228, 228n18
Appatov, Semyon, 94, 97, 99n7, 100n33
ARA. *See* American Relief Administration
Arbatov, Georgii A., ix, 96, 97, 98, 98n5, 101, 101n38, 266n5
Arendt, Hannah, 180
Armstrong, Hamilton F., 159, 161, 167n3, 167n5, 167n7, 167n15, 168
Army Specialized Training Program (ASTP), 173, 174, 179
Army's Civil Affairs Training Program. *See* Harvard University
Artsimovich, Vladimir Antonovich, 62, 72n68
Arustamova, Anna A., 125, 134n14, 134n16, 135
ASEEES. *See* Association for Slavic, East European, and Eurasian Studies
Associated Press, 47
Association for Slavic, East European, and Eurasian Studies (ASEEES), xvi, xix

Fackenthal, Frank D., 63
Fadeev, Rostislav, 25, 27, 27n57
Fahs, Charles, 183n17
Fainsod, Merle, 119, 119n14, 181,
  184n31
Fairfield University, Connecticut, 219
Fast, Howard, 132, 141, 151n12, 153
Faulkner, William, 149
Fauset, Jessie, 142
Federalism, 50, 54
Fedorov, Nikolai, 224, 225, 228, 228n12
Fedorova, Milla, 133n4, 134n17,
  134n18, 135, 263, 264, 285
Fenton, William Nelson, 182n7, 182n8,
  185
Ferber, Edna, 144
Feshbach, Murray, 207
Feuer, Lewis, 193
Filatova, Liudmila V., 151n19, 153
Fish, M. Steven, 247, 254n15, 254n19,
  256
Fisher, Harold H., 176, 182n5, 183n16,
  185, 186
Fitzgerald, F. Scott, 147
Fletcher, William C., 195, 197, 199n17,
  200
Florinsky, Mikhail Timofeevich, ix, 67,
  82, 160, 263
Foglesong, David S., xviiin11, 72n85, 74
Foner, Eric, 232
Ford Foundation, 192–193
Foreign Affairs, ix, 158–159, 160, 161,
  162–163, 164, 262
Fortunatov, Stepan Fedorovich, 48, 50,
  53, 69n11, 70n18, 71n50, 74
Francis, David Rowland, 62
Frankfurt School, 172
Franklin, Benjamin, 234
Freeman, Joseph, 140
Friche, Vladimir M., 139, 151n19, 153
Friedrich, Carl, 103, 184n24, 261
Fulbright Program, xix, 150, 232
Fuller, Harriett Bliss, 40n17, 41n19
Furaev, Victor, ix, 215–216
Fursenko, Alexander Alexandrovich,
  ix, 90, 99n15, 215–216, 225, 228,
  228n14
Fuss, Paul, 11n3

Gabuev, Alexander, xviiin11
Gaidar, Arkadii, 128
Galkin, Il'ia V., 240n1
Gamel, Iosif. *See* Hamel, Joseph
Gandhi, Jennifer, 256, 256n60
Ganelin, Raphael Sh., ix, 68n2, 74, 215,
  216
Gansovskii, Sever, 127, 128–130
Gardner, John, 183n14, 183n17, 184n26,
  184n28
Garland, Hamlin H., 140
Gehlbach, Scott, 250, 255n54, 256
Gel'man, Vladimir, 247, 253n3, 253n4,
  253n12, 254n21, 254n29, 255n40, 256,
  261–262, 266n1, 285
George, Henry, 52
Gerovitch, Slava, 92, 100n27
Gest, Morris, 36
Giddings, Franklin H., 79
Gielgud, John, 37
Gilenson, Boris A., 99n16, 149, 152n45,
  153
Gnatyuk, Olga, 82
Gogol, Nikolai V., 36, 129
Gold, Michael, 140, 143
Golder, Frank, 35, 39, 43n68, 60, 159
Golosov, Grigorii V., 250, 253n4,
  255n53, 256
Goode, J. Paul, 252n1, 256
Goralik, Linor, 132–133, 135, 135n28
Gorbachev, Mikhail S., 90, 106,
  111–112, 113–114, 115, 117, 197, 232,
  236
Gorchakov, Alexander M., 9, 236
Gorenburg, Dmitry, 250, 255n52, 256
Gorky Institute of World Literature,
  149
Gorky, Alexei Maximovich, 36, 37,
  71n45, 124–125
Gorshkov, Boris, 211n6, 212
Grace, Alonzo G., 183n10
Graham, Otis L., Jr., 241
Grand Alliance, 176
Granovskii, Timofei, 9
Grau, Shirley A., 144
Great Depression, 80, 132
Great Powers, 16, 166
Great Reforms, 9, 17, 18
Greyson, Benson L., 68n2, 74

About the Contributors

Olga Yu. Antsyferova is professor of world literature at Ivanovo State University.

Marina B. Bulanova is professor of social science at the Russian State University for the Humanities.

Richard T. De George is distinguished professor of philosophy, emeritus, at the University of Kansas.

David C. Engerman is Ottilie Springer professor and chair of the history department at Brandeis University.

Milla Fedorova is associate professor at Georgetown University.

Vladimir Gel'man is professor at the European University at St. Petersburg and Finland Distinguished Professor at the University of Helsinki.

Mark Kramer is director of Cold War studies at Harvard University and senior fellow of Harvard's Davis Center for Russian and Eurasian Studies.

Alexander I. Kubyshkin is professor at St. Petersburg State University.

Ivan Kurilla is professor of history and political science at the European University at St. Petersburg.

Vladimir V. Noskov is professor and head of the world history division at the St. Petersburg Institute of History of the Russian Academy of Sciences.

Alexander B. Okun is associate professor at Samara State University.

Norman E. Saul is professor emeritus of Russian history at the University of Kansas.

Iana V. Shchetinskaia is a graduate of Samara State University.

Vladimir V. Sogrin is professor and chair of the Center of North American Studies at the Institute of World history of the Russian Academy of Sciences.

Ivan A. Tsvetkov is associate professor at St. Petersburg State University.

William Benton Whisenhunt is professor of history at College of DuPage.

Sergei Zhuk is associate professor at Ball State University.

Victoria I. Zhurvaleva is professor of American history and international relations and director of the program on American studies at the Russian State University for the Humanities, Moscow.